Volume One

RECLAIMING
The Forgotten
BIBLICAL HERITAGE

Volume One

RECLAIMING
The Forgotten
BIBLICAL HERITAGE

Robert K. Ssebatta

WATCHMAN
Research Media Publications

Reclaiming the Forgotten Biblical Heritage: When a People Forget Their Heritage, They Are Easily Persuaded to Lose Their Identity, Volume 1
Edited by Ryan Adair
Cover Design by Lisa Hainline

ISBN Paperback: 978-0-9576276-2-8
ISBN EBook: 978-0-9576276-1-1

Disclaimer of Warranty
This published work may contain facts, views, opinions, statements, recommendations, websites and other links or references, which are not owned, controlled or reflect the views of the author and publisher. Therefore the author has made reasonable effort to include accurate, current, and historical information but takes no warranties or representations of the accuracy, safety, or value of published, or distributed through or as part of this publication and assumes no liability or responsibility for the content of linked or referenced sources or for errors or omissions in content. Neither the publisher nor author shall be liable for any loss of profit or other commercial damages, including but not limited to special, incidental, consequential, or other damages.

Dedication

With all my love to Sylvia, Ruth, Esther, Daniel, and Elizabeth.
Thanks for always being there for Dad.

In loving memory of Joshua Ssebatta.
Though you lived only forty-two short weeks, you left fingerprints of
grace on our lives. You will not be forgotten.
Joshua, the Lord knew you before you entered your mother's womb
and He had some service for you in heaven. He formed your inward
parts and covered you in your mother's womb. We shall praise the
Lord, for He fearfully and wonderfully made you.

"Unless a grain of wheat falls into the ground and dies, it remains
alone; but if it dies, it produces much grain." (John 12:24)

Contents

Acknowledgments

Every Christian writer knows that one cannot write a book without the grace of God and the assistance from numerous people. First, I would like thank the Lord Jesus Christ for having given me the grace, strength, and ability to write this book. Without Him I can do nothing.

There is also no achievement in life that is without the help and assistance of many known and unknown individuals who contribute to our lives. We are all the sum total of what we have learned from others. I am deeply indebted and thankful to the insights offered by many authors who decided to share with us what they learned. In fact, it is impossible to thank them all individually.

I have borrowed extensively from their studies and I have tried to secure their best thoughts on some of the different historical subjects I have researched and collected over many years. I believe it is better to give the best of others' thoughts than what is poor thinking, even if it is original. I apologize and give my sincere gratitude for any quote that I may have plundered, or forgotten the source of, whether in small or large amounts.

I also specifically express my appreciation for permission to reprint extensively from these many publishers and authors: Joyce Bohn—Mott Media, Pam Pugh—Moody publishers, Tom DeVries—W. B. Eerdmans Publishing, Excel Books, Ted R. Weiland, Gary North, Gary DeMar, Ludwig von Mises, Mary Eberstadt, Dave Breese, Verna M. Hall, David Barton, Frederic Bastiat, Larry Bates, Laurence M. Vance, Heinz Eduard Todt, Ken Ham, as well as many others.

I owe a special debt of gratitude to Ryan Adair who facilitated the publishing of this manuscript by critiquing, organizing, outlining, editing, and formatting. Your patience with me during the whole process of this project was a tremendous source of motivation and encouragement. In most cases, a writer fails to see the need for any addition or correction that would be expressed in a much better and more professional way, but you provided many helpful editorial comments and suggestions. Your kind, professional advice is highly appreciated.

To the first graphic and book cover designer, Kristine Cotterman, for all your efforts in the conceptual design of the book. You are part of the dream. Thank you, very much.

I am greatly indebted to the design work and humble spirit of Lisa Hainline. Thank you, Lisa, for clarifying many points at the last stages of the project and thus making it work.

I am also grateful to my mother-in-law, Rebecca, for all your prayers and support. To all my relatives and friends who encouraged and supported me, without you this project would never have been finished.

Special thanks to my wife, Juliet, for your prayers and encouragement when I wanted to give up. Thanks for being patient with me as a result of many of hours of reading, collating, compiling, studying, and researching.

Finally, I alone am responsible for any kind of errors that might be found in this book, as it is almost impossible to produce an absolutely perfect book without mistakes. I hope you will be inspired, encouraged, warned, and reproved by the message contained within so that you can know the Lord more intimately and fulfill His purpose and plan for your life.

Introduction

The West has departed so much from its biblical Christian heritage that it is almost impossible for the average person to recognize the enormous gulf that exists between the beliefs of today's modern world and those of previous generations. William Booth (1829–1912), the founder of the Salvation Army, prophesied that by the end of the twentieth century, the following dangers that would confront the church and ultimately Western society are Christianity without Christ, religion without the Holy Spirit, forgiveness without repentance, salvation without regeneration, politics without God, and heaven without hell. And that's exactly where we find ourselves today.

Europe, which was once called Christendom,[1] refuses to make any mention of Jesus Christ or recognize the clear Christian civilization throughout its history. Jesus Christ transformed Western civilization, but now He is viewed with both hostility and resentment. Europe is turning its back to its Christian roots, forgetting that the apostle Paul's Macedonian call to preach the gospel led him into Europe instead of Asia (see Acts 16:10). Without this gospel being proclaimed, the West would not have gained its high level of civilization, which people often take for granted.

Many leaders are being reminded not to exclude the values that helped forge the "soul" of the continent, but all pleas are ignored. England, which sent missionaries around the world, is spiritually at its lowest state in over 250 years, probably worse than before the awakening of John Wesley and George Whitefield. Likewise, the American nation is also losing its sense of direction, both spiritually and morally, to the point that many Americans openly oppose the name of Jesus Christ.

Why write another book on the forgotten biblical heritage? After all, most Christians and non-Christians are inundated with information on religion. Well, this book does not focus on religion. God didn't create us to practice religion. He created us to have a relationship with Him—that is the purpose of every man and woman on this earth.

Humanity is trying to make history without God, and wherever people lose God they lose themselves. Modern technology and science now serve as the basis for meaning and value in the hearts of humanity. Intelligent and thinking people are now calling the Christian faith sheer fiction, a world of the stupid, and the Word of God a collection of ancient myths and not a revelation of divine truth. This is what German philosopher Friedrich Nietzsche said when he was describing the condition reached by Western civilization: "God is dead and we have outgrown our need of Him." What about present-day Christians, however? Do we truly understand that without the lordship of Christ and His principles, society will always descend into anarchy?

In Volume 1 of Reclaiming the Forgotten Biblical Heritage, I seek to remind the West by compiling and drawing from the Bible and the work of many historians that the West has forgotten God, which also echoes several Old Testament Scriptures that decry how Israel turned from God. Over and over again, as the Israelites prepared to cross the Jordan River to enter the Promised Land, Moses charged them to remember with gratitude where they came from.

Moses continued to remind God's people of the past, taught them how to live in the present, and urged them to look ahead to the future. They were warned not to forget, especially when prosperity and wealth came:

> Remember how the Lord your God led you through the wilderness for these forty years, humbling you and testing you to prove your character, and to find out whether or not you would obey His commands.... When you have eaten your fill, be sure to praise the Lord your God for the good land He has given you. But that is the time to be careful! Beware that in your plenty you do not forget the Lord your God and disobey His commands,

regulations, and decrees that I am giving you today. (Deuteronomy 8:2, 10–11 NLT)

But sadly the lesson was not learned and "they did not understand nor appreciate His miracles…they hastily forgot His works; and did not wait for His plans to develop in the desert" (Psalm 106:7, 13).

How does this apply to the West today? Paul tells us, "Now these things are examples (warnings and admonitions) for us not to desire or crave or covet or lust after evil and carnal things as they did…. Now these things befell them by way of a figure [as an example and warning to us]; they were written to admonish and fit us for right action by good instruction, we in whose days the ages have reached their climax (their consummation and concluding period)" (1 Corinthians 10:6, 11 AMP).

Paul cautions us to remember the lessons the Israelites learned so we can avoid repeating their mistakes. We cannot read the history of God's mercy on behalf of the Israelites without reflecting on how consistently God's people failed to learn. They repeatedly turned away from God and worshiped the idols after all the great miracles they had seen.

While on the contrary, William Bradford vividly remembered God's past acts on behalf of the pilgrims when they sailed from Plymouth and decided to settle in America. "Our fathers," said Governor Bradford to his fellow Puritans who landed at Plymouth, "were Englishmen who came over this great ocean, and were ready to perish in this wilderness; but they cried unto the Lord, and He heard their voice, and looked on their adversities and the sons and daughters of the Pilgrims then remembered."[2]

We advance our knowledge and understanding of the world we live in by studying history. Since I believe, as Santayana has said long ago, that those who disregard history are condemned to repeat it, I also believe history is not about mere memorization of important people, dates, or events. History is about studying cause and effect—what causes civilizations to develop and what causes them to collapse. Unfortunately, when nations forget God, the state takes His place. And once the state takes over, a religion of humanism is established that is diametrically opposed to biblical Christianity.

The message of this book springs from a deeply burdened heart that men have forgotten God. A. W. Tozer said that the only book that should ever be written is the "one that flows up from the deep and burning conviction of the heart, forced out by…inward pressure…. You should never write a book unless you just have to."[3] It was just such pressure that produced the book you are about to read.

I gladly acknowledge my weaknesses. I have no personal agenda nor do I support any particular political group. I have diligently sought to research, record, compile, and interpret what I perceive the Lord has put on my heart. I claim no special inspiration and only the Scriptures deserve to be considered infallible. My sole desire is to be faithful to the Lord Jesus Christ and His Word. Without apology, however, I hold fast to the inerrancy and infallible inspiration of the Holy Scriptures. The Bible is the only absolute standard by which this, and all prophetic revelation, must be tested and judged (see 2 Timothy 3:16–17; 2 Peter 1:19–21).

The apostolic extortion in 1 Thessalonians 5:20–21 tells us to examine everything carefully and not to spurn the gifts and utterances of the prophets (neither to depreciate prophetic revelations nor despise inspired instruction or exhortation or warning). But we are called to test and prove everything carefully, until we can recognize what is good. We're to hold fast to that which is good, not that which is bad. If you are reading this book with the intention of looking for what is wrong with it, you will not be able to see what is right.

Reclaiming the Forgotten Biblical Heritage is to be issued in two volumes, of which this is the first. This book does not provide a complete historical analysis of how the West has forgotten God and their Christian biblical heritage—that would be too exhaustive. It merely highlights some examples of the deep influence this heritage has had on human civilization throughout history. Although there are countless contributions to this rich heritage, we should not forget that over the centuries, and recent decades in particular, there have been many sins and injustices committed and perpetrated in the name of Christianity.

Psychologists teach us that every modern society can be divided into seven spheres of influence: spiritual, economic, governmental, familial, educational, the media, and arts and entertainment. Can self-government without the lordship of Christ succeed in producing lasting good within these spheres? How does the Bible influence nations to work together? Should the Bible be used as a basis for laws? Did the Bible inspire the United States Constitution? What is separation of church and state? What is a democracy and is it the best system of government? What motivated missionaries to spread the gospel to Africa? What were the conditions that allowed slavery to be condoned? In this volume we will try to answer some of these questions by using biblical teaching and historical documentation.

Regardless of how accurate this part of history, assessment, or revelation is, one basic key to understanding any kind of prophecy or word from the Lord is found in 1 Corinthians 13:9–10, 12 (KJV):

> For we know in part, and we prophesy in part. But when that which is perfect has come, then that which is in part shall be done away.... For now we see through a glass, darkly; but then face to face: now I know in part; but then shall I know even as also I am known.

Endnotes

[1] In theory, the concept of Christendom refers to the continent or nations where Christianity was the dominant religion. So when I suggest that Europe was called Christendom, I'm saying that it refers to the world's countries that are the majority Christian. It was a vision of a government founded upon and upholding Christian values under the leadership of the church as an institution. Both church and state complemented each other by attending to people's spiritual and temporal needs.

[2] William Bradford, "Of Plymouth Plantation," *The American Puritans: Their Prose and Poetry* (New York: Double Day Achor, 1956), 18.

[3] A. W. Tozer, *The Pursuit of God: The Human Thirst for the Divine with Study Guide* by Jonathan L. Graf (Wing Spread Publishers, 1982, 1992, 1993), 135.

Part I: The Christian Heritage in England

CHAPTER 1

The West's Hostility Toward Christ

And if you forget the Lord your God and walk after other gods and serve them and worship them, I testify against you this day that you shall surely perish.

—*Deuteronomy 8:19 AMP*

If we abide by the principles taught in the Bible, our country will go on prospering and to prosper; but if we and our posterity neglect its instruction and authority, no man can tell how sudden a catastrophe may overwhelm us and bury all our glory in profound obscurity.

—*Daniel Webster*

Hostility Toward Christ

History continues to repeat itself but few heed its warnings. Western civilization no longer upholds the values it proclaims. What then is the basis for its claim to virtue? The Western world today has rejected God and embraced scientific knowledge, technology, and new age philosophies. We have rejected our Christian heritage, which is the stabilizing force in the world today. Man has elevated himself to the position of a god, thinking in his little mind that he can somehow better run this world and the forces of nature than the God who created and established it.

In one of his major works, Dietrich Bonhoeffer wrote,

What the West is doing is to refuse to accept its historical inheritance for what it is. The West is becoming hostile towards Christ. This is the peculiar situation of our time, and it is genuine decay. It is only in the Christian west that it is possible to speak of a historical heritage. The historical Jesus Christ is the continuity of our history.[1]

The Spread of the Gospel

The amazing story historians and researchers have tried to verify for us is why Jesus fixed the number of the apostles to twelve, and that of the disciples to seventy. The Bible reveals that to spread the gospel, Jesus called and trained twelve disciples, commissioning them to preach the gospel and demonstrate the signs of the kingdom (see Luke 6:12–16). And after Jesus had suffered, died, and on the third day arose from the dead, Luke records that Jesus told His followers:

> And that repentance [with a view to and as the condition of forgiveness] of sins should be preached in His name to all nations, beginning from Jerusalem. You are witnesses of these things. And behold, I will send forth upon you what My Father has promised; but remain in the city [Jerusalem] until you are clothed with power from on high. (Luke 24:47–49 AMP)

The book of Acts provides the basic history of the spread of Christianity during the three decades immediately following the death and resurrection of Jesus Christ. The Gospels tell us of the life and ministry of our Savior, but there is only one book in the New Testament that traces the expansion of the early church—the book of Acts. Luke informs us in his first book about the life, teachings, and works of Christ (the Gospel of Luke). He then made a continuous report dealing with the Acts of the Apostles in his second book.

Luke's purpose in writing his story was to offer a coordinated account of Christian origins, indicating how God revealed Himself in the work and person of Jesus Christ through the church. He reflects a keen consciousness of the Roman Empire into which early Christianity spread. How do we know Luke was accurate in his scholarship? To answer this question, we only need to look at a portion of Acts where Luke uses the pronoun "we," signifying he was with Paul during some of his missionary journeys. Thus, he is giving firsthand witness to what he wrote about.

> Therefore, sailing from Troas, we ran a straight course to Samothrace, and the next day came to Neapolis and from there to Philippi, which is the foremost city of that part of Macedonia, a colony. And we were staying in that city for some days. And on the Sabbath day we went out of the city to the riverside, where prayer was customarily made; and we sat down and spoke to the women who met there. Now a certain woman named Lydia heard us. She was a seller of purple from the city of Thyatira, who worshiped God. The Lord opened her heart to heed the things spoken by Paul. And when she and her household were baptized, she begged us, saying, "If you have judged me to be faithful to the Lord, come to my house and stay." So she persuaded us. (Acts 16:11–15)

Furthermore, Luke uses accurate historical proper names for all the various Roman officials, which researchers have recognized as a mark of firsthand knowledge.

Jesus and the Roman Empire

A great part of the world was subject to the Roman Empire when Jesus Christ came as a Man to the earth. The Romans lost every shadow of liberty and were reduced to a state of submission under Augustus Caesar. So the disciples themselves must have wanted Israel to be freed from the tyranny of Rome. During the forty days after His crucifixion, however, Jesus appeared to the apostles by a series of many convincing demonstrations that He was actually alive, talking to them about the kingdom of God.

Luke further writes:

> And while being in their company and eating with them, He commanded them not to leave Jerusalem but to wait for what the Father had promised, of which [He said] you have heard Me speak. For John baptized with water, but not many days from now you shall be baptized with (placed in, introduced into) the Holy Spirit. So when they were assembled, they asked Him, Lord, is this

the time when You will reestablish the kingdom and restore it to Israel? (Acts 1:4–6 AMP)[2]

Like all other people of the day, the apostles were fed up with the Roman rulers. They wanted Jesus to free them and all of Israel from Roman power and become their true King, establishing His dominion in the political realm. But Jesus told them not to worry about politics, but rather to focus on the mission He was giving them:

> It is not for you to know times or seasons which the Father has put in His own authority. But you shall receive power when the Holy Spirit has come upon you; and you shall be witnesses to Me in Jerusalem, and in all Judea and Samaria, and to the end of the earth. (Acts 1:7–8)

The Holy Spirit came fifty days after the resurrection, which was just ten days after Jesus's ascension. As soon as the apostles received this precious gift from the Father, their ignorance was turned into light and all their doubts evaporated. The Holy Spirit gave the apostles a variety of gifts, including the gift of tongues, which was necessary for them to have ability, efficiency, and might in being witnesses and preaching the gospel to different nations. Within a short period of time, thousands of people were converted and discipled. John Lawrence Mosheim writes of this time:

> All these apostles were men without education, and absolutely ignorant of letters and philosophy; and yet, in the infancy of the Christian church, it was necessary that should be, at least, some defender of the gospel, who, versed in the learned arts, might be able to combat the Jewish doctors and Pagan philosophers with their own arms. For this purpose, Jesus Himself, by an extraordinary voice from heaven, called to His service a thirteenth apostle whose name was Saul (afterwards Paul), and whose acquaintance both with Jewish and Grecian learning was very considerable. This extraordinary man, who had been one of the most virulent enemies of the Christians, became their most glorious and triumphant defender. Independent of the miraculous

gifts, with which he was enriched, he was naturally possessed of an invincible courage, an amazing force of genius, and a spirit of patience, which no fatigue could overcome, and which no sufferings or trials could exhaust. To these the cause of the gospel, under the divine appointment, owed a considerable part of its rapid progress and surprising success, as the Acts of the Apostles, and the Epistles of St. Paul, abundantly testify.[3]

An Organized Manner

The Bible goes on to say that instead of taking the gospel eastward into Asia, Paul's call led him to take the gospel into Europe first, where he planted his first church in Philippi. Luke again tells us:

> Now when they had gone through Phrygia and the region of Galatia, they were forbidden by the Holy Spirit to preach the word in Asia. After they had come to Mysia, they tried to go into Bithynia, but the Spirit did not permit them. So passing by Mysia, they came down to Troas. And a vision appeared to Paul in the night. A man of Macedonia stood and pleaded with him, saying, "Come over to Macedonia and help us." Now after he had seen the vision, immediately we sought to go to Macedonia, concluding that the Lord had called us to preach the gospel to them. (Acts 16:6–10)

Later, the apostle Paul sent preachers and teachers to specific areas throughout Europe: Tychius to Ephesus (see Ephesians 6:21–22), Crescens to Galatia (see 2 Timothy 4:10), and Titus to Dalmatia and Crete (see Titus 1:5). This was consistent with what later historians record about the apostles' organized movements. And early church historian Eusebius wrote that Thomas was sent to Parthia, Andrew to Scythia, and John to Asia.[4] The gospel of Jesus Christ was spread in an organized manner, not haphazardly or without purpose.

Gildas (AD 500–570) was a British cleric and one of the best-documented figures of the Christian church in the British Isles during the sixth century. In his book *The Ruin of Britain*, he reasoned that God judged the British people with the departure of the Romans and the arrival of the Vikings. He says that the coming of Christianity into Britain happened during the last years of the emperor Tiberius (AD 14–37), which means that Christianity arrived in Britain no later than AD 37—less than a decade after Christ's crucifixion.[5]

The apostles first brought Christianity to the Island, and it began in Britain within fifty years of Christ's ascension. Many historical sources confirm that the apostles took Christianity to Ireland four centuries before St. Patrick's visit ever occurred.[6]

The Purpose for the Blessing

Another great scholar of the seventeenth century, James Ussher, presented considerable evidence that James, Simon Peter, the apostle Paul, and others brought Christianity to Europe's Western Isles in the first century.[7] History also shows that Britain's rise to greatness began in the turmoil of the Protestant Reformation. Having broken from Rome and faced with the combined hostility of the continental church and imperial Spain, then the most powerful nation in the world, England began to look beyond the seas for her security and trade. Explorers were sent throughout the world during the reign of Queen Elizabeth I (1558–1603), which led to the establishment of colonies that later developed into the United States of America and the nations of the British Commonwealth.

Historians have called both Britain and America "revolutionary empires." They were not tyrannies as were earlier empires in which everyone was subject to dictators. Both have had their own Parliament or government to which voters have sent elected representatives. People could own land in both nations, practice their own religion, and even take their government to court, while newspapers were free to criticize the authorities. Books were freely published and innovative ideas flourished in what have become the most politically stable nations in modern history. I believe God blessed these nations for a specific purpose, and that was to take the gospel of Jesus Christ to all the surrounding nations. But they have forgotten God and their Christian heritage.

Historian G. M. Trevelyan wrote that when George III came to the throne in 1760, the old-world system of economic and social life had undergone little change. Prosperity and personal independence, though far from universal, were widely diffused. The agriculturist or manufacturer in his cottage accepted his lot in life, whether easy or hard, as part of the order of things. It did not occur to him to question the framework of society or to regard the oligarchy under which he lived as oppressive.[8] But a great spiritual awakening in England, Scotland, and Wales swept the land and society was changed, in turn enhancing the living standards of humanity, bringing an industrial revolution, enhancing various aspects of human life, abolishing slavery, building hospitals and schools, improving the standards of prisons, and implementing many other social reforms. The British influence was beneficial for the whole world.

The British and Foreign Bible Society was responsible for the Bible being translated into every language and made it available for the first time to peoples all over the earth. What is to be noted is that huge occupying armies did not enforce the British Empire throughout the world. As a matter of fact, during the nineteenth century the British army was so small it was called the "thin red line." A couple of historians note: "The British administered justice, collected taxes, and enforced laws. They alone came into direct contact with the native populations in those countries…they worked hard and efficiently… there was no corruption and they upheld justice, peace, and order for several decades."[9] England, as tiny as it was, emerged as the greatest, most extensive empire the world had ever seen up to that point.

Across the Atlantic

Across the Atlantic many of America's Founders knew that God was the One who blesses a nation, believing, "Blessed is the nation whose God is the Lord; and the people whom He hath chosen for His own inheritance" (Psalm 33:12 KJV). The first permanent settlement in the United States was in Jamestown, Virginia, in 1607. A number of years later, in 1620, the Pilgrims landed at Plymouth Rock in

Massachusetts. After a severe winter there, they gave thanks to God for the harvest in 1621, in what historians have called the first Thanksgiving. From 1783 to 1853, after the thirteen colonies became the United States, the nation acquired land to extend its continental reach from what has been termed "from sea to shining sea."

The greatest land expansion took place in 1803 under President Thomas Jefferson, when France sold the Louisiana Territory to the United States for only $15 million. French emperor Napoleon said, "This accession of territory affirms forever the power of the United States and I have given England a maritime rival who sooner or later will humble her pride."[10] During the seventeenth and eighteenth centuries, settlers from England flowed into what became known as the United States. From 1803 the U.S. expanded rapidly because of its combination of agricultural and mineral wealth.

But the Founders of the States looked to their religious heritage as the foundation and justification of their political philosophy. They wrote in the Declaration of Independence:

> We hold these truths to be self-evident, that all men are created equal, that they are endowed by their Creator with certain unalienable Rights, that among these are Life, Liberty and the pursuit of Happiness. --That to secure these rights, Governments are instituted among Men, deriving their just powers from the consent of the governed, --That whenever any Form of Government becomes destructive of these ends, it is the Right of the People to alter or to abolish it, and to institute new Government, laying its foundation on such principles and organizing its powers in such form, as to them shall seem most likely to effect their Safety and Happiness.[11]

And inscribed on the United States Liberty Bell are these words from Leviticus: "Proclaim liberty throughout all the land unto all the inhabitants thereof" (25:10 KJV). And the founding verses of the British Empire are, "Those who go down to the sea in ships, who do business on great waters, they see the works of the Lord, and His wonders in the deep" (Psalm 107:23–24).

Great Warnings

There were Christian statesmen from these two nations who championed social and economic change, freedom, law, and justice after having a change of heart and a personal experience with the Lord Jesus Christ. Daniel Webster (1782–1852), the great statesman, gave this warning about America's future:

> If there is anything in my thoughts or style to commend, the credit is due to my parents for instilling in me an early love of the Scriptures. If we abide by the principles taught in the Bible, our country will go on prospering and to prosper; but if we and posterity neglect its instructions and authority, no man can tell how sudden a catastrophe may overwhelm us and bury all our glory in profound obscurity.[12]

George Whitefield prophetically declared: "My heart bleeds for America. There is a plot against both your civil and religious liberties, and they will be lost. You have nothing but trouble before you."[13] Maybe George Whitefield was right. Maybe we have nothing but trouble before us and we need to repent, both nationally and individually.

The things of this world have enticed and seduced us (see 1 John 2:15–17), robbing our affections that should belong solely to Jesus Christ. Another preacher warned that the efforts to halt the West's godlessness "may be too late" as evidenced by the rising use among our political, military, banking, and celebrity elite classes of the ancient Babylonian system.[14] We are trying to fill the emptiness inside of us with material things as our source of purpose. Not that material blessings are bad in and of themselves, but God did not shower all these blessings on the Western world for us to live in extravagance, self-indulgence, and spiritual weakness.

We have neglected the only thing that could help us regain our focus and balance. What is missing in our lives is a personal relationship with Jesus Christ, allowing the power and the grace of the cross to change our hearts. The Lord warns us against trusting in our possessions and prosperity. Instead of thinking that we have gained all this wealth by our own efforts, we need to understand that it is God who gives the power to gain wealth for His purposes (see Deuteronomy 8:17–20).

A Civilization Is As Strong As Its Faith

Even "China, a communist nation, also realizes what the West is rapidly forgetting, that a civilization is as strong as its faith," writes Chief Rabbi Jonathan Sacks.[15] Toward the end of his recent book *Civilization*, historian Niall Ferguson drops into his analysis an explosive depth charge. He quotes a member of the Chinese Academy of Social Sciences, part of a team tasked with the challenge of discovering why it was that Europe, having lagged behind China until the seventeenth century, overtook it, rising to prominence and dominance. He said that at first they thought it was the West's guns, because they had better weapons. Then they delved deeper and thought it was their political system. But then they searched deeper still and concluded it was their economic system.

But for the past twenty years, Ferguson went on to say, they had realized that it was in fact their religion—Christianity—that brought about their prosperity. It was the Christian foundation that undergirded both the social and cultural life in Europe that made possible the emergence of capitalism first, then of democratic politics. Judaism and Christianity share an astonishing capacity for self-renewal. That is what happened in Judaism after every tragedy from the Babylonian exile to the Holocaust. That is also what is happening now to Christianity in many parts of the world. And it can happen here too.[16]

Men Have Forgotten God

Aleksandr Solzhenitsyn (1918–2008), a Russian novelist, historian, and critic of communism, has been considered by some as one of the most brilliant and heroic men of the twentieth century. His determination to tell the truth about the oppressiveness of the Soviet regime was, in part, responsible for its collapse. While many cheered the collapse of the Soviet Empire, few have appreciated the main weapon that brought it down: "Truth—one word of truth outweighs the whole world," and "The book is mightier than a bullet," Solzhenitsyn would say.

He was heralded as a hero in the West for his courageous and gifted writings from prison that exposed the horrors and tyranny of Soviet communism. But the reaction in the West was more subdued, at times even hostile, when he began to speak with equal candor about the sins and spiritual poverty of the West, most notably in a commencement address given at Harvard University on June 8, 1978. Among his comments, he said:

> But should someone ask me whether I would indicate the West such as it is today as a model to my country, frankly I would have to answer negatively. No, I could not recommend your society in its present state as an ideal for the transformation of ours. Through intense suffering our country has now achieved a spiritual development of such intensity that the Western system and state of spiritual exhaustion does not look attractive.[17]

He said that the Russian people lost their freedom in 1917 because "they forgot God." This is something that may happen in the Western nations as well. After decades of uninterrupted prosperity, the Western world has turned away from God. We've certainly not honored or acknowledged the Creator who gave us all these blessings. It is very tempting to forget the horrors and inhumane acts of the past twentieth century. World War II alone killed more than 50 million human beings.

The following excerpt, taken from the Templeon Address that Aleksandr Solzhenitsyn gave, can only remind us that forgetting God has very grave consequences:

> More than half a century ago, while I was still a child, I recall hearing a number of older people offer the following explanation for the great disasters that had befallen Russia: Men have forgotten God; that's why all this has happened. Since then I have spent well-nigh fifty years working on the history of our

Revolution; in the process I have read hundreds of books, collected hundreds of personal testimonies, and have already contributed eight volumes of my own toward the effort of clearing away the rubble left by that upheaval. But if I were asked today to formulate as concisely as possible the main cause of the ruinous Revolution that swallowed up some sixty million of our people, I could not put it more accurately than to repeat: Men have forgotten God; that's why all this has happened. What is more, the events of the Russian Revolution can only be understood now, at the end of the century, against the background of what has since occurred in the rest of the world. What emerges here is a process of universal significance. And if I were called upon to identify briefly the principal trait of the entire twentieth century, here too, I would be unable to find anything more precise and pithy than to repeat once again: Men have forgotten God.[18]

Endnotes

[1] Dietrich Bonhoeffer, *Ethics* (SCM Press, Ltd., 1955), 87.

[2] See also John 14:16, 26; 15:26.

[3] Quoted by Verna M. Hall, *A Compilation The Christian History of the Constitution of the United States of America, Christian Self–Government with Union, Volume II* (Foundation for American Christian Education, 2004), 110–111.

[4] Johann Lorenz Mosheim, *An Ecclesiastical History Ancient & Modern, Volume 3* (University of Michigan Library, 1826).

[5] Gildas, *The Ruin of Britain*, (Dodo Press 2010), 18.

[6] Seumas MacManus, *The Story of the Irish Race* (Devin-Adair Company: Reprint Edition, 1980), 103.

[7] Charles Richard Elrington, *The Whole Works of James Ussher, Volume 5* (NabuPress, April 1, 2010). See the whole of chapter 1.

[8] George Macaulay Trevelyan, *British History in the Nineteenth Century (1782–1901)* (New York, 1922), 1.

[9] Walter Phelps Hall and Robert Greenhalgh, *A History of England and the British Empire* (Albion Publisher Ginn: 2nd Edition 1946), 738.

[10] Chuck Morse, *An Introduction to the Louisiana Purchase of 1803* accessed from *http://www.helium.com/items/2087553-louisiana-purchase-jefferson* on March 20, 2011.

[11] Taken from the Declaration of Independence text transcription, *http://www.archives.gov/ exhibits/ charters/ declaration_transcript.html*, accessed on August 13, 2013.

[12] Henry H. Halley, *Halley's Bible Handbook* (Zondervan Publishing House, 1962), 18.

[13] William Gordon, *The History of the Rise, Progress and Establishment of the United States,* 3 Volumes, (New York: Samuel Campbell, 1794), 1:102.

[14]The article was taken from *http://www.eutimes.net/2010/03/world-mourns-as-Communist-darkness-falls-upon-america/* on July 29, 2013.

[15] Chief Rabbi Sir Jonathan Sacks, "China Realizes What the West Is Rapidly Forgetting: A Civilization Is as Strong as Its Faith," taken from *http://www.aish.com/ci/s/Christianity_ Rise_in_China.html* on June 8, 2011.

[16] Ibid.

[17] Aleksandr Solzhenitsyn, His Historic and Prophetic Address at Harvard Commencement on June 8, 1978. The Christian Catalyst Collection DVD, distributed by Vision Video, 540 Worcester, PA, 19490.

[18] Aleksandr Solzhenitsyn, The Templeon Address, "Men have Forgotten God." taken from *http://thefloatinglibrary.com/2008/10/14/men-have-forgotten-god-alexander-Solzhenitsyn/*, accessed on July 29, 2013.

CHAPTER 2

A Christian Heritage of England

For I know the thoughts that I think toward you, says the Lord, thoughts of peace and not of evil, to give you a future and a hope. Then you will call upon Me and go and pray to Me, and I will listen to you. And you will seek Me and find Me, when you search for Me with all your heart. I will be found by you, says the Lord, and…I will gather you from all the nations and from all the places where I have driven you, says the Lord, and I will bring you to the place from which I cause you to be carried away captive.

—Jeremiah 29:11–14

God's Plan for the Nations

The Bible says that it was God who divided up the peoples of the world into separate nations, and who then divided to the nations their geographical inheritance. Furthermore, it says that it was God who determined the bounds of their habitation and their lands. God's appointment of a nation's geographical position and boundaries, although a mystery to us, is directly related to its peoples' eternal salvation. For some reason known only to Him, God divided the nations and set the bounds of their habitations. He decreed that the people of England should dwell in a land that He Himself had constituted as an island, and He had a plan and purpose for that nation.

Paul confirms that God divided up the nations as He saw fit when he declared, "And He made from one [common origin, one source, one blood] all nations of men to settle on the face of the earth, having definitely determined [their] allotted periods of time and the fixed boundaries of their habitation (their settlements, lands, and abodes)" (Acts 17:26 AMP). Furthermore, Moses affirmed much the same thing when he was recounting Israel's history right before they entered the Promised Land, saying, "When the Most High assigned lands to the nations, when He divided up the human race, He established the boundaries of the peoples according to the number in His heavenly court" (Deuteronomy 32:8 NLT).

Not only does God tell us this, but the Bible gives us the reason why He chose to do it this way:

> So that they should seek God, in the hope that they might feel after Him and find Him, although He is not far from each one of us. For in Him we live and move and have our being; as even some of your [own] poets have said, For we are also His offspring. (Acts 17:27–28 AMP)

When God Almighty was dividing to the nations their inheritance and setting the boundaries of their habitations, He decided beforehand when these nations should rise and fall, and He also determined their specific purpose within the larger world context.

David Gardner wrote a book entitled *The Trumpet Sounds for Britain*. In this book, he points out that it was due to a mighty act of God, way back in the dim, distant past, that Britain became an island, or rather a group of islands. There was a time when Britain was joined together, in the geographical sense, to the continent of Europe and formed part of the European mainland. So what happened? Why did it become an island? Gardner writes,

> There was a tremendous severance which experts say that must have been before the pyramids were built, a violent earthquake caused an immense convulsion to take place in the region of the North Sea, and a great oceanic surge came sweeping around the north coasts of Scotland and down towards the east coast of England. In the midst of this convulsion, the marshy plain sank a few hundred feet beneath the waves and thus admitted the mighty Atlantic Ocean to the North Sea and the Baltic. As a result, the

British islands were severed from the Continent at a point roughly between Holland and what is now the coast of Norfolk and Suffolk.[1]

As it now stands, Britain is an island in the ocean, lying toward the northwest at a considerable distance from the coasts of Germany, Gaul, and Spain, which together form the greater part of Europe. Britain remained unknown and unvisited by the Romans until the time of Gaius Julius Caesar, who became Consul with Lucius Bibulus 693 years after the founding of Rome, and just sixty years before the birth of the Lord Jesus Christ.[2]

Christendom was in Britain far earlier than most people realize. It's been reported that before Winston Churchill wrote his book *The History of English Peoples*, he employed an army of research workers who sought to discover when it was that Christianity first came to the British Islands. The researchers found that the task was impossible because Christianity was already in Britain when the first missionaries arrived.[3]

Paul's Call to Europe

In Acts 9 we are told that after Paul's baptism, he immediately started preaching that Jesus was the Son of God in the Jewish synagogues. He confounded the Jews who lived in Damascus, proving to them that Jesus was indeed the Christ (see Acts 9:20–22). During this time, Luke doesn't tell us whether he led anyone to the Lord or not. Rather, what we know is that he incited the Jews to kill him, many watching day and night for the right moment to do so (see Acts 9:23). When the plot to kill Paul became known to him, he arranged for his disciples to lower him over the wall of Damascus at night in a large basket (see Acts 9:25), thus escaping harm. He immediately went to Jerusalem where he entered the synagogues and started "preaching boldly in the name of the Lord. He debated with some Greek-speaking Jews, but they tried to murder him" (Acts 9:29 NLT).

Finally, when the believers in Jerusalem heard about this, "they took him down to Caesarea and sent him away to Tarsus, his hometown" (Acts 9:30 NLT). When Paul left, "the church then had peace throughout all Judea, Galilee, and Samaria, and it became stronger as the believers lived in the fear of the Lord. And with the encouragement of the Holy Spirit, it also grew in numbers" (Acts 9:31 NLT).

Historians then tell us that Paul spent the next fourteen to sixteen years in his hometown of Tarsus. Many hold the mistaken assumption that Paul became a missionary immediately after his conversion. But that is not what happened. It was only when Barnabas invited him to help the church at Antioch that they recognized his calling to be a missionary, and then he was able to begin his work. Luke makes it clear that "[Barnabas] went on to Tarsus to hunt for Saul. And when he had found him, he brought him back to Antioch. For a whole year they assembled together with and were guests of the church and instructed a large number of people; and in Antioch the disciples were first called Christians" (Acts 11:25–26 AMP). What was Paul doing in Tarsus before Barnabas found him? He was probably waiting to be sent by Christ.[4]

During his second missionary journey, when Paul and his party would have turned southward, they were "forbidden by the Holy Spirit to speak the word in Asia" (Acts 16:6); and when he was intending to turn eastward, again "the Spirit suffered them not" (Acts 16:8 KJV). From that moment on, Paul found people open to the gospel message in the West, including the first convert to Christianity in Philippi, and therefore Europe—a woman named Lydia who was a merchant specializing in costly purple cloth (see Acts 16:11–15).

We don't know why the Holy Spirit told Paul that he and his companions should not go to Asia, but what we know is that the West was the geographical will of the Holy Spirit for them to preach the gospel. If the apostle Paul had not brought the gospel to Europe, foundational principles such as freedom and human dignity would not be part of the British and American heritages.

Christianity did not begin with Augustine. Though he is referred to as "the apostle of the English," Augustine did not arrive in Britain until the year AD 596, and Christianity had already been in Britain for over 500 years. This means it must have been a Christianity that was nearer to the pure New Testament form than the one which had been brought in AD 596.

Christianity Arrives in Britain

In order to further understand this, we need to ask ourselves some questions: When did Christianity arrive in Great Britain? How exactly did it come? Christianity could have arrived in Britain directly after Pentecost or very soon thereafter. It dates at least as far back as the period of the Roman occupation of the British Islands, which can be dated quite definitely. Let's try to go back in history and get some facts so we can see when Christianity entered Britain.

The Romans occupied Britain under the emperor Claudius, who is mentioned a couple of times throughout the book of Acts (see Acts 11:28; 18:2). This shows us that British history was happening simultaneously with the events of the New Testament. It was in the year AD 43 that the Roman legions landed in Kent and, after several battles, achieved a decisive victory with a long train of captives, and Claudius received from the Roman senate the title of Emperor Britannicus.[5]

From AD 43, therefore, Britannia became one of the forty-five provinces of the great Roman Empire, and remained so for 400 years, until AD 407. Historians tell us the Roman occupation of Britain gave time for the Christian faith to be planted, and it was within that period of time that there arose a British Christian church which sent its bishops to early councils. It was only fifty-five years before the birth of our Lord Jesus Christ in Bethlehem that Julius Caesar first landed in Britain, returning again the following year. This paved the way for the conquest of Britain under Claudius Caesar in AD 43 and opened the way for the arrival of the gospel.

Christianity is based on facts, and some of the facts suggest that the gospel could have arrived during the ten-year interval between Pentecost and Claudius Caesar's conquest, before Britain became a

Roman province, and perhaps not very long after the day of Pentecost. Those facts certainly suggest that Christianity came to Britain in apostolic times. All the main events relating to its beginnings can be placed against this specific timescale.

Paul writes, "When the fullness of the time had come, God sent forth his Son" (Galatians 4:4), which means that when the right time came—when everything was ready and the way had been fully prepared, when certain figures such as Pontius Pilate and Caiaphas were already on the stage of human history—then God sent forth His Son. And He did this just fifty-four years after Julius Caesar's second landing in Britain.

Britain has just 0.16 percent of the earth's land area, yet in history she was directly responsible for almost a third of the planet at various times. It was God's plan to make Britain to be one of the greatest nations for the purpose of taking the gospel to the peoples of the world. Unfortunately, this great Christian heritage and part of history have been largely forgotten.

New Testament Form of Christianity

Many historians hold the view that Christianity came to Britain directly from Pentecost, or even twenty to thirty years after Pentecost. So this means it would have been the original New Testament form of Christianity that came. Paul makes it clear that the gospel message he preached was not based on mere human reasoning, and he didn't receive it from a human source. Instead, he received it by the direct revelation from Jesus Christ (see Galatians 1:11–12). He also made it clear that if anyone deviated from this gospel, a curse would come upon them: "Let God's curse fall on anyone, including us or an angel from heaven, who preaches a different gospel than the one we preached to you. I say again what we have said before: If anyone preaches any other Good News than the one you welcomed, let that person be cursed" (Galatians 1:8–9 NLT).

It was this type of Christianity that all the apostles proclaimed and which was held in Rome by these early Christians between the years

AD 60–62. This is the gospel the apostle Paul was preaching and which became embodied in the Epistles and the Gospels. And it would have been this type of Christianity that was carried to Britain, if the speed of travel in those days allowed for it to arrive at an early date. God planned it that way not just in Britain but for the arrival of Christianity in the world itself. Just as God planned and foreordained when and where His Son should come into the world to die for men's sins, so He also foreordained the ways by which the good news concerning Jesus Christ would spread throughout the world, including when it was to arrive in different places and countries, and by what means.[6]

After our Lord Jesus Christ had been crucified and risen again, God began to put His predetermined plan into action. He had been preparing the way long before the Savior was ever born. The rise of the Roman Empire was one of the tools God used by preparing the way everywhere for the spread of Christianity to the four corners of the world in such a short period time by the roads built and guarded by the Roman soldiers.

It should be emphasized that, in all this, God was preparing the way for the arrival of Christianity in the world. So God was at work in Great Britain to ensure that this nation was truly built on Christian foundations and principles.[7]

Endnotes

[1] David E. Gardner, *The Trumpet Sounds For Britain, Volume 1: Revival or Perish* (Christian Foundation Publications, 2002), 14–15.

[2] Bede, *A History of the English Church and People,* translated and with an Introduction by Leo Sherley-Price (Penguin Books, 1955, 1968), 40.

[3] David E. Gardner, *The Trumpet Sounds For Britain,* 24–28.

[4] The church at Antioch had been established well over a year before Claudius Caesar's conquest of Britain. This is verified from reading Acts 11:19–30 and by comparing relative dates.

[5] Gardner, Ibid.

[6] Ibid., 29–30.

[7] Ibid.

CHAPTER 3

What Kind of Christianity Was It?

Martin Luther and the Reformation

There reached a period, not only in Britain but also over all Europe, when the pure, original gospel was lost and great spiritual and moral darkness followed. So England entirely lost her original biblical Jewish-Christian foundations. In 1506 the Church of Rome undertook one of the grandest and most expensive projects to date: the building of a new St. Peter's Basilica as the centerpiece of the Vatican. The church was to be so lavish and huge that, when completed 150 years later, it was the largest church ever built and remained so until 1989.

This project was too expensive to fund by normal giving, so as a source of fundraising, the Church turned to the sale of indulgences. This practice of granting indulgences, which was the remission of the punishment for sins through the intercession of the Church, already had a long history. Early on indulgences were granted when a sinner performed some hazardous duties for the Church. For example, going on a crusade to the Holy Land got an individual forgiveness for all sins ever committed. Later it became possible to buy indulgences on one's deathbed, which meant a person would enter heaven immediately, bypassing purgatory.[1]

Pope Sixtus IV's fundraising campaign touted indulgences that would free your deceased loved one's suffering from purgatory as well. Engaging in emotional extortion, Church envoys resorted to imitating the anguished wailing of parents who, in the throes of holy purification fires, pleaded with their children to buy an indulgence and ease their torment.

Auctioning of indulgences to the highest bidder—on the basis of "buy now, pay nothing later"—was another favorite tactic. The state of the affairs was so shocking that in 1512 Johann Geiler, the famed preacher from Strasbourg, predicted that God Himself would see to the much-needed house cleaning: "Since neither pope, nor emperor, kings nor bishops will reform our life, God will send a man for the purpose. I hope to see the day…but I am too old. Many of you will see it: think, then I pray you of these words."[2]

The reformer whose coming Geiler foretold was none other than Martin Luther. The Holy Spirit moved upon the heart of this man, opening him to the truth that no one can earn salvation by his or her own personal works or merit as Rome had taught. In his days as a monk, he sought to save himself by following what he understood to be appropriate practices. He prayed to three saints every day and flogged himself until he fell unconscious on the cell floor. He went on a pilgrimage and climbed the holy steps in Rome on his knees. But he found no peace. His father superior asked him, "If you take away relics and pilgrimages and prayers to saints and all the devotional practices, what will you put in their place?" Martin Luther replied, "Christ, man only needs Jesus Christ." This is how the Protestant Reformation began.

The Lord's plan was that people could be eternally saved from the guilt of sin by simply trusting in what the Lord Jesus Christ had done on the cross to atone for their sins. The scales fell off the eyes of Martin Luther and he realized he was now truly born again, which revolutionized his spiritual experience.

By this time the sale of indulgences had reached a fever pitch. Luther reacted by posting his protest—the now famous Ninety-five Theses—on the door of All Saints Church in Wittenberg on October 31, 1517. The consequence for this was that his protest reached Rome, and he was asked in no uncertain terms to recant. He refused, proclaiming his famous defense, "Here I stand, and I cannot do otherwise." He was excommunicated four years later from the Church of Rome.

The experience of his new birth sparked a movement on the Continent which became known as the Reformation. It spread from Wittenberg to Geneva, began to take root in Scotland, and then came to England. Within a space of ten years it had spread so rapidly that it overran the whole Continent.

The Church and State System in England (1558–1660)

King Henry VIII ascended to the throne in 1509 and married the older widow of his brother, Catherine of Aragon. After eight years they separated because Catherine failed to produce a male heir for him. He later fell in love with Anne Boleyn, who was a young and beautiful lady waiting to be the queen. He asked the papacy to declare the marriage to Catherine invalid, claiming that the original dispensation allowing him to marry her had been in error. But there were many obstacles that stood in the way of Henry's demand. Charles V, the Holy Roman Emperor, was related to Catherine and strongly opposed her being thrown off like a used robe. Through a series of events, King Henry took matters into his own hands, and in 1534 he declared himself the head of the Church of England and married Anne Boleyn.[3]

He was then excommunicated from the Church of Rome, but this in the end solidified English nationalism because people were asking why they were looking abroad for any part of British laws and not acting through their own Parliament. In Henry's reign, the average Englishman retained the feeling of his Welsh and Celtic Christian ancestors against the pope's interference in England. So when Henry's divorce issue was at its height and was being strongly resisted by the pope, Henry himself, in his indignation, came to understand what many Englishmen had realized long before: if England would be a nation, it must protect both spiritual and temporal jurisdiction from outside manipulation. As is so often the case in national affairs, it took a personal issue for Henry to see this clearly.[4]

Henry now found it intolerable that the interests of England should be subjected to the will of an outside power. The decisive moment had been reached. He made up his mind that England would no longer submit to being governed by a religious authority, or any other authority for that matter, sitting hundreds of miles away, judging English matters by Italian, Spanish, or French standards. Henry, therefore, took measured steps until England was wholly independent of every kind of administration from Rome.[5]

When a bill was finally passed through Parliament abolishing what still remained of papal authority in England, just a month later it was followed by a letter written personally by the "king as sovereign, recognizing no superior in earth, but only God, not subject to the laws of any earthly creature." The break between England and Rome was now complete. At this stage, the great revolution known as the English Reformation freed the English church and state from the bondage of Rome and ushered in the acceptance by England of the Protestant Christian religion. Christianity was now free to develop as it always should have been.

William Tyndale: The Bible for Every Person

It just so happened that God had prepared someone for this time: William Tyndale. Tyndale became gripped with a burning conviction that the entrance of God's Word into a person's heart brings light and revelation. For centuries the Scriptures had been denied to everyone except the priests, and besides, they were written in Latin anyhow.

So William Tyndale made sure that the Bible would be translated from Latin into the English language of the day so every person could understand and comprehend it. It was his hope that a copy of the Scriptures should be placed in the hands of every man, woman, and child. His desire was that even the poorest person should have access to the Bible and be able to read it. He was continually persecuted, and later driven from England to the Continent. There Tyndale persistently continued his work and began shipping Bibles to England. It cost him his life—he was later burned at stake as a martyr in 1536. But just before he was martyred, he uttered his now famous prayer: "O God: Open the eyes of the King of England." This prayer is inscribed on a metal plaque in front of his statue in London's Thames Embankment Gardens.

God, in His faithfulness, answered Tyndale's prayer and within a year, after the establishment of the Church of England in 1538, Henry VIII issued a proclamation that a copy of the Bible should be translated into the language that every person could read and understand, and that it should be placed in every church in the land. The clergy were encouraged to personal Bible reading and public reading of the Holy Word. Now that it was translated in English, the Bible became a regular feature of worship. Private ownership of the Bible increased, and in many homes it was the only book in the house that was read from extensively. This definitely had a significant impact on the religious and political development of England.

It was the Bible, above all, which led to the profound spiritual and moral change in the nation at that time. Historians say that the reign of Henry VIII must be credited with giving the people the English Bible. Though Henry VIII married six times, his role in the Reformation was undeniable. He defied the Catholic Church after temporarily becoming the head of the Church of England; and his authority was used to put away image worship, paying sums of money for forgiveness of sins, and other religious superstitions. He also ordered fathers everywhere to teach their children the Lord's Prayer, the Ten Commandments, and the Articles of the Christian Faith in English in their own homes.[6]

Edward VI and Mary I

King Henry VIII died at fifty-six years of age and his son Edward VI, who was the son of Henry's third wife, ascended to the throne in his place. But he also died of tuberculosis six years later at the age of twenty-four. In his short reign, Edward did much to carry on the work his father started of totally severing England from the Roman Catholic Church. He embraced the principles of the Reformation and diligently reestablished Protestantism in England; he also introduced the *Book of Common Prayer.*

Once King Edward died, Henry's first daughter by the unwanted Catherine of Aragon became the queen—Mary I. The problem was that Mary was a devout Catholic. She was only eighteen years old when her father founded the Church of England, and she would not easily forget the offense when he defied the Catholic Church and the pope in order to marry his mistress instead of Catherine's mother.

Mary felt that she had to avenge for that insult and make things right in the land. She wasted no time in her efforts to revive Catholicism in England. She did this by persecuting Protestants, which included burning some 300 Protestants at the stake, earning her nickname, "Bloody Mary." But by God's grace her reign lasted only five years and she also reportedly died at an early age of only forty-two. And much of what she had started was revoked by her half sister and successor, Elizabeth I.[7]

Elizabeth I and the Puritans

Elizabeth I became Queen of England in 1558 after the death of her sister Mary. Elizabeth took up the great issue where her father left it and with a similar understanding of it. When she became queen at the age of twenty-five, she declared her intentions in the establishment of law and order, asking for beneficial cooperation among men, saying:

> My lords, the law of nature moves to sorrow for my sister; the burden that is fallen upon me makes me amazed, and yet, considering I am God's creature, ordained to obey His appointment, I will thereto yield, desiring from the bottom of my heart that I may have assistance of His grace to be the minister of His heavenly will in this office now committed to me. And as I am but one body naturally considered, though by His permission a body politic to govern, so shall I desire you all...to be assistant to me, that I with my ruling and you with your service may make a good account to Almighty God and leave some comfort to our posterity on earth. I mean to direct all my actions by good advice and counsel.[8]

She sought to bring Ireland under the rule of her house and to establish Protestantism as the state religion, to whom every minister of God's Word was responsible for his preaching and for all his spiritual administrations, where the king or queen was head. She almost succeeded in considerable measure.[9]

The problem with Elizabeth was her compromise. She tried to return England to Protestantism by being a peacemaker between Catholicism and Protestantism. She retained the Catholic hierarchy of archbishops and bishops and also insisted that the Church of England's preachers wear uniform vestments and conduct services according to a uniform liturgy. With all these decrees, the Puritans felt that Elizabeth had betrayed them because the Catholic Church with its centralized power had already betrayed Christianity by mediating itself between God and man.

The Puritans had an intense commitment to morality, a form of worship, and a civil society strictly conforming to God's commandments as set forth in the Bible. They feared that the Anglican Church would become just another version of the Roman Church, which would only establish the supremacy of a monarchy over a church that could be easily corrupted by kings and queens. So they refused to acknowledge any authority other than the Bible. That meant no human being—not a king, not a queen, not a pope, nor a bishop—was the supreme and sole source of religious standards.[10] Queen Elizabeth died in 1603 and was succeeded by James IV, who was already King of Scotland, having reigned there from his infancy.

King James I

King James I became King of England in 1603, when he was just thirty-six years old, and with that he became the head of the Church of England. He formed a plan for bringing Scotland into the same ecclesiastical system with England. He summoned a conference of the bishops of the English church and the elders of the Scottish kirk, with the hope and purpose of carrying out his plan for the establishment of the Episcopal system with the king as its head throughout his entire realm.

While the king was in progress to London, the Puritans presented their petition entitled, "The humble petition of the ministers of the

Church of England, desiring reformation of certain ceremonies and abuses of the church…" Whereupon Dr. Raynolds, in the name of his brethren, humbly requested (1) that the doctrine of the Church might be preserved pure, according to God's Word; (2) that good pastors might be planted in all churches, to preach the same doctrine; (3) that the *Book of Common Prayer* might be fitted to more increase piety; and (4) that church government might be sincerely ministered according to God's Word.[11]

But things got worse when King James I forced conformity in ecclesiastical matters that were left unfinished by Elizabeth. The British Christian heritage was once again attacked during the Puritan period. The king then did something unbelievable—he mandated the reading of his *Book of Sports,* which permitted recreations on the Sabbath (which was supposed to be a day of rest from all earthly pleasures and pursuits, dedicated solely to prayer and spiritual matters only). The Puritans were very disappointed with this, and seeing that no good would come from the monarch's meddling in religious affairs, they decided to board to another world as a result of religious persecution. They arrived in the New World on the Mayflower in 1620, intent on establishing a community that would abide and be ruled by God's laws alone, not by those of men.

King Charles I

After King James I's death in 1625, King Charles I then ascended to the throne at the prime age of twenty-five, and in a political alliance married the Catholic princess Henrietta Marie of France. Charles also wanted to assert the divine right of kings. He believed that the monarch was God's representative on earth and should not be subject to man-made laws. He chose his judges, who instead of upholding the law as the defense and security of the subject's privileges, set it aside by distinguishing between the rule of law and rule of government so that those who could not be convicted by statute law were to suffer by the rule of government or another kind of political justice. He made use of his power by dissolving Parliament three times. In 1629 he made the decision to rule without Parliament.

During his reign he made William Laud, the archbishop of Canterbury and an avowed anti-Puritan, the head of the Anglican Church. By means of these two powerful organizations, the king administered the government and indoctrinated his subjects in the belief of the divine source of his sovereignty.[12] Bishop William Laud tried to introduce a new liturgy, and in the process riots broke out in Scotland. Charles was unable to raise the funds to stop the riots, so he had to reinstate Parliament. Parliamentary elections were then held and religion played a key role in these elections, which gave the Puritans great influence in political affairs.

This was evidenced by the first two acts of the new Parliament when it convened in 1640. One was to set aside a day for fasting, prayer, and humiliation, and the second was to appoint house preachers whose sermons urged the nation to renew its covenant with God so that England could become their Jerusalem, a praise in the midst of the earth. Of course the king would be threatened by a Parliament whose members had nothing but contempt for the temporal power of the monarchy and who strongly believed that the sole legal and moral authority came from God through the interpretation of the Bible.

Archbishop Laud began persecuting the Puritans, and without Parliament sitting, there was no accountability. The Puritans believed the Bible taught that all men were created equal and that the monarch had to be accountable to uphold its teaching. It was these principles that led the Puritans into a confrontation with the king. Eventually the dispute between Parliament and the monarch resulted in a civil war in 1642. The king believed he could rely upon Parliament for aid in such a crisis and so called its members to assemble; but the Parliament could not trust the king with an army for the purpose of quelling this insurrection, fearing that he would use it to expel the Parliament itself. Instead of the king sending members of Parliament to their homes, he himself was compelled to set up his government at Oxford. In a nutshell, the king found himself, before the end of 1642, face to face with a revolution.[13]

Oliver Cromwell and the Puritan Revolution

King Charles then realized that hostility between him and the Puritans was inevitable, so he arranged anti-Puritan forces while Parliament also got ready, recruiting the New Model Army, a force of 22,000 men under Oliver Cromwell, a Puritan and sometime member of the House of Commons. All that was needed now was a capable and determined military leader of the parliamentary forces to bring the conflict to a decision. Civil war broke out, which came to be known as the English Revolution or Puritan Revolution. The main issue was whether England should be ruled by Parliament or by a monarch claiming supreme authority by virtue of the divine right of kings. It took eight years, but Parliament eventually won.

Oliver Cromwell and his comrades defeated the royal forces at Marston Moor by their resolute action in 1644, and the king was put in prison. In January of 1649, Charles was tried and finally executed. Parliament, which was now led by Cromwell as its head, governed supreme. He sought a godly reformation involving reform of the legal and judicial system whereby the king had to be in complete subjection of the law.

Cromwell wanted to form a monarchy government, but it was to be a constitutional and a Protestant monarchy with parliamentary government, taxation, and reform of the representation; an enlightened and vigorous administration, belief in individual liberty guaranteed by common law, the service of the state freely open to merit; trial by jury, law reform, church reform, university reform, the union of the three kingdoms, and a pacified and civilized Ireland. And all of this with no halting and wavering foreign policy, but the glorious leadership of the Protestant cause in Europe.[14]

Oliver Cromwell believed in liberty of conscience, which is the freedom of all faiths to practice their beliefs without restriction. Everywhere in Ireland, Scotland, and England there was unrest and riots. There was only one way out, however, and that was for Cromwell with his army to seize the government. In 1653 he dissolved the existing Parliament and summoned a new House of Commons, elected under the control of the army. He then became the executive power in the government.

For five years he pursued with great success the work of consolidating England, Scotland, and Ireland into one national state, giving the British Commonwealth such an international standing as it had never before enjoyed. And at the end of his life, so preeminent was his popularity and prestige, that his son Richard succeeded him without any opposition worth noting. Such was briefly the course of the English Revolution.[15]

Perhaps Cromwell's greatest legacy was to permanently limit the power of the monarch and to empower the Parliament. However, his record among Catholics in Ireland is harshly criticized and his name was associated with massacre and religious persecution of the Catholic community. The Puritan political agenda that led to the revolution was overwhelmingly a product of their religious beliefs, which stressed the right of every man and woman to interpret God's law, as embodied in the Bible, and to appeal to that law above any other authority.[16]

When Cromwell died, the Puritan domination of England died with him. By 1660 there was a shift back in favor to the monarchy, and a new king, Charles II, was crowned. The Puritans once again found themselves the persecuted minority. Nevertheless, God moved again and raised up men like John Bunyan, Richard Baxter, John Milton, Thomas Goodwin, John Howe, and John Owen to keep the true light of the gospel burning. The Puritans left a lasting legacy of political reform not only in England but in the rest of the Continent as well, even as they packed their bags and fled for the safety of America, forming the moral basis of a new society in a New World.

Meanwhile, an English translation of the Bible for the Church of England, which had begun in 1604, was completed in 1611 under the sponsorship of King James. This translation has been noted for its "majesty of style" and described as one of the most important books in English culture and the driving force in the shaping of the English-speaking world.

Endnotes

---

[1] Paul Johnson Touchstone, *History of Christianity* (August 1, 1979), 233.

[2] Ibid., 267.

[3] Ken Spiro, *World Perfect: The Jewish Impact on Civilization* (Simcha Press: Florida, 2002), 222.

[4] David E. Gardner, *The Trumpet Sounds for Britain,* 54.

[5] Ibid.

[6] Ibid., 56.

[7] Spiro, *World Perfect: The Jewish Impact on Civilization*, 235.

[8] David Loades, *Elizabeth I: The Golden Reign of Gloriana* (London: The National Archives Full Document reproduced by Loades), 35–37.

[9] Verna M. Hall, A *Compilation: The Christian History of the Constitution of the United States of America, Christian Self–Government* (Foundation for American Christian Education, 2006), 196. Cited by Verna Hall from John W. Burgess's *The Sanctity of Law* (Boston, 1927).

[10] Ibid., 236.

[11] Daniel Neal, *The History of the Puritans* (London, 1735). Quoted by Verna Hall, *A Compilation: The Christian History of the Constitution of the United States of America,* 201.

[12] Ibid., Hall, *The Christian History of the United States Constitution*, 204. Cited by Verna Hall from *The Sanctity of Law* by John W. Burgess (Boston, 1927).

[13] Ibid., 205.

[14] Ibid.

[15] It seems Cromwell indefinitely limited the power of the monarch. Let us critically examine what had taken place during this world-eventful era in British history, as explained by John W. Burgess (Ibid., 207):

> In the first place, if there had ever been any connection legal, political, or moral with the Holy Roman Empire of the German Nation, as the theory of the Empire logically required, it was now completely severed, and any procession of authority from a divine source through the Emperor to the king was no longer to be thought of. In the second place, the doctrine of the papacy asserting the claim of the popes to act as the sole organ for the revelation and interpretation of the divine will throughout the world was now definitely set aside, both in spiritual and civil relations, within Great Britain. And, lastly, the assumption by the king of the authority of both Pope and Emperor as the organ of revelation of the divine commands was likewise pronounced false and blasphemous.
>
> The sanctity of law from the divinity of its origin and from its transmission through the organs of revelation, to which European belief through 800 years of history attributed authority, was lost…. What took the place of this all-embracing philosophy? The answer was that it must be the nation, within its natural geographical limits, organized in the House of Commons of the central Parliament, under the chieftaincy of the prime minister, the commander, for the moment, of the majority therein because of being the most truthful representative and most successful formulator of the consensus of its views. Every other condition, circumstance, organization, institution, trait, belief, or opinion was secondary to these fundamental requirements, or even more remote from them than that.

[16] Ibid., 242.

CHAPTER 4

The Impact of the King James Bible

The Bible is the most priceless possession of the human race.

—Halley's Bible Handbook

It is impossible to enslave mentally or socially a Bible reading people. The principles of the Bible are the groundwork of human freedom.

—Horace Greeley

The Bible is no mere book, but a Living Creature, with a power that conquers all that oppose it.

—Napoleon

Bible reading is an education in itself.

—Lord Tennyson

The authorization of the King James Version of the Holy Bible was the foundation of the state-church system of England. It has been rightly regarded as the most influential book in the history of English civilization.[1] From the nation of England, the Word of God has gone throughout the world through the missionaries who led many people to know and come into an experience with a loving Savior—Jesus Christ our Lord.

Christ and the Bible: The Word of God

The Bible is rightly considered to be the Word of God; Christ is also the Word of God. The Bible perfectly reveals Christ; Christ perfectly fulfills the Bible. The Bible is the written Word of God; Christ is the personal Word of God. Before His incarnation, Jesus Christ was the eternal Word that was with the Father. In His incarnation, however, Christ is the Word made flesh. The same Holy Spirit who reveals God through His written Word also revealed God in the Word made flesh, Jesus of Nazareth. All of the sermons in the book of Acts were about the Man Jesus Christ.

The apostles preached Jesus Christ and Him crucified—nothing more and nothing less. They preached His death, burial, and resurrection, especially emphasizing His resurrection as proof that He was God who had come in the flesh. Throughout its pages, the Bible declares itself to be the very Word of God. On the other hand, in a number of passages the same title—the Word—is given to Jesus Christ Himself. For example:

> In the beginning was the Word, and the Word was with God, and the Word was God. (John 1:1)

> And the Word (Christ) became flesh (human, incarnate) and tabernacled (fixed His tent of flesh, lived awhile) among us; and we [actually] saw His glory (His honor, His majesty), such glory as an only begotten son receives from his father, full of grace (favor, loving-kindness) and truth. (John 1:14 AMP)

> He is dressed in a robe dyed by dipping in blood, and the title by which He is called is The Word of God. (Revelation 19:13 AMP)

Jesus's life is a testimony to His belief in the divine authority of the Scriptures. At the age of twelve He confounded the spiritual leaders of Israel with His knowledge of God's Word (see Luke 2:41–51). Jesus said to the religious leaders of His day, "You search and investigate and pore over the Scriptures diligently, because you suppose and trust that you have eternal life through them. And these [very Scriptures] testify about Me!" (John 5:39 AMP). Most importantly, Jesus affirmed that the Scriptures are the inspired Word of God. On one occasion, as Jesus was teaching, a certain woman in the crowd raised her voice and said to Him:

Blessed (happy and to be envied) is the womb that bore You and the breasts that You sucked! But He said, Blessed (happy and to be envied) rather are those who hear the Word and obey and practice it! (Luke 11:27–28 AMP)

Jesus used Scripture to teach the fundamentals of kingdom living (see Matthew 5–7), He used Scripture to confront and confound Satan (see Matthew 4:1–11; Luke 4:1–13), and He used Scripture to teach His disciples after His resurrection and to open their minds to understand the Scriptures: "Then beginning with Moses and [throughout] all the Prophets, He went on explaining and interpreting to them in all the Scriptures the things concerning and referring to Himself" (Luke 24:27 AMP, see also verses 44–45).

Jesus quoted Moses, the Psalms, and the Prophets. And the disciples of Jesus evidenced the same respect for the Scriptures as He did, which can be seen by how the Gospel of Matthew quotes Old Testament passages repeatedly from beginning to end, attempting to prove to his Jewish readers that Jesus fulfilled Messianic prophecy. And Paul said:

Every Scripture is God-breathed (given by His inspiration) and profitable for instruction, for reproof and conviction of sin, for correction of error and discipline in obedience, [and] for training in righteousness (in holy living, in conformity to God's will in thought, purpose, and action), so that the man of God may be complete and proficient, well fitted and thoroughly equipped for every good work. (2 Timothy 3:16–17 AMP)

In His Sermon on the Mount, delivered early in His ministry, Jesus affirmed that He had come to fulfill the Scriptures. He said that heaven and earth would pass away before one jot would pass away from what had previously been written, thereby affirming the verbal inspiration of the Bible. At the end of His ministry, in the last prayer He prayed with His disciples, Jesus referred to the Scriptures as the Word of God and then added, "Thy word is truth" (John 17:17 KJV). At one point

Nicodemus confronted the Pharisees with their failure to keep their own laws:

> When the Temple guards returned without having arrested Jesus, the leading priests and Pharisees demanded, "Why didn't you bring Him in?" "We have never heard anyone speak like this!" the guards responded…. Then Nicodemus, the leader who had met with Jesus earlier, spoke up. "Is it legal to convict a man before he is given a hearing?" he asked. They replied, "Are you from Galilee, too? Search the Scriptures and see for yourself—no prophet ever comes from Galilee!" (John 7:45–46, 50–52 NLT)

Yet God had fulfilled this through Isaiah when he clearly predicted in Scripture: "Nevertheless, that time of darkness and despair will not go on forever. The land of Zebulun and Naphtali will be humbled, but there will be a time in the future when Galilee of the Gentiles, which lies along the road that runs between the Jordan and the sea, will be filled with glory" (Isaiah 9:1–3 NLT).

More than 3,000 times the biblical writers claim to be speaking the very words of God. Over and over the writers say, "Thus says the Lord," or "The Lord said," which are common phrases used to describe that what is recorded in God's Word are actually God's words. Peter writes in his letter:

> [Yet] first [you must] understand this, that no prophecy of Scripture is [a matter] of any personal or private or special interpretation (loosening, solving). For no prophecy ever originated because some man willed it [to do so—it never came by human impulse], but men spoke from God who were borne along (moved and impelled) by the Holy Spirit. (2 Peter 1:20–21)

And the apostle John asserted that the one who loves the Lord is he who "keeps His Word" (1 John 2:5).

A Library of Many Books

The reason why we use the Bible to interpret the Bible is because it is not just a mere book. It is a collection of sixty-six books written by more than forty authors over a period of 1,600 years. The Bible is a whole library of many kinds of books, consisting of different genres. David Pawson, a widely respected Bible teacher, tells us, "The Bible, unlike all other holy books, is full of history and geography because God unfolded His total revelation at particular times and in particular places…. God gave us His Word in books, but not in chapters and verses. That was the work of two bishops, French and Irish, centuries later. It became easier to find a text and ignore context."[2]

The authors of these sixty-six books came from every walk of life —kings, peasants, philosophers, fishermen, poets, statesmen, scholars, tax collectors, farmers, and medical doctors. They wrote in every conceivable place—palaces, dungeons, on islands, in the wilderness, in cities, and in the midst of wars. They wrote in different moods, ranging from heights of ecstasy to the depths of despair and sorrow. They spoke about hundreds of controversial subjects. They wrote in three different languages, utilizing every conceivable literary style—history, law, poetry, biography, memoir, letter, sermon, drama, parable, and prophecy. Yet, despite all their diversity, their writings interlock with a harmony and continuity from Genesis to Revelation that can only be explained by pointing to divine inspiration.[3]

The Translation of the Bible: John Wycliffe

John Wycliffe translated the Bible at a time when there was no printing press. The Catholic authorities declared him a heretic for doing so, and after his death they exhumed his remains and burned them. Why would they do this to a man who worked so hard to make the Bible accessible by all people? His crime of translating the Bible into the common English language was a threat to the established Catholic religion. It has been reported by historians that Wycliffe's favorite Scripture was Philippians 2:12–13: "Therefore, my beloved, as you have always obeyed, not as in my presence only, but now much more in my absence, work out your own salvation with fear and trembling; for it is God who works in you both to will and to do for His good pleasure."

The Bible became part and parcel of an individual's life and character in Britain to the point that even literature became steeped in it and personal letters were full of quotations from it. The Reformation in England meant that another important landmark had been reached in the history of Britain. Under Queen Elizabeth I, England became, for the first time, a Protestant Christian country by law, a position which has been attacked throughout succeeding generations and without reasonable doubt needs to be emphasized.

What should be noted is that "reformers wanted to return Christianity to its pure roots—to before the Catholic Church corrupted Christianity as they saw it. In their minds, the roots of Christianity were not in Rome, but Israel."[4] As a consequence, understanding of the Jewish roots of Christianity became a primary task of Reformation Bible study. From the sixteenth century onward, the Bible became the most influential book not only in England but in all of Europe, and especially in those areas affected by the Protestant Reformation.

The British and American people have been the instruments God used to make His Word accessible and known to most of the English-speaking world. Although we have often taken the Bible for granted, and many U.S. and British homes now have several copies each, it wasn't always this way. For many centuries, virtually the only copies available outside of the original languages were in Latin, with the Roman Catholic Church tightly controlling the common people's access to the Scriptures. Neil Lightfoot says about this: "Yet it was in England, so long deprived of the living Word, where the battle was fought and won for the right of the common man to have his Bible in his own language."[5]

After several failed attempts to produce English-language versions in the 1500s, the King of England officially approved the publication of what has become known as the King James Version of the Holy Bible in 1611. Its translators, by order of King James, produced it from its original languages by a large team of Hebrew and Greek scholars. It quickly gained the reputation of being the most accurate translation of the Bible ever attempted up to that time. For almost 400 years it has remained the best-known Bible translation in the English-speaking world. And it has been the model for Bible translations for practically all other languages. No single book has affected the history of the English-speaking people like the King James Version of the Holy Bible.

Since that time, the Bible has been translated into thousands of languages, virtually almost every tongue, with the British-descended people printing and distributing hundreds of millions of copies all over the globe. The policies and resources of America and Britain have both encouraged and enabled the true gospel of the kingdom of God to be proclaimed around the world in recent years. They have provided the climate of religious freedom, the financial resources, and most of the laborers that were needed to disseminate biblical knowledge to all the nations.

Why is it that the Bible has been so predominant in Britain and the United States? The King James Bible has influenced Britain and America's culture, literature, language, and civilization. It has also had a profound influence upon their political and constitutional laws.

God Reveals Himself to Us in His Word

The Scriptures were not written for intellectuals. People don't have to have a PhD to understand what the Holy Spirit is saying through the apostles and prophets. Rather, they were written for the common, everyday person. They were written to convict people of sin and draw them to salvation in Jesus Christ alone. The Bible is God's Word—as we hear and do it, as we study and apply it—that is able to build up within us a strong, secure edifice of faith, laid upon the foundation of Christ Himself. The Scriptures are not hard to understand if we rely on the Holy Spirit, who is the teacher and revealer of His Word.

The Bible is God's truth about Himself. God uses this Word to draw us into a deep, personal relationship with Him; it also tells us how we should relate to Him. It was originally given to the Israelites so that they would know the Lord their God from personal experience. It tells us we are all infected with a virus called sin, but that God provided a Lamb to rescue us from eternal destruction. This is why when John the

Baptist saw Jesus for the first time, he declared, "Behold! The Lamb of God who takes away the sin of the world!" (John 1:29). The Bible is the authoritative Word of God, and its message has changed millions of lives throughout history. It has survived despite the numerous efforts of so many to destroy it.

No one in the English-speaking world could be considered literate without a basic knowledge of the Bible. In Britain it was rated as one of the top fifty most interesting books to read. And in the United States it is a best-seller and the single book Americans say has most influenced their lives. The Bible is quoted by people of all walks of life, including statesmen, politicians, philosophers, poets, and even astronauts. The Lord gave us the English language to become the most widely used medium of communication in the whole world. And it is into this language that the Bible was translated, which defined and helped secure freedom of thought and speech for many people around the globe.

It was through many revivals and awakenings that England became one of the greatest empires in the history of the nations. With all its imperfections and weaknesses, it was still one of the most just and righteous empires in the history of mankind. Despite the opposition of Satan and his followers to the infallibility of the Scriptures, the Bible is still the most widely read, published, and influential book in the history of mankind. The truths found in God's Word have changed the lives and eternal destiny of billions of people worldwide. It has influenced the course of world history, specifically altering the destines of many nations and empires.

When an ambassador of an African prince was introduced to Queen Victoria, he asked her the question his monarch had requested he present to her: "What is the secret of your country's power and success throughout the world?" Queen Victoria picked up the Bible on her table and answered, "Tell your prince that this book is the secret of England's greatness."

Historians tell us that it was a surprise abdication of Elizabeth's uncle, King Edward VIII, that brought King George VI to the throne, putting Elizabeth next in line. During the reign of King George VI there was an enthusiasm for the Bible in both the leaders and the people. But after his death, the attitude toward this Holy Book changed. When she was twenty-one years old, Elizabeth made what she called "a solemn act of dedication" that would frame her entire life: "I declare before you that my whole life, whether it be long or short, shall be devoted to your service and the service of our great Imperial Commonwealth to which we all belong."[6]

It is also reported that during her coronation service on June 2, 1953, Queen Elizabeth II kissed the Bible and vowed to uphold its laws and promises—to judge with law, justice, and mercy, to maintain the laws of God, and to preserve the Church of England. But unfortunately, preceding governments have progressively rejected the instructions and laws of God and replaced them with the laws of man. This has resulted in the destruction of the family unit and subsequent social and economic problems. During her recent Christmas speech, Her Majesty the Queen reiterated the importance of family and faith, saying that the only hope for Britain—and also for Europe as a whole—is to return to the morality presented in the Bible and the gospel of Jesus Christ.

The Power and Permanence of God's Word

Many Christians are asking why preachers can't speak in the same way they used to, giving the Word of God more emphasis in their weekly sermons. We are taught everything in churches except the knowledge of how to study the Word, apply it, or how to help others study it. The discovery of truth is difficult and takes time, but God has promised that the person who seeks shall find what he or she is looking for. God's Word is the only authentic revelation of His will. All human statements of divine truth, however correct, are defective and carry a measure of human authority. In the Word of God, however, the Lord speaks directly to us.

Every child of God is called to direct fellowship with the Father through His Word. God reveals His heart and grace in it. And we can receive from God all the life and power contained in the Word into our own hearts and beings. We cannot rely on secondhand reports because they can't be trusted. Very few people report accurately what they have heard. But every one of us has the right and calling to stand in direct communication with God, reading His sacred words that were committed to paper. When the Berean believers accepted the gospel message from the apostle Paul, they searched and examined the Scriptures daily to verify if these things were so (see Acts 17:10–11). And so should it be with us.

The permanence of God's Word was attested by Isaiah when he wrote, "The grass withers, the flower fades, but the word of our God stands forever" (Isaiah 40:8). The existence of numerous specific archeological sites that are referenced in the Gospels have been confirmed throughout history, some very recently. Based on the very methods that literary and historical scholars use today, the only reasonable and logical conclusion that we can draw is that the Bible is the most reliable book of antiquity.

A. W. Tozer tells us, "Charles H. Spurgeon, the preacher from London, was invited to come and give a series of ten lectures in defense of the Bible. He wired back, 'I will not come; the Bible needs no defense.' Turn it loose, and like a lion, it will defend itself. I believe that, and I believe the Word of God needs no defense. We only need to preach it with power and authority."[7]

The King James Bible was involved in a significant way in the Great Awakening of the eighteenth and nineteenth centuries. Revivalists George Whitefield and John Wesley used a King James Bible and both were used to bring salvation to thousands and produced widespread social changes, as we shall examine in the following chapter.

Endnotes

[1] *The Encyclopedia Britannica.*

[2] David J. Pawson, with Andy Peck, *Unlocking The Bible: A Unique Overview of the Whole Bible* (Harper Collins Publishers, 2007), xvi.

[3] Dr. David Reagan, *Living for Christ in the End Times* (New Leaf Press, Inc., 2001), 73.

[4] Verna Hall, *The Christian History of the United States Constitution,* 228.

[5] Neil R. Lightfoot, *How We Got the Bible* (ACU Press: Revised Edition, 1986), 76.

[6] William Shawcross, *Queen and Country* (McClelland & Stewart, Inc.: 1st Edition, 2002), 31–32.

[7] A. W. Tozer, *Reclaiming Christianity: A Call to Authentic Faith* (Ventura, CA: Regal, 2009), 40.

CHAPTER 5

The Great Awakening with George Whitefield and John Wesley

Moral Disorder and a Powerless Church

In England, the first half of the eighteenth century was a period of moral disorder. According to one historian, this alarming and extensive lowering of moral standards stemmed from a prior indifference to the claims of the Christian faith. The bulk of the populace failed to recognize its relevance. Immanuel Kant called it "'the court duties of religion,' but comparatively few had experienced the glowing reality of personal communion with Christ. Biblically based doctrinal preaching was a discount. Evil and guilt, sin and redemption—the whole personal drama and appeal of religion was forgotten or rationalized away."[1]

According to Dr. J. H. Plumb, "It was not a religion which had much appeal to the men and women living brutal and squalid lives in the disease ridden slums of the new towns and mining villages. They needed revelation and salvation. It was this inculcation of a bare morality, unassociated with the evangelical truths of the Christian faith which alone can bring ethics to life and which made so pathetically little impact on the congregations that the nation drifted to the brink of moral bankruptcy."[2]

"We have preached morality so long," complained Thomas Jones of Southwark, "that we have hardly any morality left; and this moral preaching has made our people so very immoral that there are no lengths of wickedness which they are not afraid of running into."[3] If, however, we are to trace the source of moral decline in the twenty-first century, we must go behind the indifference of the people and the ineffectiveness of the clergy.[4]

Many people openly defied the moral laws and standards, and the whole population seemed to be given over to one kind of orgy or another. Almost every sphere of the English society was corrupt; and against all this evil, the Christian church was a totally powerless and ineffective weapon, either to fight against the evil or to stem the tide. When we look at the present situation we are facing today, we definitely get the impression that we're on the same path again, when history is repeating itself because humanity is in a fallen state unless we have been regenerated by the blood of Jesus Christ.

It has been documented by historians that the first two Georges of the royal house of Hanover were unfaithful to their wives. Because this came from the top, it soon reflected all the way down to the people of the land. The clergy were also corrupt and indifferent, and morals degenerated. The Word of God was ridiculed. The nature and character of God was attacked. Christian leaders and theologians also lacked a genuine fear of the Lord, and they chose to make Him to be a God after their own likeness and according to their twisted image. The deity and the person of Jesus Christ also came under attack during this time. He was declared to be no more than a man, and therefore no longer to be regarded as God. Christianity became a "dead" religion.

The salt that was supposed to preserve the evil was trampled down, and everywhere one turned it was being held in ridicule. When the Great Plague of 1665 killed one in every five people in London, everyone who could flee did so, including government and the official Church of England leaders. But many of the pastors ignored the laws and returned to help their dying congregations by preaching that the only hope for humanity was by trusting in the saving grace of our Lord Jesus Christ.

Then the government of England, which was now in an apostate state, passed the Five Mile Act or Oxford Act. This act forbade clergymen from living within five miles of their former church from which they had been expelled, unless they swore an oath never to resist the king. As a result of this continuing persecution, the Puritans and other non-conforming pastors were driven from their churches and from society. Over 4,000 pastors were imprisoned during this time. Eventually, in 1714, the Parliament passed the Schism Act, which prohibited anyone from teaching without being granted a license from a bishop. This was aimed against dissenters and other schools who did not want to conform to the liturgy of the Church of England.

Great Spiritual Awakening

As a result of the suppression of the free preaching of the Word of God, England descended into a moral abyss, perversion, corruption, and a widespread social and moral collapse. As society broke down, God in His mercy sent a revival through the preaching of John Wesley and George Whitefield. Through their preaching, the soul of the nation that had become a spiritual wasteland was transformed. John Wesley preached a practical gospel that changed every aspect of society. "Christianity is essentially a social religion," Wesley said, "to turn it into a solitary religion is indeed to destroy it…" Wesley declared that a "doctrine to save sinning men, with no aim to transform them into crusaders against social sin, was equally unthinkable."[5]

David Gardner, who provides a beautiful analysis of the Christian heritage of Britain, writes:

> The nation had witnessed a decline in religion and public morality scarcely to be matched in the history of the nation. England had reached an all-time low. Such an appalling corruption abounded that it seemed to call for nothing else but an outpouring of divine wrath. The nation had become ripe for judgment. But just at the point when things were at their worst, God in His mercy and grace raised up revivalists like George Whitefield, Howell Harris, and Daniel Rowland and He used all the three to bring about a great spiritual awakening in England, Scotland and Wales. This awakening is now referred to as the Eighteenth-Century Revival, and by the time that George III came to the throne in 1760, this great Evangelical Revival had swept the land.[6]

George Whitefield

Those who have studied both George Whitefield and John Wesley have considered both of them to be some of the greatest evangelists since the first century. Their compassion for souls drove them to preach and consequently reach thousands for Jesus Christ.

George Whitefield's new life began as the result of reading a book called *The Life of God in the Soul of Man* by Henry Scougal. Scougal laments that few who want to be religious understand what religion truly means:

> Some place it in the understanding, in orthodox notions and opinions. Others place it in the outward man, in a constant course of external duties and a model of performances; if they live peaceably with their neighbors, keep a temperate diet, observe the returns of worship, frequenting the church or their closet, and sometimes extend their hands to the relief of the poor, they think they have sufficiently acquitted themselves.[7]

Whitefield was astonished—all his ideas were overturned. "Alas! If this be not true Religion, what is it?" He pushed the book away. "Shall I burn this book? Shall I throw it down? Or shall I search it?" Feeling like a debtor who does not dare to look in his ledger for fear of finding himself bankrupt, he gingerly drew the book toward himself and stood up. Lifting up his eyes, he said aloud, "Lord, if I am not a Christian, for Jesus Christ's sake show me what Christianity is, that I may not be damned at last." He sat down and read on: "But certainly Religion is quite another thing…. True Religion is a Union of the Soul with God, a real participation of the divine nature, the very image of God drawn upon the Soul, or in the Apostle's phrase, it is Christ formed within us."[8]

Whitefield blinked. He read it again—and the room seemed ablaze with light. In a second he saw, as plainly as if God had written the message in letters of fire, "I must be born again—a new creature!

Christ must be formed within me! I must leave no means unused which will lead me nearer to Jesus Christ."9

The more he thought about it, the more obvious it seemed: the new birth was the point of all his devotion. He seized a pencil, sharpened it, cut some paper, and began to write one letter after another, to his brothers and sisters, to his mother and to Gabriel Harris, the bookseller. All of Gloucester must be urged toward attaining this new birth, this union with Jesus Christ. He could hardly write fast enough. "All our corrupt passions," he wrote, "must be subdued, and a complex habit of virtues such as meekness, lowliness, faith, hope and love of God and man be implanted in their room before we can have the least title to enter into the Kingdom of God.... We must renounce ourselves and take up our cross daily.... Unless we have the Spirit of Christ we are none of His."10

He tried all religious practices in order to live a holy and acceptable life before God, but all was done in vain. He tried all kinds of sacrifices and his friends became worried of his excesses about "the new birth" until he met a woman who wanted to commit suicide in the Thames River because her husband was in jail and her children were starving. This woman wanted to repent and be saved, and the only man who could understand her woes was George Whitefield. He gave her money and promised to visit them both in prison that afternoon.

True to his word, he visited them and began reading to the poor couple the third chapter of John, about the new birth, the chapter he had been puzzled over again and again. He reached the words, "And as Moses lifted up the serpent in the wilderness, even so must the Son of man be lifted up.... For God so loved the world, that He gave His only begotten Son, that whosoever believeth in Him should not perish, but have everlasting life" (John 3:14, 16 KJV). "I believe! I believe!" cried the woman. "I shall not perish because I believe in Him now! I am born again, I'm saved!" Her husband trembled, grasped Whitefield's hand, and cried out, "I am on the brink of hell!" The next moment the man's whole face changed. "I see it too! I'm saved! Oh joy, joy, joy!" he exclaimed.11

George Whitefield was astonished. He had labored nearly a year, yet these two notorious sinners seemed to have been forgiven in a second. So as he entered into a real experience of the new birth, he became a man indwelled by the Holy Spirit of God. As a result of being repeatedly endued with new power from on high, he made a tremendous impact by his life and preaching in England and on the continent of North America. His message, like that of John Wesley, was accompanied with great spiritual power. He constantly called for repentance and faith. Listen to part of one of his sermons:

> Oh my dear friends, I see thousands sitting attentive, with their eyes fixed on the poor unworthy preacher. In a few days we shall all meet at the judgment seat of Christ…every eye will behold the Judge! With a voice whose call you must abide and answer, He will enquire whether on earth you strove to enter in at the strait gate. Whether you were supremely devoted to God? Whether your hearts were absorbed in Him? My blood runs cold when I think how many of you will seek to enter in and shall not be able. O what a plea can you make before the Judge of the whole earth? It was no help that they had read the sacred Word and made long prayers and appeared holy in the eyes of men instead of loving God supremely; they had been "false and hollow Christians."[12]

He crossed the Atlantic Ocean to preach in the American colonies to many people there. Benjamin Franklin, who was a scientist, author, statesman, and inventor, measured his voice and said it could be heard at a distance of a half-mile, and that Whitefield could be heard at a distance of one mile away if conditions were good.

George Whitefield preached, as he had in England, both to win souls and to collect alms for his poor orphans. His opponents spread the word that he embezzled the offerings. Benjamin Franklin, who knew Whitefield's scrupulous honesty, thought the orphan house should be built in Philadelphia and said,

> I silently resolved he should get nothing from me. I had in my pocket a handful of copper money, three or four silver dollars,

and five pistols in gold. As he proceeded I began to soften, and concluded to give the copper. Another stroke of his oratory determined me to give the silver; and he finished so admirably that I emptied my pockets wholly into the collector's dish, gold and all.[13]

When Franklin went to his club afterward, a friend who also disapproved of George came up to him, chuckling. "I suspected," he said, "a collection would be made, so I emptied my pockets before leaving home. Toward the end of the sermon I asked a neighbor who stood near me to lend money for the collection."[14] God had given him a supernatural ability in speaking.

When he arrived back in England in 1739, he found the churches closed to him and society in England was in a wicked state. Whitefield had built on the labors of others but none doubted that from October 1740 a Great Awakening began not only among the people but among the ministers too. Whitefield emphasized repeatedly that a minister must be converted himself:

> I am persuaded by the generality of preachers' talk of an unknown and unfelt Christ. The reason why congregations have been so dead is because they had dead men preaching to them. How can dead men beget living children? Some clergy snorted at this though they had kept their strictures private…. Others frankly admitted being awakened for the first time.[15]

The Disagreement with John Wesley

John Wesley and George Whitefield parted ways on April 4, 1741. Their disagreement echoed the old dispute which split the Reformation between Luther and Calvin, while their different angles on the great Reformation doctrine of justification by faith were rendered more acute by personal weaknesses—the imperiousness of Wesley and the impulsiveness of Whitefield—and by the factiousness of followers.[16] The truth lay in both extremes rather than in the middle: the very tension between these extremes served to strengthen the gospel.[17]

Whitefield set out for a preaching tour through Gloucestershire. By this time John Wesley had gone to Bristol and Wales. They Finally reconciled in 1742 when George recognized that he was partly to blame for the breaking of their friendship by demanding agreement in doctrine as the price of fellowship; had all of them been large-hearted enough, the breach would never have opened. Wesley said:

> Why should we dispute...when there is no probability of convincing? I think this is not "giving up the faith" but fulfilling our Lord's new command, "Love one another," and our love is but feigned unless it produces proper effects. I am persuaded the more the love of God is shed abroad in our hearts, the more all the narrowness of spirit will subside and give way. Besides, so far as we are narrow-spirited, we are uneasy. Prejudices, jealousies and suspicions make the soul miserable.[18]

Reconciliation did not mean the restoration of their former unity however. John Wesley was not prepared to unite with George Whitefield in equal, total alliance for their common aim. They would love one another but work separately unless Whitefield acknowledged the leadership of Wesley. But Whitefield disagreed with too many of Wesley's teachings to acknowledge his leadership. Two streams, therefore, would flow from the Evangelical Revival, instead of one mighty river watering the land.[19]

Together they could have done so much more than they did separately. They complemented each other so well. Wesley possessed a brilliant administrative mind whereas Whitefield felt impatient with organizing although he labored to organize when necessary. Wesley was the better theologian. Both were devoted pastors; but Whitefield was by far the greater preacher of the two.[20]

John Wesley

John Wesley's discipline of study intellectually equipped him to be a defender of the faith. But most of all he failed through self-effort to be brought to salvation or a sense of fulfillment in his ministry, ultimately leading him to seek salvation where alone it can be found—namely, in an unconditional reliance on the merits of Christ the

Redeemer. It was Wesley's conversion that made him an evangelist. Until the experience at Aldersgate Street on the May 24, 1738, he was too preoccupied with the problem of saving his own soul to be effective in winning others. After that personal encounter, he resolved in his brother's words, "To spend, and to be spent, for them who have not yet my Saviour known."[21]

Christianity, at this time, was based solely on the Bible because a Bible religion demanded a thorough knowledge of the Scriptures. Wesley taught that one could never be a "thorough Christian" without extensive reading. This discipleship concept set thousands of converts to teach themselves to read so that they might search the Scriptures and other books which were designed to strengthen their moral and spiritual lives. The Bible, therefore, became central to countless people's lives. To the individual Christian, it was the handbook of moral and spiritual guidance, which became underlined because it was personal. The Bible became the medium of family worship and was regarded as both the chart and the compass in the journey of life in the British Isles.[22]

It was Wesley and Whitefield's ministry together with other Spirit—filled preachers that ushered in a period of great spiritual revival and strength. Historians have spoken of it as the great work of grace which transformed England in one of the darkest periods of its history.

National Transformation

How did this great national transformation come about? First of all, Wesley and Whitefield did not believe, as some religious and government leaders do today, that it is a person's environment, surroundings, and social circumstances that largely determine their character and the way they conduct themselves. Rather, they saw that the teaching of the Bible and their own personal experience of the new birth proved this assertion. It was not a question of changing society in order to change the behavior and character of individuals, but rather a matter of changing people's hearts so that they would change their society. They both saw what the Lord Jesus Christ had clearly taught before them, that the real problem is in the heart (see Mark 7:21–23).

The eighteenth-century revival centered Christianity in the individual heart, not in the state or the environment, or even in the church itself. We need this today if we are to experience another Great Awakening. These two men clearly saw that individual's hearts were estranged and cut off from vital union with God because of sin. So both of them constantly preached Jesus Christ and Him crucified in the power of the Holy Spirit.

They preached and called the sinners to repentance through the power of the cross, which brings individual souls into an abiding, personal communion with God. No evangelism will succeed that does not set the cross at the center. The apostle Paul was prepared to strip his message of all that was peripheral and to know nothing among his hearers except Jesus Christ and Him crucified (see 1 Corinthians 2:2).

Wesley said that the only remedy for sin was to be found at the cross. He concentrated on the death and resurrection of Christ as the essence of the saving proclamation:

> The gospel (that is, good tidings, good news for guilty, helpless sinners), in the largest sense of the word, means the whole revelation made to men by Jesus Christ; and sometimes the whole account of what our Lord did and suffered while He tabernacled among men. The substance of all is, "Jesus Christ came into the world to save sinners;" or "God so loved the world, that He gave His only-begotten Son, to the end that we might not perish but have everlasting life;" or "He was bruised for our transgressions, He was wounded for our iniquities; the chastisement of our peace was upon Him; and with His stripes we are healed." Believe this, and the Kingdom of God is thine. And again: It is the blood of Christ alone, whereby any sinner can be reconciled to God; there being no other propitiation for our sins, no other fountain for sin and uncleanness.[23]

Both of these men's greatest concern was to see the hearts of people changed as a result of individual conversion. They saw that true Christianity was the life of God Himself dwelling in the innermost soul of man by the Holy Spirit. This could then bring forth fruit in terms of new life and Christlike character. It is Jesus Christ who settles in individual's hearts through the Holy Spirit and lives out His life from within the heart of a Christian. Personal conversion and experience were the primary motives of Wesley and Whitefield preaching not social revolution or mere knowledge without a personal experience with Jesus Christ.

Wesley's Deep Concern and Effectiveness

There were so many evils and injustices in society that deeply concerned John Wesley. But he clearly understood that if the gospel could change people's hearts, and they had been brought into a personal experience with Christ in great numbers, as a result of their conversion their consciences would be awakened to all the evils and social injustices of society that surrounded them. Therefore, they would automatically begin to do something about changing the fabric of society and the evils of that day.

That is probably why John Wesley said, "Give me a hundred men who fear nothing but God and hell and we will change the world." And indeed God honored his request and gave him thousands of souls, and changed lives resulted from his labors. The moral and spiritual decline that engulfed the nation was now revived. Many people came to a saving faith in Jesus Christ, and that new faith gradually created a new conscience in all parts of the country. The revival of Christianity changed the hearts and gave a new sense of direction and purpose to the lives of a great number of people.

What really made John Wesley effective in that day when the rest of the church was not as effective? Again, "the only remedy for 'the leprosy of sin' is to be found at the cross." Here was the heart of Wesley's gospel and the final clue to his effectiveness. And the message of what happened there must be proclaimed in all the fullness with which Scripture itself has invested in it. In the New Testament, as someone observed, the cross is set forth as the climax of revelation. In consequence, thus to present it must always be the primary concern of the gospel preacher.

That was Wesley's consuming preoccupation. No historian can easily miss the immense raising of the nation's spiritual temperature by Wesley in his own movement and through the effects in the Church of England. The recovery of the national mind and character of Britain started with Wesley. The souls of many people were awakened and they became aware of the moral bankruptcy and social injustices that were so common in every sphere of society. This led to a desire and determination to put things right and, therefore, positive change was achieved and the whole fabric of society was changed.

Changing the Fabric of Society

Many reforms were ushered in by men whose hearts had been transformed by the gospel of Jesus Christ. This changed every facet of British society, set the tone of public life, the legal system, education system, and healthcare (where Florence Nightingale invented modern nursing). It was the eighteenth-century revival that changed the hospital system—the only major hospital system at that time that was supported almost exclusively by the free will gifts of an appreciative public. As a matter of fact, John Wesley started the first free medical dispensary in England, and it was he who established the first centers offering free electrical treatment to the poor. He always emphasized the sanctity of the human body as the temple of the living Spirit of God by urging the Christian to keep it healthy and pure.[24]

John Howard, who was a zealous disciple of John Wesley, reformed the British prison system and made sure that his fellow men were being treated in a more dignified manner. Most of his personal fortune was expended in reforming the prison system of the day, and it became more humanized, with the penal code also being reformed.

Before the Great Awakening, education in Britain was in great decline. Many people, both children and adults, could not read. But when the revival came, the spiritual awakening spread to many areas of the country—people longed to read and study the Bible. This led individuals to crave spiritual knowledge, instruction, and teaching, and John Wesley made sure that people had access to Bible literature by teaching thousands of his disciples to read. And he also used the printing press to supply them with good Christian literature. Wesley's teachings had such a great influence that parents desired that their own children would be educated, which resulted in an increase of schools and other learning centers.

Sunday schools were introduced that taught reading and writing as well as the knowledge of the Bible. It is reported that John Wesley found these schools springing up everywhere he went. King George III, who also promoted the revival, gave the movement a further boost when he reportedly said that it was his wish that every every poor child in his dominion shall be taught to read the Bible.

The revival of George Whitefield and John Wesley emphasized the equal and priceless value of every person in the sight of God, and the way we treat each other as individuals who are made in the image of God. Men like William Wilberforce, Zachary Macaulay, Henry Thornton, John Venn, and many others fought for the abolition of slavery, and were infused with power from on high to carry out these courageous acts.[25] It was the motivation of people to choose godliness which saved Britain from a civil war.[26]

The Awakening inspired many modern philanthropic and social movements which included Dr. Barnado's Homes, the Shaftesbury Society, the National Society for the Prevention of Cruelty to Children, the Salvation Army, and the London City Mission, as well as many others. What is to be noted is that all these organizations were brought into being by people who were possessed by an abiding love and the compassion of Jesus Christ after the revival. All of them were now motivated to do good deeds in rescuing and taking care of the less privileged, which glorified Jesus Christ. The entire industrial system was drastically improved and caused England's industrial slaves to be set free. And all of this came because of the main influence of two men: George Whitefield and John Wesley.

Endnotes

1 A. Skevington Wood, *The Burning Heart, John Wesley: Evangelist* (Bethany House Publishers 1978), 10–14.

2 J. H. Plumb, *England in the Eighteenth Century* (1950), 44–45. Cf. Lecky, Vol. I, 84.

3 *The Works of Thomas Jones*, ed. William Romaine (1763), 362.

4 A. Skevington Wood, *The Burning Heart*, 10–14.

5 Henry Carter, *The Methodist First Edition* (Kelly, 1914), 174.

6 David E. Gardner, *The Trumpet Sounds for Britain*, 64–65.

7 John Pollock *George Whitefield and the Great Awakening: The Life of George Whitefield: The Man, The Leader, The Controversial Preacher* (Lion Publishing, PLC, 1972), 10–11.

8 Ibid.

9 Ibid.

10 Ibid.

11 Ibid., 14.

12 Ibid., 160.

13 Ibid., 146.

14 Ibid.

15 Ibid., 162.

16 Ibid., 176.

17 Ibid.

18 Ibid., 190.

19 Ibid., 191.

20 John Newton, the ex-slave trader who became one of the world's finest hymn writers, came to know Wesley and Whitefield intimately. In old age he told the young William Wilberforce that Whitefield was incomparably the greatest preacher he had ever heard, saying, "He had a manner of preaching which was peculiarly his own. He copied from none, and I never met anyone who could imitate him with success; they who attempted generally made themselves disagreeable. His familiar address, the power of his action, his marvelous talent in fixing the attention of most careless, I need not describe to those who have heard him, and to those who have not the attempt would be vain. Other ministers could perhaps preach the Gospel as clearly, and in general say the same things. But, I believe, no man living could say them in his way. Here I always thought him unequalled, and I hardly expect to see his equal while I live" (Ibid.).

21 A. Skevington Wood, *The Burning Heart*, 280–281.

22 David E. Gardner, *The Trumpet Sounds for Britain*, 78.

23 A. Skevington Wood, *The Burning Heart*, 237.

24 David E. Gardner, *The Trumpet Sounds for Britain*, 79–82.

25 Ibid.

26 David Herbert Donald, *Lincoln* (Simon & Schuster, 1st Touchstone Edition, 1995), 354. Not forgetting that across the Atlantic, Abraham Lincoln called the Civil War "God's punishment for the sin of slavery," and the presidency was an office that drove him to his knees "by the overwhelming conviction that he had nowhere else to go."

CHAPTER 6

Societal Change with William Wilberforce and Ashley Cooper Lord Shaftesbury

The vigorous campaign in favor of all the above mentioned causes was mainly led by two notable men: William Wilberforce and Ashley Cooper Lord Shaftesbury, both of whom were described as evangelical of evangelicals. These two men were the direct products of the eighteenth-century Great Awakening and where either directly or indirectly influenced by George Whitefield and John Wesley's revivals.

The Western world, especially the British and Americans, need to be reminded that many of the blessings that are being enjoyed today and which have been taken for granted were the direct result of this God-given revival. It was a return to the Bible, the Word of God, that transformed England from a moral wasteland into one of the most respected nations in the entire world.

William Wilberforce (1759–1833)

William Wilberforce was an evangelical Christian and a member of Parliament. He came to faith in Jesus Christ in 1785 at the age of twenty-five, and he almost missed his high calling. His first reaction after being converted was to give up politics and join the ministry. He thought, as millions have thought before and  since that time, that spiritual affairs are far more important than secular ones. Fortunately, John Newton, the converted slave trader who wrote

"Amazing Grace," persuaded Wilberforce that God wanted him to stay in politics rather than enter the ministry.

He was counseled by John Newton to follow Christ but not to abandon public office. "It's hoped and believed," Newton wrote, "the Lord has raised you up to the good of His church and for the good of the nation. Yes, I trust that the Lord, by raising up such an incontestable witness to the truth and power of the gospel, has a gracious purpose to honor Him as an instrument of reviving and strengthening the sense of real religion where it is already, and of communicating it where it is not."[1]

This motivated Wilberforce to think about his conversion and calling. Did God call him to just rescue his own soul from hell? He could not accept that as God's sole purpose for him. If Christianity was true and meaningful, it must not only save but also serve. It must bring God's compassion to the oppressed as well as oppose the oppressors. The Bible says, "Learn to do right! Seek justice, relieve the oppressed, and correct the oppressor. Defend the fatherless, plead for the widow" (Isaiah 1:17 AMP).

After much prayer and thought, Wilberforce concluded that Newton was right. God was calling him to champion the liberty of the oppressed as a Parliamentarian. "My walk," he wrote in his journal in 1787, "is a public one. My business is in the world; and I must mix in the assemblies of men, or quit the post which Providence seems to have assigned me."[2] That was a key moment in British and world history. A few months later, on Sunday, October 28, 1787, he wrote in his journal the words that have become famous: "God Almighty has set before me two great objects, the suppression of the slave trade and the reformation of manners—in modern terms, 'habits, attitudes, morals.'"[3]

No greater reformer in Western history is so little known as William Wilberforce. His success in the first of the "two great objects" was described by a Wilberforce biographer, John Pollock, as "the greatest moral achievement of the British people"[4] and by historian G. M. Trevelyan as "one of the turning events in the history of the world."[5]

Another historian credited his success with saving England from the French Revolution and demonstrating the character that was to be the foundation of the Victorian age. An Italian diplomat who saw Wilberforce in Parliament in his later years recorded that "everyone contemplates this little old man…as the Washington of humanity."[6]

John Pollock gave a fascinating lecture at the National Portrait Gallery in London in 1996. Among his comments were:

> One evening a young English MP pored over papers by candlelight in his home beside the Houses of Parliament. Wilberforce had been asked to propose the Abolition of the Slave Trade although almost all Englishmen thought the trade necessary, if nasty, and that economic ruin would follow if stopped. Only a very few thought that Slave Trade was wrong and evil. Wilberforce's research pressed him to excruciatingly clear conclusions. "So enormous, so dreadful," he told the House of Commons later, "so irremediable did the Trade's wickedness appear that my own mind was completely made up for Abolition. Let the consequences be what they would, I would from this time determine that I would never rest until I had effected its abolition.[7]

Wilberforce's accomplishments were achieved against all odds. He was a little man with a relatively weak physical makeup with a faith that was despised. His task was almost impossible because the practice of slavery was almost universally accepted and the slave trade was as important to the economy of the British Empire as the defense industry is to the United States today. His opposition included powerful mercantile and colonial vested interests, such as national heroes as Admiral Lord Nelson, and most of the royal family. As regards to his perseverance, Wilberforce tirelessly kept on for nearly fifty years before he accomplished his goal.[8] He was constantly mocked, ridiculed, and vilified; he was twice waylaid and physically assaulted. He was criticized by slave-defending adversaries who claimed that Wilberforce pretended to care for slaves from Africa but cared nothing about "the wage slaves"—the wretched poor of England.

A Father's Pain

A. W. Tozer said, "It is doubtful whether God can bless a man greatly until He has hurt him deeply."[9] Far more painful and unbearable than any of these criticisms were the burdens of his family life. William Wilberforce and his wife Barbara were very different from each other. "While he was cheerful, Barbara was often depressed and pessimistic. She finally worried herself into very bad health which lasted the rest of her life and other women who knew her said she whined when William was not right beside her."[10]

When their oldest son William was at Trinity College, Cambridge, he fell away from the Christian faith and gave no evidence of the precious experience his father called "the great change."[11] Wilberforce wrote on January 10, 1819, "O that my poor dear William might be led by Thy grace, O God."[12] On March 11, he poured out his grief again:

> Oh my poor William. How strange he can make so miserable those who love him best and whom really he loves. His soft nature makes him the sport of his companions, and the wicked and idle naturally attach themselves like dust and cleave like burrs. I go to pray for him. Alas, could I love my Saviour more and serve Him, God would hear my prayer and turn his heart.[13]

He received a word from Henry Venn that young William was not reading for his classes at Cambridge but was spending his father's allowance foolishly. Wilberforce agonized and decided to cut off his allowance, have him suspended from school, put him with another family, and did not allow him to come home.[14] "Alas my poor William! How sad to be compelled to banish my eldest son," Wilberforce lamented.[15]

Even when William finally came to faith, it grieved Wilberforce that three of his sons became Anglicans with little respect for the dissenting church that Wilberforce, even as an Anglican, loved so much for its evangelical truth and life.[16] Worse still, his daughter Barbara died of consumption tuberculosis in the autumn of 1882 at the tender age of twenty-two. Wilberforce wrote to a friend on this occasion, "Oh my dear Friend, it is in such seasons as these that the value of the promises of the Word of God are ascertained both by the dying and attendant relatives…the assured persuasion of Barbara's happiness has taken away the sting of death."[17] It is important to note that after Wilberforce's death, three of his sons became Roman Catholic.[18]

Encouragement from John Newton and John Wesley

At one point Wilberforce became discouraged after, unexpectedly, his motion to abolish the slave trade on January 1, 1796, was defeated in Parliament by seventeen votes. He was devastated by this setback and thought of giving up his campaign for the abolishment of slavery. He received a letter from Newton, reminding him of the sovereignty of God in the midst his circumstances:

> You've acted nobly, Sir, in behalf of poor Africans. I trust you will not lose your reward. But I believe the business is now transferred to a higher hand. If men will not redress their accumulated injuries, I believe the Lord will. I shall not wonder if the Negative lately put upon your motion should prove a prelude to the loss of all our West India Islands…. But I would leave a more favourable impression upon your mind before I conclude. The Lord reigns. He has all hearts in His hands. He is carrying on His great designs in a straight line, and nothing can obstruct them.[19]

Newton kept assuring Wilberforce that God had raised him up to be His chosen servant in British public life.

Another trying moment for Wilberforce came when he fell ill in the spring of 1788. The doctors thought he was going to die, but Newton was confident about his recovery. When Newton heard the good news that his friend had somehow recovered, he wrote to him:

> When you were at the lowest, my hopes were stronger than my fears. The desires and opportunities the Lord has given you, of seeking to promote the political, moral, and religious welfare of the kingdom, has given me a pleasing persuasion that he has raised you up and preserved you to be a blessing to the public. I

humbly and cheerfully expect that you will come out of the furnace refined like gold.[20]

The most important correspondence came in July of 1796, however, when Wilberforce wrote to Newton saying that he was considering retirement from public life. Newton once again strongly opposed Wilberforce's urge to end his political career. He wrote back to him on July 21, 1796, to say that his reelection as MP for Hull was a sign that God had further work for him to do:

If after taking the proper steps to secure your continuance in Parliament you had been excluded, it would not have greatly grieved you. You would have looked to a higher hand and considered it as a providential intimation that the Lord had no further occasion for you there. And in this view I think you have received your dismissal with thankfulness. But I hope it is a token for good that He has not yet dismissed you.[21]

John Wesley, who was on his deathbed, also heard about Wilberforce desiring to give up. He asked for a pen and paper and wrote Wilberforce the following letter:

Dear Sir,

Unless the divine power has raised you as *Athanasius contra mundum,* I see not how you can go through your glorious enterprise in opposing that execrable villainy which is the scandal of religion, of England, and of human nature. Unless God has raised you up for this very thing, you will be worn out by the opposition of men and devils. But if God be for you, who can be against you? Are all of them together stronger than God? Oh, be not weary of well-doing! Go on, in the name of God and in the power of His might, till even American slavery (the vilest that ever saw the sun) shall vanish away before it.

Reading this morning a tract wrote a poor African, I was particularly struck by that circumstance that a man who has a black skin, being wronged or outraged by a white man, can have no redress; it being a "law" in our colonies that the oath of a black against a white goes for nothing. What villainy is this? That He who has guided you from youth up may continue to strengthen you in this and all things, is the prayer of, dear sir.[22]

Wesley died six days later (in 1791). Wilberforce took his words of encouragement to heart and persisted with his crusade. Another friend once wrote to him cheerfully: "I shall expect to read of you carbonadoed by West Indian planters, barbecued by African merchants and eaten by Guinea captains, but do not be daunted, for I will write your epitaph!"[23]

Newton was sympathetic with Wilberforce's inclination to enjoy a private life and avoid many things that wearied and disgusted him. But he continued reminding him of his duty to promote the cause of God and public good:

Nor is it possible at present to calculate all the advantages that may result from your having a seat in the House at such a time as this. The example and even the presence of a consistent character may have a powerful though unobserved effect upon others. You are not only a representative for Yorkshire, you have the far greater honor of being a representative for the Lord in a place where many know Him not, and an opportunity of showing them what are genuine fruits of that religion that you are known to profess.[24]

Newton's final appeal in his letter was based on a comparison between Wilberforce and Daniel:

You live in the midst of difficulties and snares, and you need a double guard of watchfulness and prayer. But since you know both your need of help and where to look for it, I may say to you as Darius to Daniel, "Thy God whom thou servest continually is able to preserve and deliver you." Daniel likewise was a public man and in critical circumstance. But he trusted in the Lord, was faithful in his departments, and therefore though he had enemies they could not prevail against him.[25]

Another final correspondence worth mentioning was Newton's constant encouragement of Wilberforce by the prayers and benedictions with which many of his letters ended. Among them was this:

> May the Lord bless and guard you, My Dear Sir, and make you yourself as a watered garden and in all your connections as a spring whose waters fail not. My prayers are particularly engaged for you that the Lord may furnish you with wisdom, grace, and strength every way equal to the importance and difficulty of your situation. May the Lord comfort you in the midst of your labours, give you the desire of your heart in promoting the good of others, and fill your soul with His wisdom, grace and consolation. My heart is often with you, and my poor prayers are often engaged for you. That the Lord may give you a double portion of His Spirit to improve the advantages and to obviate the difficulties of your situation. That you may be happy in His peace yourself and that your influence may by His blessing promote the happiness and welfare of many.[26]

Wilberforce's Prayer Life

We might all be aware of Wilberforce's role in bringing an end to slavery but we've not taken the time to examine the beliefs and motivations that inspired him . Among these were faith, prayer, and waiting on God. In the beginning of his religious career he records:

> My chief reasons for a day of secret prayer are, (1) That the state of public affairs is very critical and calls for earnest depreciation of the divine displeasure. (2) My station in life is a very difficult one, wherein I am at a loss to know how to act. Direction, therefore, should be specially sought from time to time. (3) I have been gracious supported in difficult situations and of public nature. I have gone out and returned home in safety, and found a kind reception has attended me. I would humbly hope, too, that what I am now doing is a proof that God has not withdrawn His Holy Spirit from me. I am covered with mercies.[27]

The recurrence of his birthday led him again to review his situation and employment. "I find," he wrote:

> that books alienate my heart from God as much as anything. I have been framing a plan of study for myself, but let me remember but one thing is needful that if my heart cannot be kept in a spiritual state without so much prayer, meditation, Scripture reading, etc, as are incompatible with study, I must seek first the righteousness of God…. That I have not studied the Scriptures enough. Surely in the summer recess I ought to read the Scriptures an hour or two every day, besides prayer, devotional reading, and meditation. God will prosper me better if I wait on him. The experience of all good men shows that without constant prayer and watchfulness the life of God in the soul stagnates…. I would look up to God to make the means effectual. I fear that my devotions are too much hurried, that I do not read Scripture enough. I must grow in grace; I must love God more; I must feel the power of divine things more. Whether I am more or less learned signifies not. Whether even I execute the work which I deem useful is comparatively unimportant. But beware my soul of lukewarmness.[28]

The New Year began with Holy Communion and new vows. "I will press forward," he wrote,

> and labor to know God better and love him more. Assuredly I may, because God will give His Holy Spirit to them that ask Him, and the Holy Spirit will shed abroad the love of God in the heart. O, then, pray, pray; be earnest, press forward and follow on how to know the Lord. Without watchfulness, humiliation and prayer, the sense of divine things must languish.[29]

At another time he put on record:

> I must try what I long ago heard was the rule E——, the great upholsterer, who, when he came from Bond Street to his little villa, always first retired to his closet. I have been keeping too late hours, and hence have had but a hurried half hour to myself.

Surely the experience of all good men confirms the proposition that without due measure of private devotions, the soul will grow lean.[30]

To his son William he wrote:

Let me conjure you not be seduced into neglecting, curtailing, or hurrying over morning prayers. Of all things, guard against neglecting God in the closet. There is nothing more fatal to the life and power of religion. More solitude and earlier hours— prayer three times a day at least. How much better might I serve had I cultivated a closer communion with God.[31]

Most of us are so busy and immersed even in serving the Lord and carrying out His work like Martha that we neglect the quiet seasons of prayer and communion with the Lord. Before we know it our souls are lean and impoverished. The secret of Wilberforce's determination and success was his close communion with the Lord.

Wilberforce's Determination

William Wilberforce's faith in Jesus Christ animated his lifelong passion for reform. He was convinced that Almighty God had set before him two great objectives, "the abolition of the slave trade and the reformation of manners." As Charles Colson wrote in the Preface to *A Practical View of Christianity*:

The opposition to end slavery was equally determined not to vote for its end, pointing to the jobs and exports that would be lost. Wilberforce again filled the House of Commons with stirring eloquence: "Never, never will we desist till...we extinguish every trace of this bloody traffic."[32]

When the abolitionists analyzed their battle in 1792, they were painfully aware that many of their colleagues were puppets, unable or unwilling to stand against the powerful economic forces of their day. So Wilberforce and his friends decided to go to the people, believing, "It is on the general impression and feeling of the nation we might rely...so let the flame be fanned."[33] The abolitionists distributed thousands of pamphlets detailing the evils of slavery, spoke at public meetings, and circulated petitions.

Thousands of British subjects signed the petition for the total abolition of the slave trade, making a huge difference in swaying the tide. For several years, Wilberforce introduced the motion for abolition; and each year Parliament threw it out. And so it went—1797, 1798, 1799, 1800, and 1801—the years passed with Wilberforce's motions thwarted and sabotaged by political pressures, compromise, his illness, and the war in France.

Finally, by God's grace in 1806, Wilberforce's efforts began to show some light at the end of the tunnel. His friend William Pitt, who had become prime minister in 1784 at the tender age of twenty-four, died on January 23, 1806, and William Grenville, a strong abolitionist became prime minister in his place. He reversed the pattern of the previous twenty years, and introduced Wilberforce's bill into the House of Lords. In 1807, sixteen years after he had begun, Wilberforce succeeded in getting the English slave trade abolished. It took another twenty-six years for him to achieve the abolition of slavery in England altogether. The bill was passed in 1833, which was the year Wilberforce died, at age seventy-four.

Spiritual Movement

In the years that followed, a great spiritual movement swept across England. With the outlawing of the slave trade came Wilberforce's eighteen-year battle toward the total emancipation of the slaves. Social reforms swept beyond abolition to clean up child labor laws, poorhouses, and prisons, and to institute education and healthcare for the poor. Evangelism flourished, and later in the century missionary movements sent Christians around the world. This was a result of a rich Christian biblical heritage in the public square.

Though some people are accusing Christians of imposing their personal religious views on others, again we ought to remember that in America and Great Britain it was the Christians who led the fight against slavery, enacted child labor laws, opened hospitals, and ran charitable societies to aid widows, orphans, alcoholics, and prostitutes. And it is the Christians who are acting as salt and light in society today. Wilberforce knew this quite well. He wrote in *A Practical View of Christianity:*

> I must confess equally boldly that my own solid hopes for the well being of my country depend, not so much on her navies and armies, nor on the wisdom of her rulers, nor on the spirit of her people, as on the persuasion that she still contains many who love and obey the Gospel of Christ. I believe that their prayers may yet prevail.[34]

Today world leaders are debating how to handle the host of social challenges and human crises, but one person looked beyond selfish interests and fought for the abolition of the African slave trade in the various British colonies until they were illegal in the whole of the British Empire. He truly lived out his convictions not only by working to abolish slavery but by reforming other social injustices that still influence our national values today. His tireless efforts, life, and faith in the Lord Jesus Christ serve as an inspiration and example to all disciples of the Lord Jesus Christ.

Ashley Cooper Lord Shaftesbury

Lord Shaftesbury (1801–1885) entered Parliament as an evangelical Christian and soon learned how the elite were treating the lower classes

of people in England. He was shocked by the way the insane were treated and he personally toured asylums and got firsthand information on what was going on within them. He then decided to present these facts to Parliament and to convince fellow members to take action. He profoundly influenced the social welfare system, not only of the British people but of English-speaking people everywhere, eventually becoming known as the "Great Emancipator."[35]

He then tackled the issue of children's working hours which

became almost a fifteen-year fight. There were many reforms that Ashley led that it would not be possible to list all of them here. He labored to see that Christian education was provided to "street-ragged children" at a time where there were no national schools since the time of Alfred the Great. He then pressed for improved sewage systems. There was a terrible cholera epidemic that took 50,000 lives nationwide, further justifying his cause. He backed D. L. Moody's efforts at evangelizing England. He enacted for a legislation to end the abominable practices of forcing half-naked women and children to haul coal and pump water for long hours in darkness. Often they were not even allowed above the ground level at all.

Due to his determination and hard work, boys were also freed from work as chimney sweeps. He fought sex slavery in which girls were sold into prostitution. Considering the minimal financial resources he had, he continued to feed starving children. When he became Lord Shaftesbury, he built cottages and refurbished his estate that had been neglected by his selfish and self-centered father. He advocated for better housing for the poor. On August 3, 1872, he laid the foundation stone of a large housing complex that was named after him at Battersea. He was behind the Factory Act, the Mines and Collieries Act, the Chimney Sweep's Act, and a number of other important legislative enactments which his tireless efforts on behalf of the working people in England have placed on the statute books of Britain.

Lord Shaftesbury was a product of the evangelical revival, but so too were other heroes who worked with him to free industrial slaves. The memorial to Shaftesbury that is in Piccadilly Circus serves as an abiding testimony to the eighteenth-century evangelical revival that freed the factory workers of England. It should again be noted that it was changed men who changed conditions in the factories. All their endeavors were achieved by non-violent means. It was a deeply religious and Christian spirit that permeated these men. When a national conference of factory operatives was held in London shortly after the passage of the 1847 Factory Act, a great note of thanksgiving to Almighty God was given—it is quoted here again by David Gardner:

> That we are deeply grateful to Almighty God for the success which has hitherto attended our efforts, and now that the object of our labors for the last thirty years is about to be brought to a happy consummation, we pledge ourselves to promote by every means in our power those religious and social blessings which it was the object of the Bill to extend to the factory worker.[36]

It should also be emphasized that Shaftesbury and his colleagues freed the "industrial slaves" entirely by constitutional and Christian means without a protracted strike, without a lockout, and without a civil war, and certainly without a single loss of life. All these ugly things were avoided and, because they were avoided, there is no legacy of resentment and hatred after the Factory Act had been passed. Rather, there remained a strong foundation of Christian principles, on which coming generations could build when attaining social changes in the country. In fact, Shaftesbury is given credit with possibly preventing a revolution and easing class tensions.[37]

Historians have dubbed the 1847 Factory Act as "The Magna Carta of the Industrial Worker's Liberty." Some of the things that were involved in the Act included the closing down of factories between the hours of 6:00 p.m. and 6:00 a.m., and the keeping of them closed between those hours so as to put a stop to all-night work. It suppressed the cunning practice of "shifts" and "relays." It guaranteed evening leisure, established practical immunity from Sunday labor, enforced a weekly day of rest, and won for British factory workers the Saturday half holiday, thus providing a prolonged weekly period for recreation and sport long before any other country had even dreamed of such a benefit.[38] All of these social reforms were made possible by Christian men, and none of these things had been in operation before the Act was passed. In addition, the Act suppressed the practice of the free use of women and child labor.

Those who are deeply concerned about broken families today should take note of Shaftesbury's crusade of social reform that women should be freed from the tyranny of industry, and be educated to develop homemaking to the standard of a Christian art or skill.[39] The Act also initiated the practice of compulsory education, and after this legislation had passed through Parliament, under Shaftesbury's leadership, other programs of social welfare began to flow from it. There were many friendly and benefit societies, and a hundred self-help and cooperative movements that sprang into being, as well as workers institutes, temperance guilds, literacy and debating societies, and the self-governing British trade union movement.[40]

The great lesson that the eighteenth-century awakening teaches us, therefore, is that the souls of men had to first be awakened and regenerated before all these social reforms could be set in motion. The hearts of individuals were changed first when the Christian gospel was preached in the power of the Holy Spirit. Then changed people began to change their society. That is the order in which things happened and it is what we need today. Like all other reformists, Shaftesbury had a conviction that Christ must be the center of a living faith. He preached Christ and the people did not mock him for his beliefs, but listened intently and with respect. Non-conformist chapels were established all over the country, and the British trade union movement grew out of these very chapels.

Shaftesbury Memorial and the Statue of Eros

At the southwestern side of Piccadilly Circus stands the Shaftesbury Monument Memorial Fountain. It was moved after World War II from its original position in the center, and was erected in 1892–1893 as a memorial to the philanthropic works of Lord Shaftesbury. The monument depicts an arrow of a winged statue of an archer, which is sometimes referred to as the Angel of Christian Charity. Though it is known as Eros, which is the mythical Greek god of love, others have also felt that it was too sensual and quite inappropriate to commemorate such a respectable person as Shaftesbury. But we should not lose its original meaning, which signified the great work of Shaftesbury and all that he did to obtain the emancipation of his fellow men from poor working conditions. According to one expert, the statue most importantly depicts an arrow of Christian love piercing the world, which is what Shaftesbury's love for his fellow men sought to do.

William Gladstone (1809–1898) was a British prime minister four separate times. He depended on and relied upon the direct inspiration of the Bible and had a view of the individual conscience which in turn affected and influenced his political outlook. He gave a tribute to Lord Shaftesbury that can be seen today inscribed around the base of this memorial. It states:

> During a public life of half a century he devoted the influence of his station, the strong sympathies of his heart, and the great power of his mind, to honoring God by serving his fellow men; an example to his order, a blessing to his people, and a name to be by them ever gratefully remembered.[41]

We Should Glorify God

As much we admire and appreciate these men of God, and how God greatly used them in the Great Awakening and the societal change that happened after, I must express in the fullest terms that the whole lesson from these men will be missed if it leads us to glorify an individual instead of glorifying God. As Leonard Ravenhill has noted, "Biographies are so fallible and often are incomplete. God alone knows all men's tears and their travails. The 'great day' alone will give the full score."[42]

In connection with this, I would mention that the Word of God alone is our standard of judgment in spiritual things; it alone can only be explained by the Holy Spirit in this present time, as well as throughout the past. He is the teacher of His people. Without the Holy Spirit of God, we are all nothing. Zechariah declared, "This is the word of the Lord unto Zerubbabel, saying, Not by might, nor by power, but by My Spirit, saith the Lord of hosts" (Zechariah 4:6 KJV). It is not by gifts, eloquence, or the organizational skills of any man; it is not by good music, good praying, good preaching, or anything else; but it is only by the Holy Spirit of God who works with His might through His people.

Wilberforce, Shaftesbury, and others lived at a time when Great Britain had fallen to its lowest debauchery in her history. With their resolve to make morality fashionable, they so radically transformed this nation that the period after them is known for its high morality—the Victorian Age. Could that happen again in Britain and America today, where both countries have fallen to their lowest level of debauchery, corruption, and immorality of all time? Time will tell whether the prayers of the remnant will prevail. But we are called to have hope and pray for the awakening of the West.

Endnotes

1 Quoted in Os Guinness, *The Call: Finding and Fulfilling the Central Purpose of Your Life* (W. Publishing Group, Thomas Nelson, Inc., 1998, 2003), 29.

2 Ibid., 27–28.

3 Ibid.

4 John Pollock, "A Man Who Changed His Times," in *Character Counts: Leadership Qualities in Washington, Wilberforce, Lincoln, and Solzhenitsyn,* ed. Os Guinness (Grand Rapids: Baker Book House, 1999), 87.

5 George Macaulay Trevelyan, *British History of the Nineteenth Century* (1782–1901) (Longmans Green and Company: New York, 1922).

6 Quoted in Os Guinness, *Character Counts: Leadership Qualities in Washington, Wilberforce, Lincoln, and Solzhenitsyn,* (Baker Books: Michigan, 1999), 70.

7 Ibid., 77.

8 Quoted in Os Guinness, *The Oak and the Call* (Baker Books: Michigan 1999), 28.

9 A. W. Tozer, *Mystery of The Holy Spirit*, ed. Rev. James L. Snyder (Alachua, FL: Bridge Logos Foundation, 2007), 14.

10 Betty Steele Everett, *Freedom Fighter: The Story of William Wilberforce* (Fort Washington, PA: Christian Literature Crusade, 1994), 64–65.

11 John Piper, *Amazing Grace in the Life of William Wilberforce* (Wheaton: Crossway Books, 2006), 51.

12 Ibid.

13 John Pollock, *Wilberforce* (London: Constable and Company, 1977), 267.

14 John Piper, *Amazing Grace in the Life of William Wilberforce*, 52.

15 John Pollock, *Wilberforce*, 268. From his Diary, April 11, 1819.

[16] Ibid., 280.

[17] Ibid.

[18] Ibid.

[19] Jonathan Aitken, *John Newton: From Disgrace to Amazing Grace* (Crossway Publishing: Wheaton, Illinois, 2007), 312.

[20] Ibid.

[21] Ibid., 314.

[22] A. B. Hyde, *The Story of Methodism Throughout the World* (Springfield, MA: Wiley & Co., 1889), 237.

[23] John Pollock, "A Man Who Changed His Times," in *Character Counts: Leadership Qualities in Washington, Wilberforce, Lincoln, and Solzhenitsyn,* ed. Os Guinness (Grand Rapids: Baker Book House, 1999), 83.

[24] Ibid., 314–315.

[25] Ibid., 315.

[26] Ibid., 317.

[27] Edward McKendree Bounds, *Purpose in Prayer* (New York: Fleming H. Revell Company, 1920), 88–91.

[28] Ibid.

[29] Ibid.

[30] Ibid.

[31] Ibid.

[32] Preface to William Wilberforce, *A Practical View of Christianity* (Hendrickson Publishers, Inc.: Peabody, Massachusetts, 1996), xiii.

[33] Ibid.

[34] Ibid., xvii.

[35] David E. Gardner, *The Trumpet Sounds for Britain,* 86.

[36] Ibid., 87.

[37] David E. Gardner, *The Trumpet Sounds For Britain,* 88.

[38] Ibid.

[39] Ibid., 89.

[40] Ibid.

[41] Ibid., 87.

[42] Leonard Ravenhill, *Sodom Had No Bible* (Christian Life Books, originally published by Bethany House Publishers, 1971), 146.

CHAPTER 7

Missionaries and the European Colonization of Africa: Part 1

David Livingstone

Most people believe that all missionaries were promoters of European colonization of Africa, but there were many Christian missionaries who opposed the imperialistic policies of the British Empire, especially in regards to the issue of the slave trade. These missionaries saw that the propagation of the gospel could not be combined with imperial pursuits. One of the most notable missionaries who fought against these injustices was David Livingstone (1813–1873), of the London Missionary Society (LMS). Livingstone opposed the harsh treatment of the indigenous people, which was a concept of missionary enterprise different from other members of the London Missionary Society. He also regarded the mission field not only for evangelizing the natives but also for the provision of all people's social, economic, political, and spiritual needs.

In order to achieve this end, however, he decided to define three categories that affected the whole scope of human activity: Christianity, commerce, and civilization. In an area such as central Africa, which was dominated by the slave trade both by Europeans and Arabs, Livingstone believed that all the inhumane  activities of the slave trade could be alleviated by the introduction of commerce and good government which ensured civil and religious rights for the people that guided by Christian principles. Christianity had to provide a moral compass to guide Africans, while education and commerce would encourage them to produce their own goods from their abundant fertile soils to trade with the Europeans. Livingstone believed that the development of agriculture and industry would raise the standard of living for Africans and help them overcome the scourge of the slave trade.

He found the challenges of the slave trade and illiteracy to be among the greatest blocks to Christian progress and economic empowerment in Africa. Therefore, he believed the introduction of education and lawful commerce would prepare the African people for development through the impartation of skills, combining Christian values and ethos, and which would also provoke African initiatives in the development of their natural resources.

While addressing a series of meetings throughout England, most notably before the University of Cambridge on December 4, 1857, Livingstone called on professionals consisting of graduates, undergraduates, and laymen from the neighboring towns, to go to Africa as missionaries with a view of promoting commerce, Christianity, and civilization. In one of his addresses, he concluded:

> I beg to direct your attention to Africa, I know that in a few years
> I shall be cut off in that country, which is now open; do not let it
> be shut again! I go back to Africa to make an open path for
> commerce and Christianity; do carry out the work which I began.
> I leave it with you![1]

Livingstone believed that uniting Christianity, commerce, and civilization would improve the life and prosperity of Africans and stem the loss of population which was caused by the slave trade, transforming the more violent institutions of African society.[2]

Historians tell us that though the slave trade had been abolished in 1807, smuggling continued even after Wilberforce and other campaigners had managed to push the bill for the abolition through Parliament in 1804. So abolitionist Thomas Buxton began to work for the abolishment of slavery itself. He suggested that the best way of eliminating slavery in Africa was the introduction of legitimate trade in Africa. Buxton believed that opening up the African continent to legitimate trade would undermine the slave trade at its source.

David Livingstone was strongly influenced by Buxton's arguments that the slave trade would be destroyed through the influence of legitimate commerce.[3] Buxton not only called for the total eradication of it, but he also proposed other necessary measures, like influencing of missionary enterprises, exploration of geography of the continent, study of African languages, elimination of tropical diseases, introduction of more sophisticated methods of agriculture, and the institution of legitimate commerce and of engineering projects, all of which would facilitate the elimination of the slave trade.[4]

Because the slave trade had been created and sustained through the demand for desirable European goods, these goods could now be supplied instead through commerce in agricultural produce and other products. In fact, it was after attending one of the meetings addressed by Buxton that Livingstone told his audience in England, "A prospect is now before us of opening Africa for commerce and the Gospel."[5]

Livingstone Inspired by William Wilberforce

Inspired by what William Wilberforce called "a practical view of true practical Christianity," Livingstone endeavored to open Africa for legitimate commerce. In 1854 he wrote to his brother-in-law about his determination to do so, saying, "I shall open up a path into the interior or perish. I never have the shadow of a shade of doubt as to the propriety of my course, and wish only that my exertions may be honored so far that the gospel may be preached and believed in all this dark region."[6]

When he traveled to the west coast overland, he proposed that more effective communications could be established from the east coast, up the Zambezi River and its tributaries, into the sphere of the Arab or Swahili slave trade of eastern Africa. He called on the British government to use diplomatic means to persuade the Arab Sultan of Zanzibar, the commercial center of the eastern slave trade, to prohibit the practice. It was in this context that Livingstone formulated his phrase of three Cs—Christianity, commerce, and civilization—for his lecture tour in England in December 1857, saying:

> I am going back to that country and my object is to open up traffic along the banks of the Zambezi, and also to preach the Gospel. The natives of Central Africa are very desirous of trading, but their only traffic is at present in salves, of which the poorer people have an unmitigated horror: it is therefore most desirable to encourage the former principle, and thus open a way for the consumption of free productions, and the introduction of Christianity and commerce. By encouraging the native propensity for trade, the advantages that might be derived in a commercial point of view are incalculable; nor should we lose sight of the inestimable blessings it is in our power to bestow upon the enlightened African, by giving him the light of Christianity. Those two pioneers of civilization—Christianity and commerce—should ever be inseparable.[7]

He further wrote about his first impressions of Africa and its people from a place near Port Elizabeth on May 19, 1841. He wrote,

> The Hottentots of Hankey appear to be in a state similar to that our forefathers in the days immediately preceding the times of the Covenanters. They have a prayer meeting every morning at four o'clock and it is well attended. They began it during a visitation of measles among them, and liked it so much that they still continue…[8]

David Livingstone saw a striking similarity between the African and Scottish environments, and between Africans and his own Highland ancestors. He therefore concluded that the African environment combined with education and Christianity would be a conducive environment for economic progress.[9] In his letter to J. J. Freeman, who was a missionary in Madagascar, dated on July 3, 1842, he explained how he had been inspired to promote a more civilized life as well as true religion:

Not long after our arrival it occurred to me that it would be advantageous if we could lead out for irrigation the fine stream which winds round the foot of the hill on which their town is built. And this is because it would both furnish the teachers with an available garden and also help to convince the people that they might by a little industry render themselves independent of those impostors called "rain makers."[10]

Livingstone realized how much drought affected people's economic activities and thus affected missionary work. He therefore introduced the idea of a dam to retain river water and irrigate crops during drought periods:

I declared that I could make rain too, not however by enchantment like them, but leading out their river for irrigation. The idea took off mightily and to work we went instantly. Even the chief's own doctor went at it, laughing heartily at the cunning of the foreigner who can make rain like that.[11]

Livingstone participated in village projects such as building of houses, cobbling shoes, carpentry, smithing iron, and gun and wagon mending, as well as vegetable and fruit gardening.[12] During the construction of the dam, Livingstone wrote to his sister Agnes on April 4, 1842:

I am engaged in leading out the water to irrigate a garden for Pomore, a native teacher. For this purpose we have been obliged to raise a huge dam of earth and stone and dig a canal. The Natives do it all themselves. I am only an overseer, for the first day I got my legs and arms so burnt by the sun, although in the water almost the whole time, I was unable to stimulate them by my example.[13]

The strategy was that all this development could be promoted through market economies, private property, unrestricted trade, the use of irrigation to maximize production, and increased levels of consumption. This increased trade and economic activity would in process facilitate the spread of the gospel. It is been noted that these three Cs were closely interlinked and reinforced one another. David Livingstone knew that when one tribe began to trade with another, it felt a sense of mutual dependence. He knew this could diffuse the blessings of Christianity, because one tribe would never go to another without telling the news of the gospel, and, this in this way, the knowledge of Christianity was thus spread by means of commerce.[14]

Livingstone Disappeared

A story is told of David Livingstone when he disappeared without a trace on a trip into the jungle areas of central Africa. The last reliable news of his expedition reported that Livingstone was sick, without any medical supplies, and deserted by his guides. Many people in Britain and Europe gave up, thinking he was forever lost, especially after more than a year of a frantic search ended with no news from Africa. However, a small group of dedicated Christians in London believed that they must launch a rescue mission in an attempt to save one of Scotland's finest sons.

This group sent an explorer, Henry M. Stanley, to mount an expedition to find Livingstone. Stanley embarked on a journey across the jungles and rivers of the unknown continent of Africa in his attempt to locate David Livingstone. When Stanley started his journey, he carried extensive baggage that included several cases containing seventy-three of his favorite hardbound books weighing 180 pounds.[15] As he and his group of African carriers began to succumb to fatigue after 300 miles of travel through the jungle, Stanley reluctantly began to abandon or burn his precious books to light fires each night. As they continued through the jungle, Stanley's library dwindled in size until there was only one book left, his precious Bible.

With God's supernatural assistance, Stanley finally found this great man of God and greeted him with the famous words, "Dr. Livingstone, I presume?" The two explorers shared their deep personal faith in Jesus Christ. Livingstone told Stanley about the wonderful conversions of many African tribes to faith in Jesus Christ although they had previously engaged in cannibalism. When Stanley returned from this incredible journey, he reported that he had read his beloved Bible through from Genesis to Revelation three times during his long journey.[16]

Combining the Three Cs

Livingstone's other ideas of combining Christianity, commerce, and education was that Africans could produce raw materials so they could trade with Europe for manufactured goods. In central Africa, he discovered the potential for export of materials such as seed oils, fibers, dyes (which were useful for the manufacturing of paper), sheep's wool, honey, sugarcane, coffee, millet, cotton, indigo, iron, and coal. Most critics argued that this was still a form of exploitation of Africa by Europe. For instance, when the colonists came, they brought with them magistrates, police, and their own administrators who then worked with the indigenous people to implement their colonial ambitions.

They introduced a tax for the natives and legislation for breaking these tax laws if natives wouldn't comply. Was this a more civilized way of exploiting people through slavery? Not at all. Rather, it greatly severed the relationship between the different tribes and brought strife between those who had good relations in the past. How was this done? By dividing and conquering—some tribes were considered to be superior to others, and better job opportunities would be offered to one tribe over the other, which created animosity among the different tribes. When the colonists left, these seeds of bitterness brought about events similar to the Rwandan genocide which killed over a million people. We need to understand that some colonists intended to exploit the Africans by infiltrating these noble Christian men and women. The exploiters could not pioneer anything for the purpose of freeing the slaves. They had to let the missionaries build the infrastructure of these nations, then infiltrate their established systems and change them from within, using their colonial laws.

John Philip

Another notable Scottish evangelist, John Philip (1775–1851), went to South Africa as a missionary in 1820, and in 1822 he was appointed superintendent of the London Missionary Society in South Africa, where he served until 1850.[17] Like Livingstone, he also argued that if Africans were given the opportunity of education, they would become self-sufficient. He charged the corrupt colonial system for the unfair treatment of Africans, and in 1823 he decided to go back to England to lobby for African civil rights. He argued that the source of the problem was not the wickedness of the indigenous people, but that both the Boer and British farmers had taken their land. He believed that the gospel could not be preached without developing political, social, economic, and civil right freedoms for all peoples. He wanted dignity to be restored to those Africans  who were forced to work for the colonial masters without pay by giving them legal contracts and terms of service.

The House of Commons adopted his recommendations, but his views were not popular with the Boers who became agitated because of his ideas. In 1828 an ordinance was passed granting all colored persons equal rights, just like all other British subjects were entitled to. John Philip noticed the role Christianity had played in the development of civilization in Scotland and he believed the influence of Christianity and the gospel in the development of education, civilization, industry, and trade would be incorporated the same way in Africa. Literacy, in particular, was expected to lead to economic prosperity and increase the number of skilled artisans, craftsmen, and small businessmen.

Philip saw the Bethelsdorp Mission near Port Elizabeth, whose first missionary was Johannes van der Kemp, as the model for this pattern of development. This mission center was 375 miles east of Cape Town, South Africa. It was created as a refuge to provide civil rights and social justice for the local Khoi people who were engaged on white farms. The Khoi people started their own businesses, received proper education and health services, and attended church services. The mission flourished as a Christian community.

John Philip argued that if Africans had their own freehold land and were given a chance to trade and to farm in an atmosphere of basic human rights, then they would be able to play their own part in preaching the gospel and advancing Christianity, trade, and civilization.[18]

As John Philip was one main spokesmen of LMS, his main message was aimed at bringing an individual into a warm personal relationship with Jesus Christ as Savior and a commitment to spreading the good news about redemption from the power of sin and death to all mankind, scorning all denominational differences which were a hindrance to the task. He said,

> Our motive is not to send Presbyterianism, Independency, Episcopacy, or any other form of Church Order and Government about which there may be differences of opinion among serious persons, but the Glorious Gospel of the blessed God to the Heathen: and that it should be left (as it ever ought to be left) to the minds of the persons whom God may call into the fellowship of His Son from among them to assume for themselves such form of Church government as to them shall appear most agreeable to the Word of God.[19]

These laws, in effect, placed upon every "free person of color" the need to be the servant of or dependent of someone who was white. In regards to these awful laws, Phillip responded, "There is no tyranny so cruel as that which is exercised under the pretext of law, and under the color of justice; when wretches are, so to speak, drowned on the very plank to which they clung for safety."[20]

The colored people were subjected to many impositions that did not apply to whites; impositions, as Philip came to understand, that were deliberately created to provide a cheap labor pool for white farmers and traders in South Africa. One of the impositions was the *corvee*, which is unpaid work on demand as a tax. Philip complained of its effects in checking the attempts of some of the Christians at the mission stations to improve themselves. He wrote:

> If a Hottentot, possessing one wagon by which he is able to earn 76 dollars by one journey to Grahamstown and he is liable to be dragged from his employment to serve for 4 shillings a day, the people liable to such extortions, labor under oppression.[21]

John Philip campaigned forcefully, but he was unsuccessful in changing these laws. In 1826 he returned to England determined to solicit evangelical political groups in his cause, especially the Anti-Slavery Society. He became a close friend to Thomas Fowell Buxton, who encouraged him to write a book about the situation. This book was published in 1828 and became known as *Researches in South Africa: Illustrating the Civil, Moral, and Religious Conditions of the Native Tribes.* They both waged a campaign to stop slavery and, just like with Livingstone, a victory was gained in Parliament.[22]

Livingstone's Missionary Ideas Led to Colonization

All these factors further influenced David Livingstone's missionary ideas in Africa. When he arrived at the Cape on March 17, 1841, he spent some time with John Philip before proceeding to his final destination. He soon realized that LMS missionaries at the Cape were divided over the question of church and state relations. Some missionaries sympathized with the colonists, others with the African people. Livingstone straight away took the side of those who fought to protect the civil rights of Africans.[23]

Livingstone's point of view was that salvation for Africa could be found in her fertile soil—the slave trade could be eliminated by drawing on Africa's own resources. Agricultural development and enhanced trade would help to produce conditions in which Christianity would spread. These developments would lead to literacy, printing, new technologies, roads and transport, new forms of civil organization, and good government which would lead to civilization in Africa.[24]

At the same time, there is no denial that Livingstone's

determination to open up Africa for trade, Christianity, and civilization, ultimately led to European colonization. There is no evidence that Livingstone consciously promoted the idea of imperialism—he was against any domination of Africans and he wasn't motivated by personal riches or power at the expense of poor Africans. He also declined to be associated with individuals whose main motivation was to colonize Africa and create permanent settlements for their own selfish goals.

What inspired him most was to preach the gospel and to open Africa for legitimate and lawful trade, education, and good government, and to make Africa a conducive and peaceful environment for the spreading of the gospel of Jesus Christ. But still critics were not convinced. They've dubbed Livingstone and other missionaries to have led the way for European colonization of Africa. One of those who hold this view was one of his biographers, Cecil Northcott. He wrote:

> Livingstone was a colonist and was not ashamed of it. He was in Africa to offer the benefits of the white man's civilization, and no latter day beliefs in the black man's freedom, liberation and independence may be read into his actions.[25]

African missionary Loren Davis put it this way:

> In spite of the primitive nature of some people at that time, we have to understand that African villages were very structured. Every inhabited part of Africa was communal property of each tribe. The tribal chiefs and elders allocated land to its people. The land belonged to the people but the colonizing nations coveted the land, wealth, and the labor force of the Dark Continent. Not all of the state's missionaries intentionally were working with their governments to bring in colonization, but intentional or not, they were used by their governments, and they facilitated it. When the state church missionaries came, and the colonists followed them, they always came bearing gifts and making great promises of a better life to the natives. But their gifts were only a bait used to

seduce them so they could take over their land, their lives, then rule over them. This caused Africans to lose their independence, self-rule, and freedom. Colonization was so successful because many chiefs cooperated with the wealthy foreigners who came. They sold the land and freedom for their own personal benefits. The same basic problem today is that many of the African leaders care about their own welfare, and really don't care about their own people.[26]

William Carey

 This idea of combining commerce, Christianity, and civilization was also exemplified by William Carey (1761–1834), who formulated these principles upon which his missionary service would be formed. He encouraged financial self-reliance by training the indigenous ministers. He noted: "Our finances being small, it will be necessary to live economically—industry being absolutely necessary, everyone would have his proper work allotted him, and would be employed at his post; some cultivating the land, some instructing, some learning, some preaching and the women superintending the domestic concerns."[27]

Similar to what Livingstone had done in Africa, Carey wanted missionaries to come to India to develop trade and industry in mission centers. He called on young men with appropriate training to come out to India as medical missionaries, experts in industrial development, and teachers in schools.[28] By 1794 he had opened his first primary school at his own expense and begun to develop the local people's language. He subsequently conducted scientific experiments in order to improve agricultural and horticultural practices.[29]

He also fought for women's rights, especially the banning of *suttee*, which was the practice of burning widows alive after their husbands had died. When the ban went into effect, many cried that the foundations of the Hindu society would be shaken if widows were not burned alive. Others argued that that the ban would violate Article Twenty-Five of India's constitution that gave the people freedom of religion.[30]

He faced many obstacles along the way, and among them was the East India Company, which was against his activities because they would hinder their trading. Christian missionaries have always been accused of destroying local culture, but Carey was honored in India for serving that nation, including helping the resurgence of the Bengali language. Carey also brought the first printing press to the nation and worked hard to print works in local languages. He truly affected change in that nation.

Jamaican Emancipation with William Knibb

William Knibb (1803–1845) was a missionary to Jamaica and has been called an honest friend of the Jamaican people. In the early nineteenth century, Jamaica had become one of the British Empire's chief sugar exporters, and this colonial wealth was being reaped through slavery. Because of his non-conformist evangelical views, Knibb chose the side of the slaves and the cause of emancipation. After his arrival in Jamaica, he wrote home to England, saying:

> The curse blast of slavery has, like a pestilence, withered almost every moral bloom. I know not how any person can feel a union with such a monster, such a child of hell. I feel a burning hatred against it and look upon it as one of the most odious monsters that ever disgraced the earth. The iron hand of oppression daily endeavours to keep the slaves in the ignorance to which it has reduced them.[31]

When a black slave named Sam Swiney was unjustly accused of a minor offense, Knibb spoke for him in court. In what has been described as a gross miscarriage of justice, the colonial authorities convicted Swiney and had him flogged, but Knibb refused to let it drop. He published full details in the newspaper, for which he was threatened by the prosecution for libel. The details of this case reached the secretary of state in London who decided to fire the two responsible magistrates.[32]

Knibb was so popular with the slaves that at one time the church in Falmouth needed a minister and Knibb's name was put forward. The missionary who chaired the meeting recorded that when the name of Knibb was proposed as their new minister, and when he asked the congregation for a show of hands, the entire congregation stood up, held up both hands, and wept.[33]

He enforced other social changes as thousands of slave children received free education. It is been noted that despite the overwhelming needs, Knibb did what he could but was hindered by a lack of teachers and instructors. Upon emancipation, the adult slaves were released into a world without education or institutions to support them. The church ministers were often the only people to whom the freed slaves could go for legal assistance. Knibb said, "Often I have had persons come to me for advice who have walked twenty miles to ask for it."[34]

He also helped raise money to purchase thousands of acres of land, to enable 19,000 former slaves to own their own property. Knibb was summoned to appear before committees of both houses of Parliament that had been convened to investigate the state of the West Indian colonies. Knibb's evidence was so authentic that it contributed more than that of any other witnesses to the conviction of all, that slavery must be speedily abolished.[35] In describing his efforts, he said, "I was forced from the den of infamy and from a gloomy prison, with my congregation scattered, many of the members of my church murdered, and multitudes of the faithful lashed. I came home and I shall never forget the three years of struggle, and the incessant anxiety upon my spirit as I passed through the length and breadth of the country detailing the slaves' wrongs."[36]

With the emancipation also came the revival known as the Jamaican Awakening, which had so many thousands of former slaves joining the non-conformist churches. Knibb recalled that "in those seven years, through the labour of about twenty Baptist missionaries, 22,000 people were baptised upon professing their faith in Jesus Christ."[37] Peter Masters says, "We are being told that Christian missionaries of the past were tools of colonial oppression and destroyers of culture…the story of William Knibb shows how wildly wrong this is. Persecuted by British rulers in Jamaica because he opposed settler's abuses, he was pivotal in swinging British public opinion behind legislation to end colonial slavery."[38]

Endnotes

[1] Dr. Livingstone's Cambridge Lectures together with a prefatory Letter by Edited by Revered William Monk (Deighton Bell and Cambridge Bell: London, 1858), 24.

[2] Andrew F. Walls, *The Legacy of David Livingstone* (International Bulletin of Missionary Research, Volume 11 No. 3, July 1987), 126.

[3] Thomas Fowell Buxton, *The Extinction of the Slave Trade and the Civilization of Africa: A Review of "The African Slave Trade," and its Remedy* (1840), 171–190.

[4] Oliver Ransford, *David Livingstone: The Dark Interior* (John Murray Publishers, 1978), 10.

[5] *Dr. Livingstone's Cambridge Lectures*, edited by Revered William Monk (Deighton Bell and Cambridge Bell: London, 1858), 163.

[6] Ibid., 165.

[7] R. Foskett, *The Zambezi doctors: David Livingstone's Letters to John Kirk,* 1858–1872 (Edinburg UP, 1964), 40–41.

[8] David Livingstone, *Missionary Travels and Researches in South Africa* (1857), 228.

[9] Andrew Ross John Philip, *1775–1851: Missions, Race and Politics in South Africa* (Mercat Press, 1986), 226–227.

[10] J. J. Freeman (1794–1856): A Missionary in Madagascar 1827–1836, and became a Joint Secretary of the LMS 1841–1846; Home Secretary 1846–1851 (LMS Register No. 264), 33.

[11] Harry Hamilton, *Johnston Livingstone and the Exploration of Central Africa* (George Philip & Son, 1865), 72–76.

[12] David Livingstone, *Missionary Travels and Researches in South Africa* (John Murray, 1857), 228.

[13] I. Schapera (Ed), *Family Letters of Livingstone 1841–1856* (Chatto & Windus, 1959), 53.

[14] Brian Stanley, "Nineteenth-Century Liberation Theology: Nonconformist Missionaries and Imperialism," The Baptist Quarterly 32, 1987, 9–12.

[15] Grant R. Jeffery, *The Signature of God-Astonishing Biblical Discoveries* (Frontier Research Publications, Inc., 1996), 18.

[16] Ibid.

[17] London Missionary Register No. 194.

[18] Andrew Ross John Philip, 1775–1851: *Missions, Race and Politics in South Africa* (Mercat Press, 1986), 215–227.

[19] Minutes of the Meeting of the Board of Directors, May 9, 1796, LMS Archives. John Phillip, *Researches in South Africa Illustrating the Civil, Moral, and Religious Conditions of the Native Tribes*. Reproduction of a book published before 1923.

[20] John Phillip, *Researches in South Africa Illustrating the Civil, Moral, and Religious Conditions of the Native Tribes*. Reproduction of a book published before 1923, so it is now in the public domain.

[21] London Mission Society Archives File 215, Letter 125.

[22] Andrew Ross John Philip, *1775–1851: Missions, Race and Politics in South Africa* (Aberdeen University Press 1986), 102–111.

[23] W. G. Blaike, *The Personal Life of David Livingstone* (1910), 10.

[24] Andrew F. Walls, *The Legacy of David Livingstone* (International Bulletin of Missionary Research, Volume 11 No. 3, July 1987), 126.

[25] Ibid.

[26] Loren Davis, *The Race for Africa, http://www.lorendavis.com/articles.html.*

[27] F. Deaville, Walker *William Carey: Missionary Pioneer and Statesman,* 1926, (Moody Press; Reprint edition 1960), 184–185.

[28] Ibid., 189.

[29] Ibid., 115.

[30] Alvin J. Schmidt, *How Christianity Changed the World* (Zondervan: Grand Rapids, 2004), 117.

[31] Peter Masters, *Missionary Triumph over Slavery* (The Wake Man Trust: London, 2006), 11.

[32] Ibid., 13–15.

[33] Ibid., 17.

[34] Ibid., 45.

[35] Ibid., 29.

[36] Ibid., 37.

[37] Ibid., 48.

[38] Ibid., 11–12.

CHAPTER 8

Missionaries and the European Colonization of Africa: Part 2

Alexander Mackay

Alexander Mackay (1849–1890) has been called a pioneer-missionary to Uganda, which was described by explorer Henry Stanley as the pearl of Africa. He arrived in Zanzibar in 1876 and reached Uganda in 1878. He built 230 miles of road to Uganda from the coast, translated the Gospel of Matthew into  Luganda, and he died in 1890 after spending fourteen years in Africa without once returning home to his native Scotland. Mackay's favorite Bible character was John the Baptist, and he cited Matthew 3:3 and other passages that describe John the Baptist's commission to prepare the way for the coming of the Savior. He told King Mutesa I, who reigned from 1856–1884 that:

> When in ancient days, the people failed to keep the commandments of God and continued in their sinful ways, God determined to send His only Son to earth to redeem sinners and sent John the Baptist to prepare the people for His coming. I am here, O king, to prepare a way for the coming of God's Son and I want you to join me in pointing the people of this land to the Lamb of God, who alone can take away the sin of the world.[1]

Mackay wasn't the only person who appeared before the king and his chiefs. It is been recorded by one historian that walked into the king's chamber was a tall Arab in flowing robes and a red fez, followed by a number of black men, who deposited on the floor their bales of cloth and guns. "I have come to exchange these things for men, women and children. I will give you one of these links of red cloth for one man, one of these guns for two men and one hundred of these percussion caps for one woman."[2]

Mackay knew that the king was accustomed to selling his own people, as well as his captives, as slaves. He could see that the king was especially eager to get guns and ammunition, for they would enable him to conquer and enslave his enemies. Now the question on Mackay's mind was: Should I risk the king's disfavor, and even risk his own life, by opposing this traffic in human lives? He remembered that, though it cost him his head, John the Baptist did not hesitate to reprove a king by speaking what was right. Inspired by this courageous example, Mackay declared:

> O king Mutesa, the people of this land made you their king and look to you as their father. Will you sell your children, knowing that they will be chained, put into slave-sticks, beaten with whips; that most of them will die of mistreatment on the way and the rest be taken as slaves to some strange country? Can you be a party to these crimes, even for the sake of some guns? Will you sell scores or hundreds of your people, or your captives, whose bodies are so marvelously created by God, for a few bolts of red cloth which any man can make in a few days?[3]

The Arab slave dealer scowled. If only he could plunge his dagger into the white man's heart! No man had ever dared talk to the king like this before, and the chiefs stirred uneasily, wondering if Mutesa would imprison Mackay or perhaps put him to death. Instead, he dismissed the angry Arab and announced, "The white man is right. I shall no more sell my people as slaves." With a joyful and grateful heart, the missionary went to his hut. Later the same day he wrote in his diary: "Afternoon. The king sent a message with a present of a goat, saying it was a blessed passage I read today."[4]

Mackay showed unusual interest in mechanics ever since he was a small boy. At one time, he walked back eight miles in order to look at a railway engine for at least two and a half minutes. He also liked to linger around the blacksmith's shop and the carding mill, and spent considerable time in the attic at his little printing press. Thirteen years went by, during which he completed a two years' teaching course, learned much about shipbuilding in the docks of Aberdeen, made a thorough study of engineering, and went to Germany for further study. He had read avidly all he could find about his hero, David Livingstone, and on the anniversary of Livingstone's death, he wrote in his diary: "Livingstone died—a Scotsman and a Christian—loving God and his neighbor, in the heart of Africa. Go thou and do likewise."[5]

But how could he ever go to Africa? What could an engineer do there? As he was pondering these questions in Berlin on the night of December 12, 1875, he picked up a copy of the *Edinburg Daily Review* which was sent to him from Scotland. He read a letter that sent a mighty chill through his being. Because of its author, the place of its composition, the story of its transmission, its contents, and its consequences, this was one of the most remarkable letters ever penned. It was written by the explorer Henry M. Stanley, in Uganda on April 12, 1875, at the request of King Mutesa. More than seven months transpired before it appeared in the *Daily Telegraph* of London and in all other papers.

It is the story of a pair of boots, owned and worn by a Frenchman, Colonel Linant de Balleonds, to whom Stanley entrusted the letter. Marching northward from Uganda, the Frenchman and his caravan were proceeding along the bank of the River Nile when they were suddenly attacked near Gondokoro by a band of savage tribesmen. Having killed the Frenchman, they heartlessly left his body lying unburied on the sand, where it was later discovered by some English soldiers who happened to pass that way. Before burying the Frenchman, they pulled off his long knee boots and in one of them found Stanley's letter, stained with the dead man's blood. They forwarded it to the English general in Egypt, who sent it on the newspaper office in London. This was the letter which attracted Mackay's attention that cold December night in 1875. In part it read as follows:

> King Mutesa of Uganda has been asking me about the white man's God.... Oh that some practical missionary would come here! Mutesa would welcome such. It is the practical Christian who can cure their diseases, build dwellings and turn his hand to anything—this is the man who is wanted. Such a one, if he can be found, would become the savior of Africa.[6]

Having long cherished a desire to follow in the footsteps of Livingstone and Stanley, this was for him a call from on high. Immediately he wrote to the Church Missionary Society: "My heart burns for the deliverance of Africa, and if you can send me to any of those regions which Livingstone and Stanley have found to be groaning under the curse of the slave hunter, I shall be very glad." Within four months Mackay, along with seven other young missionary volunteers, was on a ship bound for Zanzibar and Uganda, saying: "I go to prepare the way by which others more readily can go and stay and work." He had given his best, his all, to the high task of being a road maker for Christ in the heart of Africa.[7]

Mary Slessor

Mary Slessor (1848–1915) was a missionary to Africa who served in an area known as the White Man's Grave. In her neighborhood,  death stalked all missionaries and none were strangers to witchdoctors, cannibals, swarms of insects, lions, and deadly diseases. In Britain she had worked twelve hours a day in a factory, waiting for a chance to serve God. And by the age of twenty-nine she landed in West Africa. This young lady faced dangers beyond imagination and through courage not only ended much tribal warfare but changed the spiritual landscape of West Africa. It is recorded by

Paul Backholer: "Witchcraft and superstition were prevalent in a country whose traditional society had been torn apart by the slave trade. Human sacrifice routinely followed the death of a village dignitary, and the ritual murder of twins was viewed by the new missionary with particular abhorrence. Her dedicated effort to forestall this irrational superstition was to prove a resounding success."[8]

She once prayed:

O Lord, I thank Thee that I can bring these people Thy Word. But Lord, there are other villages back in the jungle where no man has gone. They need Jesus too. Help me reach them![9]

She then trekked into unknown areas to preach the gospel, even though all people including local chiefs warned her that she would die. She was shocked by local customs that included killing the wives and slaves of important people upon their master's death, and worshiping the skulls of dead men.

She preached the gospel, won the respect of all, and brought crimes to an end. She also did much to improve the rights of women who were often considered inferior to animals. Throughout her life, she suffered much through sickness and disease, which would never have afflicted her at home. At her funeral stood many who loved her, former cannibals, chiefs, warriors, and people who were saved from old sinful practices. She was given a state funeral and later honored by the Queen of Great Britain, who even made a pilgrimage to her graveside.[10]

Slessor was the driving force behind the establishment of the Hope Waddell Training Institute in Calabar, which provided practical vocational training to Africans. The school provided practical training to male students in carpentry, masonry, blacksmithing, coopering, naval engineering, brick making, and bricklaying. Female students were taught dress making and tailoring, domestic science and accountancy. The school soon became the largest vocational training institution in West Africa.[11]

In his case study about the nature and extent of the influence of the educational developments in Calabar mission in Nigeria, author William Taylor tells us that England, which was the cultural pacesetter throughout the British Empire, had developed its educational system from a different ideological starting point from Scotland. It minimized state provision and maximized parental responsibility in regards to the schooling of children. Even in their overseas missionary educational activity, Scottish missionaries of various denominations, Presbyterians in particular, encouraged as many children as possible to attend school (though they could only afford to provide limited numbers of schools), irrespective of family background, intellectual ability, religious affiliation, or career potential. This preference for comprehensive education was to cause the Scots trouble in due course with both the English-oriented colonial government and ambitious parents who demanded post-basic education for their talented offspring.[12]

While Presbyterianism has long advocated egalitarianism in the social, spiritual, and church government domains, it has simultaneously advocated elitism in the intellectual and moral domains. Yet intellectual excellence often brings material rewards as a result of higher earnings for the more educated in society. Presbyterians would provide an educational opportunity for anyone to become a member of the elite. Elitism is acceptable if its members use their talents selflessly for the benefit of the wider society. This ethic was taught in the mission schools in eastern Nigeria.[13]

In establishing a Presbyterian church in Nigeria, the missionaries had to do much more than evangelize or make people literate there. They had to train church members—especially prospective elders—to participate in these various courts and committees, a training which was relatively easy to transfer from church to civil government as colonial Nigeria prepared to make way for independent democratic Nigeria.[14]

Mary Slessor is commemorated today on bank notes issued in Scotland by the Clydesdale Bank. Her portrait appears on the obverse of the £10 note, replacing David Livingstone whose image featured on the notes prior to 1998. On the reverse, she is depicted holding children in her arms alongside a map of the Ekoi and Ibibio in Calabar, in present-day Nigeria.

C. T. Studd

The missionary, famous British athlete, and founder of Worldwide Evangelization Crusade, C. T. Studd (1860–1931) was saved in 1878 at

the age of eighteen when a visiting preacher at their home caught him on his way to play cricket. "Are you a Christian?" he asked. Studd's answer was not convincing enough, so the guest pressed the point and Studd tells what happened as he acknowledged God's gift of eternal life received through faith in Christ: "I got down on my knees and I did say 'thank You' to God. And right then and there joy and peace came into my soul. I knew then what it was to be 'born again' and the Bible which had been so dry to me before, became everything."[15] His two brothers were also saved the very same day.

But there followed a period of six years in a backslidden state. C. T. Studd relates this time:

Instead of going and telling others of the love of Christ, I was selfish and kept the knowledge to myself. The result was that gradually my love began to grow cold, and the love of the world began to come in. I spent six years in that unhappy backslidden state.[16]

In 1884 after his brother George was taken seriously ill, Studd was confronted by the question, "What is all this fame and flattery worth... when a man comes to face eternity?" He had to admit that since his conversion six years earlier, he had been in "an unhappy backslidden state." As a result of the experience, he said,

I know that cricket would not last, and honor would not last, and nothing in this world would last, but it was worthwhile living for the world to come. Still further, and what was better than all, He set me to work for Him, and I began to try and persuade my friends to read the Gospel, and to speak to them individually about their souls. I cannot tell you what joy it gave me to bring the first soul to the Lord Jesus Christ. I have tasted almost all the pleasures that this world can give…but those pleasures were as nothing compared to the joy that the saving of that one soul gave me.[17]

C. T. Studd gave up all his achievements in this life for Christ's sake. He was challenged to his commitment by an article written by an atheist. That article, in part, said:

If I firmly believed, as millions say they do, that the knowledge and practice of religion in this life influences destiny in another, then religion would mean to me everything. I would cast away earthly enjoyments as dross, earthly cares as follies, and earthly thoughts and feelings as vanity. Religion would be my first waking thought and my last image before sleep sank me into unconsciousness. I should labour in its cause alone. I would take thought for the morrow of eternity alone. I would esteem one soul gained for heaven worth a life of suffering. Earthly consequences would never stay my hand, or seal my lips. Earth, its joys and its griefs, would occupy no moment of my thoughts. I would strive to look upon eternity alone, and on the immortal souls around me, soon to be everlastingly happy or everlastingly miserable. I would go forth to the world and preach to it in season and out of season, and my text would be: "WHAT SHALL IT PROFIT A MAN IF HE GAINS THE WHOLE WORLD AND LOSE HIS OWN SOUL."[18]

It is been recorded by one historian that China was a nation that was in conflict with the Western powers, and this was a big challenge to missionaries who wanted China to open its doors to the gospel. Mission houses were being destroyed, foreigners were fleeing, and the cities were in lockdown with guards posted to keep the "foreign devils" out—for rumors had spread that the white man could kidnap people and eat them![19] Traveling through areas that no European had seen before, the team crossed rivers, navigated narrow ledges, and escaped falling rocks on their way into the cities. The British consul could not believe they had found a way in and urged them to leave immediately. C. T. Studd boldly declared that God had called them there and, without doubt, they would stay and minister for Christ.[20]

As C. T. Studd attempted to sleep that ravenous night, we can only wonder if his mind went back to the memories of home. As a first-class cricketer he often stood before thousands of adoring fans applauding every move, bringing glory to his team. In 1883 the *Cricketers Record* wrote: "C. T. Studd, must, for the second year, be accorded the premier position as an all-round cricketer."[21] He had returned cricket's greatest trophy to England and became the hero of many. In his desire to follow the Master, Studd counted fame and fortune as nothing.[22]

All had changed in his life when he accepted Christ into his heart: "At once, joy and peace came into my soul. I knew then what it was to be born again, and the Bible, which had been so dry to me before, became everything."[23] The missionary endeavor made newspaper headlines; people could hardly believe that C. T. Studd and other Cambridge graduates were off to China! One of England's most famous sportsmen had forsaken all for the sake of the call of Jesus Christ.

During his time in China, Studd received a massive inheritance, and as he prayed about what to do with it, the words of Jesus echoed in his heart: "Sell what you have and give to the poor…and come, follow Me" (Matthew 19:21). Following the command of Jesus, Studd gave all his inheritance away to Christian organizations and looked to the Lord alone to provide for his every need. For many years Studd labored in China, winning people to the Lord and teaching them the principles of Christian discipleship.

Due to his wife's illness, he returned to England and they later completed missions in India. "Cannibals Want Missionaries," brought a large smile to C. T. Studd—it was this poster that caught his attention in England. During the meeting he heard of many unreached tribes in

Africa. Now nearing the latter end of his life, with no money, poor health, and a sick wife, he picked up his cross again and responded to the call of Jesus. His plan was to go to Sudan, but God began to burn in his heart. "This trip is not merely for the Sudan," he said, "it is for the whole unevangelised world!" It took him over half a year to enter the heart of Africa; a man who grew up in a wealthy home, laughed as he now lived in a mud hut—writing home his letters were always "from Buckingham Palace."[24]

Life on the mission field was full of hazards and cruel at times, but C. T. Studd always kept a light-hearted view of things. Once a team member fired shots into the river to scare away crocodiles as he baptized new believers, and snakes found their way into his hut. Studd had left fame and fortune to serve the Lord in China, India, and Africa, and he founded the Worldwide Evangelistic Crusade (WEC). Today WEC headquarters in the U.K. are still continuing the faith, vision, and the pioneering work of Studd. His mission still lives on vibrantly in the hearts and minds of those still willing to sacrifice all for Christ and His great commission.

When the Lord divided Canaan among the tribes of Israel, Levi received no share of the land. God told them:

> At that time the Lord set apart the tribe of Levi to bear the ark of the covenant of the Lord, to stand before the Lord to minister to Him and to bless in His name unto this day. Therefore Levi has no part or inheritance with his brethren; the Lord is his inheritance, as the Lord your God promised him. (Deuteronomy 10:8–9 AMP)

To paraphrase Andrew Murray's teaching here, there is a spiritual principle here that is still valid for every priest of the Most High God, and which should be the purpose of all God's children in the midst of the perishing around us. The life of Studd composed a sign of what the character of the New Testament believer is to be. We are spiritual Levites and are to be ministers and stewards of His grace. The priestly tribes were to have no inheritance with other tribes; God alone was their inheritance.

The Levites' lives were to be lived by faith, set apart unto God. They were to live in Him and for Him. In the surrender of what may appear lawful to others in our separation from the world, we prove that our consecration of holiness to the Lord is wholehearted and complete. Above all, we consent to give up all inheritance on earth, to forsake all, and like Jesus Christ, to have only God as our portion. To possess as not possessing and hold all for God alone marks the true priest, the man who only lives for God and his fellowmen.[25]

C. T. Studd faithfully served Jesus Christ as his motto was: "If Jesus Christ is God and He died for me, then no sacrifice can be too great for me to make for Him."

The Love of Christ Compels Us

We cannot consider the different thousands of stories of Western missionary men like Andrew Murray who was opposed to *Afrikaner Nationalism*, which emphasized the unity of all African-speaking white people against such "foreign" elements as Blacks, Jews, and English-speaking South Africans. People like David Brainerd, missionary to the Native Americans, or Adoniram Judson, missionary to the Burmese people, all endured personal hardships and sacrificial living on a daily basis because the love of Christ compelled them. Working together, they kept governments and corporations accountable. They incorporated charitable societies.

We shouldn't think that today's charity and compassion in the Western world developed on its own or due to the mere progress of civilization. It was the missionaries who pioneered and helped to end the slave trade and all kinds of injustices. They started vocational schools that provided practical training to Africans; they provided many educational opportunities; they opened hospitals; they promoted women's rights and saved their children from death. They also founded orphanages, started rescue missions, built almshouses and opened soup kitchens. They changed unjust laws and gave humans a sense of dignity. The British Empire was also always kept in check by these Christian missionaries. They created civil governments and rescued victims of governments, who considered the greatest crime one could commit was that of being black.

It was the love of Jesus Christ that inspired and motivated all these missionaries to give themselves wholeheartedly to His service in order to help the unfortunate, regardless of their background, race, religion, class, or nationality. They practiced true religion, which according to James is "to visit orphans and widows in their trouble, and to keep oneself unspotted from the world" (James 1:27).

They also bore witness to the habit of prayer as exemplified by David Livingstone who was said to have lived in the realm of prayer and knew its gracious influence on his life. It was his habit every birthday to write a prayer. On his next to last birthday, this was his prayer: "O Divine One, I have not loved Thee earnestly, deeply, sincerely enough. Grant, I pray Thee, that before this year is ended I may have finished my task."[26] It was just on the threshold of the year that followed that faithful men, as they looked in to the hut of Ilala, while the rain dripped from the eaves, saw their master on his knees beside his bed in an attitude of prayer. He had died in that position.

"These early Christian missionaries set a model for their descendants in the Western world to follow," says Alvin Schmidt, "a model that today modern secular societies seek to imitate, but without Christian motivation. Sympathy toward the poor is a concept that comes from Christian values. The rich and well-to-do in Greece and Rome despised the poor,"[27] just like some of the elites in our society today. Or worse still, many leaders around the world emulate their colonial masters by keeping their people down without freedom to improve their lives.

Despite the humanitarian nature of Christian missionary work, these servants of God frequently found that non-religious people were the ones who hindered and criticized their work, just as they do today. Christians then are frequently at the forefront of relieving suffering, providing medical care and education in the developing world, including spiritual encouragement and moral guidance. These early missionaries have now become a source of inspiration and encouragement to many other Christians around the world who have taken their stories today as a testament to walking with God through all kinds of persecutions and trials in order to answer God's call (see Matthew 28:19–20).

These missionaries paved the way for future revivals by their sacrifice, prayers, death by disease, or deprivation in the Master's service. Many of them had been inspired by the revivals of the past, and it was this revival that continued to change British society in subsequent years.

Endnotes

1 Eugene Myers Harrison, *Blazing the Missionary Trail* (Chicago, Ill.: Scripture Press Book Division, © 1949).

2 Ibid.

3 Ibid.

4 Ibid.

5 Ibid.

6 Ibid.

7 Ibid.

8 Paul Backholer, *How Christianity Made the Modern World: The Legacy of Christian Liberty: How the Bible Inspired Freedom, Shaped Western Civilization, Revolutionized Human Rights, Transformed Democracy and Why Free People Owe So Much to their Christian Heritage* (Faith Media, August 2009), 231–232.

9 Ibid.

10 Ibid.

11 William H. Taylor, *Mission to Educate: A History of the Educational Work of the Scottish Presbyterian Mission in East Nigeria, 1846–1960* (E. J. Brill: Netherlands, 1996), 127–128.

12 Ibid., 5–6.

13 Ibid., 12.

14 Ibid.

15 Norman P. Grubb, *C. T. Studd: Cricketer and Pioneer* (Fort Washington, PA: Christian Literature Crusade, 1933, 1985), 241.

16 Ibid.

17 Copied by Stephen Ross for *WholesomeWords.org* from Pioneer Missionaries for Christ and His Church by Thomas John Bach (Wheaton, Ill., Van Kampen Press, © 1995).

18 William McDonald, *True Discipleship* (Kansas City: Walterick Publishers, 1975), 31.

19 Paul Backholer, 213.

[20] Ibid.

[21] Ibid.

[22] Ibid.

[23] Ibid.

[24] Ibid.

[25] Andrew Murray, *Teach Me To Pray*, edited by Nancy Renich (Bethany House, 2002), 209.

[26] Cited by E.M. Bounds, *Purpose in Prayer* (Fleming H. Revell Company, 1920), 41–42.

[27] Alvin J. Schmidt, 148.

CHAPTER 9

The Revival Changed British Society

The Revival's Far-Reaching Effects

There was a point in British history when around 260 British trade unionists attended an international conference with other leaders in France, and they carried a banner which read: "We represent 500,000 English workmen! We proclaim the Fatherhood of God and the Brotherhood of Man! Jesus Christ leads and inspires us." This was in 1910, and the British trade union had arisen in England over ninety years before—in the years immediately following 1815.

The Christian trade union origins and character had been preserved for almost a hundred years, which again shows the impact of the revival on the working conditions of the British community.[1] The majority of the leaders of this union were Christians, and some were either preachers or got involved in other Christian work in their sphere of influence. So the entire trade union movement in England is rooted and grounded in historical and biblical Christianity.

The revival continued to cause the spirit and teaching of our Lord Jesus to transform and influence the whole of society. Britain's first labor prime minister and three-time prime minister of England, J. Ramsay McDonald, was also a Christian who was a product of the evangelical revival whom God had raised up to a position of leadership. He found the materialistic, economic determinism, class hatred, and atheism of Karl Marx's doctrine to be quite repulsive, and he strongly advocated for Christian principles in Parliament. It has been reported that when he was prime minister he went so far as to say that he believed that democracy itself—true democracy—had its source in the eighteenth-century revival; that vital Christianity was indeed its very foundation; and that without Christianity, democracy is doomed to perish.

Gardner quotes Dr. Belden who wrote that "the Free Churches were one of the pure sources from which free democracy came. It was by the dynamic of free religion (by which he meant Christianity) that masses were inspired to escape from the quagmire of misery and injustice. The Christian faith preserved the masses from becoming soul-less things obedient to the convenience and advantage of economic forces."[2]

There is no doubt at all that when God sent revival in Britain in the eighteenth century, He saved her from the bloodshed that had happened in France during the time of the French Revolution. The impact that the evangelical revival of both George Whitefield and John Wesley had on this country and its people was unfathomable; it had far-reaching effects and lasted well over a hundred years.

Many firsthand accounts have been written to give full force of the impact, including well-known historian George Macaulay Trevelyan, who wrote, "It was one of the turning points in the history of the world.... After Britain had abolished the slave trade her command of the sea, her Empire, her inventive genius—above all, her increasing moral stature, and her expanding spiritual vision—won her a place of unique leadership amongst the nations. More than any other great nation in the middle of the nineteenth century, she was worthy of world power."[3]

Britain's Power Traced Directly to the Revival

So many testimonies have been written about the impact of this great revival, but what we should not forget is that Britain's rise to power can be traced directly to the God-given evangelical revival in the eighteenth century. It is because God, in His mercy and for His own purposes, had raised Britain up into that position. Although many testimonies have been written about this revival, the most inspiring testimony is the one found engraved in marble for all to see just inside the north doors of Westminster Abbey. There, on the huge memorial to William Pitt, we read these words: "During whose administration, and in the reigns of George II and George III, Divine Providence exalted Great Britain to a height of prosperity and glory unknown to any former age."[4]

According to Gardner, "This inscription is inspiring because it was precisely the period in the history of this country which coincided exactly with the Great Awakening which God granted Britain under the preaching of Whitefield and Wesley. Every English person today needs to dwell deeply on the words and implication of that inscription."[5]

Another thing worth remembering is that England sent many missionaries around the world, causing the gospel to further spread in other nations. Before that great revival there was not a single Protestant missionary apart from the Moravians; but by the end of the eighteenth century, the Baptist Missionary Society, the London Missionary Society, and the Religious Tract Society were all created within the space of twelve years. From these various societies, Britain began to send missionaries to the ends of the world. All of this happened because God intervened in the history of England to ensure that the Christian heritage and foundations that had originally been laid could be preserved for other proceeding generations.[6]

Many people are deeply concerned about the moral and spiritual decline of the West and its declining Christian influence in the world. This decline has taken place over a long period of time. Men have forgotten God. We as a people are living without God, both individually and as a nation. The only thing we need to do is humble ourselves, repent of our sins, and get right with God by asking Him to forgive our sins so He can cleanse us with the precious blood of the Lord Jesus Christ.

The Situation Demands It

In England, many times organizations and individuals have sent urgent appeals to the Queen (who is supposedly the Head of the Church of England) to call the nation to God in prayer, humiliation, and repentance. King George VI did this between 1939 and 1945, but every time the response had been the same from the prime minister (who advises the head of state on national matters): "The situation does not demand it." The question is, when will the situation demand it?

It is only through repentance and prayer that God's people can lay claim upon His mercies. We know that God uses human agents to fulfill His purposes in history, especially when it comes to dealing with His covenant people. A man that set a standard for us to follow in the ministry of intercession for his nation was the prophet Daniel. He was raised from humble beginnings to a position of prime minister of the entire Babylonian Empire, with power second only to that of King Nebuchadnezzar. He practiced regular prayer, which brought him trouble, but refused to give up his convictions, even if it meant being thrown into a den of hungry lions.

During the first year of the reign of Darius the Mede, the Babylonian king, Daniel learned from reading and studying the Word of God, as revealed by the prophet Jeremiah, that Jerusalem must lie desolate for seventy years (see Jeremiah 25:11–12; 29:10). Daniel realized that this seventy-year period was coming to an end. So what did he do? He turned to the Lord God and pleaded with Him in prayer and fasting.

In Daniel's prayer for the nation, he confessed his own sin instead of shifting the blame to someone else. He did not blame others and excuse their actions. He prayed to the Lord his God:

> And I prayed to the Lord my God, and made confession, and said, "O Lord, great and awesome God, who keeps His covenant and mercy with those who love Him, and with those who keep His commandments, we have sinned and committed iniquity, we have done wickedly and rebelled, even by departing from Your precepts and Your judgments. Neither have we heeded Your servants the prophets, who spoke in Your name to our kings and our princes, to our fathers and all the people of the land. O Lord, righteousness belongs to You, but to us shame of face, as it is this

day—to the men of Judah, to the inhabitants of Jerusalem and all Israel, those near and those far off in all the countries to which You have driven them, because of the unfaithfulness which they have committed against You.

"O Lord, to us belongs shame of face, to our kings, our princes, and our fathers, because we have sinned against You. To the Lord our God belong mercy and forgiveness, though we have rebelled against Him. We have not obeyed the voice of the Lord our God, to walk in His laws, which He set before us by His servants the prophets. Yes, all Israel has transgressed Your law, and has departed so as not to obey Your voice; therefore the curse and the oath written in the Law of Moses the servant of God have been poured out on us, because we have sinned against Him. And He has confirmed His words, which He spoke against us and against our judges who judged us, by bringing upon us a great disaster; for under the whole heaven such has never been done as what has been done to Jerusalem.

"As it is written in the Law of Moses, all this disaster has come upon us; yet we have not made our prayer before the Lord our God, that we might turn from our iniquities and understand Your truth. Therefore the Lord has kept the disaster in mind, and brought it upon us; for the Lord our God is righteous in all the works which He does, though we have not obeyed His voice." (Daniel 9:4–14)

If anyone was righteous before God, it was Daniel; but even he confessed his sinfulness and need for God's grace and mercy. Instead of looking at others, he fasted, prayed, confessed his own sins, pleading with God to reveal His will for the nation of Israel. He completely surrendered to God and was willing to be open to what He wanted to do. God had sent many prophets to speak to His people throughout the years, but the message, much like it is today, was largely ignored. People did not want to hear the painful truth.

Daniel mentioned the curses and judgments written in Deuteronomy 28, where God gave His people the choice to choose blessings or curses. (We must not forget that most of these curses in Deuteronomy 28 are being fulfilled in the Western world with the exception of just a few of them.) They refused to repent by turning from their sins and recognizing His truth. Daniel kept on reminding the Israelites how God had tried to bring them back to Himself; but they still did not heed His voice. Daniel could not hide His feelings and so he went on crying and interceding for the nation. He had a deep love and concern for the nation God placed him in.

He went on pleading for God's mercy, not because they deserved help but because he knew they deserved God's wrath and judgment. Daniel knew from a personal, intimate experience that God was merciful to His people.

> And now, O Lord our God, who brought Your people out of the land of Egypt with a mighty hand, and made Yourself a name, as it is this day—we have sinned, we have done wickedly!
>
> O Lord, according to all Your righteousness, I pray, let Your anger and Your fury be turned away from Your city Jerusalem, Your holy mountain; because for our sins, and for the iniquities of our fathers, Jerusalem and Your people are a reproach to all those around us. Now therefore, our God, hear the prayer of Your servant, and his supplications, and for the Lord's sake cause Your face to shine on Your sanctuary, which is desolate. O my God, incline Your ear and hear; open Your eyes and see our desolations, and the city which is called by Your name; for we do not present our supplications before You because of our righteous deeds, but because of Your great mercies. O Lord, hear! O Lord, forgive! O Lord, listen and act! Do not delay for Your own sake, my God, for Your city and Your people are called by Your name. (Daniel 9:15–19)

Indeed, God in His mercy answered Daniel's prayer. Since the first day he began to pray for understanding and to humble himself before his God, his request was heard in heaven and he was shown great and mighty things which he did not know (see Jeremiah 33:3). He was provided the most detailed description of the major events of the end time, being told, "Go your way, Daniel, for the words are closed up and sealed till the time of the end."

One Jewish historian has characterized Daniel's unique mission by saying that he not only predicted the future, like other prophets did, but he also specified when and where these events would actually take place.[7] In spite of the fact that God's messenger to Daniel was withheld for three weeks by the spiritual prince of the kingdom of Persia, Daniel still faithfully continued praying and fasting until he received breakthrough. God's messenger eventually arrived with the answer after being assisted by the archangel Michael.

> Suddenly, a hand touched me, which made me tremble on my knees and on the palms of my hands. And he said to me, "O Daniel, man greatly beloved, understand the words that I speak to you, and stand upright, for I have now been sent to you." While he was speaking this word to me, I stood trembling.

> Then he said to me, "Do not fear, Daniel, for from the first day that you set your heart to understand, and to humble yourself before your God, your words were heard; and I have come because of your words. But the prince of the kingdom of Persia withstood me twenty-one days; and behold, Michael, one of the chief princes, came to help me, for I had been left alone there with the kings of Persia. Now I have come to make you understand what will happen to your people in the latter days, for the vision refers to many days yet to come. (Daniel 10:10–14)

Endnotes

[1] David E. Gardner, *The Trumpet Sounds For Britain*, 91.

[2] Ibid., 95.

[3] George Macaulay Trevelyan, *British History in the Nineteenth Century (1782–1901)* (55th Avenue, New York, 1922).

[4] Gardner, 96.

5 Ibid.

6 Ibid.

7 Cited in Grant R. Jeffery, *Opening Daniel's Sealed Prophecy from Babylon: Countdown to the Apocalypse* (Water Brook Press, 2008), 25.

CHAPTER 10

Britain and the Restoration of Israel

A Unique Contribution

The first known Jews arrived in England from Normandy with William the Conqueror around AD 1144. From 1095 to 1270 the Jews fled to Spain, England, Scandinavia, and Eastern Europe as a result of severe persecution. In 1290 King Edward I issued an edict that all Jews must be expelled from the country within three months. And the Jews were once again expelled by King Charles II in 1394. England remained cleansed of Jews until Oliver Cromwell decreed that they could return in 1656. And in 1858 the British Parliament passed a law that allowed Jews to be elected without restriction. Benjamin Disraeli later became the first Jewish British prime minister in 1874–1880.

The people of Britain made a unique contribution to the establishment of the state of Israel. For more than three centuries, Christians in Britain had nourished a vision, based on the Bible, that God desired to make of the Jewish people a sovereign nation once again in their own land. Franz Kobler, in his book *The Vision Was There*, highlights Britain's leading role in the restoration of Israel as a national state. In his introduction he states that nowhere more than in Britain has the idea of the restoration of Israel been developed into a doctrine and become the object of a movement extending over more than three centuries.

It was only in Britain that creation of a Jewish national home had been a serious and almost continuous political issue that was finally translated into a reality. The British movement for the restoration of

Israel is in fact one of the rare instances of the continuous interest shown by one nation in the destiny of another people. Its specific historical significance lies in the recognition of Israel's restoration as an organic part of British political ideals.[1]

Political Expression

Politically, this vision found expression through such men as Ashley Cooper Lord Shaftesbury and Arthur James Balfour. In 1917 it was the Balfour Declaration made on the behalf of the British government that set in motion the political processes that was issued, thirty-one years later, in the establishment of the state of Israel.[2]

> The British Foreign Office, 2 November 1917. Dear Lord Rothschild, I have much pleasure in conveying to you, on behalf of His Majesty's Government, the following declaration of sympathy with Jewish Zionist aspirations which has been submitted to, and approved by the Cabinet: "His Majesty's Government view with favor the establishment in Palestine of a national home for the Jewish people, and will use their best endeavors to facilitate the achievement of this object, it being clearly understood that nothing shall be done which may prejudice the civil and religious rights of existing non-Jewish communities in Palestine, or the rights and political status enjoyed by Jews in any other country." I should be grateful if you would bring this declaration to the knowledge of the Zionist Federation. Yours Sincerely, Arthur James Balfour.[3]

Lord Balfour (1848–1930) authored the Balfour Declaration of 1917, supporting the establishment of a Jewish homeland in Palestine. His declaration caused Christian Restorationists and Jewish Zionists to rejoice together.[4]

Franz Kobler also observed and concluded that there were many government leaders and church leaders that had a vision for the restoration of the people of Israel in their land. In 1979 Thomas Witherby, commenting on a book *The Restoration of the Jews: The Crisis of All Nations*, said that he felt confident that England, under a new

Cyrus, would be chosen to perform God's purposes of mercy toward Israel.[5]

In the 1830s, among those that favored the restoration of Israel and who were active to that end were Lord Shaftesbury, Lord Palmerston, and Edward Bickersteth. Shaftesbury wrote, "The ancient city of the people of God is about to resume a place among the nations, and England is the first of all the Gentile kingdoms that ceases to tread her down."[6] And in 1840 the British ambassador to Turkey strongly recommended the Turkish government to use every encouragement to urge the Jews to return to Palestine. Shaftesbury drew up a state letter urging Turkey to hand over Palestine to the Jews for "their indestructible Messianic hope."[7]

In the 1840s Charles Henry Churchill, ancestor of Sir Winston, spoke and wrote of a "pledge of England's friendship" and bonding union with the Jewish nation. "May the Jewish nation regain its rank and position among the nations of the world...."[8] At an important public meeting he stated that "God has put into my heart the desire to serve His ancient people."[9] As others had done, he made a direct approach through Lord Shaftesbury to Western Jewry to cooperate with the British government in planning for their return to Palestine.[10]

During the eighteenth and the first quarter of the nineteenth century, a wide interest in the restoration of Israel to their own land and the subsequent return of our Lord Jesus Christ spread across the evangelical church in Britain. This event was the beginning of historical forces that had been gathering strength throughout the nineteenth century. The church leaders' interest in the restoration had a background in the prophecies of the Old Testament, and were driven by their interpretation of Scripture, a sense of justice, the desire to rectify the wrongs committed by Christians against God's chosen people, and a feeling of sympathy for the Jews and their aspirations.[11]

For example, when John Owen was preaching before the House of Commons in 1649, he spoke of "the bringing home of His ancient people to be one fold with the fullness of the Gentiles...in answer to millions of prayers put up at the throne of grace for this very glory, in all generations."[12] Revivalist and founder of the Methodist Church John Wesley stated in his notes on Romans:

> So many prophecies refer to this grand event (of the restoration of Israel), that it is surprising any Christian can doubt of it. And these are greatly confirmed by the wonderful preservation of the Jews as a distinct people to this day. When it is accomplished, it will be so strong a demonstration, both of the Old and New Testament revelation, as will doubtless convince many thousands of Deists, in countries nominally Christian.[13]

Robert Murray M'Cheyne

In 1839 the Church of Scotland sent a delegation, including R. M. M'Cheyne, to the Holy Land on a mission of enquiry. Upon his return, he preached a sermon in Dundee on "Our Duty to Israel," in which he said:

> The greatest glory and joy anyone can experience is to be like God, and to care first for the Jews is to be like God.... The whole Bible shows that God has a special affection for Israel.... There are some, of course, who will say that God has a special affection for Israel...others say that God has finished with Israel. But the whole Bible contradicts such as an idea: Did God reject His people? By no means! (Romans 11:1).... They will give life to the dead world: The remnant of Jacob will be in the midst of many peoples like the dew from the Lord, like showers on the grass, which do not wait for man or linger from mankind (Micah 5:7).[14]

Bishop J. C. Ryle

In May 1868 Bishop J. C. Ryle of the Church of England, and one of the prominent Bible teachers of the last 200 years, preached a sermon at Rectory Church, Mary-le-Bone, entitled "Scattered Israel to be Re-gathered," using Jeremiah 31:10 as his text. In it he said,

> However great the difficulties surrounding many parts of unfulfilled prophecy, two points appear to my own mind to stand out as plainly as if written by a sunbeam. One of these points is

the second personal advent of our Lord Jesus Christ before the Millennium. The other of these points is the future literal gathering of the Jewish nation, and their restoration to their own land.[15]

He goes on to say,

Out of the sixteen prophets of the Old Testament, there are at least ten in which the gathering and restoration of the Jews in the latter days are expressly mentioned. I believe there is one common remark that applies to them all. They all point to a time which is yet in the future. They all predict the final gathering of the Jewish nation from the four quarters of the globe, and their restoration to their own land.... I ask you, then, to settle it firmly in your mind, that when God says a thing shall be done, we ought to believe it.[16]

Charles H. Spurgeon

Considered to be England's most influential non-conformist preacher, Charles Spurgeon (1834–1892) voiced the question of the restoration of Israel as well. He linked the restoration of the nation of Israel with their acceptance of Christ as their Messiah. "It is certain that the Jews, as a people, will yet own Jesus of Nazareth, the Son of David as their King," he said, "and that they will return to their own land, and they shall build the old wastes, they shall raise up the former desolations, and they shall repair the old cities, the desolations of many generations."[17] Again, during a message he delivered in Southwark Cathedral, he declared:

We do not think enough of the restoration of the Jews. But certainly, if there is anything promised in the Bible, it is this, I imagine that you cannot read the Bible without seeing clearly that there is to be an actual restoration of the children of Israel. "Thither they shall go up; they shall come weeping unto Zion, and with supplications unto Jerusalem." May that happy day soon come! For when the Jews are restored, then the fullness of the Gentiles shall be gathered in; and as soon as they return, then

Jesus will come upon Mount Zion to reign with his ancients gloriously. The day shall yet come when the Jews, who were the first apostles to the Gentiles, the first missionaries to us, who were far off, shall be gathered in again. Until that shall be, the fullness of the church's glory can never come. Matchless benefits to the world are bound up with the restoration of Israel; their gathering in shall be as life from the dead.[18]

In an address delivered at the Metropolitan Tabernacle on June 16, 1864, Spurgeon stated:

There will be a native government again; there will be form of a body politic; a state shall be incorporated, and a king shall reign. Israel has now become alienated from her own land. Her sons, though they can never forget the sacred dust of Palestine, yet die at a hopeless distance from her consecrated shores. But it shall not be so for forever, for her sons shall again rejoice in her: her land shall be called Beular, for as a young man marries a virgin so shall her sons marry her. "I will place you in your land" is God's promise to them.... They are to have a national prosperity which shall make them famous; nay, so glorious shall they be that Egypt, and Tyre, and Greece, and Rome, shall forget their glory in the greater splendor of the throne of David.... If there be anything clear and plain, the literal sense and meaning of this passage (Ezekiel 37:1–10)—a meaning not to be spirited or spiritualized away—must be evident that both the two and the ten tribes of Israel are to be restored to their own land, and that a King is to rule over them.[19]

Spurgeon reminded his listeners: "If the dispersion was a mark of God's judgment, according to the prophets, then Israel's return to the land is the mark of God's grace. In fact, so astounding will be the future return of Israel that it will make the exodus from Egypt seem small in comparison."[20]

The London Society for Promoting Christianity Amongst Jews, which later came to be known as The Church's Ministry Among Jewish People, was also founded in 1809. The society began in the early nineteenth century when leading evangelicals, including members of the influential Clapham Sect, such as William Wilberforce and Charles Simeon, decided that there was an unmet need to promote Christianity among the Jews. The original vision of the society was to:

- declare the Messiahship of Jesus to the Jew first and also to the non-Jew;
- endeavor to teach the church its Jewish roots.
- encourage the physical restoration of the Jewish people to *Eretz Israel*—the Land of Israel; and
- encourage the Hebrew Christian/Messianic Jewish movement.[21]

General Edmund Henry Allenby

General Edmund Allenby was a God-fearing man who liberated Jerusalem from the Turks in 1917. He also ordered that instead of forcing their way into the city of Jerusalem, the British had to send planes to drop leaflets over the city because they did not want to shed blood in the Holy City. When the Turks received them, they were afraid and fled because they thought the God of Abraham, Isaac, and Jacob was against them, preventing even one shot from being fired. Therefore, the Ottoman rule ended and the British mandatory rule began.[22] General Allenby alighted from his horse and entered Jerusalem on foot, saying, "No one but the Messiah should enter this city mounted on a horse."[23]

By God's grace Allenby succeeded, but the Arab nationalists living in Palestine were not happy with the Balfour Declaration and its call for a national home for the Jewish people. In the early 1920s more and more Jews began to arrive in Palestine to escape the growing anti-Semitism in Europe. By April 1920 Haj El-Amin, later to become the Mufti of Jerusalem, led riots against the Jewish population of Jerusalem as Britain and France participated in a League of Nations conference in San Reno, Italy, to issue a mandate for British and French rule over the Middle East. France was awarded a mandate to rule Lebanon and Syria while Britain was given a mandate to rule over Palestine, which includes all of modern-day Israel, Jordan, and the West Bank. The Balfour Declaration is incorporated into the British mandate, giving it international legal status.[24]

The End of the Empire

In 1921 Sir Hebert Samuel took his position as the first British high commissioner of Palestine. The Churchill White Paper divides Palestine along the Jordan River, creating an Arab homeland in Palestine known as Transjordan (later Jordan). During the month of August 1929, Arab riots broke out against the Jews across Palestine, including Gaza and Hebron. In Hebron, the oldest continuously inhabited Jewish city in the world, sixty-nine Jews were brutally murdered. The British authorities responded by evacuating the Jews from both places and forbidding them to return. Serious unrest and riots continued through the 1930s as Arabs pressured Britain to halt Jewish immigration and abandon the Balfour Declaration.[25]

Although Britain played a great part in creating the nation of Israel, there was a change of direction to those who did not feel warmly about the idea of a Jewish homeland. The British became increasingly friendly toward the Arabs in an attempt to win favor from them, and this resulted in restricting Jewish immigration to Palestine.[26] The Jewish community tried to persuade the British to allow increased Jewish immigration, but not to Arabs, and they were threatening to cut off access to Middle Eastern oil supplies if immigration was increased. The British responded with another White Paper that overturned the Balfour Declaration. This White Paper specified stipulations that proved disastrous to the Jewish people:

1. It called for an independent Palestinian state established within ten years, governed by both Jews and Arabs.
2. The Jewish immigration to Palestine under the British mandate was to be limited to 75,000 over the next five years, after that it would depend on Arab consent.
3. Jews would only buy land in areas where they were already the majority population.

4. Jewish immigration would be limited to the economic capacity of the country.

Churchill, who supported the Jewish national homeland, called it "a gross breach of faith." Although Churchill reaffirmed his support to the Jewish homeland, he was the one who published the White Paper that included these four major stipulations.[27]

There was a turning point on November 9, 1938, a night that has been named the "Night of Broken Glass" because of the shattered glass as Jewish shops in Germany were destroyed by Hitler's henchmen. More than 260 synagogues were burned that night and 20,000 Jews were arrested. The Jewish community was then fined $400 million for damages inflicted by the soldiers to their property. From that moment on, Adolf Hitler began to speak openly of annihilating the Jews. In spite of the role played by Britain in reestablishing the Jewish state, it was the White Paper of 1939 that condemned millions of European Jews to the concentration camps for Hitler's "final solution."

Churchill was optimistic that the Jews would be established in the position where they belonged. He said he had an inheritance left to him by Balfour and he wasn't going to change his mind, though he did admit there were dark forces working against him, although he did not know how powerful those forces were. No matter how committed he was to the cause of the Jewish homeland, he was resisted by the British foreign office and the authorities in Jerusalem who were now in charge of the mandate.

In 1945 Churchill was forced out of office by the new labor government led by Clement Atlee. Again, when the war ended, Palestine remained closed to the survivors of the concentration camps, who had now become homeless. Their homeland was allowed to take only a few thousand immigrants each year.[28] Most of them were returned to the very concentration camps from which they had been freed.

Ernest Bevin, who was the foreign minister in the Atlee Administration, was not very happy with the Jewish immigration. He restricted many Jews who attempted to return to their Promised Land. U.S. President Harry Truman was moved by the plight of Jewish refugees and urged Britain to open Palestine and increase immigration. Bevin's response was, "The Jews have waited two thousand years; they can wait a little longer."

Out of desperation, the Jewish leadership created the Haganah in 1920 to protect Jewish farms and communities from attacks by Palestinian Arabs. They were also deployed to fight an eventual German invasion. By 1945 there were two other groups that joined the Haganah in forming the Jewish resistance movement, and these were Irgun and the Lehi. They all had one purpose now, and that was to drive the British who were blocking immigration of Holocaust survivors and banning new Jewish settlements out of Palestine.

In 1946 the Haganah sacked British military installations in attempts to destroy their communications systems. Then on July 22, 1946, the Irgun, a radical resistance group, blew up the city's most prominent hotel in Jerusalem, the King David Hotel. Many people lost their lives, including twenty-eight British. In July 1947 the refugee ship known as the *Exodus* was captured by the British in international waters off Palestine. Its cargo included 4,500 Holocaust survivors and was eventually returned to German prison camps. By the end of 1947 the British had decided they wanted nothing to do with the whole mandate. As a result, the newly formed United Nations organization went back to the drawing board. We need to remind ourselves that the British worldwide Empire disappeared within a comparatively short period of time after they refused to vote for Israel's restoration at the United Nations in November 1947.

The United Nations Resolution

In May 1947 the United Nations had created a committee to study the Palestinian question. The Arabs refused to participate and the committee recommended the partition of the remaining 23 percent of Palestine into Jewish and Arab states, with Jerusalem as a free international city. However, this committee forgot or ignored the fact that Britain had already divided Palestine in 1922 and created an Arab state called Transjordan.

Britain supported only the international status of Jerusalem in this resolution. It was submitted to the General Assembly of the United Nations, which passed the resolution thirty-three to thirteen and gave the necessary two-thirds majority. The British abstained because of her recommendation in the Balfour Declaration in 1917. The British, who had been so supportive to the Jewish homeland, were now opposed to the formation of a Jewish homeland.

Under the United Nations Partition Plan, the Jews were denied sovereignty over Jerusalem, their ancient capital, but they gracefully accepted the Partition Plan that had been recommended. The first president of Israel, Chaim Weizmann, appealed to the UN to support the partition, saying:

> We realize that we cannot have the whole of Palestine. God may have promised Palestine to the Jews; but it is up to the Almighty to keep His promise in His own time. Our business is to do what we can in a very imperfect way.[29]

The first prime minister David Ben-Gurion also reiterated that God would overrule in reclaiming the whole Promised Land by saying:

> I know that God promised all of Palestine to the children of Israel. I do not know what borders He set. I believe they are wider than the ones proposed. If God will keep His promise in His own time, our business as poor humans who live in a difficult age is to save as much as we can of the remnants of Israel.[30]

One teacher of prophecy noted that it matters very little as to how much land Israel relinquishes for peace, as ultimately they will take over all the land from the Nile River in Egypt to the Euphrates River in Iraq.[31] Since the Balfour Declaration, the Jews have been returning to their homeland from many countries where they were scattered in fulfillment of Old Testament prophecies. The British mandate was set to end at 6:00 p.m. EST, which was 8:00 a.m. in Israel, on May 14, 1948.

Then the Union Jack was lowered at Government House in Jerusalem. The British high commissioner, Sir Alan Cunningham, left for Haifa where he reportedly boarded a British warship and the British Mandate ended. At 4:00 p.m., Prime Minister David Ben-Gurion and other leaders of the new nation gathered in the Tel Aviv Museum, where they declared the state of Israel as being independent. The Declaration of Independence was as follows:

> By virtue of natural and historic right of the Jewish people and of the General Assembly of the United Nations, we hereby proclaim the establishment of the Jewish state in Palestine to be called "Medinant Yisreal," the State of Israel.[32]

Isaiah foretold long ago:

> Who has heard of such a thing? Who has seen such things? Shall a land be born in one day? Or shall a nation be brought forth in a moment? For as soon as Zion was in labor, she brought forth her children. (Isaiah 66:8 AMP)

Prime Minister Ben-Gurion concluded with a plea to the Arabs:

> We extend our hand in peace and neighbourliness to all the neighboring states…the state of Israel is prepared to make this contribution to the Middle East as a whole.[33]

Of course, the Arabs rejected the UN Partition Plan and they tried to force a vote on a last-minute resolution to prevent the establishment of a Jewish state. So Israel's only hope was for the United States to recognize the new nation. Before the 6:00 p.m. deadline, nothing had changed. Finally, the British Mandate officially ended and the United States ambassador addressed the UN by recognizing the new state. Despite the recognition of Israel and the United Nations, the Arabs declared war against the new Jewish nation, and the War of Independence officially began. Jordan, Egypt, Syria, Iraq, and Lebanon all intended to eliminate the Jews and push them into the Mediterranean Sea, but against all odds Israel survived—it was nothing short of a God-given miracle.

In spite of its imperfections, God used Christian England as His channel to fulfill His promises, and Britain answered the call by putting into effect the declaration originally made on November 2, 1917, in favor of the establishment in Palestine of a national home for the Jewish people. Furthermore, Britain was obliged to use her best endeavors to facilitate Jewish immigration and to encourage Jewish settlement on the land. Lloyd George, the British prime minister during World War I, Lord Balfour, and General Edmund Allenby, all believed that biblical prophecies were the essential factor in any decisions regarding the Jewish people and Palestine. Balfour believed the Jews were exiles who would be given back their homeland in payment for Christianity's "immeasurable debt." According to historian Hugh Kitson, Balfour wrote, "The position of the Jews is unique. For them race, religion and country are inter-related as they are inter-related in the case of no other religion, and no other county on earth."[34]

One historian has noted that "the original Balfour Declaration is now residence at the British Museum and in another amazing twist of fate, the Cyrus Cylinder–which contains the description of the previous decree that led to the restoration of the Jewish state after the Babylonian exile—is also there!"[35]

A Coincidence or a Curse?

Scottish preacher Robert Murray M'Cheyne is considered to have had a thorough knowledge of the Hebrew language so that he was able to converse with learned European Jews. He prophetically once said in a lecture that "we might anticipate an outpouring of the Spirit when our church should outstretch its hands to the Jew as well the Gentile."[36] In one letter he says: "To seek the lost sheep of the house of Israel is an object very near to my heart, as my people know it has ever been. Such an enterprise may probably draw down unspeakable blessings on the Church of Scotland, according to the promise, 'They shall prosper who love Thee' (Psalm 122:6 KJV)."[37] His words, it seems, were to be prophetic, for when he returned from the Holy Land he found that revival had broken out in Scotland.

It has been noted that in earlier times wars and revolutions have often resulted in major revivals and renewal movements. After the war and the Holocaust in 1945, revivals occurred individually and also in groups, but not on a large scale. The German preacher Eric Sauer (1898–1959) wrote, "It is an alarming fact that in spite of the mighty voice of God in the momentous happenings of recent years, there has been no really great lasting general revival, not in a single European country."[38] Is this a coincidence or a curse that needs true repentance from the church? The choice might be made individually and might be made now.

Endnotes

[1] Franz Kobler, *The Vision was There: A History of the British Movement for the Restoration of the Jews to Palestine* (World Jewish Congress, British Section, Lincolns-Prager, 1956), 7–9. Cited in *A Nation Called By God: British's Leading Role in the Restoration of Israel* (Love Never Fails CFI Communications, Eastbourne), 3.

[2] Derek Prince, *The Last Word on the Middle East* (Chosen Books, 1982), 47–48.

[3] The Balfour Declaration, November 2, 1917.

[4] Derek Prince, *The Last Word on the Middle East* (Chosen Books, 1982), 37.

[5] Franz Kobler, *The Vision Was There,* 47.

[6] Ibid., 58–59.

[7] Ibid.

[8] Ibid., 63–66.

[9] Ibid.

[10] Ibid.

[11] N. I. Matar, *The Idea of the Restoration of the Jews in English Protestant Thought: Between the Reformation and 1660* (University of Durham, 1985), 1–2.

[12] *A Nation Called by God: Britain's Leading Role in the Restoration of Israel* (Love Never Fails CFI Communications, Eastbourne), 4–6.

[13] Ibid.

[14] Ibid.

[15] Ibid.

[16] Ibid.

[17] Spurgeon, The Harvest and Vintage, MTP, 50:553, accessed from *http://www.spurgeon.org/misc/eschat2.htm#note59.*

[18] *The Restoration and Conversion of the Jews Sovereign* (Grace Advent Testimony, Chelmsford, 1970), Vol. 17: 703–704.

19 *A Nation Called By God: Britain's Leading Role in the Restoration of Israel*, 6.

20 Walter C. Kaiser, "The Land of Israel and the Future Return," in *Israel: The Land and the People: An Evangelical Affirmation of God's Promises*, edited by H. Wayne House (Grand Rapids, Michigan: Kregel Publications, 1999), 224.

21 Kelvin Crombie, *For the Love of Zion* (Hodder and Stoughton Religious 1991), 3.

22 Documentary, *Jerusalem: The Covenant City*, presented by Lance Lambert, Hatikvah Film Foundation, Distributed by Evangelical Films.

23 Derek Prince, *The Last Word on the Middle East*, 37.

24 Mike Evans, *Betrayed: The Conspiracy to Divide Jerusalem* (Bedford, Texas: Bedford Books, 2008), 186–187.

25 Ibid., 190, 192–193.

26 Ibid.

27 Ibid.

28 Ibid.

29 Ibid.

30 Hugh Kitson, *Jerusalem The Covenant City* (Hatikvah Ltd: United Kingdom, 2000), 101.

31 Barry R. Smith, *Better than Nostradamus* (International Support Ministries: Marlborough, New Zealand, 1996), 220.

32 Hugh Kitson, 103.

33 Ibid.

34 Ibid., 92.

35 Paul Backholer, 241.

36 Andrew Bonar, *Memoir and Remains of R. M. M'Cheyne* (London: Banner of Truth, 1966), 87–88.

37 Ibid.

38 Erich M. Sauer, *In the Arena of Faith* (Wm Eerdmans Publishing, Co., 1955), 9.

Part II: The History of Christianity in America

CHAPTER 11

A Brief History of American Christianity

Finally, let us not forget the religious character of our origin. Our fathers were brought hither by their high veneration for the Christian religion. They journeyed by its light, and labored in its hope. They sought to incorporate its principles with the elements of their society, and to diffuse its influence through all their institutions, civil, political, or literary.

—Daniel Webster

William Bradford

William Bradford (1590–1657) was an English leader of the settlers of the Plymouth colony in Massachusetts, and served as governor for over thirty years after John Carver died. Bradford is credited as the first civil authority to designate what popular American culture now views as Thanksgiving in the United States. William Bradford's book *Of Plymouth Plantation* was written between 1630 and 1647. The book vividly documents the Pilgrims' adventures—their first stop in Holland, the crossing aboard the *Mayflower*, the first winter in the new colony, and the help from friendly Native Americans who saved their lives.[1]

William Bradford was born at the village of Austerfield, near Scrooby, in Nottinghamshire, and the baptismal entry in the registers of the church is dated March 19, 1590. His first wife, (Dorothy May), was drowned in the harbor soon after the arrival of the *Mayflower* by falling overboard. He was an avid reader of the Geneva Bible version by the age of twelve, and he became the first governor of the colony a few months after their arrival. He died May 9, 1657, at sixty-nine years of age.

No words could more vividly depict the feelings in the heart of Bradford's descendants on the return to American soil of this precious relic by the free gift of England than those of Senator Hoar. Bradford wrote:

> I do not think many Americans will gaze upon it without a little trembling of the lips and a little gathering of mist in the eyes, as they think of the story of suffering, of sorrow, of peril, of exile, of death and of lofty triumph, which that book tells—which the hand of the great leader and founder of America has traced on those pages. There is nothing like it in human annals since the story of Bethlehem. These English men and women going out from their homes in beautiful Lincoln and York, wife separated from husband and mother from child in that hurried embarkation for Holland, pursued to the beach by English horsemen; the thirteen years of exile; the life at Amsterdam in alley foul and lane obscure; the dwelling at Leyden; the embarkation at Delfthaven; the farewell of Robinson; the terrible voyage across the Atlantic; the compact in the habour; the landing on the rock; the dreadful first winter; the death roll of more than half the number; the days of suffering and of famine; the wakeful night, listening for the yell of the wild beast and the war-whoop of the savage; the building of the State on those sure foundations which no wave nor tempest has ever shaken; the breaking of the new light; the dawning of the new day; the beginning of the new life; the enjoyment of peace with liberty—of all these things is the original record by the hand of our beloved father and founder.[2]

William Bradford writes: "The suppression of religious liberty in England was the first cause of the foundation of the New Plymouth Settlement."[3] As is well known, England was the first country to be thus enlightened with the gospel of Jesus Christ after the gross darkness of the papal system. In every age of history, darkness has threatened to extinguish the light of God shining in the world. But also in every age of history, heroes and heroines of the faith rise up to hold high the torch of their testimony—witnesses to the truth of the gospel of Jesus Christ.

From the Pilgrims who sought liberty for themselves to the Founders like Thomas Jefferson who wrote the Declaration of Independence, they all believed that God the Creator gives human rights, and, as such, they are universal and absolute for every person on earth. They are the rights of all people, in all places, at all times, regardless of one's nationality, race, or religion.

One Aim: Advancing the Kingdom of God

According to Bradford, the Pilgrims came into these parts of America with one aim, namely, to advance the kingdom of our Lord Jesus Christ and to enjoy the liberties of the gospel in purity and peace. The strong grasp of the intellectual and practical side of his and other Pilgrims' ideas of religious liberty they owed, no doubt, a deep debt to that splendid apostolic figure, their old pastor at Leydon, John Robinson. This is evidenced by the clear exposition of their claims in the answer they gave to charges against them of dissembling in their declaration of conformity to the practices of the French Reformed Churches, and of undue license in differing from those professed forms of worship.

> In attempting to tie us to the French practices in every detail, you derogate from the liberty we have in Christ Jesus. The apostle Paul would have none follow him but wherein he followed Christ; much less ought any Christian or Church in the world do so. The French may err, we may err, and other churches may err, and doubtless do in many circumstances. That honour of infallibility belongs, therefore, only to the Word of God and pure Testament of Jesus Christ, to be followed as the only rule and pattern for direction by all Churches and Christians.

It is great arrogance for any man or Church to think that he or they have so sounded the Word of God to the bottom as to be able to set down precisely a Church's practices without error in substance or circumstance and in such a way that no one thereafter may digress or differ from them with impunity.[4]

Bradford's Disparagement of an Utopian Government

On the other hand, it is interesting to mark Bradford's disparagement of Utopian schemes of communal, or socialistic, forms of government. Here is his conservative argument, based on the experience of the first few years of their colonization in the New World:

The failure of this experiment of communal service, which was tried for several years, and by good and honest men, proves the emptiness of the theory of Plato and other ancients, applauded by some of later times—that the taking away of private property, and the possession of it in community by commonwealth, would make a state happy and flourishing; as if they were wiser than God. For in this instance, community of property (so far as it went) was found to breed much confusion and discontent, and retard much employment which would have been to the general benefit and comfort.... If (it was thought) all were to share alike, and all where to do alike, then all were on an equality throughout, and one was as good as another; and so, if it did not actually abolish those very relations which God himself has set among men, it did at least greatly diminish the mutual respect that is so important and which should be preserved amongst them. Let none argue that this is due to human failing rather than to this communistic plan of life itself. I answer, seeing that all men have this failing in them, that God in His wisdom saw that another plan of life was fitter for them.[5]

Thus in civil as in religious matters, "Bradford's and other Pilgrims' instinct led him always to follow the guidance of a wise and benevolent Providence, working for the rational and natural evolution of mankind, which humanity could expedite only by a plain, unsophisticated reliance upon truth and goodness, as incarnate in the divine character and life of Jesus Christ."[6]

As President Reagan reiterated in his "City on a Hill" speech in 1974: "You can call it mysticism if you want to but I have always believed there was some divine plan that placed this great continent between two oceans to be sought out by those who were possessed of an abiding love of freedom and a special kind of courage."[7]

What Did the Pilgrims Have in Mind?

Although historically the Pilgrims were initially associated with the Puritans, there were important differences between the two. Both saw the need for religious reform, but they differed concerning the means by which reform was to be achieved. The Puritans determined to remain within the established church and to impose reform from within—even by compulsion, if necessary. The Pilgrims sought liberty for themselves and declined to use the machinery of secular government to enforce their views upon others. These differing views are expressed in Leonard Bacon's book *Genesis of the New England Churches*:

> In the old World on the other side of the ocean, the Puritan was a Nationalist, believing that a Christian nation is a Christian church, and demanding that the Church of England should be thoroughly reformed; while the Pilgrim was a Separatist, not only from the Anglican Prayer Book and Queen Elizabeth's episcopacy, but from all national churches.... The Pilgrim wanted liberty for himself and his wife and little ones, and for his brethren, to walk with God in a Christian life as the rules and motives of such a life were revealed to him from God's Word. For that he went into exile; for that he crossed the ocean; for that he made his home in a wilderness. The Puritan's idea was not liberty, but right government in church and state—such government as should not only permit him, but also compel other men to walk in the right way.[8]

The difference between Puritans and Pilgrims could be expressed in the two words reformation and restoration. The Puritans sought to reform the church as it existed in their day; they believed that the ultimate purpose of God was to restore the church to its original condition, as portrayed in the New Testament. The Pilgrim vision of restoration according to Bradford was that "the Church of God revert to their ancient purity and recover their primitive order of liberty and beauty."[9]

Again, Bradford returned to the same theme when he declared the Pilgrims' purpose:

> The one party of reformers endeavored to establish the right worship of God and discipline of Christ in the church, according to the simplicity of the Gospel without mixture of men's inventions; and to have and be ruled by the laws of God's Word, dispensed in those offices, and by those officers of Pastors, Teachers and Elders, etc., according to the Scriptures.[10]

With this purpose in view, these people became two distinct bodies and congregated separately, for they came from various towns and villages in Nottinghamshire, Lincolnshire, and Yorkshire. They were persecuted on every side; some were imprisoned; others had their houses watched day and night, and they escaped with much difficulty. Again, Bradford explains,

> The reformers who saw the evil of these things and whose hearts the Lord had touched with heavenly zeal for His truth, shook off this yoke of anti-Christian bondage and as the Lord's free people joined themselves (by a covenant of the Lord) into a church estate, in the fellowship of the gospel, to walk in all His ways made known, or to be made known unto them, according to their best endeavours, whatsoever it should cost them, the Lord assisting them. And it cost them something, the ensuing history will declare.[11]

Later, when the congregation moved to Leyden, Holland, Bradford described their way of life there:

First for these reformers to be thus constrained to leave their native soil, their lands and livings, and all their friends, was a great sacrifice, and was wondered at by many. But to go into a country unknown to them, where they must learn a new language, and get their livings they knew not how, seemed an almost desperate adventure and a misery worse than death. Further they were unacquainted with trade, which was the chief industry of their adopted country, having been used only to a plain country life and the innocent pursuit of farming. But these things did not dismay them, though they sometimes troubled them; for their desires were set on the ways of God, to enjoy His ordinances; they rested on His providence, and knew whom they had believed…. They had other work in hand, and another kind of war to wage. For though they saw fair and beautiful cities, flowing with abundance of all sorts of wealth and riches, it was not long before they saw the grim and grisly face of poverty coming upon them like an armed man, with whom they must buckle and encounter, and from whom they could fly; but they were armed with faith and patience against him and all his encounters; and though they were sometimes foiled, yet, by God's assistance, they prevailed and got the victory.[12]

American Calvinists

Just like the Puritans, American Calvinists of the last century believed that the Bible should be used in every area of life and thought. In political theory, for example, they rejected the theories of popular and state sovereignty and insisted instead that God was sovereign over all nations:

Though they supported the separation of church and state, Calvinists and many other evangelicals living in the late nineteenth century proclaimed that religion should not and could not be divorced from politics. Underlying all governments were central presuppositions that either supported or undermined Christianity; there was no intermediate option.[13]

They also insisted that the Bible be central to all education. They argued "that religious substance could not simply be tacked on to a neutral curriculum by Bible reading and prayer; rather, a biblical world and life view must undergird and inform the study of all subjects in the public schools."[14] Again, like the Puritans, American Calvinists worked for comprehensive reform. The Calvinist understanding of the kingship of Christ was especially important.

William Greene (professor at Atwater and Princeton Seminaries) emphasized that the doctrine of God's sovereignty in history and salvation stimulated Christians to serve God through their vocations, homes, and statecraft in order to bring the affairs of society under the rule of Christ. Calvinists, who believed that biblical principles should guide all human activities, denounced efforts to confine the influence of Christianity to the church and family life.[15]

Reasons for Settlement in America

Again, in his fourth chapter, Bradford described the main reasons that led the Pilgrims to decide upon undertaking the journey to America. I will summarize his views below.

First, they saw by experience that the hardships of the country were such that comparatively few others would join them, and fewer still would remain with them. Many who came and many more who desired to come could not endure the continual labor and hard fare and other inconveniences that they themselves were satisfied with. For, though many desired to enjoy the ordinances of God in their purity, and the liberty of the gospel, yet they preferred to submit to bondage, with danger to their conscience, rather than endure these privations.

Some even preferred the prisons in England to this liberty in Holland with such hardships. But it was thought that if there could be found a better and easier place of living, it would attract many and remove this discouragement. Their pastor would often say that if many of those who both wrote and preached against them were living where they might have liberty and comfortable conditions, then they would practice the same religion as they themselves did.[16]

Secondly, they saw that though the people generally bore these difficulties very cheerfully, and with resolute courage, being in the best strength of their years, yet old age began to steal from many of them, and their great and continual labors, with other crosses and sorrows, hastened it before their time. This was so that it was not only probable but certain that in a few more years they would be in danger of scattering by the necessities pressing upon them. Therefore, according to Proverbs 22:3, "A prudent man foresees the evil and hides himself, but the simple pass on and are punished." They, like skillful and hardened soldiers, were wary of being surrounded by their enemies so that they could neither fight nor flee, and thought it wiser to dislodge in good time to some place of better advantage and less danger, if any such could be found.[17]

Thirdly, as necessity was a taskmaster over them, so they themselves were forced to be not only over their servants but in a sort over their dearest children. This wounded the hearts of the parents and produced many sad and sorrowful effects within the community. Many of their children, who were of the best disposition and who had learned to bear the yoke in their youth and were willing to bear part of their parents' burden were often so oppressed with their labors that though their minds were free and willing, their bodies bowed under the weight and became worn out in early youth.

But still more lamentable, and all of sorrows most heavy to be borne, was that many of the children, influenced by these conditions, and the great licentiousness of the young people of the country and the many temptations of the city were led by evil examples into dangerous courses, leaving their parents. Some became soldiers, others embarked upon voyages by sea, and others upon worse paths tending to dissoluteness and the danger of their souls, to the great grief of the parents and the dishonor of God. So they saw their posterity would be in danger to degenerate and become corrupt.[18]

Lastly (and which is not least), a great hope and inward zeal they had of laying some good foundations for the propagating and advancing of the gospel of the kingdom of Christ in those remote parts of the world, though they should be but as steppingstones unto others for the performing of so great a work. The place they fixed their thoughts upon was somewhere in those vast and unpopulated countries of America, which were fruitful and fit for habitation, though devoid of all civilized inhabitants and given over to savages, who range up and down, differing little from the wild beasts themselves. Besides the causalities of the seas, they asserted that the length of the voyage was such that women, and other weak persons worn out with age and travail, could never survive it.

Even if they should survive it, they contended that the miseries that they would be exposed to in such a country would be too hard to endure. They would be liable to famine, nakedness, and want. The change of air, diet, and water would infect them with sickness and diseases. Again, all those who surmounted these difficulties would remain in continual danger from the savages, who are cruel, barbarous, and treacherous, furious in their rage, and merciless when they get the upper hand; not content to kill, they delight in tormenting people in the most bloody manner possible; flaying some alive with the shells of fishes, cutting off the members and joints of others piecemeal, broiling them on the coals, and eating scallops of their flesh in their sight whilst they live, with other cruelties too horrible to be related.[19]

All great and honorable actions are accompanied with great difficulties, and must be both met and overcome with answerable courage. It was granted that the dangers were great but not desperate; the difficulties were many but not invincible. For many of the things feared might never come to pass. Others, by provident care and the use of good means, might in a great measure be prevented; and all of them, through the help of God, by fortitude and patience, might either be borne or overcome.[20]

True it was that such attempts were not to be undertaken without good ground and reason, rashly or lightly, or, as many had done, for curiosity or hope of gain. But their condition was not ordinary, their ends were good and honorable, their calling was lawful and urgent. Because of this, they expected the blessing of God on their proceedings. Though they would lose their lives in this action, yet might they have the comfort of knowing that their endeavor was worthy.[21]

John Robinson's Address

Edward Winslow (1595–1655), a Puritan who traveled over to the New World on the *Mayflower*, gave a message where he summed up John Robinson's address, revealing the theological position of the Pilgrims:

> We are now ere long to part asunder, and the Lord knoweth whether he [Robinson] should live to see our face again. But whether the Lord had appointed it or not, he charged us before God and His blessed angels, to follow him no further than he followed Christ; and if God should reveal anything to us by any other instrument of His, to be ready to receive it, as ever we were to receive any truth by his ministry; for he was very confident the Lord had more truth and light yet to break forth out of His Holy Word. He took occasion also miserably to bewail that state and condition of the Reformed churches who had come to a period of [standstill] in religion, and would go no further than the instruments of their reformation [i.e. those who had been leaders in the Reformation]. For example, the Lutherans could not be drawn to go beyond what Luther saw; for whatever part of God's will He had further imparted and revealed to Calvin, they [the Lutherans] would rather die than embrace it. And so also, saith he, you see the Calvinists, they stick where he [Calvin] left them, a misery much to be lamented; for though they were precious shining lights in their times, yet God had not revealed His whole will to them; and were they now living, saith he, they would be as ready and willing to embrace further light, as they had received. Here also he put us in mind of our church covenant, at least that part of it whereby we promise and covenant with God and one another to receive whatsoever light or truth shall be made known to us from His written Word; but withal [he] exhorted us to take heed what we received for truth, and well to examine and

compare it and weigh it with other Scriptures of truth before we received it. For saith he, it is not possible [that] the Christian world should come so lately [recently] out of such thick antichristian darkness, and that full perfection of knowledge should break forth at once.[22]

Robison's message shows that the Pilgrims did not claim to have arrived at a final understanding of all the truth. They were on a pilgrimage, looking for the further revelation of truth that lay ahead as they walked in obedience to the truth already received. From the study of the Scriptures, Derek Prince summarizes this by saying, "The Pilgrims learned two great truths that they have in turn bequeathed to their spiritual descendants in America and other lands. First, the end-time purpose of God is the restoration and completion of the church. Second, the source of power for achievement of this purpose is united prayer and fasting."[23]

Endnotes

1 Bradford's *History of the Plymouth Settlement 1608–1650*, Rendered into Modern English by Harold Paget E. P. (Dutton and Company, 681 Fifth Avenue ,1920), xxiii–xxiv.

2 Ibid., 1.

3 Ibid., xxvii.

4 Ibid., xxviii.

5 Ibid.

6 Ibid.

7 This quote, "We will be as a city upon a hill," was originally attributed to John Winthrop, the Puritan governor of the Massachusetts Bay colony. President Ronald Reagan reiterated it on January 25, 1975, in his speech to the first Conservative Political Action Conference (CPAC), accessed from *http://www.calvin.edu/academic/history/katerbergneh /Web%20ready/ berg%20adina.pdf*.

8 Leonard Bacon, *The Genesis of the New England Churches* (Nabu Press, 2010). This is a reproduction of a book published before 1923.

9 Bradford's *History of the Plymouth Settlement*, 2.

10 Ibid., 3–4.

11 Ibid., 7.

12 Ibid., 9, 14.

13 Gary Scott Smith, *The Seeds of Secularization: Calvinism, Culture, and Pluralism in America, 1870–1915* (Grand Rapids, MI: Christian University Press Eerdmans, 1985), 55–56.

14 Ibid., 78.

15 Ibid., 144.

16 Bradford's *History of the Plymouth Settlement*, 19–23.

17 Ibid.

18 Ibid.

19 Ibid.

20 Ibid.

21 Ibid.

22 Quoted by Verna M. Hall, *A Compilation: The Christian History of the Constitution of the United States of America, Christian Self-Government* (The Foundation for American Christian Education, 2006), 184.

23 Derek Prince, *Shaping History Through Prayer and Fasting* (Whitaker House, 1998), 448.

CHAPTER 12

Christianity's Influence on the Founders

Defining "Christian"

There may have been Christian men among the Founding Fathers, but if we confine the founding of the American nation to the foundation of the New Plymouth Settlement by the Pilgrims, then we might get a more accurate account upon which the American nation was founded. But why do some Christians in America think these men (what have become known as the Founders, primarily after 1776) were Christians? Some believe it would be easier to justify their political agenda, whereby instead of introducing Christian principles into the government, they tried to restore the principles that were lost, which probably took place around 1830.

Other historians have also argued that during the American Revolution, some of these statesmen were not Christians at all, but they used religion and the Scriptures as instruments to gain political capital. Whereas other historians claim that these great men were deists, which according to the Oxford dictionary "is the belief of a supreme being arising from reason rather than *personal* revelation." According to deists, God the Creator of the universe does not intervene in earthly or human affairs or suspend the natural laws of the universe. They don't believe in spiritual gifts like miracles or personal prophetic revelations either. For them, human beings can only know God through reason and the observation of nature, not by personal revelation or supernatural manifestations.

Let's try to remind ourselves what it means to be a Christian because we cannot exchange deism for Christianity by any means.

Some of these honorable men believed in one God, but believing in God or being educated in theological training without the personal experience of salvation does not mean they were Christians by any sense of the word. A Christian's personal experience is something that cannot be explained by human reason alone: "You say you have faith, for you believe that there is one God. Good for you! Even the demons believe this, and they tremble in terror" (James 2:19 NLT).

Christianity was founded upon the person and work of Jesus Christ. If anyone claims to be a Christian, they cannot separate themselves from the Man Jesus Christ. A Christian has to acknowledge that they have sinned, and then make a personal response in faith to the lordship and person of Jesus Christ as the only One who can save them and redeem them from their sins. And by repenting of their sins, they receive the gift of the Holy Spirit.

The basic facts of the gospel and the response which each person is required to make are simplified as (1) Jesus Christ was delivered by God the Father to die on the cross for our sins; (2) Jesus Christ was buried; (3) God raised Him from the dead on the third day; (4) we must therefore repent, be baptized, and receive the Holy Spirit; and, (5) we are also marked by an eager expectation for the Lord to return at any time.

Some of these Founders believed that the "Supreme Architect" doesn't alter the universe by intervening in it. In other words, they believed God designed and created the universe but then stood aside to let it run on its own accord. Yet the psalmist tells us of God's sovereignty over all His creation—He has supreme, unlimited power over the entire universe. He creates, He preserves, and He governs. Our every breath depends on the life He has breathed into us.

> He appointed the moon for seasons; the sun knows its going down. You make darkness, and it is night, in which all the beasts of the forest creep about. The young lions roar after their prey, and seek their food from God. When the sun rises, they gather together and lie down in their dens. Man goes out to his work and to his labor until the evening. O Lord, how manifold are Your

works! In wisdom You have made them all. The earth is full of Your possessions—this great and wide sea, in which are innumerable teeming things, living things both small and great. There the ships sail about; there is that Leviathan which You have made to play there. These all wait for You, that You may give them their food in due season. What You give them they gather in; You open Your hand, they are filled with good. You hide Your face, they are troubled; You take away their breath, they die and return to their dust. You send forth Your Spirit, they are created; and You renew the face of the earth. (Psalm 104:19–30)

The Age of Enlightenment

Deism became more prominent in the seventeenth and eighteenth centuries during the Age of Enlightenment, which took place most notably in France, Britain, Germany, and the United States. This age was for the so-called "intellectuals" who were raised as Christians and believed in one God but could not believe in supernatural miracles, the infallibility of Scripture, or the mystery of the Trinity. It has been noted by historians that deistic ideas influenced several leaders of the American and French Revolutions.

Deists varied in what they believed. Some deists rejected prophecies and miracles but still considered themselves Christians because they believed Christianity was corrupted by additions of miracles, prophecies, and the doctrine of the Trinity. For instance, in his work *The Life and Morals of Jesus of Nazareth*, Thomas Jefferson removed some sections of the New Testament that contained supernatural aspects and other Holy Spirit inspired revelations that he believed were personal interpretations that were added by the four writers of the Gospels.[1] But again, Peter assures us in Scripture:

[Yet] first [you must] understand this, that no prophecy of Scripture is [a matter] of any personal or private or special interpretation (loosening, solving). For no prophecy ever originated because some man willed it [to do so—it never came by human impulse], but men spoke from God who were borne along (moved and impelled) by the Holy Spirit. (2 Peter 1:20–21 AMP)

In his second letter to Timothy, Paul was saying that the whole Bible is God's Word and that all Scripture is inspired by God:

> Every Scripture is God-breathed (given by His inspiration) and profitable for instruction, for reproof and conviction of sin, for correction of error and discipline in obedience, [and] for training in righteousness (in holy living, in conformity to God's will in thought, purpose, and action), so that the man of God may be complete and proficient, well fitted and thoroughly equipped for every good work. (2 Timothy 3:16–17 AMP)

The First President: George Washington

George Washington was also attracted by these principles of rationality and reason. He was an outspoken leader in calling for religious liberty and tolerance, and he promoted goodwill among all religions. He rejected signs of prejudice, intolerance, and all kinds of religious persecution, hoping that bigotry would be overcome by truth and reason. It has been noted that Washington's religious beliefs have been debated by historians, researchers, and biographers alike for over 200 years because he rarely discussed his religious beliefs in any great detail. Yet he was a humble man, having great respect toward God, which was proven in his diaries, personal letters, and public speeches. His biographer Jared Sparks recorded an account from the George W. Lewis, who was Washington's nephew:

> Mr. Lewis said he unintentionally witnessed Washington's private devotions in his library kneeling in a position with an open Bible and Lewis believed this was the president's daily practice. Historians have different views on the faith of George Washington. Paul F. Boller a professor of history at Texas Christian University has argued that Washington was in fact an 18th century deist.[2]

Whereas Peter A. Lillback, historian and president of Westminster Theological Seminary, argues in his book *George Washington's Sacred Fire* that Washington was an orthodox Christian within the framework of his time. He explained that earlier historians did not have all the evidence that reveals this:

> Within this vast collection of Washington's own words and writings, we now have a remarkable ability to uncover what earlier scholars were unable to access. And when we let Washington's own words and deeds speak for his faith, we get quite a different perspective than that of most recent modern historians. Washington referred to himself frequently using the words "ardent," "fervent," "pious," and "devout." There are over one hundred different prayers composed and written by Washington in his own hand, with his own words, in his writings. He described himself as one of the deepest men of faith of his day when he confessed to a clergyman, "No man has a more perfect reliance on the all wise and powerful dispensations of the Supreme Being than I have, nor thinks His aid more necessary." Although he never once used the word "Deist" in his writings, he often mentioned religion, Christianity, and the Gospel. Historians should not turn Washington into a deist, even if they found it necessary and acceptable to do so in the past. Simply put, it is time to let the words and writings of Washington speak for themselves.[3]

Although Washington was a member of the Anglican Church all his life, there is very little evidence in his public discourse that he accepted the doctrine of the Trinity. According to Boller, not one of his letters mentioned the name of Jesus Christ.[4] Washington refused to commit to public pronouncements any statement of his personal faith besides a commitment to divine providence. Except during the war, he reportedly attended church once a month.[5] Boller says, "If to believe in the divinity and resurrection of Christ and His atonement for the sins of man and to participate in the sacrament of the Lord's Supper are requisites for the Christian faith, then Washington, on the evidence which we have examined, can be considered a Christian, except in the nominal sense."[6]

It is possible that he may have been a Christian in private, though his attitude toward the church betrays a woeful misunderstanding of Christian responsibilities. He did posses a personal prayer book, written in his own hand, which he called the "Daily Sacrifice." It contained familiar formal set prayers.[7] He was perhaps a "closet Trinitarian" in the way that John Locke was. Publicly, Washington was a Mason-Unitarian. Of him it can legitimately be said, as Mark Noll in fact says, "In short, the political figures who read the Bible in private rarely, if ever, betrayed that acquaintance to the public."[8]

David. L. Holmes describes Washington as a Christian deist by stating that "his religion fell somewhere between that of an orthodox Christian and a strict deist, whatever their beliefs, the Founders came from similar religious backgrounds, most were Protestants and the largest number of them was raised in the three largest Christian traditions of colonial America. Most of them were baptized listed on church rolls, married to practicing Christians, and in public statements, most invoked Divine assistance."[9]

But the widespread existence in eighteenth-century American deism complicates the actual beliefs of the Founders. Leaders on both sides of the constitutional debate were members of Masonic lodges, though it is hard to know precisely the number of those who were Masons. One person has said that eighteen of the fifty-six signers of the Declaration were Masons, as were eighteen of the thirty-nine signers of the Constitutional Convention.[10] When we look at the scientific and philosophical work of such figures as Isaac Newton, John Locke, and Jean-Jacques Rousseau, deists like Thomas Paine all argued that human experience and rationality, rather than religious principles and mystery, determine the validity of human beliefs.[11]

John Adams

John Adams was the second president of the United States and a close friend of Thomas Jefferson. Adams, Jefferson, and Benjamin Franklin all worked together on the first committee to design the Great Seal for the United States of America. The reverse of the Great Seal is the all-seeing eye above the pyramid, which has been described as a Masonic symbol. While there is no evidence that Adams was a member of any secret group, he was a Unitarian and shared views of Christianity not unlike those of Paine, Jefferson, and Franklin.[12] On February 22, 1756, John Adams recorded the following in his diary:

> Suppose a nation in some distant region should take the Bible for their only law book, and every member should regulate his conduct by the precepts there exhibited! Every member would be obliged in conscience, to temperance, frugality, and industry; to justice, kindness, and charity toward his fellow men; and to piety, love, and reverence toward Almighty God. What a Paradise this region would be.[13]

John Adams began as a Congregationalist and ended his days as a Christian Unitarian, accepting the central tenets of the Unitarian creed but also accepting Jesus as the redeemer of humanity and the biblical account of His miracles as true.[14]

Thomas Jefferson

Thomas Jefferson was the principal author of the Declaration of Independence and the third president of the United States. He epitomized what it meant in America to be a man of enlightenment. At his estate of Monticello, he displayed busts of Bacon, Locke, and Newton. Jefferson was sufficiently interested in religious matters, so much so that one scholar has described him as "the most self-consciously theological presidents."[15] A priest of the Church of England baptized him as an infant, and his mother used to teach him prayers from the *Book of Common Prayer*. His religion has been described by David L. Holmes as "monotheistic, restorationist, reason-centered, Jesus-centered, combative toward mystery, outwardly Episcopalian, but probably Unitarian."[16]

He was introduced to Enlightenment thinkers by William Small, a man who influenced his thinking and sparked a lifelong passion in him for their teachings. In 1803 he wrote to Benjamin Rush, saying,

To the corruptions of Christianity, I am indeed, opposed, but not to the genuine precepts of Jesus Himself. I am a Christian in the only sense in which I believe Jesus wished anyone to be; sincerely attached to His doctrines, in preference to all others; ascribing to himself every human excellence, and believing he never claimed any other.[17]

He revered Jesus as a reformer and moral exemplar, but he did not see Jesus as John and Samuel Adams, John Jay, and Elias Boudinot did —namely, as a Savior. He distrusted Trinitarian Christian clergy, viewing them as enemies of the simple teachings of Jesus. Because Jefferson's God was a God of reason, not of irrationality, Jefferson removed from the Gospels anything that appeared unreasonable.[18] He specifically removed the virgin birth, the miracles of Christ, the resurrection of the Lord Jesus, and His ascension into heaven. These he believed came from inferior minds.[19] Having disagreed with Jesus, Jefferson then indicated what he admired about Him:

> It is the innocence of His character, the purity and sublimity of His moral precepts, the eloquence of His inculcation, the beauty of His apologues in which He conveys them that I so much admire.... Among the sayings and discourses imputed to Him by His biographers, I find many passages of fine imagination, correct morality, and of the most lovely benevolence.[20]

When Jefferson lived in Philadelphia, he attended Joseph Priestley's Unitarian church. In some famous correspondence with the Unitarian minister, he predicted that Unitarianism would soon sweep the nation. He wrote:

> I rejoice that this blessed country of free inquiry and belief which has surrendered its creed and conscience to neither kings or priests, the genuine doctrine of only one God is reviving, and I trust there is not a young man now living who will not die an Unitarian.[21]

In his last years, Jefferson clearly moved toward a more traditional interpretation of Christianity. He valued Jesus as a person even more highly. Unlike some deists, he came to believe in prayer and in a life after death. But beliefs in an afterlife, according to David Holmes, were standard Unitarian beliefs of the time.[22]

James Madison

James Madison was the fourth president of the United States and has been referred to as the "Father of the Constitution" for being instrumental in the drafting of the United States Constitution. He was educated by a Presbyterian clergyman, and as a student at Princeton (1769–1772) he seemed to have developed a transient inclination to enter the ministry. In a 1773 letter to a college friend, he made the zealous proposal that the rising stars of his generation renounce their secular prospects and publicly declare their dissatisfaction by becoming fervent advocates in the cause of Christ.

Two months later Madison renounced his spiritual prospects and began the study of law. The next year he entered the political arena serving as a member of the Orange County Committee of Safety. Public service seems to have crowded out of his consciousness the previous imprints of his faith. For the rest of his life there is no mention in his writings of Jesus Christ or any of the issues that might concern a practicing Christian. Late in to his retirement, there are a few enigmatic references to religion, but nothing more.[23]

Scholars, nevertheless, have tried to construct from this unyielding evidence a religious identity for Madison. He is such a commanding figure in the founding period's controversies over religion's relation to government that knowledge of his personal religious convictions is sought as a key to his public posture on church-state issues. The very paucity of evidence has permitted latitude of interpretation in which writers have created Madison in the image of their own religious convictions. To Christian scholars, Madison is a paragon of piety; and to those of a more secular bent, he is a deist.[24]

Benjamin Franklin

Benjamin Franklin was a leading figure in the American

Enlightenment. He was a scientist and is credited for discovering and inventing the lightning rod, the Franklin stove, and many other scientific discoveries. A few weeks before he died, Franklin wrote a letter to Ezra Stiles, who was then president of Yale University. Stiles had inquired about Franklin's views on Christianity and of the Lord Jesus Christ. In response, Franklin wrote:

> Here is my creed. I believe in one God, Creator of the universe. That He governs it by His providence. That He ought to be worshipped. That the most acceptable service we render Him is doing good to other children. That the soul of man is immortal, and will be treated with justice in another life respecting conduct in this. These I take to be the principal principles of sound religion, and I regard them as you do in whatever sect I meet them. As to Jesus of Nazareth, my opinion of whom you particularly desire, I think the system of morals and His religion, as He left them to us, the best He ever saw or is likely to see; but I apprehend, it has received various corrupt changes and I have, with most of the present dissenters in England, some doubts as to His Divinity; though it is a question I do not dogmatize upon, having never studied it, and I think it needless to busy myself with it now, when I expect soon an opportunity of knowing the truth with less trouble. I see no harm, however, in its being believed, if that belief has the good consequence, as probably it has, of making His doctrines more respected and better observed; especially as I do not perceive that the Supreme Being takes it amiss, by distinguishing the unbelievers in His government of the world with any particular marks of His displeasure.[25]

Thomas Paine

Thomas Paine immigrated from England in 1774, just in time for the War for Independence. He never held elective office in America, although he did serve as secretary to a congressional committee. He returned to Europe around 1787, alternately claiming French citizenship while serving in the French Parliament and American citizenship when he was jailed by the French revolutionists and wanted American help. He ultimately returned to America in 1802. He was so ostracized by Americans because of his attacks on Christianity that when he died in 1809, only six people attended his funeral.

In his widely read work *The Age of Reason*, Thomas Paine called Christianity a "fable." He blasphemed the Lord Jesus Christ to such a degree that some of the quotes I've come across are not worth repeating. It has been noted by some historians that his famous pamphlet *Common Sense* is by far the most influential tract of the American Revolution, some maintaining that it influenced Jefferson's writing of the Declaration of Independence.[26] Paine's pamphlet sold 100,000 copies in the first three months after its publication.

Paine was also a protégé of Benjamin Franklin and denied that the Almighty ever communicated anything to man, either by speech, language, or a vision. His reasoning led him to assume that God was just a distant deity by calling Him "Nature's God," a term also used in the Declaration of Independence. According to David L. Holmes, Paine reportedly declared in a profession of faith: "I believe in one God, and no more; and I hope for happiness beyond this life. I believe in the equality of man; and I believe that religious duties consist in doing justice, loving mercy, and in endeavoring to make our fellow-creatures happy."[27]

He was also termed as an "insolent blasphemer," but Thomas Paine also acknowledged that liberty and independence was God's plan for America. Regardless of what he believed, Paine based his arguments for American independence and against the monarchy squarely upon the Bible:

> Government by kings was first introduced into the world by the heathens, from whom the children of Israel copied the custom. It was the most prosperous invention the devil ever set on foot for the promotion of idolatry.... Monarchy is ranked in Scripture as one of the sins of the Jews, for which a curse in reverse is denounced against them.... All anti-monarchical parts of Scripture have been very smoothly glossed over in monarchical

governments, but they undoubtedly merit the attention of countries which have their governments yet to form.... But where, say some is the king of America? I'll tell you, friend: He reigns above, and does not make havoc of mankind like the royal brute of Britain.... The Jews, elated with success (in Gideon's victory over the Midianites), and attributing it to the generalship of Gideon, proposed making him king, saying: Rule over us—you and your son's son also—for you have delivered us from the hand of Midian (Judges 8:22–23). Here was the temptation in its fullest extent; but Gideon, in the piety of his soul, replied: "I will not rule over you, and my son will not rule over you. The Lord will rule over you." Gideon does not decline the honor, but denies the right to give it.... These portions of Scripture are direct and positive; they admit of no equivocal construction. That the Almighty has here entered his protest against monarchical government is true, or the Scriptures are false.[28]

God's Plan for America

England has had a long history of Christian influence that resulted in the advance of civilization around the world. Therefore, America's earliest Founders did not break from their original heritage. In fact, they sought to establish old England in the state of New England.[29] New England was consciously founded by patriots seeking the glory of England, who first called the attention of their countrymen to these shores. Commercial enterprise made the first attempt at settlement. Puritanism overlaid these feeble beginnings by a proud, self-governing commonwealth dedicated to the glory of God and the happiness of a peculiar people. These three main streams in the life of old England—the patriotic, the commercial, and the religious—mingled with waters on every slope.[30]

John Adams recognized God in the establishment of the new nation. He believed that the independence of the United States would be a momentous event, and wrote to that intent to his wife, Abigail, on July 3, 1776, saying, "I am apt to believe that it will be celebrated by succeeding generations as the great anniversary festival. It ought to be commemorated, as the day of deliverance, by solemn acts of devotion to God Almighty."[31]

Thomas Paine further argued that independence was God's plan for America: "Even the distance at which the Almighty hath placed England and America is a strong natural proof that the authority of one over the other, was never the design of heaven.... The Reformation was preceded by the discovery of America, as if the Almighty graciously meant to open a sanctuary to the persecuted in future years, when home should afford neither friendship nor safety."[32]

Oscar S. Straus, secretary of commerce under President Theodore Roosevelt, declared that among the American colonists, "the Bible was studied as no people except only as the Jews had studied it. Like the Hebrews of old, the American colonists were the people of the Book."[33] They learned to read using the Bible as their basic text, and from the Bible they derived their worldview, their knowledge of right and wrong, and the way of salvation. Paine recognized that the American colonists were a deeply Christian people who would never assert their independence unless convinced the Scriptures justified them in doing so.

According to John Quincy Adams, the glory of the American Revolution was that "it laid the cornerstone of human government upon the first precepts of Christianity."[34] John Eidsmoe concludes, "And so, as this unbeliever used the Scriptures to make his case to a Bible-believing people, Thomas Paine's infidelity is in itself a strong testimony to America's Christian heritage."[35] And historian David Barton has observed,

> It is very unfortunate, that if you ask most American Christians who vote in leaders why America separated from Great Britain, the overwhelming response will be "taxation without representation." That answer is acceptable as far it goes, but taxation without representation was only one of twenty-seven grievances listed in the Declaration of Independence; and it was one of the lesser of the twenty-seven complaints. Listed in the Declaration eleven times more often than taxation without

representation was the abuse of representative powers; the abuse of military powers was listed seven times as often; the abuse of judicial powers four times as often; and stirring up domestic insurrection twice as often taxation without representation was merely grievance number seventeen out of twenty seven listed alongside Great Britain's suppression of immigration and her interference with our foreign trade. The taxation issue was given little emphasis in the Declaration, yet it is one issue that everyone knows about today. The question is why aren't most Americans familiar with rest?[36]

And Barton continues,

Since the 1920–1940s, and to the present day, the Americans have been sold a lie that the only motivating factor in life is money.... The modern historians began teaching American history, putting an emphasis on economics as the basis of the Constitution and the Revolution. In other words, economics became the basis. Since the sole economic clause in the Declaration was "taxation without representation," this has become the one clause that Americans have learned about in their history books for the past half-century.[37]

Today, after two generations of having been taught that economics is the only thing that matters, the behavior of Americans now seems to conform to that viewpoint. In elections, a big number of evangelical Christians who vote say that economic issues are more important than moral ones. And the leaders are often today judged not on the basis of their personal competency, moral character, or other positive leadership traits, but rather on the basis of how the economy is doing. Yet when we read of the Pilgrims, Puritans, and some of the Founders' original intent, it presents a completely different view of history from that which is taught today. It reveals that other, more important, issues motivated most of these great men.

For example, according to historian David Barton, in 1762 America's very first missionary society was chartered: The Society to

Propagate the Gospel among Indians and Others in North America.[38] Americans thought it was a great idea, but King George III apparently thought that it would compete with the work of the nationally established church, so he vetoed the charter.[39] This type of action by the King alarmed a number of the Founders who contended for religious liberties in America—including the ability to start their own missionary societies, Bible societies, or Sunday school societies. Consequently, the early Founders such as Carroll of Carrollton and Samuel Adams, both of whom became signers of the Declaration, cited religious freedom as a reason they became involved in the American Revolution.[40]

Endnotes

[1] R. P. Nettelhorst Notes on the Founding Fathers and the separation of church and state. Quartz Hill of Theology, accessed from *http://www.theology.edu/journal/volume2/ushistor.thm.*

[2] Paul F. Boller Jr., *Not So! Popular Myths About America from Columbus to Clinton* (New York: Oxford University Press, 1995), 31.

[3] Peter A. Lillback "Why Have Scholars Underplayed George Washington's Faith?" History News Network Saturday, 10, February 2007, accessed from *http://hnn.us/articles/34925.html.*

[4] Paul F. Boller, Jr., *George Washington and Religion* (Dallas: Southern Methodist University Press, 1963), 75.

[5] Ibid., 28–29.

[6] Ibid., 90.

[7] Gary North, *Political Polytheism: The Myth of Pluralism* (Institute for Christian Economics, 1989), 425. He cites Benjamin Hart, *Faith & Freedom: The Christian Roots of American Liberty* (Dallas: Stanley, 1988), 274. Some of Washington's prayers were such as this one: "I beseech Thee, my sins, remove them from Thy Presence, as far as the east is from the west, and accept me for the merits of Thy Son Jesus Christ…"

[8] Gary North, *Political Polytheism*, 425, cites Mark A. Noll, *The Bible in Revolutionary America: The Bible in America Law, Politics, and Political Rhetoric,* (Philadelphia: Fortress Press, 1985), 43.

[9] David L. Holmes, *The Founding Fathers, Deism and Christianity.* Encyclopedia Britannica Inc., *http://www.britannica.com/EBchecked/topi/1272214/The-Founding-Fathers-Deism-and-Christianity,* accessed January 19, 2012.

[10] J. Hugo Tatsch, *The Facts About George Washington as a Freemason* (New York: Macoy, 1929), XIV.

[11] David L. Holmes, *The Founding Fathers, Deism and Christianity.*

12 Thomas Horn, *Apollyon Rising 2012: The Lost Symbol Found and the Final Mystery of The Great Seal Revealed, A Terrifying and Prophetic Cipher Hidden from the World by The U.S. Government for Over 200 Years is Here!* (Defender Crane, 2009), 11.

13 John Adams, Charles Francis Adams, ed., *The Works of John Adams—Second President of the United States*, 10 vols. (Boston, MA: Little, Brown & Co., 1854) Vol. 9, 229.

14 David L. Holmes, *The Faith of the Founding Fathers* (Oxford University Press, 2006), 73–78.

15 Ibid., 79–80.

16 Ibid.

17 Ibid., 83.

18 Ibid.

19 Thomas Horn, *Apollyon Rising*, 7.

20 David L. Holmes, 84.

21 Ibid., 88.

22 Ibid.

23 James Hutson, *James Madison and the Social Utility of Religion: Risks vs. Rewards,* James Madison, *Philosopher and Practitioner of Liberal Democracy*, Library of Congress, accessed from *http://www.loc.gov/loc/Madison/hutson-paper.htm.*

24 Ibid.

25 Norman Cousins, ed., *In God We Trust: The Religious Beliefs and Ideas of the American Founding Fathers,* (New York: Harper and Brothers, 1958), 19.

26 Thomas Horn, *Apollyon Rising*, 4.

27 David L. Holmes, *The Founding Fathers, Deism and Christianity.* Encyclopedia Britannica Inc., *http://www.britannica.com/EBchecked/topi/1272214/The-Founding-Fathers-Deism-and-Christianity*, accessed January 19, 2012.

28 John Eidsmoe and Ben DuPré, *Thomas Paine: Involuntary Christian Witness?* Thomas Paine acknowledged independence was God's Plan for America, *http://www.wnd.com/index.php?fa=PAGE.view&pageID=123418,* accessed January 29, 2010.

29 Gary DeMar and Peter Leithart, *The Reduction of Christianity: A Biblical Response to Dave Hunt* (Ft. Worth: Dominion Press; Atlanta: America Vision, 1988), 326.

30 Samuel Eliot Morison, *Builders of the Bay Colony* (Boston, MA: Northeastern University Press, 1930, 1981), 3.

31 Henry H. Halley, *Halley's Bible Handbook* (Zondervan Publishing House, Twenty-Third Edition, 1962), 18.

32 John Eidsmoe and Ben DuPré, *Thomas Paine: Involuntary Christian Witness?*

33 Ibid.

34 Ibid.

35 Ibid.

36 David Barton, *The Role of Pastors and Christians in Civil Government* (Texas: Wall Builder Press, 2003), 4.

37 Ibid.

---

[38] Peter Thacher, *Brief Account of the Society for Propagating the Gospel Among the Indians and Others in North America* (Boston: 1798), 2. Cited in David Barton, *The Role of Pastors & Christians in Civil Government* (Texas: Wall Builder Press, 2003), 4.

[39] Ibid.

[40] David Barton, *The Role of Pastors & Christians in Civil Government* (Texas: Wall Builder Press, 2003), 5.

CHAPTER 13

Deism and Divinity: The Truth About Jesus Christ

Deism and Enlightenment Doctrine

Deism eventually subverted orthodox Christianity in the United States. Persons influenced by the movement had little reason to read the Bible, pray, attend church, or participate in such rites as baptism, Holy Communion, and the laying on of hands. How do we differentiate between those who were influenced by deism and those who were from orthodox Christian backgrounds?

David Holmes answers this question by writing that it was because deistic thought was so popular in colleges from the mid-eighteenth into the ninetieth century that "it influenced many educated as well as uneducated males of the Revolution generation. So these young men continued their public affiliation with Christianity after college but they might have inwardly held unorthodox religious views. They mainly fell into three categories: non-Christian deism, Christian deism, and orthodox Christianity."[1]

Holmes then gives us four points on how we can differentiate a Founding Father who was influenced by deism from one influenced by orthodox Christianity, which I've summarized here. First, an inquirer should examine the Founder's church involvement. Founders who were believing Christians would be more likely to go to church than those influenced by deism. Secondly, they had to participate in the sacraments of the church like baptism or communion. Few of the Founders who were deists would have participated in either rite. George Washington's refusal to receive communion in his adult life indicated deistic beliefs to many of his pastors and peers.

Third, the religious language they used varied greatly. Non-Christian deists such as Paine did not use the Christian terminology and he described God with such expressions as "Providence," "the Creator," "the Ruler of Great Events," and "Nature's God." Founders who were considered to be Christian deists added a Christian dimension to their terms—such as "Merciful Providence" or "Divine Goodness." Whereas Founders who were not affected by deism like John Adams were Unitarians and shared views of Christianity not unlike those of Thomas Paine, Thomas Jefferson, and Benjamin Franklin.[2]

In contrast to other Founders stands the example of Patrick Henry, who was a member of the Protestant Episcopal Church and who took regular communion. While he was governor of Virginia, he had printed some books at his own expense so that he could give them to skeptics he would meet: one was the *View of the Internal Evidence of Christianity* and an edition of Butler's *Analogy*.[3] He never joined the Masonic fraternity either. Rather, he wrote to his daughter in 1796, saying, "Amongst other strange things said of me, I hear it said by the deists that I am one of their number; and, indeed, some good people think I am no Christian. This thought gives me more pain than the appellation of Tory."[4] He is also quoted to have said:

> It cannot be emphasized too strongly or too often that this great nation was founded, not by religionists, but by Christians; not on religions, but on the Gospel of Jesus Christ. For this very reason peoples of other faiths have been afforded asylum, prosperity, and freedom of worship here.[5]

Lastly, consideration needs to be taken from what friends, family, and, most importantly, what the clergy said about any Founders' faith. David Holmes again writes, "Washington's pastors in Philadelphia clearly viewed him as someone who was significantly influenced by Deism, which says more about his faith than the opposite views of later writers."[6]

This Enlightenment doctrine played a big role in creating the principle of religious freedom as expressed in the First Amendment of the United States Constitution. Some of the Founders who were especially influenced by such a philosophy included Thomas Jefferson, Benjamin Franklin, George Washington, and Thomas Paine. But to put intellectual ability in the place of divine grace, as one Bible teacher has observed, "You exalt the carnal above the spiritual and this effect will be manifested in some of these areas: Theology will be exalted above Revelation; Intellectual education above Character building; psychology above Spiritual discernment; program above the leading of the Holy Spirit; Eloquence above Supernatural power; Reasoning above the Walk of faith; Laws above Love."[7]

This problem was not new in the era of the Founders however. In Paul's letter to the Colossians, Paul clearly teaches that Christ had paid for our sins and reconciled us to God, which means we have a union with Him that can never be broken (see Colossians 2:3–9). In our faith connection with Him, we identify with His death, burial, and resurrection. False teachers were promoting a heresy that stressed legalism and Gnosticism; this heresy was a fusion of religion and philosophy that modified the gospel message.

The Colossian church insisted that important secret knowledge was hidden from at least some of the believers. Paul told them that Christ provides all knowledge and wisdom, and that He lived in a body and therefore the body wasn't evil in and of itself. The church thought that Christ was only human, but Paul insisted that Jesus was fully human *and* fully God. In Christ are all the hidden treasures of wisdom and knowledge (see Colossians 2:3–9).

Paul was writing against any philosophy of human life that is based only on human ideas and experiences. Let's not forget that Paul himself was a gifted philosopher, so he was not condemning knowledge, science, or philosophy. In fact, science and philosophy are both inherently godly. They are both God-given gifts, but the only problem is that they can be idolatrous and can be a tool against the God who gave them to humanity in the first place. So Paul is condemning the teaching that exalts and credits humanity but not Jesus Christ as the answer to life's problems.

This approach becomes a false religion then. Paul asserts the deity of Jesus Christ by saying that in Him lives all the fullness of God in a human body. Historian John Von Muller says Jesus Christ is God's purpose in history: "The gospel is the fulfillment of all hope, the perfection of all philosophy, the interpreter of all revolutions; the key to all the seeming contradictions of the physical and moral world; it is life; it is immortality. Since I have known the Savior everything is clear; with Him there is nothing I cannot solve."[8]

The Deity of Jesus Christ

In 1999 during the presidential Republican debates in the campaign for the presidential nomination, President George W. Bush was asked to name his favorite "political philosopher." He replied that it was Jesus Christ. From that point on, most evangelical Christians in America voted for him because they thought he would represent their values based on his faith in Jesus Christ. President Bush should have countered the statement that Jesus Christ was not a political philosopher, but rather the very Son of God. It is not surprising that evangelical Christians are realizing that many political ties to evangelical Christianity appear to be simply for the purpose of producing political advantages.

What is a philosopher? The Oxford dictionary defines a philosopher "as a person engaged or learned in philosophy or a branch of it." But couldn't the same be said for Karl Marx or Plato or Socrates? To call Jesus a political philosopher is disrespectful to say the least. Jesus Christ is Lord and God because He is the exact representative of God the Father. God said, "Let Us make man in *Our* image, according to *Our* likeness" (Genesis 1:26). Jesus is God because He is the Word, explaining God the Father as the I AM. When Moses met God at the burning bush and received his assignment to be God's spokesman before Pharaoh, he asked God a question and received an answer:

Then Moses said to God, "Indeed, when I come to the children of Israel and say to them, 'The God of your fathers has sent me to you,' and they say to me, 'What is His name?' what shall I say to them?"

And God said to Moses, "I AM WHO I AM." And He said, "Thus you shall say to the children of Israel, 'I AM has sent me to you.'" Moreover God said to Moses, "Thus you shall say to the children of Israel: 'The Lord God of your fathers, the God of Abraham, the God of Isaac, and the God of Jacob, has sent me to you. This is My name forever, and this is My memorial to all generations.'" (Exodus 3:13–15)

The Jews wanted to stone Jesus when He said to them, "Most assuredly, I say to you, before Abraham was, I AM" (John 8:58). They understood clearly that Jesus was blaspheming the name of God by claiming to be God Himself. They knew that I AM was the memorial name of God to all generations, and they did not believe Jesus was God. They refused to believe in the deity of Jesus Christ, which means they would die in their sins. Again, on another occasion, Jesus said, "I and the Father are one," and again the Jews renewed their efforts to stone Him.

Jesus answered them, "Many good works I have shown you from My Father. For which of those works do you stone Me?" The Jews answered Him, saying, "For a good work we do not stone You, but for blasphemy, and because You, being a Man, make Yourself God." (John 10:30–33)

According to the law, they had every right to stone Jesus because He was claiming to be the exact representation of the Father (see Leviticus 24:16).

Jesus Christ is God because He is eternal. He always has been and He will always be. There is only one Man in all of time who was both God and Man—the Lord Jesus Christ. He was crucified on the cross as the only begotten Son of God, explaining the unconditional love of God the Father to a lost and broken world. John tells us that the promised Messiah is the very Son of God, and that Jesus, like the Father, is eternal: "In the beginning was the Word, and the Word was with God, and the Word was God. He was in the beginning with God. All things were made through Him, and without Him nothing was made that was made" (John 1:1–3). John further says: "And the Word became flesh and dwelt among us, and we beheld His glory, the glory as of the only begotten of the Father, full of grace and truth" (John 1:14).

The prophet Isaiah says:

> I saw the Lord sitting on a throne, high and lifted up, and the train of His robe filled the temple. Above it stood seraphim; each one had six wings: with two he covered his face, with two he covered his feet, and with two he flew. And one cried to another and said: "Holy, holy, holy is the Lord of hosts; the whole earth is full of His glory!" And the posts of the door were shaken by the voice of him who cried out, and the house was filled with smoke. So I said: "Woe is me, for I am undone! Because I am a man of unclean lips, and I dwell in the midst of a people of unclean lips; for my eyes have seen the King, the Lord of hosts." (Isaiah 6:1–5)

After this experience, Isaiah's sin was forgiven and his iniquity was taken away. Then after this he writes: "Also I heard the voice of the Lord, saying: 'Whom shall I send, and who will go for Us?'" (vs. 8). The "Us" implies more than one. The Father is there, the Son is there, and the Holy Spirit is there. Remember that God had said, "Let Us (Father, Son, and Holy Spirit) make mankind in Our image" (Genesis 1:26). But that likeness and image was destroyed when Adam and Eve chose to believe the devil rather than God, and man was separated from Him.

Intimacy and communion with God were exchanged for enmity because humanity wanted to be like God. As a result, Adam and Eve could no longer eat the fruit of the Tree of Life. But access to this tree was restored through Jesus Christ. And through one man sin entered the world, leaving all of us without hope apart from the mercy and grace of God (see Romans 5:12). But "God so loved the world that He gave His only begotten Son, that whoever believes in Him should not perish but have everlasting life" (John 3:16).

In Philippians we are once again given a confirmation of the deity of Jesus Christ:

> Let this mind be in you which was also in Christ Jesus, who, being in the form of God, did not consider it robbery to be equal with God, but made Himself of no reputation, taking the form of a bondservant, and coming in the likeness of men. And being found in appearance as a man, He humbled Himself and became obedient to the point of death, even the death of the cross. (Philippians 2:5–8)

In John 14:6–7 Jesus was talking to His disciples and said, "I am the way the truth, and the life. No one comes to the Father except through Me. If you had known Me, you would have known My Father also; and from now on you know Him and have seen Him." Then Philip responded to Him:

> Philip said to Him, "Lord, show us the Father, and it is sufficient for us."

> Jesus said to him, "Have I been with you so long, and yet you have not known Me, Philip? He who has seen Me has seen the Father; so how can you say, 'Show us the Father'? Do you not believe that I am in the Father, and the Father in Me? The words that I speak to you I do not speak on My own authority; but the Father who dwells in Me does the works." (John 14:8–10)

The Exact Representation

To see Jesus is to see God the Father because Jesus is the exact representation of His nature. When we get to know Jesus, we will get to know the Father, for they are one in essence. Paul brings this out so powerfully in the book of Colossians when he writes:

> He is the image of the invisible God, the firstborn over all creation. For by Him all things were created that are in heaven and

that are on earth, visible and invisible, whether thrones or dominions or principalities or powers. All things were created through Him and for Him. And He is before all things, and in Him all things consist. And He is the head of the body, the church, who is the beginning, the firstborn from the dead, that in all things He may have the preeminence. (Colossians 1:15–17 AMP)

Those who do not believe in the deity and incarnation of Jesus Christ normally take Colossians 1:15 out of context, for as the Bible makes it very clear, Jesus is eternal. "Firstborn of all creation" refers to a priority of position. Paul is telling us that Jesus rightfully has "first place" or preeminence "in everything" because He is God Almighty "and He is the head of the body, the church, who is the beginning, the firstborn from the dead, that in all things He may have the preeminence" (Colossians 1:18).

Again, Paul references the same point in Colossians 2:9–10: "For in Him dwells all the fullness of the Godhead bodily; and you are complete in Him, who is the head of all principality and power." And John writes in Revelation, "He is the Alpha and the Omega; He is the Beginning and the End" (Revelation 21:6).

The most important issue that we will ever have to deal with about Jesus is the question of His deity. Everyone who has ever studied about Jesus must confront this issue because of His claims to be God. C. S. Lewis wrote:

I'm trying…to prevent anyone saying the really foolish thing that people often say about Him: "I'm ready to accept Jesus as a great moral teacher, but I don't accept His claim to be God." That is one thing we must not say. A man who was merely a man and said the sort of things Jesus said would not be a great moral teacher. He would either be a lunatic—on a level with the man who says he is a poached egg—or else he would be the devil of hell. You must make your choice. Either this man was, and is, the Son of God: or else a madman or something worse. You can shut Him up for a fool; you can spit at Him and kill Him as a demon; or you can fall at His feet and call Him Lord and God. But let us not come with any patronizing nonsense about His being a great human teacher (or philosopher). He has not left that open to us. He did not intend to.[9]

The Resurrection of Jesus

After Jesus had physically risen from the dead, three women who were friends of the disciples went to the tomb early Sunday morning to anoint His body with spices. When they arrived at the tomb, they were shocked to find the stone rolled aside and the tomb empty. It was only the linen cloths in which Jesus's body had been wrapped that lay empty in the tomb (see Luke 24:10–12).

Likewise Peter and John decided to go and see for themselves where Jesus was buried. Indeed, they too were also surprised that Jesus was not in the tomb. The Bible tells us that until then they still hadn't understood the Scripture that He must rise again from dead (see Psalm 16:10). As Peter and John returned home, Mary was still standing at the tomb crying, and as she was weeping, she stooped down and looked into the tomb. Suddenly, the angels asked her why she was crying, and she replied that it was because they had taken away her Lord and she didn't know where they put Him.

She decided to leave and saw someone standing there. Thinking it was the gardener, she asked Him where He had put the body of Jesus. The man then called Mary by her name. At that moment, she realized that she was not talking to the gardener but to her risen Lord.

Jesus said to her, "Mary!"

She turned and said to Him, "Rabboni!" (which is to say, Teacher).

Jesus said to her, "Do not cling to Me, for I have not yet ascended to My Father; but go to My brethren and say to them, 'I am ascending to My Father and your Father, and to My God and your God.'"

Mary Magdalene came and told the disciples that she had seen the Lord, and that He had spoken these things to her. (John 20:16–18)

That Sunday evening, the disciples were meeting in secrecy behind closed doors because they were afraid of the Jewish leaders. Suddenly, Jesus appeared to them. As He appeared to them, He said, "'Peace be with you.' When He had said this, He showed them His hands and His side. Then the disciples were glad when they saw the Lord" (John 20:19–20). Soon after Christ had appeared to His disciples, they told Thomas, who was absent, that the Lord had appeared to them. Thomas refused to believe them, saying he needed to see and touch Christ's wounds and His side before he could believe such a report (see John 20:25). He did not want to accept their account on the basis of faith only.

The faith of Thomas, much like the disciples', was gone so he could not believe by mere faith alone. The time of three special years of personally walking with the Messiah had come to an end. Jesus was dead, so were the dreams that were once filled with hope and purpose. So unless he could put his hands into Jesus's side where he had watched the spear being thrust into the breast of his Master, he could not believe. He wanted concrete evidence.

Eight days later, the disciples were again in the same room, and this time Thomas was present.

> And after eight days His disciples were again inside, and Thomas with them. Jesus came, the doors being shut, and stood in the midst, and said, "Peace to you!" Then He said to Thomas, "Reach your finger here, and look at My hands; and reach your hand here, and put it into My side. Do not be unbelieving, but believing."
>
> And Thomas answered and said to Him, "My Lord and my God!"
>
> Jesus said to him, "Thomas, because you have seen Me, you have believed. Blessed are those who have not seen and yet have believed." (John 20:26–28)

Thomas believed. He saw Jesus for who He was—his Lord and his God. His confession of faith is the most significant one in the Bible. In it he declared the deity of Jesus Christ: Jesus was not just a Man but also God. Jesus Christ is God because He is Lord.

We need to understand that there are two fundamental doctrines that the enemy seeks to twist because they are so critical to salvation: the deity of Jesus Christ and the humanity of Jesus Christ. Satan hates His deity because it places Jesus outside and above the realm of created man. However, the incarnation of deity makes our redemption possible. That is the reason why Satan did all he could to annihilate the woman's seed from Genesis 3 onward.

When humanity sinned, only a sinless person could come and redeem us. When Jesus became Man, He had to be tempted by the devil just as Adam was. But Jesus never yielded to sin; therefore, He was offered as the Lamb of God, unblemished and spotless, to redeem us from sin and death. The Bible tells us, "For He made Him who knew no sin to be sin for us, that we might become the righteousness of God in Him" (2 Corinthians 5:21).

The Appointed Day

Paul was troubled by all the idols he saw everywhere in the city of Athens in the book of Acts. Athens, at the time, was the capital city of Greece. It was also one of the most noted places in the world for education, philosophy, and human wisdom. It continued for many years until the Romans conquered Greece. The Romans were then influenced by the education system of Greece and began to rival in the arts and science.

During the time of Jesus Christ and the apostles, it remained a place where the wise and learned men in the world would gather for debate. These people spent all their leisure time in seeking some type of new knowledge. Regardless of how educated the Athenians were, they were still ignorant of the one true God. They placed their intellect and knowledge above feeling, and nature and reason above faith in Jesus Christ.

As Paul stood there and spoke about the one true God, his audience could look down on the city and see the many idols representing gods Paul knew were worthless. Paul had all the credentials to debate with these philosophers; he was an educated rabbi taught by the finest scholar of his day, Gamaliel. He probably excited their curiosity because they loved discussing new intellectual ideas.

These Epicurean and Stoic philosophers thought that Paul was trying to be an announcer of foreign deities because he preached Jesus and the resurrection (see Acts 17:18). So they took hold of him and brought him to the Mars Hill auditorium, which has been considered by modern interpreters to be the supreme court of Athens, custodians of teachings that introduced new religions and foreign gods.

So Paul began to preach to them about Jesus Christ, a man who had recently been crucified in Jerusalem. He drew their attention to a natural debate before he could engage them about the death, burial, and resurrection for sinners. After he had gained their attention, he began revealing the one true God to these educated men of Athens. And although these men were very religious, they did not know the one true God. Luke tells it like this:

> So Paul, standing in the center of the Areopagus [Mars Hill meeting place], said: Men of Athens, I perceive in every way [on every hand and with every turn I make] that you are most religious or very reverent to demons. For as I passed along and carefully observed your objects of worship, I came also upon an altar with this inscription, To the unknown god. Now what you are already worshiping as unknown, this I set forth to you. The God Who produced and formed the world and all things in it, being Lord of heaven and earth, does not dwell in handmade shrines. Neither is He served by human hands, as though He lacked anything, for it is He Himself Who gives life and breath and all things to all [people]. (Acts 17:22–25 AMP)

He further declared to them that from one Man, Jesus Christ, He created all nations throughout the whole earth and decided beforehand when they should rise and fall and determined their boundaries (see Acts 17:26–28). Paul goes on to tell us that we should not think of God as an idol designed by craftsmen from gold or silver or stone, or a representation of human art and imagination. But rather,

Since then we are God's offspring, we ought not to suppose that Deity (the Godhead) is like gold or silver or stone, [of the nature of] a representation by human art and imagination, or anything constructed or invented. Such [former] ages of ignorance God, it is true, ignored and allowed to pass unnoticed; but now He charges all people everywhere to repent (to change their minds for the better and heartily to amend their ways, with abhorrence of their past sins), because He has fixed a day when He will judge the world righteously (justly) by a Man Whom He has destined and appointed for that task, and He has made this credible and given conviction and assurance and evidence to everyone by raising Him from the dead. (Acts 17:29–31 AMP)

Paul concludes that God overlooked people's ignorance about these things in earlier times, but now commands all men everywhere to repent. In the past God permitted all nations to walk in their own ways, but He did not leave them without any evidence of Himself and His goodness. He sent rains from heaven and fruitful seasons, satisfying their hearts with nourishment and happiness.

However, the appointed time has come when He expects and charges all men everywhere to repent, and turn from their ignorance, idolatry, and superstition, because He has appointed a day in which He will judge the world in righteousness by a Man Jesus Christ, whom He has proved to everyone who this is by raising Him from the dead.

Endnotes

1 David L. Holmes, *The Founding Fathers, Deism and Christianity*. See also Encyclopedia Britannica Inc., *http://www.britannica.com/EBchecked/topi/1272214/The-Founding-Fathers-Deism-and-Christianity*, accessed January 19, 2012.

2 Ibid.

3 Gary North, *Political Polytheism*, 425, which was cited in Moses Coit, *Patrick Henry* (New Rochelle, New York: Arlington House, 1887, 1975), 392–395.

4 Ibid., 392.

5 M. E. Bradford, *The Trumpet Voice of Freedom: Patrick Henry of Virginia* (Plymouth Rock Foundation; First Edition, 1991), iii.

6 Ibid., David Holmes.

7 Derek Prince, *Blessing or Curse You Can Choose* (Chosen Books, 1990, 2000, 2006), 103.

8 James Foster Mitchell, *Reformation Principles Stated and Applied* (Chicago and New York: F. H. Revell, 1890), 200.

9 C. S. Lewis, *Mere Christianity* (Harper Collins Publishers, 2003), 52.

CHAPTER 14

Jewish Influence on America's Founding

A Major Role

Jesus Christ was the promised Messiah of the Jewish people. For that reason our lineage extends to before the appearance of Jesus, all the way back to the people of Israel. Western history is, by God's will, indissolubly linked with the people of Israel. Jesus Christ is the sign of the free mercy-choice and of repudiating the wrath of God. Paul reminds us of this, "Therefore consider the goodness and severity of God: on those who fell, severity; but toward you, goodness, if you continue in His goodness. Otherwise you also will be cut off" (Romans 11:22). That is why an expulsion of the true Jews from the West must bring with it the expulsion of Christ, for Jesus Christ is first and foremost a Jew.[1]

Most historians agree that one of the reasons why America and the British were so blessed is because they had blessed and protected God's chosen people. God promised Abram, "I will bless those who bless you, and I will curse him who curses you; and in you all the families of the earth shall be blessed" (Genesis 12:3).

The history of the Jews in America began before the United States was an independent country. It actually began in 1654 with the arrival of twenty-three refugees to New Amsterdam (later to be known as New York), who were fleeing from the Portuguese who had conquered Recife, Brazil. By the time the colonies fought the War of Independence in 1776, there were about 2,000 Jews living in America at the time. Though they were few in number, they played a major role in ratifying the Constitution of the United States of America.

The majority of the earliest settlers were Puritans. Beginning with the *Mayflower,* 16,000 Puritans migrated to the Massachusetts Bay colony over the next twenty years, and many more settled in Connecticut and Rhode Island. Like their cousins back in England, these American Puritans strongly identified with both the historical traditions and customs of the ancient Hebrews of the Old Testament. They viewed their emigration from England as a virtual reenactment of the Jewish exodus from Egypt.

To them, England was Egypt, the king was Pharaoh, the Atlantic Ocean was the Red Sea, America was the Land of Israel, and the Native Americans were the ancient Canaanites. They viewed themselves as the new Israelites, entering into a new covenant with God in a new Promised Land. Thanksgiving was first celebrated in 1621, a year after the *Mayflower* first landed. It was initially conceived as a day parallel to the Jewish Day of Atonement, Yom Kippur, and it was to be a day of fasting, introspection, and prayer.[2]

Previously, during the Puritan Revolution in England, the Puritan identification with the Bible was so strong that some Puritan extremists sought to replace the English common law with biblical laws of the Old Testament but were prevented from doing so. In America, however, there was far more freedom to experiment with the use of biblical law in the legal codes of the colonies, and this was exactly what these early colonists set out to do. The earliest legislation of the colonies of New England was determined by Scripture alone. The New Haven legislators adopted a legal code—the Code of 1655—which contained some seventy-nine statutes, half of which contained biblical references, virtually all of them taken from the Hebrew Bible.[3]

Jewish Influence on American Education

The Hebrew Bible played a central role in the educational system of America. In addition to Harvard, many other colleges and universities were established under the auspices of various Protestant sects: Yale, William and Mary, Rutgers, Princeton, Brown, King's College (later to be known as Colombia), John Hopkins, Dartmouth, etc. The Bible played a central role in the curriculum of all these institutions of higher learning, with both Hebrew and Bible studies offered as required courses. So popular was the Hebrew Language in the sixteenth and seventeenth centuries that several students at Yale delivered their commencement orations in Hebrew.[4]

Bible study and Hebrew were course requirements in virtually all these colleges, and students had the option of delivering commencement speeches in Hebrew, Latin, or Greek. Many of these colleges even adopted some Hebrew word or phrase as part of their official emblem or seal. When Harvard was founded, the Hebrew language was taught along with Latin and Greek. Also, a significant number of the constitutional framers were products of these American universities. Thus, we can be sure that a majority of these political leaders were not only well acquainted with the contents of both the Old and New Testaments, but also had some working knowledge of the Hebrew language. Most remarkable of all, a motion was made in the Continental Congress that Hebrew become the official language of the land. But needless to say, the motion was lost.[5]

The Centrality of the Bible in America

America was created from the ideals that its early settlers revered the Hebrew Bible as the Word of God. Patriotic speeches and publications during the period of the struggle for independence were often infused with biblical motifs and quotations. Even the basic framework of America clearly reflects the influence of the Bible and power of Jewish ideas shaping the political development of America. The biblical story of mankind's creation in the image of God is clearly evident in the opening words of the Declaration of Independence.[6]

In the seventeenth century, the patriot Patrick Henry gave another testament to the centrality of the Hebrew Bible. At one time he said, "This is all the inheritance I can give to my dear family. The religion of Christ can give them one which will make them rich indeed."[7] His declaration regarding the seriousness of slavery and freedom can be noted in his words on March 23, 1775, where he refereed to the

Hebrew Scriptures in his famous speech:

> Should I keep back my opinions at such a time, through fear of giving offense, I should consider myself as guilty of treason towards my country and of an act of disloyalty toward the Majesty of Heaven, which I revere above all earthly kings…. They tell us, sir that we are weak; unable to cope with so formidable an adversary. But when shall we be stronger? Will it be the next week, or the next year? Will it be when we are totally disarmed, and when a British guard shall be stationed in every house? Shall we gather strength by irresolution and inaction? Shall we acquire the means of effectual resistance by lying supinely on our backs and hugging the delusive phantom of hope, until our enemies shall have bound us hand and foot? Sir, we are not weak if we make a proper use of those means which the God of nature hath placed in our power. The millions of people, armed in the holy cause of liberty, and in such a country as that which we possess, are invincible by any force which our enemy can send against us. Besides, sir, we shall not fight our battles alone. There is a just God who presides over the destinies of nations, and who will raise up friends to fight our battles for us (2 Chron. 32:8). The battle, sir, is not to the strong alone (Eccl. 9:11); it is to the vigilant, the active, the brave. Besides, sir, we have no election. If we were base enough to desire it, it is now too late to retire from the contest. There is no retreat but in submission and slavery! Our chains are forged! Their clanking may be heard on the plains of Boston! The war is inevitable--and let it come! I repeat it, sir, let it come. It is in vain, sir, to extenuate the matter. Gentlemen may cry, Peace, Peace--but there is no peace (Jer. 6:14). The war is actually begun! The next gale that sweeps from the north will bring to our ears the clash of resounding arms! Our brethren are already in the field! Why stand we here idle (Matt. 20:6)? What is it that gentlemen wish? What would they have? Is life so dear, or peace so sweet, as to be purchased at the price of chains and slavery? Forbid it, Almighty God! I know not what course others may take; but as for me, give me liberty or give me death![8]

William Henry Seward (1801–1872), the American secretary of state who purchased Alaska from Russia, said, "The whole hope of human progress is suspended on the ever growing influence of the Hebrew Bible."[9] The Hebrew Bible continued to play a significant cultural and ethical role in America's founding, and continued to shine as a major inspiration to the American people throughout the eighteenth century. American Jews were also eager that the rights guaranteed all Americans under the federal constitution were to be made a reality for citizens of Jewish faith.

There were probably fewer than 3,000 Jews in the United States when George Washington became president. During the colonial period, Jewish settlers in America had first encountered much of the same kind of discrimination and legal restrictions that they had been accustomed to in Europe. Nevertheless, by the time of the American Revolution, they had gradually won civil, political, and religious rights that far exceeded anything that their fellow religionists in Europe enjoyed.

By the end of the Revolution, Jews had been chosen not only to local posts in some cities, but had also been selected for more responsible positions in many parts of the country. There was no inclination to bar these people from public office. The Jews of Philadelphia led by Jonas Phillips in 1783–1784 protested the requirement that members of the general assembly take an oath affirming belief in the New Testament.

A Revision to the Constitution

This led to the revision of the Constitution of Pennsylvania a few years later, explicitly barring the disqualification on account of religious sentiments of any person who acknowledges the Being of a God and future state of rewards and punishments.[10] The *Universal Jewish Encyclopedia* affirms that this petition proved later on to be instrumental in the revision of the Pennsylvania State Constitution in such a manner as to abolish the religious test oath.[11] On September 7, 1787, Jonas Phillips, a founder of Philadelphia's Mikveh Israel Synagogue, also petitioned the framers at the federal Constitutional Convention:

> It is well known among all citizens of the 13 United States that the Jews have been true and faithful Whigs, and during the late contest with England they have been foremost in aiding and assisting the States with their lives and fortunes. They have supported the cause and bravely fought and bled for liberty which they cannot enjoy. Therefore if the honorable convention shall in their wisdom think fit and alter the said oath as found in the altered Pennsylvania Constitution and leave out the words to viz: and I do acknowledge the Scripture of the New Testament to be given by divine inspiration, the Israelites (Jews) will think themselves happy to live under a government where all religious societies are on an equal footing. Your most devoted obedient Servant, Jonas Phillips Philadelphia, 24th Ellul, 5547, or September 1787.[12]

Phillips's petition undoubtedly bore weight with the framers, as did the personal relationships many of the framers shared with the Jews. Under the heading, "Jewish Influence on the Framing of the Constitution," *The Jewish People's Almanac* brags about George Washington, Benjamin Franklin, and James Madison's personal relationship with the Jews.[13] Had the Constitutional Convention been open to the public, more than one eminent Jew would have had no difficulty in mingling on terms of equality with many of the best-known delegates.

To George Washington,[14] who presided over the sessions, Jews were of course no strangers. During the Revolution he had on his personal staff Manuel Mordecai Noah of South Carolina, David Salisbury Franks of Philadelphia, and Major Benjamin Nones, a French volunteer. In his General Orders for April 18, 1783, announcing the cessation of hostilities with Great Britain, George Washington congratulated his soldiers "of whatever condition they may be," for, among other things, having "assisted in protecting the rights of human nature and establishing an asylum for the poor and oppressed of all nations and religions."[15]

The "bosom of America," he declared a few months later, was "open to receive...the oppressed and persecuted of all nations and religions; whom we shall welcome to a participation of all our rights and privileges."[16] It is recorded that the following year, in 1784, when asking his aide-de-camp Tench Tilghman to secure a carpenter and a bricklayer for his Mount Vernon estate, he said:

> If they are good workmen, they may be of Asia, Africa, or Europe. They may be Mohometans, Jews, or Christians of any Sect, or they may be Atheists. I had always hoped that this land might be become a safe and agreeable Asylum to the virtuous and persecuted part of mankind; to whatever nation they might belong.[17]

Washington emphasized that religious freedom is something more than mere toleration of opposing and differing religions. The most famous of the exchanges that American Jews had with President Washington was on August 17, 1790, by the Newport congregation who welcomed Washington to the city and then declared:

> Deprived as we have hitherto been of the invaluable rights of free citizens, we now...behold a Government which to bigotry gives no sanction, to persecution no assistance but generously affording to all liberty of conscience, and immunities of citizenship-deeming everyone, of whatever nation, tongue, or language equal parts of the great governmental machine.... For all the blessings of civil and religious liberty which we enjoy under an equal and benign administration we desire to send up our thanks to the Ancient of days.[18]

In his reply, George Washington told the Newport Jews:

> They have a right to applaud themselves for having given to Mankind examples of an enlarged and liberal policy, a policy worthy of imitation. All possess alike liberty of conscience and immunities of citizenship. It is now no more that toleration is spoken of as if it was by the indulgence of one class of people, that another enjoyed the exercise of their inherent natural rights.

For happily the Government of the United States, which gives to bigotry no sanction, to persecution no assistance, requires only that they who live under its protection should demean themselves as good citizens, in giving it on all occasions their effectual support…. May the children of the stock of Abraham, who dwell in this land, continue to merit and enjoy the good will of other inhabitants, while everyone shall sit in safety under his own vine and fig tree, and there shall be none to make him afraid.[19]

Washington's statement has been called "immortal" and "memorable," naturally delighting the Newport congregation and the Jewish congregations elsewhere in the United States. Historian Rabbi Morris Aaron Gutstein, best known for his work on the history of the Jewish community of colonial Newport, called it one of the "most outstanding expressions on religious liberty and equality in America" and insisted that it "will be quoted by every generation in which religious liberty is cherished."[20]

The Jews and the American Revolution

In the 1760s the government of Poland persecuted and targeted the Jews. Desiring freedom, most of them fled the country and traveled throughout Europe. One of those Jews was a man by the names of Haym Salomon (1740–1785), who believed America to be a country where Jewish people could safely live. It has been noted by different historians that a number of Jews played significant roles in the founding of the American nation, men like Francis Salvador, a Jew who was the first patriot to be killed in Georgia.

In Charleston, South Carolina, almost every adult Jewish male fought on the side of freedom. Many historians believe that had it not been for the faithful efforts of Haym Salomon and other Jews, things would have turned out differently. Not only did Salomon use personal finances to provide interest free loans to James Madison, Thomas Jefferson, and numerous other public figures, he also personally paid the salaries of some government officials and army officers. He was twice arrested by the British, who suspected him of being a spy, and was thrown into a disease-infested prison where he became ill, probably with the tuberculosis that later claimed his life.[21]

Virtually all of the delegates knew Haym Salomon. Six of the delegates had long been dependent on his generosity for their own livelihoods or for the maintenance of the particular government function for which they were responsible. James Madison, the future president, sought out Salomon. Madison's papers record his indebtedness to the Jewish financier, who refused both a note and interest.

Though Article 6 dispelled the cloud of bigotry and gave freedom of each of the American people to express their individual faith according to the dictates of their own hearts, we should not forget that it was the same that opened the door for Jews, Muslims, and other non-Christians to serve in official governmental capacities. It became the initial means by which America was transformed from a monotheistic Christian nation to a polytheistic one.[22] Article 6 and the First Amendment's impact upon equal rights for American Jews is summed up by Michael Alexander:

> Although the Constitution of the United States does not specifically mention Jews, its religious liberty provisions in essence granted Jews the honor of citizenship. The United States was thus the first non-Jewish country, ancient or modern, that included Jews as political equals. The Constitution of the United States prohibited a religious test for government (Article VI), and the First Amendment prohibited Congress from establishing any religion, thus permuting Jews to participate as equal citizens on the federal level. By 1820, most state constitutions eliminated religious qualifications that had kept Jews from participating in public affairs and government office.[23]

To quote Ted Weiland, once more "compromise is a journey halfway down the road to surrender…. Though many Christians today laud the constitutional idea of freedom of religion, which allows gods other than God to be worshipped in America. Thanks to Article 6 and so-called Christians then and now, the ambassadors of those other gods are now government leaders who are helping to establish their god's morality as the laws of the nation."[24]

The ban on the Religious Test Clause was not because the federal test was deemed unnecessary in light of the states' constitutions, but instead to pave the way for deists, atheists, and even anti-Christians to hold public office. It was not the intent of the constitutional framers to leave the decision of religion solely to the states. While it is true that the prime motivation for the two religious clauses found in the Constitution appears to have been liberty of conscience in religious matters, the framers were not opposed to non-Christian or even antichrist religions. The framers had liberty for all religions in mind when they forbade Christian test oaths, as evidenced in their writings.[25]

This compromise led to a more secular state that replaced piety as the spirit of science fostered critical thinking and rationalism. What followed was the unequal yoking with other religious beliefs and following Jesus Christ, and Christian test oaths were considered religious extremism and fundamentalism. God's eternal principles were slowly replaced by an atmosphere of open-mindedness and tolerance, and it became more acceptable for faith to assume different forms.

The Enlightenment preached the sacredness of every individual—a principle that would become a cornerstone of the American democratic ideal that all men are created equal, and that their Creator endows them with certain unalienable rights. Marquis de Lafayette, who fought with the colonists during the American Revolution, wrote the Declaration of the Rights of Man and Citizen, which was adopted by the French National Assembly on August 16, 1789—a document that served as the key philosophic foundation of the French Revolution, drawing on the American Declaration of Independence. It declared, "All men are born, and remain, free and equal in rights." This theory of natural rights is related to the theory of natural law.

During the Age of Enlightenment, natural law theory challenged the divine right of kings. The term "natural rights" is a humanistic concept and is not compatible with the Bible. Deuteronomy 30:19–20 specifies that we don't have a human or civil right to do anything we want. Rather, we are given the choice between life and death, blessing and cursing.

If any of us have embraced new age thinking or Enlightenment views, then we might be having a very different idea of who or what God might be to us. We possibly believe in polytheism—that there is a multiplicity of gods. God has not only revealed who is He is in the Scriptures, but He clearly tells us that there is no salvation outside of the Lord Jesus Christ. Jesus states, "I am the way, and the truth, and the life. No one comes to Father except through Me" (John 14:6). And Isaiah declares:

> Thus says the Lord, the King of Israel, and his Redeemer, the Lord of hosts: "I am the First and I am the Last; besides Me there is no God. (Isaiah 44:6)

> I, even I, am the Lord, and besides Me there is no savior. (Isaiah 43:11)

Who Are the Real Jews?

Some hold the view that the modern-day "Jews" did not physically descend from Abraham, Isaac, and Jacob, but they instead descended from the Khazars, which are a Turkish, non-Semitic race that ruled the Khazar Empire located between the Caspian and Black Seas (now southern Russia). They believe they converted to Judaism during the early centuries. Others believe that occupants of modern-day Israel are Jews who are mainly the descendants of the tribe of Judah and Benjamin, as these were the main tribes living in Israel at the time of Christ and were then dispersed after the revolt against the Roman Empire in AD 70.

Another common view is what some have termed as "British Israelism," which is the belief that many of the world's English-speaking peoples, like the United States, Great Britain, Canada, Australia, and New Zealand, are direct descendants of the ten lost tribes of Israel. Furthermore, since God looks kindly upon the descendants of Israel, those who claim this relationship often believe

God favors them. Those who hold this view believe that this is the main reason why they've come to possess the richest portions of earthly wealth. Most of these maintain that when the Assyrians conquered Samaria, Israel's capital in 721 BC, the northern tribes of Israel were captured and enslaved by the Assyrians.

So these northern tribes never returned from their captivity and they contend that these "ten lost tribes" of Israel made their way to Northern Europe, the British Islands, and some migrated as far as to North and South America, Australia, New Zealand, South Africa, and around the world.

These theological doctrines have been attributed to Mr. Herbert M. Armstrong (1892–1986), who is the founder of the Worldwide Church of God. Though his interpretation is very complicated and tedious, he concludes that England descended from Ephraim and the United States from Manasseh. Some prophecy teachers reject his interpretation and have claimed that he takes passage after passage out of context. Mark Hitchcock rightly notes:

> The northern tribes have been not been lost. Many of them have been dispersed, but not lost. God knows where every man, woman, and child of them is located. Those who doubt that God will literally appoint 144,000 Jewish males during the end times are lacking a biblical view of God (see Revelation 7:4–7). Even though tribal identities may be forgotten by mankind, God has never lost track of them—who or where they are. And in our time we are witnessing the initial stages of the final regathering of the Jewish people to their ancient homeland.... These ten tribes are not, nor have they ever been lost. And they are not in any way related to the United States. The United States is not the ten lost tribes of Israel, nor the tribe of Manasseh. Israel is still Israel and will fulfill its central role in the events of the end times, just as the Bible predicts.[26]

God Has a Special Plan for His People

The Lord Jesus Christ, all the twelve apostles, and the original

Christian church were all Jews, as were the Old Testament patriarchs, Abraham, Isaac, Jacob, along with his twelve sons. Moses was also Jewish, as were the prophets Ezekiel, Jeremiah, Isaiah, Daniel, and the kings of Israel, like David, Solomon, and Hezekiah. Without the Jews, there would be no Bible, no gospel, and no salvation presented to the entire world. In fact, without the Jewish Jesus, there would be no Christianity. Jesus Christ is the greatest blessing the world has ever possessed. And all the true blessedness the world is now or ever shall be possessed of is owing to Abraham and his posterity.

The Jews are the stock on which the Christian church is grafted. There is a story concerning Frederick the Great who, in frustration, demanded from his cabinet that somebody provide him with proof of the existence of God. There was a momentary silence before one of his counselors spoke up: "Have you considered the Jew, your Majesty?" he asked.[27] The continuing existence of the Jew is one of the many evidences of God's existence. They are the physical evidence of God on the earth. We can dispute and scientifically explain away the Hebraic-Christian concept and every human evidence of God's existence, but we cannot explain away the Jew. John Adams, America's second president, said:

> The Jews have done more to the civilization of mankind than any other Nation. They are the most glorious Nation that ever inhabited the earth. The Romans and their Empire were but a bauble in comparison to the Jews. They have given religion to three-quarters of the globe and have influenced the affairs of mankind more, and more happily than any other Nation, ancient or modern.[28]

Throughout many of the past centuries, the church openly taught that the Jews were enemies of the cross of Christ. And in recent times, many preachers of the gospel have not preached Romans 9–11, which clearly teach God's plan for His chosen people. Early Christians were Jewish Christians who gave their lives preaching the gospel to the non-Jewish world (Gentiles).

The national policy of America and Britain since the establishment of the state of Israel doesn't mean that we are all supposed to support everything the Jewish nation does. As Christians, we have to remember that some of Israel's leaders are just as secular as American humanists. Those who think that it's the Jewish or Zionist conspiracy that is creating the New World Order should understand this conspiracy involves participants of all races, tribes, and tongues.

The historical involvement of many Jews in the Bolshevik Revolution in Russia, and the reality of many Jews in the political landscape in America and in Western Europe, has led many to conclude that Jews want to take over the world. The Bible describes a time when Israel will be isolated from the rest of the world and attacked by kings of the north, east, south, and west. Does this sound like a nation that will secretly take over the world? Just like some of the framers who wanted to replace Christianity by a religion of human reason, even today there many other humanist Jews and Gentiles who hate anything that has to do with Yeshua and Christians.

This is essentially a struggle between good and evil. It is not a Jewish problem as people are portraying it—it is anti-Semitism, and on a deeper level occultic, as it was in Nazi Germany. There is overwhelming evidence in the Word of God to indicate that anyone who curses the true descendants of Abraham, whether individually or as a nation, is on a very slippery slope indeed (see Genesis 12:3 AMP). The laboratory is Europe. Aleksandr Solzhenitsyn believed:

> The failings of human consciousness, deprived of its divine dimension, have been a determining factor in all the major crimes of this century. The first of these was World War I and II and much of our present predicament can be traced back to it. It was a war (the memory of which seems to be fading) when Europe, bursting with health and abundance, fell into a rage of self-mutilation which could not but sap its strength for a century or more, and perhaps forever. The only possible explanation for this war is a mental eclipse among the leaders of Europe due to their lost awareness of a Supreme Power above them.[29]

Consider their record on religious freedom and commitment today. Secular humanists exercise more control in positions of leadership in Europe than they do across the Atlantic. Four percent of the British people attend church services. Why is this? I believe it is because Bible-believing Christians understand the spiritual implications of blessing Israel; therefore, they've been blessed in many spiritual ways. In spite of its many mistakes, America has experienced more religious freedom and prosperity than any other nation partly because of the churches desire to support the Jewish nation. And some of its political leaders recognized that the Jews are God's chosen people, not because they deserve it, but because He chose them like He chose the church. As can be seen throughout this chapter, there has been tremendous Jewish influence on the founding of America.

Endnotes

1 Dietrich Bonhoeffer, *Ethics*, edited by Eberhard Bethge (SCM Press, Ltd., 1955), 70.

2 Rabbi Ken Spiro, *World Perfect: The Jewish Impact on Civilization* (Deerfield Beach, Florida: Simcha Press, 2002), 246–247.

3 Ibid., 248.

4 Ibid., 251.

5 William Wirt, *Sketches of the Life and Character of Patrick Henry* (James Webster, 1818), 119–123.

6 "We hold these truths to be self-evident, that all men are created equal; that they are endowed by their Creator with certain unalienable rights; that among these are life, liberty, and the pursuit of happiness..." The inscription on the Liberty Bell at Independence Hall in Philadelphia in 1773 is a direct quote from Leviticus (25:10 KJV): "Proclaim liberty throughout the land unto all the inhabitants thereof."

7 George Mason, *The True Patrick Henry* (Publisher J.B. Lippincott Company 1907), 457.

8 Ibid.

9 *Haley's Bible Handbook*, 18.

10 Jonathan D. Sarna, Benny Kraut, Samuel K. Joseph, eds., *Jews and the Founding of the Republic* (New York: Markus Weiner Publishing, 1985), 25. Cited in Ted Weiland, *Bible Law Versus The United States Constitution*, 203.

11 Salomon, Haym, *The Universal Jewish Encyclopedia*, 10 Vols. (New York: The Universal Jewish Encyclopedia, Inc., 1941), Vol. 9, 324.

12 Jonas Phillips, quoted in Jacob Rader Marcus, ed., *The Jew in the American World: A Source Book* (Detroit, MI: Wayne State University Press, 1996), 99–100.

13 Ted Weiland, *Bible Law Versus The United States Constitution: The Christian Perspective* (Scottsbluff, NE: Mission to Israel Ministries, 2012), 204.

14 "Jewish Influence on the Framing of the Constitution," *The Jewish People's Almanac*, David C, Gross, ed. (New York: Hippocrates Books, Inc., 1988), 3. It is important to note here that Benjamin Franklin, the oldest member of the Constitutional Convention, numbered many Philadelphia Jews among his friends. He was sufficiently friendly with them to be one of the contributors to the building fund for Philadelphia's first synagogue, Mikveh Israel. Not only that, but Samuel Keimer, an English printer who was one Franklin's first employers, was a Jew.

15 John F. Boller, *George Washington and Religion* (Dallas: SMU Press, 1963). Cited in Os Guinness, *Character Counts: Leadership Qualities in Washington, Wilberforce, Lincoln and Solzhenitsyn* (Michigan: Baker Books, 1999), 42.

16 Ibid.

17 Quoted in Os Guinness, *Character Counts: Leadership Qualities in Washington, Wilberforce, Lincoln and Solzhenitsyn* (Michigan: Baker Books, 1999), 43.

18 Ibid., 58.

19 Rabbi Benjamin Blech, *Eye Witness to Jewish History* (John Wiley & Sons, 2004), 177.

20 Quoted in Os Guinness, *Character Counts: Leadership Qualities in Washington, Wilberforce, Lincoln and Solzhenitsyn* (Baker Books, Michigan 1999), 60–61.

21 This excerpt of Haym Salomon was from an article that appeared in the *Believer's Voice of Victory Magazine*, Published monthly by Eagle Mountain Church, Inc./Kenneth Copeland Ministries, Inc., (October 2009), 22–23.

22 Ibid., "Jewish Influence on the Framing of the Constitution," 3.

23 Michael Alexander, *Jews, 1754–1820s, Encyclopedia of American History: Revolution and New Nation, 1761 to 1812,* Paul A. Gilje and Gary B. Nash, eds. (New York: Facts on File, Inc., 2003). American History Online, accessed from *www.fofweb.com*.

24 Ted Weiland, *Bible Law Versus The United States Constitution*, 199.

25 Ibid.

26 Mark Hitchcock, *The Late Great United States: What Bible Prophecy Reveals About America's Last Days* (Multnomah Books, 2009), 17–18.

27 Hal Lindsey, "I will bless them that bless thee," accessed from *http://www.wnd.com/2008/01/45604/*, accessed April, 18, 2008.

28 Quoted by Rabbi Ken Spiro, *World Perfect: The Jewish Impact on Civilization* (Deerfield Beach, Florida: Simcha Press, 2002), 71.

29 "Men Have Forgotten God," The Templeon Address, accessed from *http://www.roca.org/OA/36/36h.htm*.

CHAPTER 15

Freemasonry and the Founders

Many historians claim that many of the American Founders were Freemasons and that the nation itself was dedicated to the god of Freemasonry. It is true that some might have belonged to this group, but we have to understand that Freemasons started well—it was mainly a male club, or fraternity of stonemasons, who had social work that was commendable. However, so has been the work of many other organizations that have lost their original vision.

One known researcher of these groups claims that the Freemason lodges were infiltrated by persons involved in the curious arts, occult practices, and Luciferianism, as their writings make clear.[1] Historian David Barton says,

> There was a connection with Freemasonry for a few of the founders but the overwhelming majorities were not involved with Freemasonry. Furthermore, what Freemasonry has become today with its anti-Biblical teachings and oaths was definitely not what Freemasonry was at the time. Freemasonry was introduced into America in 1734, and went through major transformative philosophical changes in 1799, 1813, 1825, and especially in the 1840s and 1850s, when it finally became the organization it is and adopted the anti-Biblical teachings and practices that characterize it today; teachings and practices adopted decades after the death of the Founders.[2]

It is reported by one historian that Rev. G. W. Snyder, who said he was with the Reformed Church of Fredericktown, Maryland, sent Washington a letter on August 22, 1798, saying, "A Society of Free

Masons, that distinguished itself by the name of 'Illuminati,' whose Plan is to over throw all Government and all Religion…it might be within your power to prevent the Horrid plan from corrupting the brethren of the English Lodges over which you preside."[3]

On September 25, 1798, Washington wrote back to Snyder, including the following language, referring to Masonic lodges:

> I have little more to add than thanks for your wishes, and favorable sentiments, except to correct an error you have run into of my presiding over the English lodges in this country. The fact is I preside over none, nor have I been in one more than once or twice within the last thirty years. I believe, notwithstanding, that none of the lodges in this country are contaminated with the principles ascribed to the society of the Illuminati.[4]

Evangelist and revivalist Charles G. Finney (1792–1875), who was a Freemason before he was converted to Jesus Christ, also noted that Freemasons have paraded the fact that General George Washington was a Mason before the public. Before his death he warned the whole country to beware of secret societies. The above letter quoted by the historian needs no comment.[5]

Christian J. Pinto, an award-winning filmmaker of the documentary series *Secret Mysteries of America's Beginnings*, says that Christians have been told by their church leaders, pastors, and teachers that America was founded as a Christian nation. This assertion would not be bad if it were confined to the arrival of the Pilgrims and Puritans at Plymouth and the early development of the new world. If that were the case, it would be an accurate statement. But then he goes on to say:

> The problem arises when one marks the foundation of the country at the American Revolution and the establishment of the United States. It is at this point where all Bible-believing Christians should be wary, since the working of occult societies during this era was at an unprecedented height. Some historians even argue that you simply cannot understand the history of the world for the past few hundred years if you do not take these

societies into account. Their members have been the planners, leaders, and engineers of the global agenda, one that they do readily share with the rest of the world. Most importantly they often use "religion" as an instrument to manipulate the masses, their belief being that the end justifies the means.[6]

Some have speculated that the Founders' aim was to replace Christianity with a religion of reason. The Illuminati New World Order was organized along Jesuit lines and kept an internal discipline and a system of mutual surveillance based on that model. The Illuminati were the designers of the two seals found on the reverse side of every U.S. $1 bill, dated from 1933 onward.[7] The date in Roman numerals—1776—on the base of the pyramid does not stand for July 4, the Declaration of Independence, but for the inauguration of the Illuminati. *Illuminati* means the "Enlightened Ones."

What Is the Meaning of the Great Seals?

When we examine all the information, literature, and history publicly available on the Internet, documentaries, and other books on the Great Seal, we note that there is a consistent agreement among historians and researchers concerning the interpretation of the primary symbols. Directly above the capstone of the pyramid are words in Latin, *"Anniut Coeptis,"* and directly beneath the base of the pyramid is another expression, again in Latin, *"Novus Ordo Seclorum."* When these are translated into English, they mean "Announcing the Birth or

Arrival" and "New World Order." This is a secular, heathenistic, ungodly, one world religion, one world law system, and the one world economic system.

There is an eagle with its head turned toward its right wing with a bundle of arrows in its left claw, while its right claw is holding an olive branch. This eagle is looking to the right, indicating that while the United States prefers peace, it is always ready to go to war if necessary.[8] The American eagle upon the great seal is a phoenix. According to Barry Smith, "It is a mystical bird that rises from man's first attempt to set up a similar system of a One World Order, which is the Tower of Babel."[9]

The thirteen arrows in the bird's talon are the thirteen original colonies. There is a ribbon in its mouth with three Latin words—"*E Pluribus Unum*" which means "*Out of many—one.*" The original aim was to unite the thirteen original colonies into the United States of America, but others hold the view that because the Illuminati was formed out of many groups, it was only the finest members with the best intellectual potential that were to be kept.

The meaning of the mystical occult that shows the eye of Lucifer above the pyramid waiting to come down has many meanings as well. Those who probably designed it expect a time when this "god" would descend on his chosen people. We know it represents the world structure as we have it today and which is to become the capstone of history. And right alongside it there are words clearly written, "In God We Trust." What kind of god would be inserted between two pagan symbols?

Leading researcher, Christian J. Pinto says, "Manly P. Hall who has been considered to be a great Masonic writer wrote that in the past secret societies intentionally made a pretense or mockery of the Christian faith in order to avoid persecution. By being persecuted they were driven further into greater secrecy. So what happened is they decided to rephrase their ideas in a tone of Christian terminologies, but those who were initiated had to make vows to remain secret."[10]

Are They Really "Secret Societies"?

Bible teacher Derek Prince noted that Masons claim that the nature of their association is a secret, but that is not correct. All the major rites and formulas of Freemasonry have been publicized at various times, both by people who were formerly Masons (including some who had advanced to the highest degree) and by others who have carefully examined the material that is available to any competent researcher. Prince points out two facts about Freemasonry:

> First, in order to be initiated, a person has to bind himself by the most cruel and barbarous oaths never to reveal any of Masonry's secrets.... Secondly, Masonry is a false religion because it acknowledges a false god. Some Masons would deny that it is a religion, but here are some of the main features that clearly mark it as such: Masonry has its *revelation*; its own *temples*; its own *altars*; its own religious *symbols* and *emblems* (which include a *ring*); its own *confession of faith*; its own *priests*; its own *rituals*. Finally, it has its own *deity*, a false god, whom it calls a "Creative Principle" or "the Great Architect of the Universe."[11]

Some have dubbed Freemasonry a religious institution that has many components of being a religion. It accepts individuals of many different religions and it teaches other routes to God, which is essentially universalism. They believe anyone of any religion can go to heaven as long as they believe in one God and have good works that accompany their lives.

But the Bible tells us Jesus Christ became the sinner's sacrifice before God the Father when He shed His blood and died as the propitiation for the sins of all those who would ever believe (see 1 John 2:2; Romans 5:8; Ephesians 2:8–9). The Freemasons appear to promote belief in the God of Abraham, Isaac, and Jacob. But when we closely examine their beliefs, they don't believe in Jesus Christ but in the existence of a "Supreme Being." Derek Prince continues to point out:

Many of the objects and symbols associated with Christianity—including the Bible are used in Masonry—but this is a deliberate deception. The god whom Masonry acknowledges is *not* the God of the Bible. Although the sacred, biblical name of four letters—JHVH (commonly spelled out as "Jehovah")—is used in Masonic literature, it is interpreted as referring to a divine entity that combines in itself both male and female principles. Again, the Royal Arch degree uses an abbreviated form of the name Jehovah in combination with abbreviated forms of two heathen deities, Baal and Osiris, and acknowledges this "combined" being as god. This is nothing short of a deliberate insult to the one true God revealed in the Bible as Jehovah.[12]

Charles G. Finney wrote a book in 1869 entitled *Character, Claims and Practical Workings of Freemasonry*, and a series of articles, giving his views of the character and tendency of the institution. In one of his articles explaining why he left Freemasonry, he wrote these words:

I found that in taking these oaths I had been grossly deceived and imposed upon. I had been led to suppose that there were some very important secrets to be communicated to me; but in this I found myself entirely disappointed. Indeed I came to the deliberate conclusion that my oaths had been procured by fraud and misrepresentations; that the institution was in no respect what I had been informed it was; and as I have had the means of examining it more thoroughly, it has become more and more irresistibly plain to me that Masonry is highly dangerous to the State, and in every way injurious to the Church of Christ.[13]

If David Barton's assertion is right, that Freemasonry went through several transformations between 1799 and the 1850s, and adopted anti-biblical teachings and other practices that have been revived today, maybe Charles Finney's statement should be considered here as well:

I was aware, as Masons generally were at that time, that nearly all the civil offices in the country were in the hands of Freemasons;

and that the press was completely under their control, and almost altogether in their hands. Masons at that time boasted that all the civil offices in the country were in their hands. I believe that all the civil offices in the country where I resided while I belonged to them were in their hands. I do not recollect a magistrate, or a constable, or sheriff in that county that was not at that time a Freemason.[14]

The Same Today

Thomas Horn, one of the best researchers of these secret fraternities, asserts in his book that when President George W. Bush, who is considered to be a born-again Christian, was giving his second-term inaugural speech, he gave a clue about the Masonic involvement in the American Revolution. He said, "For half a century, America defended our own freedom by standing watch on distant borders. After the shipwreck of communism came years of relative quiet, years of repose, years of sabbatical—and then there came a day of fire." A few paragraphs later, Bush added, "By our efforts, we have lit a fire as well —a fire in the minds of men. It warms those who feel its power, it burns those who fight its progress, and one day this untamed fire of freedom will reach the darkest corners of our world."[15]

Horn says "the phrase, 'a fire in the minds of men,' is from Fyodor Dostoyevsky's 19th century book, *The Possessed*, a novel set in pre-revolutionary Russia, where civil resistance is seen championed by nihilist Sergei Nechaev, who tries to ignite a revolution of such destructive power that society will be completely destroyed…. The fact that a United States president would quote this phrase in an official speech of record was astonishing to many analysts, given that *The Possessed* is about violent crackdown on dissent that sparks civil unrest and revolution marked by public violence."[16]

Fire in the Minds of Men, according to Horn is also the title historian James H. Billington chose for his famous book on the history of revolutions, including the origin of occult Freemasonry and its influence in the American Revolution. In his closing comments, Bush himself concealed the meaning of his statement in a way that is not obvious or mysterious to his listeners. He said: "When our Founders declared a new order of the ages, they were acting on an ancient hope that is meant to be fulfilled." The phrase, "a new order of the ages," is taken from the masonically designed Great Seal, and Bush further acknowledged that the secret society members were acting on an "ancient" hope that is "meant to be fulfilled."[17]

Maybe the president might have been unaware of parts of his speech as Horn has noted because he was not the author of his speeches in the conventional sense. "Members of his staff, with input from unnamed guides, crafted most of these words. But he should have delivered these speeches after reviewing them, contemplating them, practicing them and probably making personal margin notes."[18] So whether he was aware of his actions or not, what most experts agree on is that most United States president's choice of words, actions, and speeches are received from members of an elite, top-secret cell of spiritual authorities in Washington. But this does not include Christian groups or faith councils that meet with U.S. presidents.

As a matter of fact, there is growing a consensus that many of the U.S. presidents' ties to evangelical Christianity appear to be simply for the purpose of producing political advantages. This should be a warning to Christians not to focus on Democrats, Republicans, or any political leader or party, but to put their hope and trust in the Lord Jesus Christ. Jesus said that in the last days "false christs and false prophets will arise, and they will show great signs and wonders so as to deceive and lead astray, if possible, even the elect (God's chosen ones)" (Matthew 24:24).

Christian Pinto acknowledges that there were most certainly Christians who came into America through the Puritan and Pilgrim movement, but they were not alone. With them came the secret societies that saw America as "*The New Atlantis*, a vision that was outlined by Sir Francis Bacon for the perfect society; a democratic commonwealth governed by scientific achievement."[19] Whether America is being driven by this vision today remains to be seen. No wonder Paul says we should not be deceived because Satan himself transforms himself into an angel of light (see 2 Corinthians 11:14). Pinto goes on to say:

> It was Bacon who said, "Knowledge is power," and the pursuit of knowledge through scientific discovery has guided the success of America. If one reads *The New Atlantis,* where Bacon describes a society with tall buildings, flying machines, weapons of mass destruction, health spas, the magnification of sound, and experiments with poisons on animals for the purpose of curing human beings, it becomes readily discernable that America has followed his blueprint from the start. A Freemason or Rosicrucian can readily quote the Bible and make references to Christ, Jesus, the Savior, and so forth, but he will also exalt the teachings of Plato and the philosophers of old, and will look upon the gods of the ancient world as examples of virtue and justice.[20]

Was George Orwell right or was his prediction just a good story? Do all the proponents of the New World Order have evil intentions? Not all of them are evil; in fact, I would venture to say that most of them have sincere goals, but they are ignorant of the outcome of their enterprise. What should be noted is that I am not in any way trying to speak ill of any political leader on this planet. I have a true sympathy for and a duty to pray for our leaders as all these problems that confront them on a daily basis are spiritual problems, but most of these leaders are not aware of this fact (see 1 Timothy 2:1–6).

Ephesus: Spiritual Warfare

Many people wonder why they elect politicians to power, and then after they are elected, they never seem to keep their pre-election promises. Why is this, even though many of them seem sincere and are highly honorable people? The reason is that most of them are trapped and cannot decide on important legislations because all sides—conservatives and liberals and progressives—are "not wrestl[ing] against flesh and blood, but against principalities, against powers, against the rulers of the darkness of this world, against spiritual wickedness in high places" (Ephesians 6:12).

Paul wrote the book of Ephesians, addressing the warfare and emphasizing the Christian's relationship to the principalities and powers behind it. Historians claim that Ephesus was the fourth largest city in the Roman Empire in Paul's day. It was the home of the magnificent temple of the goddess Artemis, who was a fertility deity whose image was said to have come from heaven. This statue was represented by a carved female figure with many breasts and was housed in the great temple at Ephesus, which was one of the wonders of the ancient world. Of all the deities worshiped in Asia, none was sought after like Artemis. People came from all over the world to worship in her temple.

Ephesus relied upon two important assets for its wealth. The first one was her position as a center of trade; the second was the worship of Artemis. Both were lost by the time Paul arrived there because many who became believers confessed their sinful practices (see Acts 19:18–20). All those whose wealth came from manufacturing silver shrines came to a halt. One of the businessmen who had a large manufacturing business employing many craftsmen, called all the craftsmen together and addressed them, saying that they were going to go out of business if this preaching continued (see Acts 19:25–27).

Demetrius's appeal for a riot was only motivated by the love of money and greed, which they had to hide behind the mask of patriotism and religious loyalty. The people involved in the rioting could not see their selfish motives, but they viewed themselves as fighting for their motherland. Even the temple treasury served as a bank, loaning massive amounts of money to many people, including kings. And since Artemis was the patroness of sexual instinct, prostitutes sold their bodies without condemnation. Yet for all the wealth it brought to Ephesus, the worship of Artemis left a big void in the hearts of men.

Ephesus was filled with symbolism and people turned to all sorts of magic, charms, and witchcraft. This is similar to what the West is experiencing with all these occult symbols in our capital cities that were so typical in Asia during Paul's day. There is an increased fascination with the occult; and make no mistake about it, it originates from the top leadership of these supposedly Christian nations.

This chapter should not be considered to be a personal attack on any individual. We are all fallen human beings who need to be saved by the shed blood of Jesus Christ. Many of us have also done horrible things in the past that we are not proud of. As Christians our job is to pray and intercede for Masons without judging them, because most of these men and women have no spiritual discernment or perception of what they have gotten themselves into. Most people who are members of this fraternal society are sincere and honorable persons, but they are completely unaware of the link of this institution to the occult and satanic spiritual realm.

We need to bring their sins to God in an attitude of love, crying and pleading to God for His mercy and grace, binding the spirits of deception, the antichrist, the occult, and death in the name of Jesus Christ. There are many people who were once Freemasons that Jesus Christ has saved and filled with Holy Spirit, experiencing dramatic conversions.[21]

We cannot deny the fact that the Pilgrims and some of the early Founders paid a very great price for the freedoms we enjoy today in the West. Regardless of how history portrays them, most of them were seeking to do the will of God and were seeking to incorporate Christian values in all spheres of society. They had flaws like all others human beings, but they deserve to be honored nonetheless.

Religious Liberty and the Freedom of Conscience

The constitutional framers were all committed to religious liberty and freedom of conscience. Though some of them represented enlightenment views and values, they all looked upon the new nation in which people with varied religious persuasions and nationality backgrounds learned to live peacefully and rationally together instead of resorting to violence. Some hold the view that Madison was opposed to Christianity as demonstrated in his Memorial and Remonstrate document (1785) in which he argued that the establishment proposed by the bill is not a requisite for the support of the Christian religion.[22]

Others like John Eidsmoe argue that "the Memorial and Remonstrate actually demonstrates the very opposite because Madison believed that Christianity flourished best when it operated free of government support and control."[23] Madison stated, "Whilst we assert for ourselves a freedom to embrace, to profess, and to observe the Religion which we believe to be of divine origin, we cannot deny an equal freedom to those whose minds have not yet yielded to the evidence which convinced us."[24]

Roger Williams (1603–1638), who began the colony of Rhode Island, had the same view as well. He regarded and declared any effort by the state to promote any religious idea to be "forced worship which stinks in the nostrils of God."[25] His own experience of persecution by Archbishop Laud and the Anglican establishment, including the bloody wars of religion that went on in Europe at that very time, convinced him that a state church had no basis in Scripture.

He believed the state could legitimately concern itself only with matters of civil order but not religious belief. The state had no right in trying to enforce the first table of the Ten Commandments. Those commandments dealt with the relationship between God and individual persons. The state had to confine itself to the commandments that related between people: murder, theft, adultery, lying, honoring parents, and so forth.[26]

Roger Williams said he saw no warrant in the New Testament to use the sword to promote religious belief: Constantine had been a worse enemy to true Christianity than Nero because Constantine's support had corrupted Christianity and led to the death of the Christian church. He believed that the moral principles found in the Scriptures ought to inform the civil magistrates, but he observed that well-ordered, just, and civil governments existed where Christianity was not present. All governments were required to maintain civil order and justice, but none had a warrant to promote any religion.

Freedom of religion to Roger Williams and other religious minorities had to mean that citizens had the genuine freedom to believe or not believe, to accept any religion or none at all.[27] In their opinion, what was unique about the United States, in fact, in addition to "cheapness of land," was the existence of "civil and religious liberty," which "stand perhaps unrivaled by any civilized nation on earth." Philip L. Ostergard explains:

> For centuries, the great majority of common people, living under a blanket of submission to landlords, accepted the life they were born into as their lot. Only the elite, the exclusive upper class, could try new ideas, make changes in lifestyle, and pursue dreams. When the early colonists ventured to traverse the ocean and disembarked from their ships, theirs was a new world. They could cultivate crops or starve, build shelters or freeze, succeed or fail. They owed nothing to a landlord, and they could expect help from no one (except the Lord Almighty). Early Americans had a strategic advantage, entering a land with virgin forests and hills of minerals; a land with ribbons of natural waterways simultaneously inviting and daunting exploration. Rocky Mountains beckoned the adventurous. The future belonged to these pioneers. Fueled by the high octane of liberty, they invented machines, published papers, and leveled forests for fast-growing cities. Freedom of enterprise pumped through their bodies to work longer hours, out producing workers of the old country. The explosion of new ideas and vigorous labor lifted the standard of living. The virgin soil produced men and women inclined to hard work and willing to dig deeply into rich mineral veins. The powerful dynamic of free enterprise energized them.... No quality has so marked the character of American social life as individual aspiration, turning the United States into a magnet for immigrants and a wellspring of hope for the adventurous.[28]

The American idea of union is unique to the world, and came about through the leadership of the clergy and the responsiveness of the citizenry as they learned to live the two commandments of our

Lord: "You shall love the Lord your God with all your heart, with all your soul, and with all your mind. This is the first and great commandment. And the second is like it: 'You shall love your neighbor as yourself.' On these two commandments hang all the Law and the Prophets" (Matthew 22:37–40).

Verna Hall has noted in her compilation *Christian Self-Government with Union*:

> To conceive of the thirteen colonies in 1765 being able to voluntarily form themselves into the world's first Christian republic in less than twenty-five years would seem humanly impossible, and so it would be. But in God's time-table of events, He and He alone knew when the hearts and minds of enough Christians were ready to put the matter of Christian self-government with union to the test.[29]

And again she writes:

> The way Christian unity worked between the thirteen diverse colonies is one of God's "wondrous works," which has almost been forgotten two hundred years later. Since 1830 the Christians in America began to fall away with their earlier convictions as to their responsibilities for the quality of civil government, we see the ever-increasing return to compulsory union as the nation's method for social and civil action. This trend cannot be reversed until American Christians once again assume their proper responsibility for their Christian republic.[30]

Another great writer has noted,

> Yes the British and American early leaders made many mistakes. But in the context of the era in which they lived, they still did extraordinarily well, and this world is immensely better off because of their contributions. We cannot dismantle the very tangible and beneficial accomplishments of these men by defaming them yet they cannot defend themselves because they are long dead. But we should try to know more about the characters of the figures involved, other than knowing only

historical events or dates. We should not blindly idolize them even if they fought for justice, freedom and equal opportunity, on the contrary, we should endeavor to see them as real human beings with strengths, as well as flaws. Those flaws do not discredit what they built. What men are able to achieve in spite of their flaws is often far more meaningful and valuable than what they lose because of them.[31]

At the same time we cannot disregard the enormous difference and investments many American Founders, leaders, and patriots have made in America and other nations, especially in spreading the gospel. Although the United States numbers only 5 percent of the total world population, in the last century probably more than 50 percent of the missionaries and money spent has come from America. Mark Hitchcock, author of *The Late Great United States*, wrote,

> Yes the United States has done more things right than wrong and God has been faithful in blessing the nation…. Present secular humanists have tried to distort the history of America, but they cannot alter the truth the nation was rooted on biblical (Christian) principles than any nation in the history of the world. Why? Because it was founded by more dedicated Christians than any other nation. Atheists do not pioneer the building of a new nation in pursuit of freedom, and enduring the hazards of pioneering is not their style. They prefer to let the Christians build a nation, and then they infiltrate her; alter her laws; take over her government, media, and school system; and change her culture to conform to their humanistic or pagan ideas. This has been their program in America, and that is why the nation is currently living on the outskirts of Sodom and Gomorrah.[32]

The nation's laws are filled with biblical principles because the (original) framers of the Constitution were themselves either Christians committed to the Word of God or citizens whose thinking process was saturated with basic biblical precepts. Dr. Francis Schaeffer says they had a "Christian conscience." Most of them emigrated from Europe which was, in large part, influenced by the Reformation. But as David

Holmes has clearly noted, "no examination or evaluation of history can capture the inner faith of any person."[33]

Washington unquestionably deserves major credit, along with Jefferson and Madison, for establishing the ideals of religious liberty and freedom of conscience (without which there can be no genuine cultural and intellectual freedom) for Protestants, Catholics, and Jews—and for deists and freethinkers as well—firmly in the American tradition.[34]

It is very tempting to judge others and run to conclusions about other people by evaluating whether or not they were Freemasons, deists, Christians, or committed followers of Christ; we don't know the exact eternal destiny of these Founders. What we know is that God presented them with a challenge to do what is right, and by His grace a good number of them met that challenge. It is only God who knows a person's heart, and He is the only one with the right to judge.

Our deepest loyalty should be to Jesus Christ and not to any human agent. That is why even the apostle Paul urged the Corinthians not to "make judgments about anyone ahead of time—before the Lord returns. For He will bring our darkest secrets to light and will reveal our private motives. Then God will give to each one whatever praise is due" (1 Corinthians 4:5).

Endnotes

[1] Barry R. Smith, *Better than Nostradamus* (Marlborough, New Zealand: International Support Ministries, 1996), 46.

[2] David Barton, *The Question of Freemasonry and the Founding Fathers* (Wall Builders, 2005), 21.

[3] George Washington and Free Masonry, accessed from *http://chuckbaldwinlive.com/Resources/Quotes.aspx#gw*.

[4] Ibid.

[5] *Character, Claims and Practical Workings of Freemasonry* (1869, Part 3), accessed from *http://www.matthew548.com/FFree3.html*.

[6] Preface by Christian J. Pinto in Thomas Horn's, *Apollyon Rising 2012: The Lost Symbol Found and the Final Mystery of The Great Seal Revealed, A Terrifying and Prophetic Cipher Hidden from the World by The U.S. Government for Over 200 Years is Here!* (Defender Crane, 2009), 3–4.

7 Barry Smith, who was a Christian occult researcher, has given some interesting dates and history behind the Egyptian pyramid and the eye seal that appear on the U.S. one dollar bill:

In 1782 a small group of Illumined Masons designed the two seals and handed them in a red velvet bag to a messenger. This messenger now hooded, handed the velvet bag to Thomas Jefferson on the 17th June, in his drawing room in Virginia. Then in 1784 Thomas Jefferson was appointed U.S. Ambassador to France where he was able to study European Illuminism in great detail. Jefferson and John Adam Weishaupt, the founder of the Illuminati of Bavaria in 1776, adopted a common policy and Jefferson returned to the U.S. and became Secretary of State. It was Weishaupt's belief that only a chosen few had enough "illumination" to guide and rule the world.

So on September 15th 1789, the Congress accepted the Great Seal of the United States of America that was in two parts, but until 1933, only the "eagle" was the emblem of the U.S.A. The pyramid with its "eye in the triangle" was not used officially until much later on. During the period of the year 1792, the Congress debated the cancellation and deletion of the pyramid and eye seal but all objections to what an Egyptian pyramid has to do with the U.S.A. were squashed and the seal remained (Barry R. Smith, *Better than Nostradamus* (Marlborough, New Zealand: First Published by International Support Ministries, 1996), 16–17).

8 Thomas Horn, *Apollyon Rising 2012* (Defender Crane, 2009), 124.

9 Barry R. Smith, *Better Than Nostradamus* (Marlborough, New Zealand: International Support Ministries, 1996), 30.

10 Thomas Horn, *Apollyon Rising 2012* (Defender Crane, 2009), 19.

11 Derek Prince, *Blessing or Curse You Can Choose* (Chosen Books, 1990), 146–147.

12 Ibid.

13 Charles Finney, *Character, Claims and Practical Workings of Freemasonry,* (1869, Part 3), accessed from http://www.matthew548.com/FFree3.html.

14 Ibid.

15 Thomas Horn, *http://www.newswithviews.com/Horn/thomas101.htm#_ftn2,* accessed on April 28, 2009.

16 *The Possessed*, accessed from *http://ebooks.adelaide.edu.au/d/dostoyevsky/d72p/*.

17 Thomas Horn, *Apollyon Rising 2012* (Defender Crane, 2009), 34–35.

18 Ibid., 37–38.

19 Preface by Christian J. Pinto in Thomas Horn's *Apollyon Rising*, 26.

20 Ibid., 27.

21 Knowledge about the history and current status of these secret societies is so vast and satanic that unless the Lord has called you to do research work in this area and to warn people about the dangers of Freemasonry, it is very spiritually and physically overwhelming. If you cannot present it in a logical and intelligent manner, as Barry Smith and others have done, you will be written off as having mental or psychological problems. So if you want to know more about this mystery of the great seal, the Illuminati, the New World Order, secret societies, and all these other symbols, you need to do your own investigative research. Anyone interested in a comprehensive study of this subject can refer to the writings of Thomas Horn, Grant Jeffrey, Barry Smith, film and documentary maker Christian J. Pinto, and author Martin L. Wagner.

22 James Madison, "Memorial and Remonstrate," in *The Papers of James Madison*, ed. Robert A. Rutland (Chicago: University of Chicago Press, 1977), 10:98.

23 John Eidsmoe, *Christianity and the Constitution: The Faith of Our Founding Fathers* (Grand Rapids: Baker, 1987), 107.

24 Madison, "Memorial and Remonstrate," 300.

25 Accessed from *http://en.wikipedia.org/wiki/Roger_Williams_%28theologian%29*.

26 Ibid.

27 Ibid.

28 Philip L. Ostergard, *The Inspired Wisdom of Abraham Lincoln: How Faith Shaped an American President* (Illinois: Tyndale House Publishers, Inc., 2008), 10–11.

29 Verna M. Hall, A *Compilation The Christian History of the Constitution of the United States of America: Christian Self -Government* (Published by the Foundation for American Christian Education, 2006), III, V.

30 Ibid.

31 Accessed from *http://www.infowars.com/constitutional-judo* on December 15, 2010, by Giordano Bruno.

32 Mark Hitchcock, *The Late Great United States: What Bible Prophecy Reveals About America's Last Days* (Multnomah Books, 2009), 158, 161.

33 David L. Holmes, "The Founding Fathers, Deism and *Christianity,*" *Encyclopedia Britannica Inc., accessed from http://www.britannica.com/EBchecked/topi/1272214/The-Founding-Fathers-Deism-and-Christianity* on January 19, 2012.

34 Os Guinness, *Character Counts: Leadership Qualities in Washington, Wilberforce, Lincoln and Solzhenitsyn,* (Michigan: Baker Books, 1999), 64.

Part III: According to Whose Laws?

CHAPTER 16

God's Laws or Man's Laws?

Humanity cannot make a law that will bind the conscience of the all the people of the land. God alone can make that type of law. Public opinion must be brought up to God's law; it must never be lowered to suit the unpredictable human nature of mankind. The institution of the state, as God's minister (see Romans 13:4), must therefore enforce the divine law as it pertains to civil life alone. The state punishes murder because it is a crime against humanity, not because they thought it was a good idea. But the question must be asked, According to whose laws? They are according to God's laws. Law is a rule of civil conduct prescribed by the supreme in a state, obedience to which is enforced, if necessary, by the infliction of physical penalty for disobedience or the lack of obedience.

Logically, with the assumption of the major premise, there are several conclusions connected that are in the nature of self-evident truths. For example, if the source of law is God, then humans can gain knowledge of what God requires only through revelation and His Word; and after it is understood, a person would be necessary to interpret the divine words in which the law may be framed. To what particular individual or individuals should that mind belong? Here was the great problem of the Middle Ages—the Roman Catholic Church held that it was divinely created and the appointed organ for the revelation of all truth to man.[1]

The emperor Charlemagne and his successors to the throne of the Holy Roman Empire of the German nation claimed that they were the divinely constituted and appointed minds to whom, in turn, the revelation of truth for the government of the larger part of Europe and the transformation of the same into law had been committed. This contradiction of authority went on for 800 years to the ruin of both parties, the emperors backing their authority with the power of physical punishment administered at the time and visible to all, and the pope and his cardinals and bishops backing theirs with the threat of what was far more terrible to the medieval mind, namely, the supposed punishments of the hereafter through all eternity controlled and manipulated of the church.[2]

What Is Law?

Laude Frederic Bastiat (1801–1850) has been dubbed as one of the most brilliant economic journalists who ever lived. In one of his most famous works, *The Law,* which was originally published as a pamphlet in 1850, he defined through development a just system of laws and demonstrated how such law facilitates a free society. Bastiat insisted that the sole purpose of government was to defend and protect the right of an individual to life, liberty, and property. He wrote in his book:

We hold from God the gift, which includes all others. This gift is life—physical, intellectual, and moral life. But life cannot maintain itself alone. The Creator of life has entrusted us with the responsibility of preserving, developing, and perfecting it. In order that we may accomplish this, He has provided us a collection of marvelous faculties. And He has put us in the midst of a variety of natural resources. By the application of our faculties to these natural resources we convert them into products, and use them. This process is necessary in order that life may run its appointed course. Life, faculties, production—in other words, individuality, liberty, property—this is man. And in spite of the cunning of artful political leaders, these three gifts from God precede all human legislation, and are superior to it. Life, liberty and property do not exist because men have made laws. On the contrary, it was the fact of life, liberty and property existed beforehand that caused men to make laws in the first place. So law is the collective organization of the individual right to lawful defense. Each of us has a natural right—from God—to defend his person, his liberty, and his property. These are three basic requirements of life, and the preservation of any one of them is completely dependent upon the preservation of the other two. For what are our faculties but the extension of our individuality? And what is property but an extension of our faculties?[3]

Bastiat insisted it is morally wrong for government to interfere with individual private matters, like private property, because he knew the home, above all other places, is where a man most truly reveals himself. So the law becomes perverted and guilty of the evils it is supposed to punish. This is legalized plunder, which is essentially taking from other people what rightfully belongs to them, and giving it to others to whom it does not belong.

No One Is Above the Law

One of the oldest means of depriving individuals of liberty and justice was for the top ruler (often a king or emperor of a country) to set himself above the law. Functioning above the law meant he was a law unto himself, often curtailing and even obliterating the natural rights and freedoms of the country's citizens. The pages of history are filled with examples of such rulers: Hebrew kings in the Old Testament era and most of the Roman emperors who arbitrarily snuffed out the lives of individuals who were perceived to be opposed to their policies. Whether such individuals were a threat to the welfare of the nation was irrelevant. What a ruler wanted was what he got. These rulers were not accountable to anyone (in Rome, not even to the senate) for their arbitrary and often bloody acts.[4]

Two or More Witnesses

More than a thousand years before the birth of Christ, Moses told the Israelites that a sentence could never be passed upon the testimony of one witness alone. A false witness should suffer the same punishment which he sought to have inflicted upon the person he accused. Nor could any law be more just. He said to the people, "One witness shall not rise against a man concerning any iniquity or any sin that he commits; by the mouth of two or three witnesses the matter shall be established" (Deuteronomy 19:15).

This biblical requirement became a vital component in the principle that "no one is above the law." In the New Testament, Jesus fulfilled this when He said:

> Moreover if your brother sins against you, go and tell him his fault between you and him alone. If he hears you, you have gained your brother. But if he will not hear, take with you one or two more, that by the mouth of two or three witnesses every word may be established. And if he refuses to hear them, tell it to the church. But if he refuses even to hear the church, let him be to you like a heathen and a tax collector. (Matthew 18:15–17)

Today the criminal and civil justice systems of Great Britain, the United States, Canada, and many other free countries, employ this Christian requirement of having witnesses testify in a court of law before a sentence is passed. In British and American jurisprudence, witnesses are part of what is legally called the "due process of law," which is a legal concept that first appeared in the fourteenth century under King Edward III.[5]

In AD 390 some people in Thessalonica rioted, arousing the anger of the Christian emperor, Theodosius the Great. He overreacted, slaughtering some 7,000 people, most of whom were innocent. Bishop Ambrose, who was located in Milan at the time did not turn a blind eye to the emperor's vindictive and unjust behavior. He asked him to repent of his massacre. When the emperor refused to do so, the bishop excommunicated him from the Church. After a month of stubborn hesitation, Theodosius prostrated himself and repented in Ambrose's cathedral bringing tears of joy to fellow believers.

It is unfortunate that Ambrose's action against Theodosius has often been portrayed as a power struggle between church and state rather than being the first instance of applying the principle that no one, not even an emperor or king or president, is above the laws of the state. The facts, indeed, support the latter interpretation. This is evident from Ambrose's letter to the emperor, which shows that he was solely concerned for the emperor's spiritual welfare in the matter. Like King David before him, who deliberately had Uriah killed in battle, the emperor had placed himself above one of God's laws and committed murder, and for that Ambrose demanded genuine repentance.

Today modern democracies take pride in saying that no one is above the law, but they fail to note that this landmark of civilization, which is now commonly imitated in free societies, was first implemented by a courageous, uncompromising Christian Bishop some 1,600 years ago. In a sense, Ambrose also set the stage for the Magna Carta that followed some 800 years later in England.[6]

The Magna Carta

The Magna Carta, presented by the Barons of England to King John in 1215, opens with this:

> Article 1: We have, in the first place, granted to God, and by this our present charter have confirmed, for us and our heirs forever, that the English Church shall be free, its rights undiminished, its liberties unimpaired; and that we wish this to be observed appears from the fact that we of our own free will, before the outbreak of the disputes between us and our barons, granted and confirmed by Charter the freedom of elections, which is considered most important and necessary to the English Church. We have also granted to all the free men of our kingdom, for us and our heirs forever, all the liberties underwritten, to have and to hold to them and their heirs of us and our heirs.

These are the other articles of the Magna Carta that are still law today:

> Article 13: The city of London shall enjoy all her ancient liberties and free customs, both by land and water. We also decree and

grant that all other cities, boroughs, towns and ports shall have all their liberties and free customs.

Article 39: No free man shall be taken, imprisoned, outlawed, banished, or in any way destroyed, nor will we proceed against or prosecute him, except by the lawful judgment of his equals and by the law of the land.

Article 40: To no one will we sell, to no one will we deny or delay, right or justice.[7]

When the barons forced King John to consent to and sign the Magna Carta (the Large Charter) at Runnymede in Surrey, outside of London, they obtained a number of rights that they did not have before this historic occasion. Specifically, the charter granted that (1) justice could no longer be sold or denied to freemen who were under the authority of barons; (2) no taxes could be levied without representation; (3) no one would be imprisoned without a trial; and (4) property could not be taken from the owner without just compensation.[8]

These achievements were monumental and history making. The era of the king being above the law had effectively come to an end. Commonly, this document is hailed as ushering in English liberty and justice; and some 500 years later it also served as a courageous precedent to the American patriots to establish liberty and justice in the newly founded United States of America. The early advocates of American independence often referred to the Magna Carta in support of their arguments.[9]

The Magna Carta, like many other highly beneficial phenomena that lifted civilization to a higher plateau in the Western world, had important Christian ties. Its preamble began: "John, by the grace of God…" and then it stated that the Charter was formulated out of "reverence for God and for the salvation of our souls and those of all our ancestors and heirs, for the honor of God and the exaltation of the Holy Church and the reform of our realm, on the advice of our reverend [church] fathers."[10]

Habeas Corpus Act of 1679

The Habeas Corpus Act of 1679 is considered by many as one of the most important legal documents in the history of the English-speaking world. It was embodied in England's charter of freedom, the Magna Carta, and allowed for a prisoner to be released from prison by following established legal procedures. Upon this foundation, citizens of Great Britain, Australia, Canada, New Zealand, and the U.S. feel confident that their individual freedom is safeguarded against arbitrary state action. Habeas Corpus gives people a basic civil right of protection against illegal imprisonment. The writ ordered that prisoners must have their case brought before a judge so that they can receive a speedy and fair trial.

The authorities had to have Habeas Corpus—the body of evidence—before imprisonment could take place. The prisoner should be charged with a crime within three days or be released. Winston Churchill wrote of the importance of Habeas Corpus: "No Englishman, however great or however humble, could be imprisoned for more than a few days without grounds being shown against him in open court according to the settled law of the land."[11] This act has been updated many times, apart from when Abraham Lincoln suspended it during the American Civil War. But since then the act has been suspended several times.

Natural Law

The concept of natural law goes back to the Greco-Roman philosophers. Natural law was understood as the process in nature by which human beings, through the use of sound reason, were able to perceive what was morally right and wrong; it was seen as the eternal, unchangeable foundation of all human laws several hundred years before the birth of our Lord Jesus Christ.

Likewise, the Christians believed that natural law was not an entity by rational human beings aware of what is right and wrong. The apostle Paul himself also said that the natural law contains God's commandments, which, although not communicated in a visible or audible manner, tell the natural human being what is right and wrong.

> For when Gentiles, who do not have the law, by nature do the things in the law, these, although not having the law, are a law to themselves, who show the work of the law written in their hearts, their conscience also bearing witness, and between themselves their thoughts accusing or else excusing them). (Romans 2:14–15)

Christianity had a rich theological and philosophical influence on the American early statesmen just as it has shaped the thinking of philosophers and kings for many generations before Columbus reportedly discovered the Americas in 1492, before Spain planted colonies on its shores in the sixteenth century, and before English trading settlements were established in Virginia in the later part of the sixteenth century. Historian Alvin Schmidt wrote, "Although some of the Founders might have been deists, it doesn't mean that they were not influenced by Christian ideas. This is especially true because deists two hundred years ago were much more influenced by Christian teachings and values than are modern deists or Unitarians today."[12]

As a result of the solid biblical foundation from the Pilgrims, these early statesmen signed the Declaration of Independence because they recognized that there was a higher authority—the Creator to whom they could appeal to establish objective moral grounds for their independence. Had they begun the Declaration with, "We hold these opinions as our own" (rather than "self-evident" and "truths"), they wouldn't have expressed an objective moral justification for their Declaration of Independence. This would have been their opinion against that of King George. They appealed to their Creator because they believed His moral law was the ultimate standard of right and wrong that would justify their cause—to end the rule of King George in the American colonies. They were convinced that George's rule needed to be ended because he was violating the basic human rights of the colonists.[13]

In a sense, the early statesmen were in the same position as were the allied countries after World War II. When the Nazi war criminals were brought to trial in Nuremburg, they were convicted of violating basic human rights as defined by the moral law (which is manifested in international law). This is the law that all people inherently understand and to which all nations are subject. If there was no such international morality that transcended the laws of the secular German government, then the allies would have had no ground to condemn the Nazis. In other words, we couldn't have said that the Nazis were absolutely wrong unless we knew what was absolutely right. But we do know they were absolutely wrong, so the moral law must exist.[14] And it must be God's law not man's law. "Without the moral law, there would be no human rights and without a belief in God, nothing is unconditionally wrong."[15] According to some analysts, the military in the West has abandoned the principles articulated by the Nuremburg Trial at the end of World War II, asserting the Nazi military and government officials had a responsibility of conscience to adhere to a higher order of morality than simply follow orders.

The Western world, as well as other countries around the world, have changed their laws to exclude whole classes of people from constitutional protection. Under the court's ruling, the courts have held that as long as a baby was in the womb it was not human and thus could be killed. However, a court can make abortion legal, but it cannot make it moral. A group of pro-life protestors who were outside an abortion clinic were sued for slander for calling abortionists murderers. The abortionists argued, just as Hitler's emissaries had done before them, that they could not be murderers because they were not breaking any laws.

This understanding that no laws are being broken is why many people are willing to do whatever they are told to do by the state. The experience of Nuremberg and the silent holocaust in our abortion clinics bear witness to the fact that when a state is accountable to no one except itself, it simply assumes that whatever is legal is moral. The law is simply whatever the courts or dictators say it is. Show me your laws and I will show you your God. It's a frightening scenario when we consider that a number of Christian leaders have joined the bandwagon with others who believe in the theory of natural law above God's laws. They are being told that natural law has a rich Christian history. But they are completely wrong.

Endnotes

[1] John W. Burgess, *The Sanctity of Law* (Ginn and Company Proprietors Boston 1927), 328–329.

[2] Ibid.

[3] Frederick Bastiat, *The Law* (Old Chelsea Station, New York: Originally published in 1850, Cosimo Classic, 2006), 6.

[4] Alvin J. Schmidt, *How Christianity Changed the World* (Grand Rapids: Zondervan, 2004), 249.

[5] Ibid.

[6] Augustine, *The City of God Against the Pagans* (Harvard University Press, 1963), 5:273.

[7] The article numbers indicated above relate to the original Magna Carta of 1215 as displayed in Lincoln Castle. In the final version, as placed on the Statute Book, chapter 1 remained as such, but article 13 became 9 and articles 39 and 40 were combined as article 29.

[8] J. C. Holt, *Magna Carta* (Cambridge University Press, 1965), 317.

[9] Ibid., Alvin J. Schmidt, 251.

[10] J. C. Holt, *Magna Carta*, 317.

[11] Winston Churchill, *History of the English Speaking Peoples, Habeas Corpus* (Orion Publishing Co. 1956, 2002). Quoted in Paul Backholer, *How Christianity Made the Modern World: The Legacy of Christian Liberty* (Faith Media, 2009), 159–160.

[12] Ibid., Alvin J. Schmidt, 256.

[13] Norman L. Geisler and Frank Turek, *I Don't Have Enough Faith to Be an Atheist* (Wheaton, Illinois: Crossway, 2004), 176.

[14] Ibid.

[15] Ibid.

CHAPTER 17

Is Democracy the Best Form of Government?

Democracy becomes mob rule, chaos, and dictatorship…when people rule, they choose someone bold and unscrupulous who curries favor with the people by giving them other men's property.

—Cicero, as summarized by Will Durant

The Bible Doesn't Teach Democracy

Even though those of us in the West live under a democratic system of government, the Bible doesn't teach the idea or concept of democracy. Although many of the principles of democracy are biblical, such as individual human rights, liberty, and human dignity, democracy itself is not a biblical concept. What then is democracy? How is it defined and how do we use it today?

The word *democracy* is derived from the same Greek word we get *humanism* from. It originates from the Greek word *demokratia*, which is the "rule of the people." *Demokratia* comes from two root words: *demos*, which is "people," and *kratos*, which is "power." Democracy means that all people, regardless of their social class, have political equality and are given full and absolute control of power and government while they respect the laws and institutions.[1]

In God's mind, a democracy is not His kind of government, but rather a monarchy is. However, the monarchy, which He will set up on the earth someday, will actually be a theocracy, where God is the true King and Ruler of all the earth. The reason we have a democracy now is because we don't have a "righteous rule" monarchy. Therefore, we need some kind of checks and balances in place, which is why most governments are established on this basis.

When the thirteen colonies were still part of England, Professor Alexander Tytler wrote about the fall of the Athenian republic over a thousand years ago:

> A democracy cannot exist as a permanent form of government. It can only exist until the voters discover that they can vote themselves money from the public treasure. From that moment on, the majority always votes for the candidates promising the most money from the public treasury, with the result that democracy always collapses over loose fiscal policy, followed by a dictatorship.[2]

The authenticity of this quote is often disputed and cannot be verified, but the words of the original author are still relevant to what is going on in the West today. The author noted that the average age of the world's greatest civilizations from the beginning of history has been about 200 years (the comparative data cannot prove this span of years). During those 200 years, however, these nations have always progressed "from bondage to spiritual faith; from spiritual faith to great courage; from courage to liberty; from liberty to abundance; from abundance to complacency; from complacency to apathy; from apathy two dependence; from dependence back into bondage."[3]

This progression can be seen throughout the historical books of the Bible, as well as in Greece, Persia, Babylon, and in Rome. Each of these Empires passed through the above series of stages from their inception to their decline. Where are we today on the scale? Today we have a deteriorating form of government, no matter what party is elected or who is president.[4] Politicians criticize each other, but they both play for the same team; the losers are always the people who vote for them.

In 1776 America supposedly came out of bondage with faith, understanding, and courage. Even against great odds, and with much bloodshed, they battled their way to achieve liberty. Liberty is that delicate area between the force of government and the free will of man. Liberty brings freedom of choice to work, to trade, to go and live wherever one wishes. In fact, liberty leads to abundance. Abundance, if made an end in itself, will result in complacency, which in turn leads to apathy. Apathy is the "let someone do it" philosophy that always brings dependency. For a period of time, dependents are often not aware they are in fact dependent. Rather, they delude themselves by thinking that they are still free—"We can still vote, can't we?" they ask themselves.

Eventually abundance diminishes and dependency becomes bondage once again. Most people prefer to live in a democracy rather than a tyranny, but even a democracy is not God's original choice of government. The Greek philosopher Plato gave an overview of the different forms of government. He started with the best form of government and ended with the worst. Here is how he ranked them:

- Theocracy: The rule of God over all the affairs of humanity.
- Monarchy: The rule of one good person.
- Aristocracy: The rule of a few good people.
- Oligarchy: The rule by the elite or a few individuals.
- Democracy: The rule of the people by themselves.
- Republic: The rule by a constitutional republic.
- Tyranny: The rule of one evil individual.
- Anarchy: The rule of none.

Common Political Systems

Abraham Lincoln, in his Gettysburg Address, resolved that "government of the people, by the people, for the people shall not perish from the earth."[5] Was the president right in saying that this government will not perish? I don't think he was correct because it will in fact perish because it is not God's type of government or God's perfect nation to reign through. Theocracy is the form of government established by God, visible throughout the nation of Israel in the Old Testament. It is He alone who created and redeemed humanity and He is the One qualified to govern each of us.

A society where a king rules is called a monarchy, and this form of government rejected a theocracy when Israel demanded a king to rule over them. Had the Israelites submitted to God's leadership, they would have prospered in every area of their lives. The Bible says:

> But the thing displeased Samuel when they said, "Give us a king to judge us." So Samuel prayed to the Lord. And the Lord said to Samuel, "Heed the voice of the people in all that they say to you; for they have not rejected you, but they have rejected Me, that I should not reign over them. According to all the works which they have done since the day that I brought them up out of Egypt, even to this day—with which they have forsaken Me and served other gods—so they are doing to you also. Now therefore, heed their voice. However, you shall solemnly forewarn them, and show them the behavior of the king who will reign over them." (1 Samuel 8:6–9)

Samuel explained all the consequences of being led by a king, but the Israelites refused to listen. They instead demanded a king to judge them like all other nations around them; yet Israel was called to be a holy nation separate from and unique among all the other nations (see Leviticus 20:26). In making this demand, God told Samuel, "Heed the voice of the people in all that they say to you; for they have not rejected you, but they have rejected Me, that I should not reign over them" (1 Samuel 8:7). The choice of security by repenting and turning to God as their Savior, Lord, and Provider was rejected. Instead, they turned to the false security offered to them by a civil government that would subject them to slavery in the name of security. Instead of turning to God in repentance, people with slave mentalities turned to political rulers for earthly security, even after God warned them of the consequences of their rejection of Him.

God's form of government will eventually be a monarchy of one perfect King—His name is Jesus Christ. Isaiah declared, "Behold, a king will reign in righteousness, and princes will rule with justice" (Isaiah 32:1). Jesus will lead a righteous rule and He will share His authority with His church, which is a governmental assembly. He purchased His church with His own blood and has trained it through suffering, affliction, and discipline.

God has His chosen ones, and they come from every tribe, nation, people, and tongue. If we are members of the church, we can expect to be part of a governmental assembly that will rule the world, headed by one righteous Man Jesus Christ, who will establish the kingdom of God on earth.

Therefore, democracy without the lordship of Christ is simply another form of tyranny, where the majority frequently deprive the minority through the institution of unjust laws. Philip Schaff, a German-American theologian and church historian, once wrote:

> Republican institutions in the hands of a virtuous and God-fearing nation are the very best in the world, but in the hands of a corrupt and irreligious people they are the very worst and most effective weapons of destruction. An indignant people may rise in rebellion against a cruel tyrant; but who will rise against the tyranny of the people in possession of the ballot-box and the whole machinery of government? Here lies our great danger, and it is increasing every year. Destroy our churches, close our Sunday-schools, abolish the Lord's Day, and our republic would become an empty shell, and our people would tend to heathenism and barbarism. Christianity is the most powerful factor in our society and the pillar of our institutions. It regulates the family; it enjoins private and public virtue; it builds up moral character; it teaches us to love God supremely, and our neighbor as ourselves; it makes good men and useful citizens; it denounces every vice; it encourages every virtue; it promotes and serves the public welfare; it upholds peace and order. Christianity is the only possible religion for the American people, and with Christianity are bound up all our hopes for the future.[6]

Americans believe that the Founders, with divine wisdom from the Bible, gave America a constitutional form of government called a republic—not a democracy, as some would suggest. But there is little difference between the two. A republic, is defined by *Merriam-Webster's*

Collegiate Dictionary as a "government having a chief of state who is not a monarch and who…is unusually a president," and "a government in which supreme power resides in a body of citizens entitled to vote and is exercised by elected officers and representatives responsible to them and governing according to law."

This clearly embodies the central principles of a democracy, which is a government by the people and for the people—especially the rule of the majority. *Webster's* goes on to define a *democracy* as a "government in which the supreme power is vested in the people and exercised by them directly or indirectly through a system of representation usually involving periodically held free elections."

The Founders and Democracy

The constitutional framers gave America a republic because they thought a republic was designed to be a lasting and permanent form of government. For example, in 1787, when Benjamin Franklin left the Constitutional Convention, he was asked by a woman named Mrs. Powel of Philadelphia, "Sir, What have you given us?" His immediate response was, "A republic, Mum, if you can keep it."[7] He said this because certain inalienable rights granted by the Creator (life, liberty, and property) would be protected by law; therefore, government was simply man's agent for the protection of God's good gifts.

A good number of these early statesmen knew that a democracy was only a temporary and transitional form of government that was on the way to a total government or totalitarianism. They developed democratic principles but not a majority-rule kind of democracy. John Winthrop (1588–1649), the first governor of the Massachusetts Bay colony, declared democracy to be the meanest and worst of all forms of government.[8] John Cotton (1584–1652), an English clergyman and colonist, wrote in 1636, "Democracy, I do not conceive that ever God did ordain as a fit government either for church or commonwealth. If the people be governors, who shall be governed?"[9]

John Adams, the second president of the United States, is reported to have reminded Virginia legislator John Taylor, "Remember, a democracy never lasts long. It soon wastes, exhausts and murders itself. There never was a democracy yet that did not commit suicide."[10] He is also quoted to have said, "The voice of the people is sometimes the voice of Mahomet, of Caesar, of Catiline, the Pope, and the devil."[11] And according to Thomas Jefferson, "A democracy is nothing more than mob rule, where fifty-one percent of the people may take away the rights of the other forty-nine."[12] James Madison also wrote much the same thing: "Democracies are spectacles of turbulence and contention. Pure democracies are incompatible with personal security or the rights of property…. In general they have been as short in their lives as they have been violent in their deaths."[13]

Although many of the arguments of the constitutional framers rested on the power of a constitutional republic, it was not a Christian government and could not work because it was fashioned according to Roman civil law and relied on the integrity of one person whose deciding vote has often been in contempt of God's morality. Even the much more admired republic was shoved aside and Americans have almost given up these principles completely. America is now considered a socialist democracy.

Theocratic Government

Theocracy is the rule of God over all His creation, including the angels, both Christians and non-Christians, the family, local church governments, businesses, economics, civil governments at all levels, and every other conceived created thing in this world. Jesus is "the ruler over the kings of the earth" (Revelation 1:5). The Triune God is described as "He who is the blessed and only Sovereign, the King of kings and Lord of lords" (1 Timothy 6:15 NASB).

Theocracy doesn't refer to the church as God's sole governmental rule in society. In a theocracy law is not administered by a priestly order nor is law administered by a priestly order as God's ministers and agents. While the church is under the rule of God in a theocracy, it is not the sole agent of rule in the earth. This would be an ecclesiocracy, a church-state. Theocracy is God's government in, of, and over the entire created universe. It is synonymous with the kingdom of God. The church is not the kingdom of God, and the state is not the kingdom of God; the church is under God's kingdom, and the state too is under God's kingdom.[14]

Theocracy means that all governments—"self-government, family government, and civil government—are theocratic governments. God rules them all in terms of His revealed law. Biblical theocracy therefore does not mean tyranny. Humanist theocracy means tyranny which is the rule of a self-proclaimed sovereign man."[15] The Puritans who founded America defended Christian theocracy and established theocratic systems of government while they were settling here. In 1892 the U.S. Supreme Court announced with pride that the purpose of the Founders of America was "the establishment of the Christian religion." This is because eighteenth-century America was still predominately Christian.

In the words of Gary De Mar, humanists usually think of "government" as a top-down bureaucracy that controls almost everything in society. The Bible teaches that government is actually a general term for self-government, family government, church government, and civil government. The Bible teaches that government is a bottoms up appeals court structure. Thus, when humanists paint a picture of theocracy as tyrannical, they are using a false model— indeed, an ancient human model—to guide their painting."[16]

What the Bible says is that every area of life is to be ruled by God's permanent principles. This is the biblical meaning of theocracy: "An earthly reflection of what the Bible says has always existed, namely, the rule of God in every area of life, not just civil government.... Therefore the proper goal of biblical theocracy—in a family, church, and state—is personal independence and self-responsibility."[17]

This is why biblical theocracy is hated by modern humanist theocrats who want to make the state into a god, and then rule other men through a system of top-down political power. Biblical theocracy kills humanist theocracy, for it destroys the economic, legal, and psychological dependence of the masses of people on their elite rulers.

Is it an accident that there is a Pharaoh-like pyramid on the back of the $1 bill with the all-seeing eye of Lucifer in its center?

In the humanistic system people become slaves to the world's Babylonian system. When we look at the pyramid, we notice a symbol of a large number of people who are slaves to this humanistic world system. Besides, all humanistic theocracies eventually die anyway, for they cannot stand the competition that they receive from newer, hungrier, more energetic institutions. This is the fate of every human empire in history.[18]

Government Under God

Only the innovation and flexibility of self-governed people under the rule of God's law can sustain the growth of God's kingdom over time. Men will be ruled by God or else they will be ruled by men who imitate God. There is no escape from the rule of other men; the question is, By what standard will rulers rule and also be governed? Everyone is under another person's authority in most areas of his or her life. Everyone answers for his or her own actions. The doctrine of "divine rights" applies only to God—God alone answers to no one else.

There is no divine right of kings, priests, parents, or voters. There is no divine right of anyone on earth. Every person is accountable to someone else. But this accountability is judicial, essentially an appeals court system. Initiative still remains with the individual. God has the ultimate authority to govern (see Jeremiah 27:5; Proverbs 8:15; 21:1; Matthew 28:18). Parents exercise authority over their children, employers over employees, teachers over students, elders or bishops over church members, and civil servants over citizens—but God still reigns over all of those.

Gary DeMar gives the fundamental aspects of God's designated units of government: self-government, church government, and civil government. He makes it clear that the Bible designates all four as true forms of government. One of the major errors of the modern world is to treat civil government as *the* government. This should not be surprising to us who have a Christian and biblical worldview.

There is an intellectual war going on in the earth today, a war between two rival views of God, man, law, and society. On one side is Christianity with its doctrine of plural governments, plural institutional sovereignties, checks and balances, and the Bible as the Word of God. On the other side are the anti-Christians. They hold a completely different view of the world. They believe that man, not God, is the sovereign agent of lawful authority, or at least man's institutions are: the state, the party, science, etc.[19]

The biblical pattern of authority establishes that God is our ultimate authority. Here then is the hierarchy diagram illustration as developed by Gary DeMar in his excellent book, *Ruler of Nations*.[20]

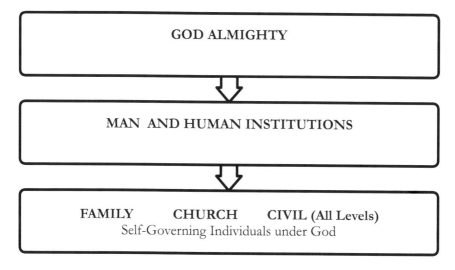

All Power and Authority Come from God

Jesus Christ is Lord of every sphere of life. Without His lordship, democracy leads to tyranny. Humanists who deny God's government over all of life work to implement instead of man's government over the same. Since man sees himself as god, we may legitimately say that humanism is "theocratic." The Humanist Manifesto II states: "No deity will save us; we must save ourselves." How do humanists hope to save us? Well, they want humanist laws, humanist schools, humanist courts, a humanist civil government, and humanist economics. In fact, they want the world to be humanistic. And who do we suppose they believe ought to run the world? Humanists, of course.

Remember, theocracy is simply the "rule of God in the world." If we believe in the lordship of Jesus Christ, then we believe in theocracy as defined by Gary above. This does not mean, however, that we believe in a church-state or state-church.

What about those who say Christians are trying to impose theocratic principles on the rest of society? The church government has a very limited jurisdiction in our world today. It does not rule over the state, business, education, or the civil courts, but individual Christians, who make up the body of Christ. The church should exercise dominion at every level of society. They do not rule as an institution—a government—but as individuals. So what do Christian reconstructionists mean when they talk about the church taking dominion in the world? They are simply referring to individual Christians as they serve God faithfully in the areas where God has granted them a calling; they don't mean the institutional church as a whole.21

Everything in life is a spiritual battle for the souls of humanity. It is the reason we cannot separate the church's battles from the state's. Paul again reminds us, "For we do not wrestle against flesh and blood, but against principalities, against powers, against the rulers of the darkness of this age, against spiritual hosts of wickedness in the heavenly places" (Ephesians 6:12). And again he writes to the Corinthians,

> For though we walk in the flesh, we do not war according to the flesh. For the weapons of our warfare are not carnal but mighty in God for pulling down strongholds, casting down arguments and every high thing that exalts itself against the knowledge of God, bringing every thought into captivity to the obedience of Christ. (2 Corinthians 10:3–5)

All God-given freedoms—personal, economic, political, and spiritual—are interconnected. The moral issues of the day are also the political issues. No one can escape the tyranny that follows once these freedoms are lost. Another writer carefully observes:

> Everything in life is a moral issue, if only because God remains
> involved in every aspect of this life. Everything is under His
> sovereign oversight and control. There is, therefore, so such thing
> as separation of church from state as it is usually thought of....
> Either non-Christians will be ruled by Christians, or Christians
> will be ruled by non-Christians. Thanks to the Constitution, most
> American Christians have adopted the two-kingdom concept and
> relegated civil authority to the non-Christians. Consequently, the
> non-Christians judiciary determines conflicts between the two. No
> wonder the tide has turned against Christianity under
> constitutional government.[22]

Paul describes the ideal government by the saying that there is no
power or authority except from God. All powers are ordained by God
and for God. Power is not established in the people and the people are
not the highest authority, as some of our statesmen allege. Nations are
moral ordinances of God, created and regulated by the moral law.
Therefore, all nations are under law to Christ and their duties and
functions are fully explained by the apostle Paul in his letter to the
Romans:

> Let every soul be subject to the governing authorities. For there is
> no authority except from God, and the authorities that exist are
> appointed by God. Therefore whoever resists the authority resists
> the ordinance of God, and those who resist will bring judgment
> on themselves. For rulers are not a terror to good works, but to
> evil. Do you want to be unafraid of the authority? Do what is
> good, and you will have praise from the same. For he is God's
> minister to you for good. But if you do evil, be afraid; for he does
> not bear the sword in vain; for he is God's minister, an avenger to
> execute wrath on him who practices evil. Therefore you must be
> subject, not only because of wrath but also for conscience' sake.
> For because of this you also pay taxes, for they are God's
> ministers attending continually to this very thing. Render therefore
> to all their due: taxes to whom taxes are due, customs to whom

customs, fear to whom fear, honor to whom honor. (Romans 13:1–7)

God has established numerous authorities for the proper ordering of society. In verse 1 we are instructed to be subject "to the government authorities," each of which are "established by God." There are many authorities and we owe no single earthly authority our total allegiance. When we look at verses 4–6, we find that the Holy Spirit is declaring through Paul on three separate occasions that those who are in civil government are "ministers of God." Authority to govern is delegated by God; therefore, those who govern are obligated to govern according to God's laws, for they are ministers of God.

The church and state are separate God-ordained monopolies in their respective realms. The church has been given the keys of the kingdom of heaven (see Matthew 16:19; 18:15–18), whereas the state is God's "minister" in executing wrath on him who practices evil (see Romans 13:3–4). All rulers are designated as ministers of God. So as Christians we must submit ourselves to those who rule because God has established them in their positions of authority by His own sovereign will. We cannot escape theocracy. A government's laws reflect its morality, and the source of that morality is its god. Gary DeMar again helpfully points out:

The rejection of one god leads inescapably to the choice of another god. If any person, group, court, etc., establishes himself/ themselves as the final arbiter of right and wrong, then he/they have assumed the attributes of a god. Thus, he/they are theocratic. Democracy can become theocratic if absolute power is given to the people. (That is what happened to America—by electing their officials, they become the source of their laws and therefore America's god is "We The People.") You've heard the phrase: *vox populi, vox dei,* "the voice of the people is the voice of God." Those who promote a particular worldview and want to see it implemented socially, educationally, politically, and judicially have elevated the majority to the status of gods. Their political advocates have theocratic tendencies. Only their choice of God has changed.[23]

Democracy will never sustain a civilization. Hitler came to power democratically. Abortion, gay marriage, eugenics, and other deplorable things in the West have happened under democratic means as well. Remember that Jesus Christ was put to death by the voice of the people, which just happened to be the majority vote (see Luke 23:13–24). God desires to set up a theocracy in the earth once again, where He reigns supreme over all spheres of life.

Endnotes

[1] Ian Morris, Kurt Raaflaub, David Castriota, *Democracy 2500? Questions and Challenges* (Kendall Hunt Pub. Co. 1997), 34.

[2] Dr. David Jeremiah with C. C. Carlson, *The Handwriting on the Wall: Secrets from the Prophecies of Daniel* (Thomas Nelson, Inc. 1992, 2008), 62.

[3] Ibid.

[4] Ibid.

[5] Philip L. Ostergard, *The Inspired Wisdom of Abraham Lincoln: How Faith Shaped an American President* (Carol Stream, Illinois: Tyndale House Publishers, Inc., 2008), 223.

[6] A compilation by Verna M. Hall, Edited by Joseph Allan Montgomery, *The Christian History of the Constitution of the United States of America, Christian Self-Government with Union* (Foundation for American Christian Education, 2004), 40.

[7] Accessed from *http://www.freerepublic.com/focus/news/2328118/posts.*

[8] Marvyn A. Davies, *Foundation of American Freedom: Calvinism in the Development of Democratic Thought and Action* (Nashville, TN: Abingdon Press, 1955), 11.

[9] Edwin Powers, *Crime and Punishment in Early Massachusetts: A Documentary History: 1620–1692* (Boston, MA: Beacon Press, 1966), 55.

[10] John Adams's *Works*, Volume VI, 484, to John Taylor, April 15, 1814.

[11] John Adams, quoted by Gilbert Chinard, *Honest John Adams* (Boston, MA: Little, Brown and Co., 1993, 1961), 241, in John Eidsmoe, "The Christian American Response to Confessionalism," in Gary Scott Smith, ed., *God and Politics: Four Views on the Reformation of Civil Government* (Phillipsburg, NJ: Presbyterian and Reformed, 1989), 227–228.

[12] Quoted in commentaries by Ken Schoolland and Janette Eldridge, *The Adventures of Jonathan Gullible A Free Market Odyssey: The Democracy Gang* (Leap Publishing, Cape Town, 2004), 235.

[13] Jacob E. Cooke, ed., *The Federalist 10* (Middletown, CT: Wesleyan University Press, 1961), 61.

14 Gary DeMar, *Ruler of Nations* (Dominion Press 1987), xvi.

15 Ibid.

16 Ibid.

17 Ibid.

18 Ibid.

19 Ibid., x.

20 Gary Demar, *Ruler of Nations* (Dominion Press, 1987), 31

21 Gary DeMar and Peter J. Leithart, *The Reduction of Christianity: A Biblical Response to Dave Hunt* (Dominion Press: Ft. Worth, Texas, 1988), 322.

22 Ted R. Weiland, *Bible Law Versus The United States Constitution: The Christian Perspective* (Scottsbluff, NE: Mission to Israel Ministries, 2012), 240.

23 Gary DeMar, "Defining Terms: Theocracy," February 26, 2007, accessed from *http://americanvision.org/1629/defining-terms-theocracy*.

CHAPTER 18

Separation of Church and State

The Origins of the Separation of Church and State

The question of church and state has been a debated issue for many ages. That is why most people are confused when it comes to church and state relations. They are separate jurisdictions, but the Bible defines their limits of jurisdiction because the Word of God is the supreme and ultimate authority in both the church and the state. Both kings and priests are commanded to follow the same standards of law and government, even though not all laws apply to each in the same way.

From the time of Jesus church and state were separate. When the Pharisees tried to entrap Jesus by asking Him whether it was lawful to give tax money to Caesar or not, Jesus asked them to show Him a Roman coin.

And He said to them, "Whose image and inscription is this?"

They said to Him, "Caesar's."

And He said to them, "Render therefore to Caesar the things that are Caesar's, and to God the things that are God's." (Matthew 22:20–21)

Does this mean Christians are not to be involved with state affairs? Not at all. We are to render our due to the government and our due to God. Christians live in two kingdoms and have responsibilities in both areas of life. In Israel there was a theocratic government—the church and the state were one and the same thing. For example, the Jewish church was not the state, nor was the state the church. Each had its distinct rulers, courts, laws, subjects, penalties, and duration. Moses, Joshua, David, Solomon, Hezekiah, and Zerubbabel represented the state; Aaron, Eleazar, Abiathar, Zadok, Azariah, and Joshua represented the church.

Formerly, it was not considered improper that the three basic functions of government—making laws, enforcing the laws, and interpreting the laws—in the settlement of controversies should be exercised by one supreme authority. Thus it will be seen that Moses not only made or promulgated the law, but was also a leader or king, and that he sat as judge over the people.[1] But this does not apply in the New Testament where the church and state are separate from one another. Therefore, we have to be careful when applying Old Testament prophecies to our modern age.

Church and state are each supreme in their own sphere, the church in spiritual things and the state in things that are temporal. The church gives effect to her spiritual laws and the state to its civil laws. On February 15, 1584, when Andrew Melville was brought before the Privy Council, unclasping his Hebrew Bible from his girdle and throwing it on the table, he said:

> These are my instructions: see if any of you can judge of them, or show that I have passed my injunctions. This was the watchword of the Second Reformation. God alone is Lord of conscience. Only His will is law for it. Man's conscience is contrary to the plainest intuitions of the human soul. Any law, either in Church or State that contravenes the law of God is no law at all. To the law and to the testimony, if they speak not according to this Word it is because there is no light in them.[2]

The apostle Paul in the book of Romans calls the leaders of both church and state "ministers of God" who are to execute judgment as God's delegated representatives or servants on the earth.

If the American political history from the Pilgrims/Puritans is Christian, then where did the separation of church and state come from? It came from infidel politicians and minority churches that did not want to be taxed for the benefit of other churches, so they gave up the idea of ruling in the civil sphere.³ The term "separation of church and state" is not in the U.S. Constitution itself. It originated in a letter from Thomas Jefferson to a group of Danbury Connecticut Baptists who called him an "infidel." He responded on January 1, 1802, by writing:

> Believing with you that religion is a matter which lies solely between man and his God, that he owes account to none other for faith or his worship, that the legislative powers of government reach actions only, and not opinions, I contemplate with sovereign reverence that act of the whole American people which declared that their legislature should "make no law respecting an establishment of religion, or prohibiting the free exercise thereof," thus building a wall of separation between church and state.⁴

Jefferson wanted to be re-elected, so he knew that he was dead politically if Christians ever found out what his true beliefs were, for Christians were the overwhelming political majority. What were his beliefs? According to some historians, he did not believe in the deity of Jesus Christ, in His miracles, or in whole Bible as the Word of God. That is why he put together his version of the Bible without any miracles in it. So he covered his tracks and hid behind a smokescreen of false concern over religious integrity and a free conscience, which has been described as a smart tactic.⁵ Since Baptists did not belong to any state religious establishment, they resented the fact that they had to pay taxes that went to support state churches. So he appealed to their sense of injustice by understanding their fears and therefore wrote that letter.

That "wall of separation" language appealed to what was then a small religious sect that was discriminated against—the Baptists. Fifty years later, they had become the numerically dominant Protestant group, as they remain today. Jefferson wanted nothing more than to get Christians out of his hair, politically speaking. So, in effect, he offered them a political deal: you get out of my hair politically, and I will get out of your hair ecclesiastically.[6] When Jefferson gave his inaugural address in 1805, he backed off on his private 1802 position to conform publicly to the Constitution. He publicly admitted that the states did not possess lawful jurisdiction over many religious matters:

> In matters of religion I have considered that its free exercise is placed by the Constitution independent of the powers of the general (federal or national) government. I have therefore undertaken on no occasion to prescribe the religious exercises suited to it, but have left them, as the Constitution found them, under the direction and discipline of the church or state authorities acknowledged by several religious societies.[7]

In a letter to Samuel Miller, Thomas Jefferson further clarified his position:

> I consider the government of the United States as prohibited by the Constitution from intermeddling with religious institutions, their doctrines, discipline, or exercises. This results not only from the provision that no law shall be made respecting an establishment or free exercise of religion, but from that also which reserves to the states the powers not delegated to the general government. It must rest with the states, as far as it can be in any human authority…[8]

Jefferson had nothing to do with the drafting of the First Amendment. The United States Constitution says, "Congress shall make no law neither respecting an establishment of religion nor prohibiting the free exercise thereof." Recent court and humanist politicians have illegitimately substituted Jefferson's anti-constitutional phrase in place of the First Amendment, which added to the Constitution to protect the church from a national establishment of religion. Increasingly this has been interpreted to mean what religious freedom has meant in Russia.

This phrase—"church is separated from the state"—is found in the Soviet Constitution. We could believe anything we wanted to in the former Soviet Union, but we would not try to act in terms of our belief. In the Soviet Union, freedom of religion was not allowed. There was nothing but the state; the Soviet regime was committed to the complete annihilation of religious institutions and ideas. Therefore, the separation of church and state meant the separation of church and everything else in all of society. This is now happening on a very escalating pace in the West.

Christianity has to be eradicated from every area of public responsibility and authority. The goal of humanists since Jefferson's day has been to intrude every area of public life, and, while the state gets bigger, it also gets less and less restrained by biblical law. The myth of separation of Christianity and the state led inevitably to the secularization of every area of life and the centralization of power in the national government. There can be no freedom without Christ. Take Christ and the Bible out of any institution of government, and we thereby lose our freedom.[9]

Freedom of Religion

The framers realized that one must be able to exercise his or her religion in order to have freedom of religion. The Constitution was designed to prevent the intrusion by Congress into state and local church affairs. Christians who have never learned the Christian history of the United States have ignorantly and complacently gone along with this deliberate rewriting of American judicial history. These infidels spoke of separation of church and state, which has been considered the greatest myth in history, but what they were really after was the separation of God and state, the separation of God's law and state, and (if they could achieve it) the separation of Christians and state. They wanted Christians to disenfranchise themselves voluntarily, and to achieve this, they invented a new slogan: "the separation of church and state."[10]

The doctrine of separation of church and state is a modern development. In primitive society, the patriarch was both priest and temporal ruler. And in most ancient communities, the priest was also king and judge. Theocracy was a government of priests. In the

American colonies, church and state were closely related, but the Founders of the federal and most of the state governments were careful to distinguish exactly the business of civil government from that of religion, and to settle the just bounds that lie between the one and the other. Any religion other than God's law degrades government because only God's perfect law provides for a perfect government.

The strict separation of church and state did not exist prior to the age of enlightenment. It is, however, a mainstay of Freemasonry.[11] Separation of church and state is a Masonic goal that dates back to the framers of the Constitution and the Bill of Rights. Freemasons have defended this concept throughout American history.[12]

The Danger of the Union of Church and State

When the courts are Christian, the church has jurisdiction over its members. In fact, I would go so far as to say that the church has primary jurisdiction over its members. When the state courts are corrupt, the church offers a refuge for those seeking justice. A Christian civilization means more than converting the state so that it will follow the dictates of God's law. All institutions must be guided by biblical law. Individuals, families, and churches are not to turn jurisdiction over to the state for security. The church does not relax its duties in society because the state becomes more Christian. There is always the danger of accommodation by the church, becoming part of the status quo because Christians have won some political battles.[13] Church historian Philip Schaff warns us by mentioning the corrupting influences of pagan Rome on the church:

> But the elevation of Christianity as the religion of the State presents also an opposite aspect to our contemplation. It involved great risk of degeneracy to the church. The Roman state, with its laws, institutions, and usages, was still deeply rooted in heathenism, and could not be transformed by a magical stroke. The Christianizing of the State amounted therefore in great measure to a paganizing and secularizing of the church. The world overcame the Church, as much as the church overcame the

world, and the temporal gain of Christianity was in many respects cancelled by spiritual loss. The mass of the Roman Empire was baptized only with water, not with the Spirit and fire of the gospel, and it smuggled heathen manners and practices into the sanctuary under a new name.[14]

Philip Schaff gave the distinctive character of American Christianity in its organized social aspect and its relation to the national life, as compared with the Christianity of Europe. He wrote that although the American history has its roots in Europe, the American relationship of church and state differed from all previous relationships in Europe and the colonial period of its history.

The relationship of church and state in the United States secures full liberty of religious thought, speech, and action, within the limits of the public peace and order. This, according to Philip Schaff, made persecution impossible. In the Protestant states of Europe, the civil government protects and supports the church, but at the expense of her dignity and independence, and deprives her of the power of self-government. In America the state had no right whatsoever to interfere with the affairs of the church, her doctrine, discipline, worship, and the appointment of ministers. It would be a great calamity if religion were to become a subject to our ever-changing politics.[15]

Christians all over the world in the mid-eighteenth century still believed that it was necessary for the state to finance the church. This economically placed the church under the state to some degree. Christians, then as now, did not understand that the state is a ministry of God for the suppression of evil—a covenant institution that is supposed to impose exclusively negative sanctions. By making the state into an organization like the family or Church—an institution imposing positive sanctions—Christians created a perverse institution that was considered a blessing yet it was a curse in disguise, a wolf in sheep's clothing. And it it still is today (fortunately, it is a nearly bankrupt wolf).[16]

This powerful state has always been a threat to the existence and influence of the church. Whether the threat be Nazism, communism, or humanism, a state that is hostile to religion will always attempt to push the church toward forced irrelevancy.[17] That is why the Nazi regime intended to destroy Christianity in Germany, if it could, and substitute the old paganism of the early tribal Germanic gods and the new paganism of the Nazi extremists. As Martin Bormann, one of the men closest to Hitler, said publicly in 1941, "National Socialism and Christianity are irreconcilable."[18] In his book *Hitler's Cross*, Erwin W. Lutzer writes:

> This uneasy relationship between church and state (sometimes cozy, sometimes competitive, and often corrupt) did not end with the Reformation of 1517. Even today the church of Europe (both Catholic and Protestant) is supported through taxes. Of course the so-called golden rule applies: whoever has the gold has the rule! The marriage of church and state is always detrimental to the mission of the church. Either the church will change its message to accommodate the state's political agenda, or the political rulers will use the church to their own ends. Regardless, the purity of the church is compromised. This unholy unity contributed to the paralysis of the church during the Hitler era. At the very moment when the church should have been condemning the politics of the day with one unified voice, the church found its existence dependent upon the goodwill of the state. The church had a history of allegiance to its militaristic Prussian heroes. In the fourth century Constantine had the cross of Christ emblazoned on the shields of his soldiers; in the twentieth century, the Nazis wrapped the Cross in the swastika, making the cross a weapon to further Hitler's agenda.[19]

Constantine imposed a top-down state religion on the disintegrating Roman Empire. The Edict of Milan in AD 313 secured for Christianity many privileges and guaranteed the right of all to profess the faith, removing any legal disabilities they might suffer in consequence.[20] Numerous freedoms were granted to Christians, including the restoration of status lost because of a conscientious objection to certain pagan practices, freedom of assembly and worship, and restitution for the confiscation of land and other property.

The church was also recognized as a corporation—it was authorized to own property.[21] Constantine's reign, however, came on the heels of an already established Christian revival throughout the Empire. Even persecution could not stop the growth of God's kingdom.[22] Despite persecution, Christianity had grown to such a degree that it was now considered a threat to the state.[23] In time, Constantine went beyond these basic freedoms that set the stage for Theodosius and a state-imposed pyramid society. Rushdoony points out:

> Christianity represented strength, and Constantine believed in strength; it represented the power of God, and Constantine believed in the power of God as a Roman. As Constantine saw it, the function and calling of the church was to revivify the Roman Empire and to establish on a sound basis the genius of the emperor. Constantine was respectful, kindly, and patient with the church, but in all this he saw the church still as an aspect of the Empire, however central a bulwark. The evidence indicates that he saw himself somewhat as Eusebius.... Even as God was sovereign and monarch over all in heaven, so Constantine was sovereign and monarch on earth. Eusebius wrote, "Thus, as he was the first to proclaim to all the sole sovereignty of God, so he saw himself as sole sovereign of the Roman world, extended his authority over the whole human race."[24]

In time, the Eastern church (which refers to those churches that developed in the eastern half of the Roman Empire) "gladly surrendered herself to the care and protection" of the state.[25] While the state should have a protective function regarding the church, the church does not surrender herself to the state, giving up its jurisdiction and rights given by God. The church has its own courts, rulers, and jurisdiction. That is why Paul teaches how the church would handle individual problems between believers.

Dare any of you, having a matter against another, go to law

before the unrighteous, and not before the saints? Do you not know that the saints will judge the world? And if the world will be judged by you, are you unworthy to judge the smallest matters? Do you not know that we shall judge angels? How much more, things that pertain to this life? If then you have judgments concerning things pertaining to this life, do you appoint those who are least esteemed by the church to judge? I say this to your shame. Is it so, that there is not a wise man among you, not even one, who will be able to judge between his brethren? But brother goes to law against brother, and that before unbelievers!

Now therefore, it is already an utter failure for you that you go to law against one another. Why do you not rather accept wrong? Why do you not rather let yourselves be cheated? (1 Corinthians 6:1–7)

The state has set up a legal system in which disagreements can be resolved in courts, but Paul declares that the church should not have to go to a state court to resolve their differences. As Christians, we have both the Holy Spirit and the mind of Christ, so why should we turn to those who are unlikely to be sensitive to Christian values or who would hold the church in contempt? Paul tells us we need to realize that someday believers will judge the world, and since we are going to judge the world, we need to resolve these disputes among ourselves instead of going to judges who do not respect the church.

Besides the jury and judge are likely to be non-Christians, and these lawsuits harm the cause of Christ and make the church look foolish, causing unbelievers to focus on the weaknesses of the church rather than on Jesus Christ. The basis for going to court is often revenge, which should never be a Christian motive anyhow. Paul makes it clear that there should be people in the church who are wise enough to decide on legal issues instead of suing one another right in front of unbelievers. Paul was simply imitating what the Lord Jesus Christ had already said about this issue (see Matthew 18:15–17).

The Whole Community Is Responsible

Just like the Israelites, when a crime was committed and the criminal caught, the whole community was held responsible. God wanted His children in the whole community to have a sense of responsibility for what was going on around them and to resolve all situations that were harmful to the community. It was the Levitical priests, whom the Lord had chosen to minister before Him and pronounce blessings in the Lord's name, who would step forward to decide all legal and criminal cases. All of this composed a sign of what the character of the New Testament priest was to be when handling legal matters in the church:

> One witness shall not rise against a man concerning any iniquity or any sin that he commits; by the mouth of two or three witnesses the matter shall be established. (Deuteronomy 19:15)

> Then the Levitical priests must step forward, for the Lord your God has chosen them to minister before Him and to pronounce blessings in the Lord's name. They are to decide all legal and criminal cases. (Deuteronomy 21:5 NLT)

The Western church maintained its own courts because of rampart paganism in the legal system. Administratively and institutionally, the Eastern church "merged with the empire to form with it but one politico-ecclesiastical organism and acknowledged the emperor's right to administer her."[26] When Christianity became the religion of the Empire under Constantine, the church gladly closed down her courts and gave everything over to the transformed Christian courts of the state. Thus, the checks and balances of church courts and state courts was lost in the East, and this led in practice to a social monism, a viewpoint that eventually led to one ultimate principle.

In the West, because the church continued to exist in a pagan environment, she maintained her own courts, which continually discipled and checked the actions of the state courts.[27] Even when the state is Christian and its courts function on a Christian basis, the church must maintain itself as a complimentary government. The church's courts should function regardless of the spiritual condition of the state. In a nutshell, the purpose of the New England colonies was, with respect to church and state, twofold: First, to establish the true and free church, free of the control of the state, free to be a coworker in terms of the kingdom of God, to establish God's Zion on earth. And secondly, to establish godly Christian state magistrates as ordained by God.28

God Uses Human Rulers

When trying to find the type of civil government that is most pleasing to God, and one that is also appropriate for every nation, it is important to note that the church does not seek to overthrow the government by violent means. Power and promotion come from God Almighty and He controls every aspect of world history (see Psalm 75:4–7). That is why our Savior said to Pilate, "You could have no power at all against Me unless it had been given you from above" (John 19:11).

The Psalmist calls rulers "gods" because they represent God and Paul calls them "God's ministers" because they are His agents. Paul stated that the government is established by God, but how that government will affect Christians depends upon the attitude and conduct of the Christians who live under the rule of that government. If Christians are walking in obedience to the will of God, then the governments "are God's agents working for their good." But if Christians are not walking in the path of God's will, then the government becomes God's agent of punishment. Therefore, Christians get the kind of government they deserve.

But what if Christians find themselves under a government that is evil, corrupt, and cruel against Christians? How should we react then? The Word of God doesn't give Christians the liberty to complain or to disobey our governments, unless of course they contradict the Word of God. The Word does, however, impose on us to pray for our government. If we humble ourselves and pray, God will hear our prayers and bring about the change that will ensure the conditions that will be conducive for the gospel to be preached. Why? Paul gives us the answer in writing to Timothy:

> For this is good and acceptable in the sight of God our Savior, who desires all men to be saved and to come to the knowledge of the truth. For there is one God and one Mediator between God and men, the Man Christ Jesus. (1 Timothy 2:3–5)

The apostle Peter, writing to God's chosen people who were living as foreigners in the provinces of Rome, reiterates respecting human authority—whether the king as head of state or the officials he has appointed:

> Therefore submit yourselves to every ordinance of man for the Lord's sake, whether to the king as supreme, or to governors, as to those who are sent by him for the punishment of evildoers and for the praise of those who do good. (1 Peter 2:13–14)

And Paul again says,

> Therefore I exhort first of all that supplications, prayers, intercessions, and giving of thanks be made for all men, for kings and all who are in authority, that we may lead a quiet and peaceable life in all godliness and reverence. (1 Timothy 2:1–2)

We can't preach the gospel without freedom. As an example of this, just look at North Korea and other countries that restrict and persecute Christians. This is one of the reasons why the apostle Paul also admonished us to pray for those in authority, so that we can live peaceful and godly lives in every sphere of life. Paul knew that peace can only be realized through the life-transforming gospel of Jesus Christ. But for the gospel to be preached without hindrance we need to make intercessions for kings and all those God has put in authority. This is the element of self-government. Peace with God brings peace with others.

God designed the civil government as the arm that administers the affairs of the divine government among the nations. Jefferson's assertion that "rulers receive their just powers from the consent of the governed" is true but not the whole truth because rulers are God's ministers. They represent Him and their authority comes only from Him. The family, the church, and the state are authorities ordained by God to perform tasks in their prescribed jurisdictions.

The family has no authority or power to perform the tasks commissioned by God for the church and state. The church is not called to usurp either the family or the state in their appointed tasks; likewise, the state has no authority over families or churches as they perform their God-ordained duties. Of course, if a family member commits murder, is tried and convicted, then the state is duty-bound to execute or imprison the murderer. But the church has a task to perform as well: it must "restore the brother" and seek God's guidance in resolving conflicts within the church (see Matthew 18).

The Main Role of Civil Government

Since the fall of humanity, the state is to be the judge "that does not bear the sword in vain" (Romans 13:4). It is God's minister that takes vengeance (punishment, justice) to those who do wrong and to encourage those who do good service (see 2 Peter 2:13–14). Jesus Christ is the center around which the family, the church, and the state revolve, and His providential government is simply the blueprint for developing and perfecting these divine institutions. Another answer is given by the Holy Spirit through David in 2 Samuel:

> The Spirit of the Lord spoke by me, and His word was on my tongue. The God of Israel said, the Rock of Israel spoke to me: "He who rules over men must be just, ruling in the fear of God. And he shall be like the light of the morning when the sun rises, a morning without clouds, like the tender grass springing out of the earth, by clear shining after rain." (2 Samuel 23:2–4)

The ruler must be just and must rule in the fear of God. Today in the United States and Great Britain, Christians have allowed themselves to be influenced by party principles more than divine principles. God does not promise to bless a Republican, a Democrat, a Conservative, or

Labor; He only promises to bless a government whose leaders are just, ruling righteously and in the fear of God. Christians who respect God's principles should not vote for any man or woman who is not just and God-fearing, no matter what party that leader belongs to.

This same idea was prophetically pointed out by revivalist Charles Finney, who reminded Christians of this important lesson:

> The Church must take right ground in regard to politics…. The time has come that Christians must vote for honest men and take consistent ground in politics…. Christians have been exceedingly guilty in this matter. But the time has come when they must act differently…. God cannot sustain this free and blessed country which we love and pray for unless the Church will take right ground…. It seems sometimes as if the foundations of the nation are becoming rotten, and Christians seem to act as if they think God does not see what they do in politics. But I tell you He does see it, and He will bless or curse this nation according to the course Christians take in politics.[29]

If the church ignores God's requirements and votes for men who are morally unworthy, we are inviting God to make those men, if elected, and to be agents of His judgment against the very people who voted them into office. The question is, Where do we find leaders that are just, righteous, and God-fearing in our generation? We still suffer from Constantine's decision of combining church and state, and his legacy still remains in European nations. But as far as the Bible is concerned, church and state are indeed separate. We might apply Old Testament principles, but we must remember that the two institutions are not directly compatible.

Endnotes

[1] H. B. Clark, *Clark's Biblical Law* (Portland, OR: Binfords & Mort, 1943), 57–58. Cited in Ted R. Weiland, *Bible Law Versus The United States Constitution: The Christian Perspective* (Scottsbluff, NE: Mission to Israel Ministries, 2012), 234.

[2] Foster, *James Mitchell Reformation Principles Stated and Applied* (Chicago and New York: F. H. Revell, 1890), 19.

[3] Gary DeMar, *Ruler of Nations* (Dominion Press, 1987), 233.

[4] Ibid.

[5] Ibid., 234.

[6] Ibid.

[7] Ibid.

[8] Ibid.

[9] Ibid., 236.

[10] Ibid., 234.

[11] Ted R. Weiland, *Bible Law Versus The United States Constitution*, 236.

[12] Henry C. Clausen, *Masons Who Helped Shape Our Nation* (San Diego, CA: Neyenesh Printers, 1976), 67–71. Cited in Ted R. Weiland, *Bible Law Versus The United States Constitution*, 234.

[13] Quoted by Gary DeMar and Peter Leithart, 309.

[14] Ibid.

[15] Verna M. Hall, *The Christian History of the Constitution of the United States of America*, 36–38. The excerpts are from *Church and State in the United States* by Philip Schaff, 1888.

[16] Gary North, *Political Polytheism: The Myth of Pluralism* (Institute for Christian Economics, 1989), 526.

[17] Dr. Erwin W. Lutzer, *Hitler's Cross: The Revealing Story of How the Cross of Christ Was Used as a Symbol of the Nazi Agenda* (Chicago, IL: Moody Publishers, 1995), 19.

[18] William L. Shirer, *The Rise and Fall of the Third Reich: A History of Nazi Germany* (Published by Book Club Associates by Arrangement with Secker & Warburg, Ltd., 1959, 1960), 240.

[19] Dr. Erwin W. Lutzer, *Hitler's Cross*, 21–22.

[20] Gary DeMar and Peter Leithart, *The Reduction of Christianity*, 307. Cited in Charles Norris Cochrane, *Christianity and Classical Culture* (New York: Oxford University Press, 1980), 178.

[21] Ibid.

[22] Gary DeMar and Peter Leithart, *The Reduction of Christianity*, 307.

[23] Marcellus Kik, *Church and State: The Story of Two Kingdoms* (New York: Thomas Nelson & Sons, 1963) 34. Cited in Gary DeMar and Peter Leithart, *The Reduction of Christianity*, 307.

[24] R. J. Rushdoony, *The One and Many: Studies in the Philosophy of Order and Ultimacy* (Nutley, NJ: Craig Press, 1971), 149. Cited and quoted in Gary DeMar and Peter Leithart, 307–308.

[25] Alexander Schmemann, *Church World: Mission* (Crestwood, NY: St. Vladimir's Seminary Press, 1979), 37. Cited in Gary DeMar and Peter Leithart, 307–308.

[26] Ibid.

[27] Quoted by Gary DeMar and Peter Leithart, 308, in James B. Jordan, *Workshop on Church Law and Government Supplement to The Geneva Review* (Tyler, Texas, February, 1985).

[28] R. J. Rushdoony, *This Independent Republic: Studies in the Nature and Meaning of American History* (Fairfax, Virginia: Thoburn Press, 1964, 1978), 97–98.

[29] Charles G. Finney, *Lectures on Revivals of Religion* (New York: Fleming H. Revell Company, 1868, first published in 1835), Lecture XV, 281–282.

CHAPTER 19

Christian Origins of the United States Constitution: Part 1

The First Charter of Virginia that was drafted on April 10, 1606, is a document from King James I of England to the Virginia Company to assign land rights to the colonists for the stated purpose of propagating the gospel of Jesus Christ:

> We, greatly commending and graciously accepting of their desires for the furtherance of so noble a work, which may, by the providence of Almighty God, hereafter tend to the glory of His Divine Majesty, in propagating of the Christian religion to such people, as yet live in darkness and miserable ignorance of true knowledge and worship of God, and may in time bring the Infidels and savages, living in those Parts to human Civility, and to a settled and quite Government...[1]

Fundamental Orders of Connecticut

In 1635–1636, settlements were planted at Windsor, Wethersfield, and Hartford, Connecticut. In 1637 the three towns assumed the control of their own affairs. And on January 14, 1639, they drew up the constitution known as the Fundamental Orders of Connecticut, which has been considered the first full-fledged written constitution that created a government in the Western tradition known to history.[2] It was written by Thomas Hooker, who reportedly founded the colony of Connecticut in 1639. Its longevity is also remarkable. Whereas other documents in the colonies were later modified or replaced, the Connecticut Constitution remained intact up to and well beyond the adoption of the national Constitution, exactly 150 years later.[3]

It reads in part:

> For as much as it hath pleased Almighty God by the wise disposition of His divine providence so to order and dispose of things that we the Inhabitants and Residents of Windsor, Hartford and Wethersfield are now cohabiting and dwelling in and upon the River of Connecticut and the lands thereunto adjoining; and well knowing where a people are gathered together the Word of God requires that to maintain the peace and union of such a people there should be an orderly and decent Government established according to (Almighty) God, to order and dispose of the affairs of the people at all seasons as occasion shall require; do therefore associate and conjoin ourselves to be as one Public State or Commonwealth; and do for ourselves and our successors and such as shall be adjoined to us at any time hereafter, enter into Combination and Confederation together, to maintain and preserve the liberty and purity of the Gospel of our Lord Jesus Christ which we now profess, as also, the discipline of the Churches, which according to the truth of the said Gospel is now practiced amongst us; as also in our civil affairs to be guided and governed according to such Laws, Rules, Orders and Decrees as shall be made, ordered, and decreed as followeth.[4]

The Fundamental Agreement of the Colony of New Haven, Connecticut, 1639, Agreement also attested that early Americans formed Christian governments designed around God's laws. It stated:

> We all agree that the Scriptures hold forth a perfect rule for the direction and government of all men in duties which they are to perform to God and to man, as well in families and commonwealth as in matters of the Church; so likewise in all public officers which concern civil order, as choice of magistrates and officers, making and repealing laws, dividing allotments of inheritance, and all things like nature, we will, all of us, be ordered by the rules which the Scripture holds forth; and we agree that such persons may be entrusted with such matters of government

as are described in Exodus 18:21 and Deuteronomy 1:13 with Deuteronomy 17:15 and 1 Corinthians 6:1, 6 & 7.[5]

The 1636 agreement makes no reference to any other government as it source of authority:

> It is worthy to note that this document contains none of the conventional references to a dread sovereign or a gracious King, nor the slightest allusion to the British or any other government outside of Connecticut itself.[6]

The Mayflower Compact

This followed the first republican document known as The Mayflower Compact (covenant) that was drawn up on a shipboard off Cape Cod on November 11, 1620. It was intended not only as a basis for the government of the colony on the absence of a patent, but also according to Bradford, as an effect to "discontented and mutinous speeches" of some of the company, so that when they landed "they would use their own liberty; for none had the power to command them, the patent they had being for Virginia, and for New England, which belonged to another government, with which the Virginia company had nothing to do."[7] It has been considered a predecessor to the United States Constitution. It states in part:

> In the name of God, Amen, We, whose names are underwritten, the loyal subjects of our dread sovereign lord King James, by the grace of God, of Great Britain, France and Ireland, King Defender of the Faith, etc., having undertaken for the glory of God and advancement of the Christian faith, and the honor of our king and country, a voyage to plant the first colony in the northern parts of Virginia; do by these presents, solemnly and mutually in the presence of God and one another, covenant and combine ourselves together into a civil body politic, for our better ordering and preservation and furtherance of other ends aforesaid and by virtue hereof to enact, constitute, and frame, such just and equal laws, ordinances, acts, constitutions, and offices, from time to time, as shall be thought most meet and convenient for the

general use of the Colony, unto which we promise all due submission and obedience. In witness whereof we have here under scribed our names at Cape Cod, 11th of November…A.D. 1620.[8]

The New England Confederation, which was put into effect on May 19, 1643, (composed of Massachusetts, Connecticut, New Plymouth, and New Haven) established a union of like-minded civil bodies.

> Whereas we all came into these parts of America with one and the same end and aim, namely, to advance the Kingdom of our Lord Jesus Christ and to enjoy the liberties of the Gospel in purity with peace; and whereas in our settling (by a wise providence of God) we are further dispersed upon the sea coasts and rivers than was first intended, so that we cannot (according to our desire) with convenience communicate in one Government, and Jurisdiction; and whereas we live encompassed with people of several Nations, and strange languages, which hereafter may prove injurious to us and our posterity…[9]

The Main Objective of Drafting the Constitution

It is true that America is the only country in the world founded by believers in Jesus Christ who made a covenant with God dedicating a new nation to God Almighty. Because of this covenant, the nation has been blessed with systems of law and economics that have made the country both rich and free. But when we ponder on all of this, we need to ask ourselves, What was the real objective of those who originally drafted the Constitution?

The founders of America (the Puritans and Pilgrims) intended to create a "city on a hill," a nation governed by God's laws, giving glory to God and spreading the gospel across the world. The original intent of the settlers and founders of the New World was to form a godly nation. In order to create a godly society, however, they made sure that the government would promote the teachings of Jesus Christ, not paganism or atheism. It was therefore forbidden for any but the followers of Christ to hold political offices.

The Delaware Constitution of 1776 established a godly state by requiring in Article 22:

> Every person who shall be chosen a member of either house, or appointed to any office or place of trust...shall...make and subscribe the following declaration, to wit: "I_____, do profess faith in God the Father, and in Jesus Christ His only Son, and in the Holy Spirit, one God Blessed for evermore; and I acknowledge the Holy Scriptures of the Old and New Testaments to be given by divine inspiration."[10]

This proves that it was only the followers of Christ who could hold any public office under the Delaware Constitution. The Delaware oath of office is known as a "test oath," because it requires the one swearing to affirm—either explicitly or implicitly—a particular set of religious beliefs. This was the case in virtually all of the states, in varying degrees of doctrinal specificity. It was done because the Bible was understood to require it. Legislators used to insert biblical references in the margins of the statute books to prove the validity of their laws. For example:

> Pennsylvania Frame of Government, Section 10. And each member (of the legislature), before he takes his seat, shall make and subscribe the following declaration: "I do believe in one God, the Creator and Governor of the Universe, the rewarder of the good and the punisher of the wicked, and I do acknowledge the Scriptures of the Old and New Testament to be given by Divine Inspiration."[11]

These early documents, according to Gary DeMar, have several things in common:

1. They are not revolutionary documents, calling on men to overthrow the existing order through armed conflict.

2. God is acknowledged as King and Sovereign, and earthly kings must bow in submission to His revealed will.

3. The adherents of these documents came to the New World to "advance the kingdom of the Lord Jesus Christ" and not some

utopian, state-sponsored political order.

4. The Bible was accepted as the standard for an "orderly and decent government" as well as "for the discipline of churches."

5. The gospel preceded the advance of civilization.

6. The people covenanted with God before they "combined and confederated together."

7. The future depended upon faithfulness to God's commands.

8. Liberty was the fruit of a Christian world order.[12]

The Ratification of the U.S. Constitution: 1787

The constitution does not say, "The United States is a Christian nation." Historians believe the Constitution document drafted in 1787 in Philadelphia is not the biblically compatible document we have been told it is. When the Founders ratified the Constitution, they specified that "no religious test shall ever be required as a Qualification to any Office or public Trust under the United States" (Article VI, clause 3).

The first criterion for a Christian civil government is recognition of God as sovereign of the affairs of that government. Not only is Christ not recognized in the Constitution, there is no hint of God at all. The sovereign recognized in the Preamble is not God; it is the people. It is truly a covenant, but not one with God.

The U.S. Constitution bans all religious tests, which means it rejects the rule of God in Article VI, clause 3:

> The Senators and Representatives before mentioned, and the Members of the several State Legislatures, and all executive and judicial Officers, both of the United States, and of the several States, shall be bound by Oath or Affirmation, to support this Constitution; but no religious Test shall ever be required as a Qualification to any Office or public Trust under the United States.

What is remarkable is that Article VI, prohibiting any religious test for public office, was not only "historically unprecedented and was a radical departure from the established pattern of religious discrimination throughout the world at the time, but it was at variance with the prevailing patterns and practices in all of the original colonies, and during their early years of statehood."[13]

Henry Abbot recognized that those who are hostile to Article VI, clause 3, suspected what might happen: "If there be no religious test required, pagans, deists, and Mahometans might obtain offices among us, and that the senators and representatives might all be pagan."[14] He goes on to write, "We must understand what this means: It means that civil officers are not under an oath to the God of the Bible. It means that in the exercise of various offices, civil magistrates are bound by an oath to a different god."[15] That god is the American people, considered as an autonomous sovereign who possesses original and final earthly jurisdiction.[16]

Charles Pinckney, who introduced the clause, clearly recognized that Article VI was a break with the Christian covenants of over a thousand years. It was "a provision the world will expect from the establishment of a system founded on republican principles and in an age so liberal and enlightened as the present."[17]

According to some interpreters, this provision was to ensure that no religion could make the claim of being the official, national religion, such as England had done. But the framers' goal was that each citizen of the republic was free to pursue God and to order their relationships according to the dictates of their own conscience without government interference.

John Adams (1735–1826), the first vice president and second president of the United States, wrote, "Our Constitution was made only for a moral and religious people. It is wholly inadequate to the government of any other."[18] And again, "Rights come from God not the State—you have rights antecedent to all earthy governments; rights that cannot be repealed or restrained by human laws; rights derived from the Great Legislator of the Universe."[19]

Patrick Henry (1736–1799), another Founder who is well remembered for his "give me liberty, or give me death" speech, also noted that "the Constitution is not an instrument for the government to restrain the people; it's an instrument for the people to restrain the government."[20] Though this quote has been widely attributed to Patrick Henry, it has not been sourced to any document before the 1990s, and it appears to be at odds with his beliefs as he opposed the U.S. Constitution because he feared that it threatened the rights of the states, as well as the freedoms of individuals.

Others believe that those who ratified the original document had as their objective a state in which every citizen would be free to pursue his or her own legitimate interests without interference from other citizens or the government, but with the protection of the government and its officers. They viewed such a state as being possible only under the sovereign protection and favor of Almighty God. They wanted the basic charter of the new nation to agree so exactly with the purposes and principles of government ordained by the Holy Scriptures.

The world's best example of how to maintain Christian self-government and achieve voluntary union among diverse individuals occurs in America between 1620 and 1789, from the Pilgrims through Patriots, and from Mayflower Compact to the Constitution. As Verna M. Hall has noted:

> The knowledge of how to maintain individual freedom and union at the same time did not come about easily or in a short time. It took centuries for Christians to think through the practical application of their biblical precepts. Even after 1620 when the Pilgrims arrived in America, one hundred and fifty more years were needed for Christian Self-Government with Union to permeate the thirteen colonies to the degree necessary to enable these diverse colonies to work together voluntarily through the seven long years of the War for Independence. Never in the history of the world has there been such an example of Christian voluntary union in civil affairs as was exhibited by the colonists between 1775 and 1783. This costly experience laid the groundwork for the adoption of the Constitution six years later in 1789.... No wonder, as George Bancroft says, kings sat still in awe, and nations turned to watch the issue. Through the

American Constitution, the church was free from the dictates of the state for the first time in history; the American state (the body politic) was established for the protection of the church---a concept entirely new to the world, yet longed for by Christians throughout the centuries.[21]

God gave this honor to America. The church was expected to be a blessing to the state by continuing to raise up generations of men and women capable of maintaining the Christian republic.

Alexis de Tocqueville

In 1830 the government of France sent Alexis de Tocqueville (1805–1859), a well respected lawyer, political thinker, and historian who is best known for his book on democracy in America. He studied the society, the beliefs, and the prisons of the United States of America to find out why there was so little crime and so few prisons. After several years of study, he ended up writing about the American continent and character in his famous book *The Democracy of the United States* in 1840. During his study from the earliest historical and legislative records of New England, he said,

> The new early settlers did not derive their incorporation from the head of the empire, although they did not deny its supremacy; they constituted a society of their own accord. They perpetually exercised the rights of sovereignty; they named their magistrates, concluded peace or war, made police regulations and enacted laws, as if their allegiance was due only to God.[22]

He further wrote about the reason for America's greatness as a nation and her low crime rate during that time:

> I sought for the greatness of the United States in her commodious harbors, her ample rivers, her fertile fields, and boundless forests—and it was not there. I sought for it in her rich mines, her vast world commerce, her public school system and in her institutions of higher learning—and it was not there. I looked for it in her democratic Congress and her matchless Constitution

—and it was not there. Not until I went into the churches of America and her pulpits flame with righteousness did I understand the secret of her genius and power. America is great because America is good, and if America ever ceases to be good, America will cease to be great![23]

This observant French lawyer further recognized the contributions that Christianity made to American individual liberty:

The Americans combine the notions of Christianity and of liberty so intimately in their minds, that it is impossible to make them conceive the one without the other…. Upon my arrival in the United States, the religious aspect of the country was the first thing that struck my attention; and the longer I stayed there, the more did I perceive the great political consequences resulting from this state of things, to which I was unaccustomed. In France I had almost always seen the spirit of religion and the spirit of freedom pursuing courses diametrically opposed to each other; but in America I found that they were intimately united, and that they reigned in common over the same country.[24]

The Preamble to the Constitution

The Preamble to the Constitution of the United States gives the purpose for which it was written, as recorded by Bruce and Esther Findlay in their well-written book *Your Rugged Constitution:*

We the people of the United States in order to form a more perfect union, establish justice, insure domestic tranquility, provide for the common defense, promote the general welfare, and secure the blessings of liberty to ourselves and our posterity, do ordain and establish this Constitution for the United States of America.[25]

These words, according to Bruce and Esther, are extremely important to all American citizens. They go on to say, "In many countries, governments are not run by all of the people, but by small groups of people for their own selfish purposes. In the famous

Preamble to the Constitution, we the people of the United States proclaim to the world that our government belongs to the people, is run by the people, and exists for the good of the people."[26]

But Ted Weiland, in his well-researched book *Bible Law Versus The United States Constitution: The Christian Perspective*, has different viewpoint that needs contemplating. He writes:

> When the Constitutional framers spoke of justice in the Preamble, they were not speaking of the Preamble, or of the justice that originates with God, but rather justice that originated with themselves. Otherwise, they would have followed the example of our Christian forefathers in the 1600s and early 1700s and cited, or at least mentioned, the laws of God upon which their justice was based.... In contrast with New Haven 1639 Agreement (we all agree that the Scriptures hold forth a perfect rule for the direction of government), one of the purposes for this new Constitution was to form a more perfect union. What the framers had in mind was a union more perfect than that of the Articles of Confederation. However because the Articles of Confederation and the Constitution were both based upon the imperfect laws of man, both were a far cry from the governments of the New England Colonies.[27]

The authors of *The Search for Christian America* address some key issues in regard to the worldview of the framers of the Constitution, whom history defines as the "Founding Fathers." It is difficult for modern Americans to recapture the religious spirit of the country's great early leaders—George Washington, Thomas Jefferson, Benjamin Franklin, and their colleagues. The difficulty arises because these brilliant leaders, surely the most capable generation of statesmen ever to appear in America, were at once genuinely religious but not specifically Christian.

Virtually all these great men had a profound belief in the "Supreme Judge of the world" and in the "protection of Divine Providence," to use the words of the Declaration of Independence. Yet only a few believed in the orthodox teachings of traditional Christianity—that, for example, Christ's death atoned for sin, that the Bible was unique revelation from God, or that the miracles recorded in the Scripture actually happened.[28] They do list a few exceptions—John Witherspoon, Patrick Henry (who reportedly "smelled a rat" in Philadelphia and who opposed the ratification of the Constitution), and John Jay—but the major figures were not Trinitarians. This is certainly true of Jefferson, John Adams, Benjamin Franklin, and Madison. And it is also probably true of Washington too.[29] If they were not Christians, then did they change the covenant the Puritans had previously made with God?

Again Ted R. Weiland presents clear and well-substantiated views of how the Constitutional framers abandoned their original covenant with God: "You cannot have any civil government anywhere in the world without an establishment of religion. All laws represent morality. So it is inescapable that when you enact a law you are enacting your moral and religious faith."[30]

America was founded on Christian principles and, during the seventeenth century, it was a predominately Christian nation. Many historians concur, however, that during the eighteenth century America departed from the supreme law of God and the "we the people" became the national replacement of God. The Preamble states:

> WE THE PEOPLE of the United States, in order to form a more perfect union, establish justice, ensure domestic tranquility, provide for the common defense, promote the general welfare, and secure the blessings of liberty to ourselves and our posterity, do ordain and establish this Constitution for the United States of America.[31]

An Apostate Covenant

Article VI, clause 3, of the Constitution judicially closed the door to any transcendent god beyond the political order itself. The Constitution is therefore an apostate covenant, a wholly new god is ordained in it, a god acknowledged by the framers in order to ordain it and ratify it—the American people.[32] R. J. Rushdoony gives five points regarding the role of government and religion:

1. Law in every culture is religious in origin.
2. The source of law is the god of that society.
3. In any society, any change of law is an explicit or implicit change of religion.
4. No disestablishment of religion as such is possible in any society.
5. There can no tolerance in a law-system for another religion.[33]

Rushdoony observes that behind every system of law there is a god. "If the source of law is the individual, then the individual is the god of that system…if the source of law is our court then the court is our god. If there is no higher law beyond man, then man is his own god…. When you choose your authority, you choose your god, and when you look for your law, there is your god."[34]

While the Preamble has received considerable attention, Article VI, clause 3, has almost been universally ignored. Despite the silence of the commentators and historians, there is no single covenantal cause of the suppression of Christianity in America in the modern world that has had greater impact than the test oath clause.

It is this clause that judicially established the anti-Christian nature of the Constitutional experiment. While "we the people" is viewed by some Constitutional scholars as having no legal impact, the oath clause is so sacred that it receives little attention. Its legitimacy and normality is assumed by everyone who reads it. This fact testifies to the impact of natural law philosophy in the history of Christendom. Ideas have consequences—in this case, disastrous ones. But few people recognize the cause of the disasters. Like the Israelites in Egypt, Christians would rather serve as slaves in the household of God's enemies than serve those who profess biblical religion. The politics of Christian envy begins with Article VI, clause 3.[35]

The Constitution is a broken covenant. To preserve its judicial continuity, a national covenant must establish the Bible as the law of the land. The Bible is a permanent covenant document. Its stipulations do not change. A nation's civil courts must therefore enforce the Bible's civil laws. Any statute not in conformity to the Bible must be declared unconstitutional. An oath of allegiance to the national government is a promise to uphold the national constitution, which must automatically be an oath to uphold and enforce the Bible.

A national constitution is required by God to serve as the bylaws of the ultimate source of legitimate civil law—the Bible. A constitution's preamble is the appropriate place to declare this publicly. The preamble should be a nation's declaration of absolute dependence on the Trinitarian God of the Bible; it should therefore declare the Bible as the unchanging law of the land. Furthermore, it should declare this law as being immune to any subsequent alteration. Thus, any public rejection of this judicial standard would be identifiable as a breaking of the national covenant.

The Constitutional Convention

Christian historian and economist Gary North asserts that the Constitution was a rejection of the rule of God for the rule of man. What was foremost in the mind of the framers was not Christianity. The Constitutional Convention began as a convention to propose changes to the Articles of Confederation, which would be reported back to Congress and voted on by them. The Convention did not create a new form of government or a Christian civil covenant. The argument Gary North presents is that 1787 was indeed a *coup detat*. But this coup had a side to it that the history books refuse to mention— religion.

The Constitutional Convention was a successful attempt by a small group of men whose most eloquent leaders had long-since rejected the doctrine of the Trinity. The voters were Christians; the Convention leaders were what two decades later would be called Unitarians. They had assimilated their theology not from the creeds of the nation's churches but from dissenting Whig political theory—Newtonian to the core—and from the secret rites of the Masonic lodges to which many of them belonged. What the Constitutional Convention was all about was a national political transformation by a group of men who really believed in secrecy and oaths.[36]

Americans think of the Philadelphia Convention as the place where all the giants of the Revolutionary War era met to settle the fate of the republic experiment. Some giants did show up; not all of them did. The list of distinguished Americans certain not to come was large. Only one of the great diplomats of the Revolution, Benjamin Franklin, would be there; John Jay of New York and Henry Laurens of South Carolina had not been chosen, and Thomas Jefferson and John Adams were in Europe as ambassadors during that time. Most of the Republicans were missing. Thomas Paine was in Europe hoping to spread the gospel of republican revolution. Neither Sam Adams nor John Hancock of Massachusetts, nor Richard Henry Lee and Patrick Henry of Virginia chose to come. Henry did not come because, he said, "I smelt a rat"; the others offered no excuses.[37]

It is important to note that Henry was a dedicated, Bible-believing Christian. Sam Adams, who also refused to attend, was either a Calvinist or at least highly influenced by Calvinism.[38] John Hancock and Richard Henry Lee were both Freemasons; but Adams and Henry were not.[39]

Conclusion

The question is, Why do some Christians believe the United States Constitution is based upon biblical principles and is a great Christian document? It is primarily because those who wrote it wanted us to perceive it as a Christian document. They knew few Americans would have the time to read it or give it any serious thought. When we study its contents and compare them to Scripture, we will be astounded with what we will find. Even Benjamin Franklin predicted the document would end in despotism.[40]

The document promoted the will of the people over God's will for His people. Whatever is good and honorable about America can be traced back from the 1600s when many of the original colonies were governed by God's laws alone. Things changed when the United States ratified the Constitution. But this is hard to believe because we've been told repeatedly that is one of the most important documents in the history of humankind.

Endnotes

[1] *Select Charters and other Documents Illustrative of American History, 1606–1775*, edited with notes by William Macdonald (New York: The Macmillan Company, London, 1904), 2–3.

[2] Ibid., 60–61.

[3] Ted R. Weiland, *Bible Law Versus The United States Constitution*, cited in Mark A. Beliles, Douglas S. Anderson, *Contending for the Constitution: Recalling the Christian Influence on the Writing of the Constitution and the Biblical Basis of American Law and Liberty* (Charlottesville, VA: Providence Foundation, 2005), 95.

[4] *Select Charters and other Documents Illustrative of American History*, 60–61.

[5] Donald S. Lutz, *Colonial Origins of the American Constitution: A Documentary History* (Liberty Fund, Inc., 1998), 210.

[6] John Fiske, *The Historical Writings of John Fiske*, 12 Vols. (Boston, MA: Houghton Mifflin Company, 1902), vol. 6, 155.

[7] *Select Charters and other Documents Illustrative of American History*, 33.

[8] Bradford's *History of the Plymouth Settlement 1608–1650*, rendered into modern English by Harold Paget E. P. (New York: Dutton and Company, 1920), 75–76.

[9] *Select Charters and other Documents Illustrative of American History*, 95.

[10] Thomas T. Skillman, *The Constitutions of All the States According to the Latest Amendments* (Lexington, 1817), 181. Cited in David Barton, *The Myth of Separation: What Is the Correct Relationship Between Church and State?* (WallBuilder Press: Fifth Edition, 1992), 23.

[11] *Sources and Documents Illustrating the American Revolution, 1764–1788* and the *Formation of the Federal Constitution*, 166 (S. Morison Ed. 1923). Cited in Barton, *Myth*, 23.

[12] Gary DeMar, *Ruler of Nations* (Dominion Press, 1987), 229.

[13] James E. Woods, "No Religious Test Shall Ever Be Required: Reflections on the Bicentennial of the U.S. Constitution," Volume 29, No. 2 (Spring 1987), 201.

[14] Gary North, *Political Polytheism*, 391.

[15] Ibid.

[16] Ibid.

[17] James E. Woods, "No Religious Test Shall Ever Be Required: Reflections on the Bicentennial of the U.S. Constitution," Volume 29, No. 2 (Spring 1987), 199.

[18] Charles Frances Adams, *The Works of John Adams* (Boston: Little Brown and Company, 1856) Volume IX, 229, to the officers of the First Brigade of the Third Division of the Militia of Massachusetts on October 11, 1798.

[19] Ibid.

[20] Though this quote has been widely attributed to Patrick Henry, it has not been sourced to any document before the 1990s.

21 Verna M. Hall, *A Compilation The Christian History of the Constitution of the United States of America: Christian Self-Government with Union* (Foundation for American Christian Education, 2004), III.

22 Alexis de Tocqueville, *The Republic of the United States of America and Its Political Institutions, Reviewed and Examined*, translated by Henry Reeves, two volumes in one (New York: A. S. Barnes & Company, 1856), 37.

23 Ibid., 335.

24 Ibid.

25 Bruce Allyn Findlay and Esther (Blair) Findlay, *Your Rugged Constitution: What It Says, What It Means to Americans Today* (University Press, Second Revised, 1969), 2–3.

26 Ibid.

27 Ted R. Weiland, *Bible Law Versus The United States Constitution: The Christian Perspective* (Scottsbluff, NE: Mission to Israel Ministries, 2012), 72–73.

28 Mark A. Noll, and George M. Marsden, *The Search for Christian America* (Helmers & Howard Publishing, 1983, 1989), 72.

29 Gary North, citing Paul F. Boller Jr., *George Washington & Religion* (Dallas, Texas: Southern Methodist University Press, 1963).

30 Ted R. Weiland, *Bible Law Versus The United States Constitution*, 53. Cited in R. J. Rushdoony, *Lecture: The U.S. Constitution Changed.*

31 Accessed from *http://constitutionus.com.*

32 Gary North, *Conspiracy in Philadelphia: The Broken Covenant of the U.S. Constitution* (Draper, VA: Nicene Council.com, 2004), 322.

33 R. J. Rushdoony, *The Institutes of Biblical Law* (The Presbyterian and Reformed Publishing Company, 1973), 4–5.

34 R. J. Rushdoony, *Law and Liberty* (Fairfax, Va: Thoburn, 1971), 33.

35 Gary North, *Political Polytheism*, 410.

36 Ibid., 461.

37 Forest McDonald, *E Pluribus Unum: The Formation of the American Republic, 1776-1790* (Indianapolis: Liberty Press, 1965, 1979), 259–260. Cited in Gary North, *Political Polytheism: The Myth of Pluralism*, 415.

38 Gary North, *Political Polytheism*, 416.

39 Ronald E. Heaton, *Masonic Membership of the Founding Fathers* (Silver Spring, Maryland: Masonic Service Association, 1965, 1988), 25, 110, 88, 92. Cited in Gary North, *Political Polytheism: The Myth of Pluralism*, 416.

40 Benjamin Franklin, Ormond Seavey, ed., *Speech in the Constitutional Convention at the Conclusion of its Deliberations, Autobiography and Other Writings* (Oxford: Oxford University Press, 1998), 350.

CHAPTER 20

Christian Origins of the United States Constitution: Part 2

The Nature of an Oath

As we've already mentioned, all states required candidates to be biblical Christians in order to take the oath of office. They were not required to affirm to any kind of denomination in particular, but they had to at least be Christians. What kind of oath did they have to take to take to enter into political office? The 1828 edition of the *Webster's American Dictionary* defines an oath as:

> A solemn affirmation or declaration, made with an appeal to God for the truth of what is affirmed. The appeal to God in an oath implies that the person imprecates God's vengeance and renounces His favor if the declaration is false, or if the declaration is a promise, the person invokes the vengeance of God if he should fail to fulfill it. A false oath is called perjury.

Most everyone understands that citizenship requires an oath. The question is, To whom is the oath made? Is it made to God or to some other authority? The humanist says that the oath must be taken for the state, the people, the Constitution, or to some other natural authority, which are all man-made deities. But the Bible says that the oath must be taken to God; it must call down on the oath-taker eternal as well as temporal sanctions. When people are taking an oath of allegiance to the Crown to become British citizens, they are required to affirm to take this oath:

> I (name) swear by Almighty God that on becoming a British citizen, I will be faithful and bear true allegiance to Her Majesty

Queen Elizabeth the Second, her Heirs and Successors, according to law…[1]

Likewise, in every country where an oath of office is required, as is required in the United States by the Constitution, the oath has reference to swearing by Almighty God to abide by His covenant, invoking the curses and blessings of God for obedience and disobedience to the government.[2] Did you know that the oath of the president of the United States excludes the name of the Supreme Being? It does not appeal to God at all. It contains nothing by which presidents can be held accountable by their word. It states, "I do swear (or affirm) that I will faithfully execute the Office of President of the United States, and will to the best of my ability, preserve, protect and defend the Constitution of the United States."[3]

A True Oath

The oath of office, according to Timothy Baldwin, comes from the notion first that there is a Creator God who implements justice on earth and in life thereafter; that He rewards good and punishes evil. It comes from the belief that humankind has a tendency to be evil and will use power at the expense of the people and the individual's freedom and rights. It comes from the notion that constitutions, elections, and even threats of revolts do not adequately prevent politicians from abusing power. Therefore, an oath of office is required to ensure that political leaders will bind themselves to the supreme law of the land.

More specifically, an oath is a solemn promise made by the politician to God Almighty, where if the politician breaks his or her promise, they are calling the wrath of God's punishment upon their life in whatever proportion God deems justified. It is no wonder that federal politicians ignore their oath of office—they have no fear of God before their eyes, and they have no fear of the people either. How can we expect a person to fear people if they don't fear God?[4]

Jesus Christ is the supreme and ultimate authority, the ultimate appeal of all things. But in our Constitution, "we the people" have arrogated to ourselves this prerogative. Isn't that political atheism at its core? When the president is inaugurated into office, he shall either swear or affirm that he will uphold the Constitution. Every president after George Washington and before R. B. Hayes, who took the oath of office, never took an oath without an appeal to God, which is the the very essence of the oath. Rev. A. M. Milligan wrote President Lincoln in 1861, asking why he would not take the presidential oath in the name of God. He replied: "The relations between the Northern and Southern States are so strained I would not dare violate the letter of the Constitution. The name of God is not in that instrument."[5]

President Lincoln took the oath without an appeal to God, omitting the very essence of the oath. The Bible says, "Thou shalt fear the Lord thy God, and swear by His name" (Deuteronomy 6:13 KJV). J. M. Foster claimed that the framers of our Constitution took this Bible oath, and with the penknife of Jehoiakim, cut off the name of God and introduced the mutilated oath into that instrument.[6]

In 1844 Daniel Webster testified before the Supreme Court regarding the pluralism of constitutional oaths: "What is an oath?" he asked. "It is founded on a degree of consciousness that there is a Power above us that will reward our virtues or punish our vices. We all know that the doctrine of the law is that there must be in every person who enters court as a witness, he be Christian or Hindu, there must be a firm conviction on his mind that falsehood or perjury will be punished either in this world or the next or he cannot be admitted as a witness."[7]

Self-Government Without Christ Is Impossible

Originally, the spirit of voluntary Christian union in America came primarily through the education of the clergy. This type of education in biblical principles of self- and civil government had a positive effect in America's domestic life, which extended to other nations as well. In regards to the nature of self-government, Verna Hall says, "The first lesson the American Christian must learn if he would successfully develop, maintain or restore the Christian republic, is Christian self-government. Self-government without the modifier 'Christian' in its full biblical meaning is nothing more than self-will regardless of initial intent to be or do good. Man without Christ cannot succeed in producing lasting good."[8]

The second lesson is in many ways far more difficult than the first. We must learn how to live properly with our neighbors. Our Lord Jesus gave us His law for accomplishing this when He answered the lawyer's question regarding the most important commandment: "And the second is like it: 'You shall love your neighbor as yourself'" (Matthew 22:39). Thus there is not just one great commandment in the law (see Matthew 22:36), but there are two. And the failure to live by the second causes one's failure in upholding the first.

The centuries attest to the fact that humankind is far more willing to try to love and worship God than to properly love one's neighbor.[9] Miss Hall says that she began her intellectual journey when she was employed by a federal bureaucracy, which she recognized as socialistic in intent.[10] She wondered how this had come about, given the existence of the Constitution in governing the country. The correct answer, and the one that pained her greatly, was that it was *because* of the Constitution this was taking place.

The Constitution framers unquestionably began their historic efforts with the presupposition of the indispensability of moral self-government. Nevertheless, the document they produced categorically and formally rejects the concept of Christian self-government. Miss Hall again says, "Self-government without the modifier 'Christian' in its full biblical meaning is nothing more than self-will regardless of initial intent to be or do good. Man without Christ cannot succeed in producing lasting good."[11] The good that the Constitution was intended to do could not survive unscathed. The hard question that is never faced clearly and decisively by those who defend the theory of the Christian origins of the Constitution is this:

Why were the Articles of Confederation inherently less Christian than the Constitution, and so ineffective that a conspiracy had to be entered into, organized initially in 1785–87 by Freemasons,

Deists, and proto Unitarians, in order to restore inherently Christian principles of national government? To put it another way, why were the lawyers in charge of the Convention and the pastors absent? Why were the pamphlet debates of 1787–88 conducted in terms of Roman historical examples and not biblical examples? Why was there never any appeal to specific biblical laws, but endless appeals to natural laws? Why were the symbols adopted by the Continental Congress, the Convention, and post War nation systematically non-Christian? Why, if the Constitution is Christian, is the name of Jesus Christ missing? There is only one sensible answer: the U.S. Constitution is not Christian.[9]

Seeking Christian Roots

Many conservative Christians today are seeking the previously hidden Christian roots of the U.S. Constitution. These are not hidden roots; they are missing roots. The roots of the Constitution are Rhode Island political theory, Newtonian philosophy, Deist-Unitarian-Whig social theory, Scottish Enlightenment rationalism, and Masonic universalism. The Constitution's structure, according to Gary North, was Christian-Puritan; but its content was humanist. There may well be trappings that are Christian, for the framers were men of their era, and that era was Christian at its very foundation. But the Christianity of eighteenth-century America was deeply schizophrenic (contradictory, inconsistent, or incoherent). Newton was the favored model, not Paul on Mars Hill (see Acts 17).[12]

Gary North further argues that the framers were greatly committed to a specific historic model: republic Rome. You can see that in the adoption of Roman classical architecture. The pantheon of Rome was polytheistic in appearance but monotheistic in substance. The many gods of the expanding republic were united by their place in Rome's religious order. They publicly manifested the unifying power of the Roman state. By the time of Christ, the republic had become the Empire. The Roman pantheon was then international in scope. Every god of every captive people had a lawful place within the pantheon, testifying publicly to the subordination of each god's city to the Empire. But one God was conspicuously absent from this pantheon: the God of the Bible. This God acknowledged no other gods and no other kingdoms but His own. Rome was under the authority of this God, not over it. And so there was from the beginning an inevitable civil war between Christ and Caesar, church and state. This war was eventually won by the earthly representatives of the ascended Christ.[13]

Eighteenth-century America was still predominately Christian in its religion, but its national government was neither Christian nor biblical. In 1808 President Jefferson was petitioned by the New England ministers to proclaim a fast throughout the land. He refused, saying, "I am interdicted by the Constitution from doing anything that pertains to religion."[14] Although it was inevitable that Christian influence affected government in 1788, as evidenced by all the other national days of fasting, prayer, and humiliation proclaimed by George Washington, John Adams, James Madison, Abraham Lincoln, and others, unfortunately that influence has diminished significantly as time passed.

The American government has become more strictly constitutional since that time. Most believe the Constitution is Christian in nature even though it has been exploited by secular humanists. But, unfortunately, the opposite is all too true. Gary North again comments:

> The Constitution removed religious test oaths as judicial requirements for judges and officers of the new national government. This, in and of itself, delivered the republic into the hands of the humanists. Nothing else was necessary after that. From that point on, the secularization of America was a mopping-up operation. This operation is still in progress. Those being mopped up are unappreciative, but they cannot seem to identify when the turning point came. It came in 1788.[15]

In setting up this government, they ignored the claims of the King of kings. The Constitution does not contain the name of God. It is silent as the grave respecting the authority and law of the reigning

Mediator. It is a secular instrument.[16] Morally, it is a compact of political atheism. Insofar as it is the people's right to make the Constitution, elect their own officers, and determine the policy of the administration, civil government is "an ordinance of man."[17] But it is also an ordinance of God. Jesus Christ says (as wisdom personified), "By Me kings reign, and rulers decree justice. By Me princes rule, and nobles, all the judges of the earth" (Proverbs 8:15–16).

All Nations Have a Covenant with God

All nations have a covenant with the God of the Bible, even though those nations might not necessarily be conscious that they are dealing with the God of the Bible. The problem is that most of the Western nations have damaged their covenant with God and declared that the only legitimate form of government is a democracy—which means man is a god and we cannot have the God who created us to rule over us. We can do whatever we want and everything is permitted under a democracy. Even though some may argue with me, I don't think this is an overstatement. One author tells us:

> Civilizations are not neutral. An analysis of any nation at any point in time will tell us what gives meaning to the people and their institutions. A nation's religious foundation can be determined by looking at its economic system, judicial pronouncements, educational goals, and taxing policy. Culture is "religion externalized." Look at a nation's art and music and there you will find its religion. Read its books and newspapers. Watch its television programs. The outgrowth of civilization will be present on every page and in every program. The habits of individuals and families are also indicators of a nation's religious commitments. The sum of all these expressions will lead us to a nation's religious commitments. While it may be beneficial to look at the creeds of the churches, the actions of the people who subscribe to the creeds are a more accurate barometer of what the people really believe.[18]

Gary North argues that two features of the U.S. Constitution mark it as a humanist covenant. What are they? The Preamble and the religious test oath clause of Article VI. While the famous phrase of Jefferson's regarding "a wall of separation between church and state" is not in the Constitution in this familiar form, it is nonetheless judicially in the Constitution. What then is required for the Constitution to be a truly Christian covenant? According to Weiland:

> If a national organic document is in fact a covenant with God, then it must state clearly in the Preamble. A covenant as opposed to a contract includes God as party to the government. Second, there must be delineation of how the covenant is to be administered. If a covenant is made with God, then it must spell out the nature of the authority to whom God has delegated administration of the covenant. Who represents the people before God? If these two elements are missing, it is impossible to claim that the document represents a covenant with God. In fact, if these elements are absent or distorted, it is possible to argue that the Constitution represents a national break from covenant with God, since this covenant had been established earlier in the Mayflower Compact and various colonial charters.[19]

A government that is covenanted with God is not, therefore, a social contract as taught by Locke and Rousseau, or Jefferson in the Declaration of Independence. Civil government is established by the sovereign will of God, not the "consent of the governed."[20]

In order to protect the Constitution from biblical condemnation, some constitutionalists attempt to neutralize its moral implications. The Constitution contains little moral prescription. It does not address ethical issues. At best, it is a written set of political rules that will implement whatever moral precepts the people generally hold at any given time.[21] While serving as president of the United States, George Washington declared that the United States government protects all in their religious rights.[22] This is similar to what President Barack Obama wrote after declaring that America was no longer an exclusively Christian nation:

I think that the right might worry a bit more about the dangers of sectarianism. Whatever we were, we're no longer a Christian nation. At least not just. We are also a Jewish nation, a Muslim nation, and a Buddhist nation, and a Hindu nation, and a nation of nonbelievers.... When we're formulating policies from state house to the Senate floor to the White House, we've got to work to translate our reasoning into values that are accessible to every one of our citizens, not just members of our own faith community.[23]

President Obama is essentially advocating a world religion. American Christians should not criticize or be angry with President Obama for telling the truth. Instead, they should be angered at the origin of Obama's statements: the First Amendment of the Constitution of the United States.

So how could presidents swear by God's name since they don't have it in their conscience that God governs the nations and leaders are accountable to Him? The no religious test clause of the United States Constitution is found in Article VI, paragraph 3, and states that:

The Senators and Representatives before mentioned, and the Members of the several State Legislatures, and all executive and judicial Officers, both of the United States and of the several States, shall be bound by Oath or Affirmation to support this Constitution; but "No religious test shall ever be required as a qualification to any office or public trust under the United States."[24]

This has been interpreted to mean that no federal employee, whether elected or appointed, career or political, can be required to adhere to or accept any religion or belief system. Moreover, the First Amendment—"Congress shall make no law respecting the establishment of religion, nor prohibit the free exercise thereof"— prohibited Congress from establishing any religion and thus permitting all religions to participate as equal citizens on the federal level.[25] By 1820 most state constitutions eliminated religious qualifications that had kept people of other religions from participating in public affairs or offices.

Eight years after the adoption of this Constitution, Congress made a treaty with Tripoli that has never been called into question as to its constitutionality. It says: "This government is no sense founded on the Christian religion, and makes no distinction between the Christian and the Mussulman (Muslim)."[26] Chief Justice Joseph Story, in his *Commentaries on the Constitution*, said, "This provision means the Pagan, the Mohammedan, the Jew, the Christian and the Infidel shall sit down in common at the tables of our national council."[27] But the Bible says, "Moreover you shall select from all the people able men, such as fear God, men of truth, hating covetousness; and place such over them to be rulers of thousands, rulers of hundreds, rulers of fifties, and rulers of tens" (Exodus 18:21).

A talent for politics, integrity, and a heartfelt regard for the will of God are required to hold office according to God's standards, but our Constitution sets aside these qualifications and makes way for the enemies of truth and righteousness. What is the union of religion and state? No state can live without a religion. There is no neutrality on these issues. The question is: Which religion will the state choose? The choice for Christians in the West has been this one since 1636: God's law or man's law, civil covenant keeping or civil covenant breaking?

Conclusion

For over three centuries, the West has made the wrong choice. But before we judge their decisions, it is important to say that so has virtually everybody else on earth. God's law is our standard, both individually and corporately. There are covenantal institutions God has established to declare and enforce His law. All institutions must obey, but these are those that are exclusively governed by formal oaths before God.[28] The Constitution is nothing other than a compact of political atheism. In adopting it, we virtually said, "O King of kings, we propose to run this nation independent of You, in the name of we the people."

The Lord Jesus Christ has a controversy with this nation, and unless we put away our rebellion and bow to His scepter, we shall be broken in pieces: "The adversaries of the Lord shall be broken in pieces. Out of heaven shall He thunder upon them."[29] Dr. Schaff says, "Take away Jesus Christ, and the human race is left without an animating soul, without a purpose, an inexplicable enigma."[30] That is something we cannot afford.

Endnotes

1 Accessed from *http://www.ukba.homeoffice.gov.uk/birthcitizenship/applying/ceremony.*

2 R. J. Rushdoony, *The Theism of the Early Church* (Blackheath, New South Wales: Logos Foundation, 1983), 77.

3 Accessed from *http://www.inaugural.senate.gov/days-events/days-event/presidents-swearing-in-ceremony.*

4 Timothy N. Baldwin, JD. April 6, 2010, accessed from *http://www.newswithviews.com/Timothy/baldwin130.htm.*

5 James Mitchell Foster, *Reformation Principles: Stated and Applied* (Chicago and New York: F. H. Revell, 1890), 234–235.

6 Ibid.

7 Daniel Webster, *Mr. Webster's Speech in Defense of the Christian Ministry and in Favor of the Religious Instruction of the Young, Delivered in the Supreme Court of the United States, February 10 1884, in the Case of Stephen Girard's Will* (Washington, DC: Gales and Seaton, 1884), 43. Cited in Ted Weiland, 145.

8 Verna M. Hall, *The Christian History of the Constitution of the United States of America, Christian Self-Government with Union,* edited by Joseph Allen Montgomery, compiled by Verna M. Hall (San Francisco: Foundation for American Christian Education 1962, 1979), Preface, II–III.

9 Ibid.

10 Gary North, *Political Polytheism,* 533. Cited in Verna M. Hall, *Christian History of the Constitution* (San Francisco: American Constitution Press, 1960), Preface, III.

11 Gary North, *Political Polytheism,* 534–536.

12 Ibid.

13 Ibid.

14 James Mitchell Foster, 236.

15 Gary North, *Conspiracy in Philadelphia: The Broken Covenant of the U.S. Constitution* (Draper, VA: Nicene Council.com, 2004), 90. Cited in Ted Weiland, 196.

16 Ibid.

17 Ibid.

[18] Gary DeMar and Peter Leithart, *The Reduction of Christianity: A Biblical Response to Dave Hunt* (Fort Worth, TX: Dominion Press and Atlanta, GA: American Vision, 1998), 300.

[19] Ted R. Weiland, 63–64. Cited in Dennis Woods, *Discipling the Nations: The Government Upon His Shoulder* (Franklin, TN: Legacy Communications, 1996), 25.

[20] Ted R. Weiland, 64. Cited in Dennis Woods, 134–135.

[21] Gary DeMar, *Says Who? Biblical Worldview* (Powder Springs, GA: American Vision, March 2003), vol. 19, no. 3, 7.

[22] George Washington, Jared Sparks, ed., *The Writings of George Washington*, "Letter to the Synod of the Reformed Dutch Church of North America," October 1789, vol. 12, 167.

[23] Barak Obama quoted in Aaron Klein, "Obama: America No Longer Christian Democrat," says also for Muslims and nonbelievers. WorldNet Daily, June 24, 2008, accessed from *http://www.worldnetdaily.com/index/php?pageid=67735*.

[24] Accessed from *https://en.wikipedia.org/wiki/No_Religious_Test_Clause*.

[25] Accessed from *en.wikipedia.org/wiki.org/wiki/First_Amendment_to_the_United_States_ Constitution*.

[26] James Mitchell Foster, 235–236.

[27] Ibid.

[28] Gary North, *Political Polytheism*, 539.

[29] James Mitchell Foster, 238.

[30] Ibid., 201.

CHAPTER 21

We the People

The Key Words

Warren Burger, who was the 15th Chief Justice of the United States from 1969 to 1986, said that "we the people" are the Constitution's most important words.[1] The United States Preamble precisely follows the biblical covenant structure: The (1) sovereign creating agency, "we the people," (2) acts in history (history prologue) to establish a union that will (3) establish justice and insure the common defense (boundaries) in order to secure (4) the blessings of liberty for ourselves and (5) our posterity.[2]

Meredith G. Kline, in her book *The Structure of Biblical Authority*, uses the word *preamble* in describing the Ten Commandments section of Exodus 20:2 (KJV): "I am the Lord thy God. You shall have no other gods before or besides Me." The purpose of these words was to inspire awe and reverential fear in the Lord God.[3] It means that God was more powerful than all the others gods of Egypt put together, which was made clear by the name God gave to Himself. The context tells us that the legal system should have been based on the Ten Commandments; without them the people would lose the fear of God, inevitably leading to idolatry and injustice.

There is no historical prologue in the Preamble to the Constitution because the Constitution was literally announcing the advent of a new covenantal divinity whose prior existence had no independent legal status in the American system of laws. The people had been referred to time and time again in colonial political theory but had no independent legal status. They had always been under a god of some kind. But this was about to change.

This new independently sovereign divinity would formally announce its advent as the sole covenantal agent of national incorporation by means of public ratification. The people, the Preamble states, "ordain and establish this Constitution for the United States of America." The new god of the Constitution was both suzerain (a feudal overlord) and vassal—something covenantally unique in the history of humanity prior to 1787. It elevated the people from point two in the covenant structure (representation) to point one (the Creator). Warren Burger is correct: "we the people" are the key words *conceptually*.[4]

Constitutional Convention Framers

Both the federalists and anti-federalists of those who attended the Constitutional Convention put the emphasis on the people, which is evidence that they had lost sight of God and His ultimate authority over their lives. Such an emphasis on the people cannot be found anywhere in the Bible.[5] Let's look at some of the framers who attended the convention:

George Washington (who presided over the Constitutional Convention) confirmed this self-originating authority in his farewell address: "This government, the offspring of our own choice uninfluenced and unawed, adopted upon full investigation and mature deliberation, completely free in its principles, in the distribution of its powers, uniting security with energy, and containing within itself a provision for its own amendment, has a just claim to your confidence and support."[6]

Alexander Hamilton stated, "The fabric of American empire ought to rest on the solid basis of the Consent of the People. The streams of national power ought to flow immediately from that pure, original fountain of all legitimate authority."[7]

In Gary D. Barnett's opinion, Hamilton and his followers were able to fool and then co-opt enough of the political leaders of the time to bring about a massive change, a change that ushered in a much more powerful central governing system. This was entirely by design and was never intended to advance and protect the freedom of the individual. Had this been the case, slavery would never have been sanctioned by that same document. Why this system is so revered is beyond me. It can only be due to long-term indoctrination. I have been told since childhood of the greatness of the Constitution by peers, the school system, politicians, the media, and by virtually everyone else who is able to utter the spoken word. Considering this, it is no wonder that many worship this document.[8]

In one of his many arguments on behalf of the Constitution, Madison revealed where ultimate power resides—in a constitutional republic. He said, "As the people are the only legitimate fountain of power it is from them that the constitutional charter under which the power of the several branches of government is derived."[9]

Madison, who is often called the "Father of the Constitution," had a dream of creating a secular republic. He had spent an extra year in post-graduate study with Witherspoon, studying Hebrew, ethics, and theology, so he knew what Christianity was. He wanted no part of an explicitly Christian republic. He worked hard to see to it that such a republic, which existed at the state level under the Articles of Confederation, would not survive. What had long motivated him was his commitment to remove the religious test oath from Virginia politics. He achieved both of these goals within a three-year period, between 1786–1788.[10]

James Madison was a covenant-breaking genius, and the heart and soul of his genius was his commitment to religious neutralism. He devised a Constitution that for two centuries has fooled even the most perceptive Christian social philosophers of each generation into thinking that Madison was not what he was he really was: a Unitarian theocrat whose goal was to snuff out the civil influence of the Trinitarian churches wherever they did not support his brainchild. For two centuries his plan worked.[11]

John Adams confessed to the same humanism regarding each state's constitution:

It will never be pretended that any persons employed in that service (the establishment of the states' Constitutions) has interviews with the gods, or were in any degree under the inspiration of Heaven. It will forever be acknowledged that these governments were contrived merely by use of reason and the senses.... Thirteen governments (of the original states) thus founded on the natural authority of the people alone.[12]

John Adams also played a part because of his detailed studies of state constitutions—especially his pre-convention, three-volume work, *Defense of the Constitution of the Government of the United States*. His model of the "balanced constitution" was an important influence at Philadelphia. But it was Madison who was the father of the convention, with Washington sitting silently as the godfather. It was Madison who, more than any other man, broke the national covenant with God.[13] Likewise, the constitutional republic's fifth president, James Monroe, agreed, "The people, the highest authority known in our system, from whom all our institutions spring and on whom they depend, formed it."[14]

It has been noted that during the Constitutional Convention, Benjamin Franklin proposed prayers imploring the assistance of heaven and its blessing upon their deliberations.[15] His proposal did not even merit a vote.[16] It is said that after the Convention had adjourned, Rev. Dr. Miller, a distinguished professor at Princeton College, met Alexander Hamilton in the streets of Philadelphia and said, "Mr. Hamilton, we are greatly grieved that the Constitution has no recognition of God or the Christian religion." "I declare," said Hamilton, "we forgot it!"[17] Franklin wrote later, "The Convention, except three or four persons, thought prayers unnecessary."[18] Franklin's proposal included his famous acknowledgement of God's sovereignty in the affairs of men:[19]

I have lived, sir, a long time, and the longer I live, the more convincing proofs I see of this truth that God governs in the affairs of men. And if a sparrow cannot fall to the ground without His notice, is it probable that an empire can rise without His aid? We have been assured, sir, in the Sacred Writings, that except the Lord build the house, they labor in vain that build it. I firmly believe this; and I also believe that without His concurring aid we shall succeed in this political building no better than the builders of Babel.[20]

Patrick Henry on the Debate Over Ratification

Patrick Henry was convinced that the Constitution would fail to protect liberty. He insisted the conventioneers had no right to claim they represented the people. He voiced his concerns to the Virginia Ratifying Convention in 1788, saying:

> I say our privileges and rights are in danger. The new form of Government will effectually oppress and ruin the people. In some parts of the plan before you, the great rights of freemen are endangered, in other parts, absolutely taken away. There will be no checks, no real balances, in this Government: What can avail your specious imaginary balances, your rope-dancing, chain-rattling, ridiculous ideal checks and contrivances? And yet who knows the dangers that this new system may produce: they are out of the sight of the common people: They cannot foresee latent consequences.... I see great jeopardy in this new Government.[21]

Henry was the primary opponent in the debate over ratification. For this historians have relegated him into the "outer darkness." He saw the constitutional implications of what was being proposed by the federalists in 1788. His protest was not sufficiently persuasive at Virginia's ratification convention, but in retrospect, he seemed prophetic. Patrick Henry had been invited to attend the Philadelphia Convention but refused. A year later he spoke out against ratification. He had seen the meaning of "we the people," and he warned against its implications during the debates over ratification:

> And here I would make this inquiry of those worthy characters who composed a part of the late federal Convention. I am sure they were fully impressed with the necessity of forming a great

consolidated government, instead of a confederation. That this is a consolidated government is demonstrably clear; and the danger of such government is, to my mind, very striking. I have the highest veneration for those gentlemen; but sir, give me leave to demand, what right had they to say, *We the People?* My political curiosity, exclusive of my anxious solicitude for the public welfare, leads me to ask, who authorized them to speak the language of, *We the People,* instead of, *We the States?* States are the characteristics and the soul of a confederation.... If the States be not the agents of this compact, it must be one great consolidated national government of the people of all the States.... Had the delegates, who were sent to Philadelphia a power to propose a consolidated government instead of a confederacy? Were not they deputed by States, and not by the people? The assent of the people, in their collective capacity, is not necessary to the formation of a federal government. The people have no right to enter into leagues, alliances, or confederations: they are not proper agents for this purpose: States and sovereign powers are the only proper agents for this purpose: Show me an instance where the people have exercised this business: has it not always gone through the legislatures? ...This, therefore, ought to depend on the consent of the legislatures.[22]

He also told the delegates at the Constitutional Convention in Philadelphia, "The People gave them no power to use their name. That they exceeded their power is perfectly clear."[23] In modern terminology, this was a form of property infringement. He reminded his listeners of the nature of the original authorization of the Convention:

I have the highest respect for those gentlemen who formed the Convention, and, were some of them not here, I would express some testimonial of esteem for them. America had, on a former occasion, put the outmost confidence in them—a confidence which was well placed; and I am sure, sir, I would give up anything to them; I would cheerfully confide in them as my representatives. But sir, on this great occasion, I would demand the cause of their conduct. The people gave them no power to use their name. That they exceeded their power is perfectly clear. It is not mere curiosity that actuates me: I wish to hear the real, actual, existing danger, which should lead us to take those steps, so dangerous in my conception. But notwithstanding this, we are wandering on the great ocean of human affairs. I see no landmark to guide us. We are running we know not whither. Difference of opinion has gone to a degree of inflammatory resentment in different parts of the country which has been occasioned by this perilous innovation. The Federal Convention ought to have amended the old system; for this purpose they were solely delegated; the object of their mission extended to no other consideration. You must, therefore, forgive the solicitation of one unworthy member to know what danger could have arisen under the present Confederation, and what are the causes of this proposal to change our government?[24]

A handful of men decided to take the new nation down a different path. It was not enough to amend the Articles by taking such steps as repealing all internal tariffs and making gold or silver legal tender for a national currency. They wanted a completely new system of national government, and this would be achieved through a coup. Congress was unwilling and probably unable to undertake such a radical revision of the Articles in 1787. Yet the Articles of Confederation, as the legal bylaws of the national government, specified that all changes would have to be approved by Congress and then by all of the state legislatures (Article XIII). Both congress and the state legislatures would have to be bypassed. This required some special preparations; in short, a conspiracy.[25] The people of the colonial era recognized that an oath to God and an affirmation of the authority of the Bible were basic to the preservation of Christian social order, political freedom, and economic prosperity.[26]

Patrick Henry knew where this government was headed. The Constitution was ratified under the presumption of the sovereignty of the people. But it was more than mere presumption; it is right there at the beginning of the document. This is why there is no Trinitarian oath in the Constitution: the framers were operating under the legal fiction that the sovereign people, not the God of the Bible, had authorized the new covenant.[27] Henry said in reference to this:

> If I shall be in the minority, I shall have those painful sensations which arise from a conviction of being overpowered in a good cause. Yet I will be a peaceable citizen. My head, my hand, and my heart, shall be at liberty to retrieve the loss of liberty, and remove the defects of that system in a constitutional way. I wish not to go to violence, but will wait with hopes that the spirit which predominated in the revolution is not yet gone, nor the cause of those who are attached to the revolution yet lost. I shall therefore patiently wait in expectation of seeing that government changed, so as to be compatible with the safety, liberty, and happiness of the people.[28]

Patrick Henry remained true to his word. He remained loyal to the United States even when he opposed the federalist party's Alien and Sedition Act at the end of his life. He was also opposed to anarchy.[29] The framers who were the dominant voices at the Constitutional Convention had a definite goal, and that was to issue a death warrant against Christianity, but for tactical reasons they and their spiritual heirs refused for several generations to deliver it to the intended victims. They covered this covenantal death sentence with a lot of platitudes about the hand of Providence, the need for morality, the grand design of the universe, and similar Masonic shibboleths.[30]

The Fourteenth Amendment officially delivered the death sentence; it has been carried out with escalating enthusiasm since the 1950s.[31] That is the reason why humanist institutions deny the reality of sin—they would rather believe that people can save themselves once they are given enough time, resources, money, technology, and education.[32]

People Cannot Be Sovereign

But some would argue that the constitutional framers considered the people sovereign under the Declaration of Independence and the

Constitution. According to *Webster's Dictionary*, the word *sovereign* is defined as "1. chief or highest; supreme; 2. supreme in power, superior in position to all others; 3. independent of, and unlimited by, any other, possessing or entitled to, original and independent authority or jurisdiction." This means the Constitution was written by and for "sovereigns" who were deemed as the highest authority, not God.

The problem is that "this government of the People, by the People and for the People" cannot be sovereign; neither can the government itself be sovereign. The nation had broken with its Christian judicial roots by covenanting with a new god, the sovereign people. There would be no other God tolerated in the political order. There would be no appeal beyond this sovereign god. The collective god, speaking through the federal government, began its inevitable expansion, which was predicted by the anti-federalists, most notably Patrick Henry.

The secularization of the republic began in earnest, and this process has not yet ceased. Surrender to secular humanism was not an overnight process. The rise of Unitarian abolitionism, the coming of the Civil War, the advent of Darwinism, the growth of immigration, the spread of the franchise, the development of the public school system, and a host of other social and political influences have all worked to transform the interdenominational American civil religion into a religion not fundamentally different from the one set up. The golden calves may not be on the hilltops today, but the theology is much the same: religion exists to serve the needs of the state, and the state is sovereign over the material things of this world. There are many forms of idol worship. The worship of the U.S. Constitution has been a popular form of this ancient practice, especially in conservative Christian circles.[33]

The Constitution's provisions were written by self-consciously apostate men and conspiratorial Christian colleagues whose understanding of the biblical covenant had been eroded by a lifetime of Newtonian philosophy and training in the pagan classics.[34] Nevertheless, these men were under restraints: both political (a Christian electorate) and philosophical (natural rights doctrines). Both of these restraints have almost completely disappeared in the twentieth century. Thus, the evils implicit in the ratified national covenant have grown more evil over time.[35] Christians lost the battle in 1788—the lawyers in Philadelphia won it. Christians accepted the ratification of the Constitution not just as good losers but as enthusiastic cooperators. They have yet to identify their problem.

Decade by decade, the American republic grows ever more consistent with the apostate foundation of the Constitution. Christians even find themselves besieged today, and they vainly expect to get rid of their problems by returning to the "original intent" of the framers. On the contrary, what we have today is the outcome of their political intent as Patrick Henry warned so long ago. Darwinism, socialism, and several major wars sped up the process of moral disintegration, but the judicial foundation of this disintegration had been established in 1787–1788.[36]

"We the people" was not the vassals of the Great King in this treaty; "we the people" are the great king, and we shall have no other gods beside "we the people." Thus, the framers outlawed religious oaths. Yet this crucial constitutional provision is rarely mentioned today. The humanist defenders of the Constitution automatically assume it, and the Christian defenders either do not recognize its importance or else do not want to face its obvious implications. Instead, the debate has focused on Congress and the freedom of religion. This provision is not the heart of the constitutional covenant; it is merely an application of it.[37]

The Declaration of Independence

What about the Declaration of Independence where we read, "Government is subject to the consent of the governed"? Jefferson's Declaration of Independence compromised the original Christian covenant of the states by joining them together in an alliance of independent states under the authority of nature and nature's god, a myth of Unitarian theology.[38] The Articles of Confederation completed the Declaration's halfway covenant by creating the United

States of America: a true covenant document rather than a mere alliance of judicially independent states. Therefore, rights that are given by men can easily be taken away. Gary Barnett accurately tells us:

> The widespread belief by most Americans that this document grants us our rights, and protects our freedom is in my opinion absurd. Natural rights, or any rights for that matter, are inherent due to our very humanity. Our freedoms and rights did not come from any political class or due to any drafting of a political document. Our rights and freedoms are God-given and inherent. They are natural human rights, and cannot be bestowed by men! For if men can bestow rights, then they are not rights at all, because they can just as easily be taken away. To believe then, that a group of men that some men call "founders," could with a stroke of a pen grant rights to another group of men, is ludicrous.[39]

It is the reason why the Puritans' idea of rights and liberty was quite different from what the framers had in mind.[40]

Differences of the Puritans and Constitutional Framers

There was a difference between the Christianity of the 1600s and that of the 1700s in America. The Puritans were theologically minded and preferred to apply their biblical worldview to every sphere of society. They often referred to the Ten Commandments, and the Bible became the law of their life, especially the books of Exodus, Kings, and Romans. During the mid- and late eighteenth century, Christianity of the Puritans was all but dead, which meant government was based upon the laws of God was also dead.[41] The eighteenth-century conception of Greco-Roman paganism had completely replaced the Puritanical Hebraism concept of self-government. What were the theological differences between the worldviews of the Puritans and the Constitutional framers?

The Puritans' political views and thoughts centered in the doctrine of divine sovereignty. The early magistrate was a minister of God under common grace for the execution of the laws of God among the people at large, for the maintenance of law and order, and for ruling the state. In Puritan political theory, the magistrate derived his powers from God and not from the people.[42] Yale historian Edmund Morgan describes the Puritans as men who made a strong demand on human nature, for they were engaged in a mission that required great exertion. They had undertaken to establish a society where the will of God would be observed in every detail, a kingdom of God on earth.

Every nation existed by a virtue of a covenant with God in which it promised to obey His commands. They had left England because England was failing in its promise. In high hopes that God was guiding them and would find their efforts acceptable, they had promised to form a "special overruling providence." By staying His wrath so long and allowing them to depart in peace by delivering them safe across the water, He had sealed a covenant with them and given them a special responsibility to carry out the good intentions that had brought them into the wilderness.

Theirs was a special commission from God: "And when God gives a special commission," Winthrop warned them, "He looks to have it strictly observed in every Article."[43] The whole concept of government that would later be proclaimed by John Locke and others, which placed the sovereignty in the hands of the people and which found the origin of government in a human compact, was utterly unknown to the Puritans. They did not believe in a government by the people; they sensed that in the democratic philosophy, with its emphasis upon the sovereignty of the people, lay a fundamental contradiction to the biblical doctrine of the sovereignty of God. They clearly perceived that democracy was the fruit of humanism and not the reformation concept.[44]

Richard Mosier has well observed that the late seventeenth-century revolutionary age demanded that both the absolute God and the absolute king must "henceforth rule by the consent of the governed. The God of Puritanism, stripped of His antique powers, had no recourse but to enter as a weakened prince into the temple of the individualism and there to seek refuge."[45] This sovereignty he once claimed, and was accorded by the Puritans, was now claimed by humanity itself. This was the philosophical and theological outlook of many of the leaders of the Revolution—theirs was a secular political philosophy and its roots are to be found in the enlightenment in general and deism in particular. Most of the revolutionary leaders desired to retain the Christian ethic but to separate it from the biblical revelation and to find a new basis for it in natural law.[46]

The change of law and government in the late 1700s brought about a change of religion. And because the former law and government represented God, both He and His laws were necessarily discarded for the new god and its laws. This is difficult to accept, especially since we have incessantly been told the constitutional framers were such godly men.[47] Today's Christian constitutionalists are quick to share the framers' Christian-sounding quotations. Hundreds of books, replete with such quotations, have been compiled, and no one can question that many of them often said the right things regarding God, His Son, Christianity, and occasionally even His law. But such statements mean nothing by themselves without a personal relationship with Jesus Christ.

Thomas Jefferson made Christian-sounding statements, but no one would argue that he was a Christian. Politicians are famous for saying the right things at the right times but doing completely the opposite. Two hundred years from now, Christian historians will be using Christian-sounding statements from Bill Clinton, George W. Bush, and Barack Obama to buttress declarations that these men were great Christians too.[48] It's a regular occurrence to hear a U.S. president quoting Scripture or publicly giving an invocation of God. This dangerous assumption opens the door to political abuse in the name of Christ and the Christian sanction of ungodly actions—including those of the constitutional framers.[49]

A good example would be from the author of the *Faith of Barack Obama,* who wrote, "His religion…frames his worldview, frames his sense of justice, frames his sense of right and wrong and therefore frames his policies."[50] Archbishop Desmond Tutu said, "Obama has such a passion for justice and equality, such a gift for filling people of different generations with newfound hope that things can and will change for the better. His inspiration comes from his faith; he is an ardent believer. Yes, he is a Christian."[51] But if they call themselves Christians, then why don't they repent, turn to God, and live lives consistent with and worthy of their repentance (see Acts 26:20; 2:38)?

Conclusion

Many analysts believe that the destruction of America's founding principles can be traced to the country's willful rejection of the Bible as the source of divine authority. As we've seen, this officially began with the ratification of the Constitution. Of course there are a few biblical principles contained in the Constitution, but we also find instances in which the document conflicts with biblical laws and attacks the sovereignty and authority of God Almighty. The original sin of man was to be independent from God. He chose to be as "god" by making decisions for himself that were based upon the tree of knowledge. Since that day man became a law unto himself.

The Preamble's opening words, "we the people," were a new declaration of independence, in which the framers consciously or unconsciously declared themselves sovereign. It is true that ideas have consequences. The Founders took the ideas from polytheism, where all gods are equal, which ultimately leads to relativism and humanism, where man now makes his own laws. And humanism has now led to antichrists in the halls of legislation. This should not be.

Endnotes

[1] Gary North, *Conspiracy in Philadelphia Origins of the United States Constitution* (Harrisonburg, Virginia: Dominion Educational Ministries, Inc., 2004), 256–257. Cited in the Orlando Sentinel (September 8, 1988), A-2.

[2] Ibid.

[3] Meredith G. Kline, *The Structure of Biblical Authority*, rev. ed. (Grand Rapids, Michigan: Eardmans, 1972), 114.

4 Gary North, *Conspiracy in Philadelphia*, 257.

5 Ted R. Weiland, *Bible Law Versus The United States Constitution*, 68.

6 George Washington, Worthington Chauncey Ford, ed., *The Writings of George Washington*, 14 Vols. (New York; NY: G. P. Putman's Sons, 1892) Vol. 13, 297. Cited in Ted R.Weiland, *Bible Law vs The United States Constitution The Christian Perspective*, 68.

7 Alexander Hamilton, *The Federalist, No. 22* (New York, NY: G.P. Putnam's Sons 1888), 135. Cited in Ted R. Weiland, *Bible Law Versus The United States Constitution*, 68.

8 Gary D. Barnett, "I'm Fed up with Constitution Worship," accessed from *http://www.lewrockwell.com/barnett26.1.html*.

9 James Madison, *The Federalist, No. 46* (New York, NY: G. P. Putman's Sons, 1888), 127. Cited in Ted R. Weiland, *Bible Law Versus The United States Constitution*, 68.

10 Gary North, *Political Polytheism*, 427. Cited in Robert A Rutland, "James Madison Dream: A secular Republic," (Free Inquiry 1983), 8–11, and Bradford, *A Worthy Company*, 142, 144.

11 Gary North, *Political Polytheism*, 696.

12 John Adams, *The Works of John Adams*, 10 Vols. (Boston, MA: Little, Brown, and Company, 1865) Vol. 4, 292–293.

13 Gary North, *Political Polytheism*, 428, cited in Gordon S. Wood, *The Creation of the American Republic, 1776–1787* (Williamburg, Virginia: Institute of Early American History, published by the University of North Carolina Press, 1969), chapter 14.

14 Views of the President of the United States on the Subject of Internal Improvements May 4, 1822, Richardson 2:147–49, accessed from *http://press-pubs.uchicago.edu/founders/documents/preambles20.html*.

15 Ted R. Weiland, *Bible Law Versus The United States Constitution*, 79.

16 Robert Yates, "Secret Debates of the Federal Convention of 1787," *Secret Proceedings and Debates of the Constitutional Convention 1787, Entered according to Act of Congress in the Year 1838* (Hawthorne, CA: Omni Publications, 1986) 197–198. Cited in Ted R.Weiland, *Bible Law Versus The United States Constitution*, 78.

17 Benjamin F. Morris, *The Christian Life and Character of the Civil Institutions of the United States* (Powder Springs, GA: America Vision, Inc., 2009, originally published in 1864), 296–297. Cited in Ted R. Weiland, *Bible Law Versus The United States Constitution*, 81.

18 Benjamin Franklin, quoted in William Templeton Franklin, *Memoirs of the Life and Writings of Benjamin Franklin* (London: Henry Colburn, 1818, 3rd Edition), 195. Cited in Ted R. Weiland, *Bible Law Versus The United States Constitution*, 79.

19 Timothy Dwight, quoted in Isaac Kramnick and R. Laurence Moore, *The Godless Constitution: A Moral Defense of the Secular State* (New York: W. W. Norton & Company, 1966), 105–106. In 1812, in a speech to students assembled in the Yale College chapel, Pastor Timothy Dwight summed up this mockery: "The nation has offended Providence. We formed our Constitution without any acknowledgment of God; without any recognition of His mercies to us, as a people, of His government, or even of His existence. The convention, by which it was formed, never asked even once His direction, or His blessings, upon their labors. Thus we commenced our national existence under the present system without God."

20 Speech to the Constitutional Convention, June 28, 1787, accessed from *www.saferschools.org/pdfs/Franklin.pdf*.

21 Patrick Henry, Ralph Ketcham, ed., "Speeches of Patrick Henry (June 5 and 7, 1788)," *The Anti-Federalist Papers and the Constitutional Convention Debates* (New York, NY: Penguin Books, 2003, 2nd ed.), 200–208. Cited in Ted R. Weiland, *Bible Law Versus The United States Constitution*, 74.

22 Jonathan Elliot (ed.), *The Debates in the Several State Conventions on the Adoption of the Federal Constitution as Recommended by the General Convention at Philadelphia in 1787,* 5 Vols. (Philadelphia: Lippencott, 1836, 1907), III, Virginia, 22–23.

23 This statement appears in *The Debates in the Several State Conventions on the Adoption of the Federal Constitution as Recommended by the General Convention at Philadelphia in 1787,* edited by Jonathan Elliot, 5 Vols. (Philadelphia: Lippincott, 1836, 1907), III, 22.

24 Jonathan Elliot (ed.), 22–23.

25 Gary North, *Political Polytheism*, 416.

26 Ibid., 464.

27 Edmund S. Morgan, *Inventing the People: The Rise of Popular Sovereignty in England and America* (New York: Norton, 1988). Cited in Gary North, *Conspiracy in Philadelphia*, 378–379.

28 Jonathan Elliot (ed.), 652.

29 Norine Dickson Campbell, *Patrick Henry: Patriot and Statesman* (Old Greenwich, Connecticut: Devin-Adair, 1969) 426–428.

30 Gary North, *Political Polytheism*, 691.

31 Ibid.

32 Look at the excerpt from *The Preamble to the Charter of the United Nations*. It is an example of people's attempt to govern and live at peace in this world without the lordship of Jesus Christ:

We the Peoples of The United Nations determined:
- to save succeeding generations from the scourge of war, which twice in our lifetime has bought untold sorrow to mankind, and
- to reaffirm faith in fundamental human rights, in the dignity and worth of the human person, in the equal rights of men and women and of nations large and small, and
- to establish conditions under which justice and respect for the obligations arising from treaties and other sources of international law can be maintained, and
- to promote social progress and better standards of life in larger freedom, and for these ends,
- to practice tolerance and live together in peace with one another as good neighbors, and
- to unite our strength to maintain international peace and security, and
- to ensure, by the acceptance of principles and the institution of methods, that armed force shall not be used, save in the common interest and to employ international machinery for the promotion of the economic and social advancement of all peoples...have resolved to combine our efforts to accomplish these aims (*http://www.un.org/en/documents/charter/preamble.shtml,* accessed on December 3, 2013).

33 Gary North, *Conspiracy in Philadelphia*, 382.

[34] Carl J. Richard, *The Founders and the Classics: Greece, Rome, and the American Enlightenment* (Cambridge, Massachusetts: Harvard University Press, 1994). Cited in Gary North, Conspiracy in Philadelphia, 302.

[35] Gary North, *Conspiracy in Philadelphia*, 302.

[36] Ibid., 301.

[37] Ibid., 379.

[38] Gary North, *Political Polytheism: The Myth of Pluralism* (Published by Institute for Christian Economics, 1989), 531.

[39] Gary D. Barnett, "The Constitution Does Not Grant Rights," accessed at *http://www.lewrockwell.com/barnett53.1.1,html.*

[40] C. Gregg Singer, *A Theological Interpretation of American History* (Phillipsburg, NJ: Presbyterian and Reformed Publishing Co., 1964), 19. "John Winthrop reminded his fellow-citizens of Massachusetts that a doctrine of civil rights (as in the Declaration of Independence) and the Bill of Rights which looked to natural or sinful man as its source and guardian (as in the Preamble) was actually destructive to the very liberty which they were seeking to protect. True freedom can never be found in institutions which are under the direction of sinful men, but only in the redemption wrought for man by Jesus Christ. Christ, not man, is the sole source and guarantee of true liberty."

[41] Daniel J. Boorstin, *The Americans: The Colonial Experience* (Norwalk, CT: The Easton Press, 1987), 5–6, 18–19, 24, 28.

[42] Ted R. Weiland, *Bible Law Versus The United States Constitution*, 59. Cited in C. Gregg Singer, *A Theological Interpretation of American History* (Philipsburg, NJ: Presbyterian and Reformed Publishing Co. 1964), 13–14.

[43] Edmund S. Morgan, *The Puritan Dilemma: The Story of John Winthrop* (Publisher: Little, Brown and Company Boston 1958), 69–70.

[44] C. Gregg Singer, *A Theological Interpretation of American History* (Philipsburg, NJ: Presbyterian and Reformed Publishing Co. 1964), 18–19. Cited in Ted R. Weiland, 59.

[45] Ted R. Weiland, 59–60.

[46] Ibid.

[47] Ibid., 61–62.

[48] Ibid.

[49] Ibid.

[50] Paul Backholer, *How Christianity Made the Modern World* (Faith Media, 2009), 147.

[51] Paul Backholer, Cited on *Christianitytoday.com,* where author Daniel Blake predicts faith will play a big role in Obama's presidency, on November 10, 2008.

CHAPTER 22

Was the Constitution Inspired By the Bible?

God Voted Out

When the war for independence was over and the victory over our enemies won, and when the blessings and happiness of liberty and peace were secured, the Constitution was framed and God began to be neglected in the lives of the people. He was not merely forgotten; He was absolutely voted out of the Constitution. The proceedings as published by Charles Thomson, the secretary of the Continental Congress between 1774 and 1789, and the history of the day, show that the question was gravely debated whether God should be in the Constitution or not. And after a solemn debate, He was deliberately voted out.[1]

It's hard to say that the Constitution is not Bible-based, especially when so many sources appear to authenticate it as a document created by Christian men. For example, historian David Barton, the founder of Wall Builders, an organization dedicated to presenting America's forgotten history, writes:

Noah Webster, the Founder personally responsible for Art. I Sec. 8 of the Constitution specifically cites Exodus 18:21 and John Jay and George Washington also attributed God's providence as the reason that America elected its own leaders. Since so many of the ideas that found application in the American government were taken from the Bible, it is not surprising that John Adams had identified Christians and ministers as being so influential in American independence. Nearly four decades after the

Revolution, he reaffirmed this position, declaring: The general principles on which the fathers achieved independence were...the general principles of Christianity.... Now I will avow that I then believed, and now believe, that those general principles of Christianity are as eternal and immutable as the existence and attributes of God.[2]

Not just John Adams, but many early American political leaders also declared that America was guided by or founded on Christian principles.[3] John Adams also believed that America's government could function well only for a moral people. He wrote:

We have no government armed with power capable of contending with human passions unbridled by morality and religion. Avarice, ambition, revenge, or gallantry would break the strongest cords of our Constitution as a whale goes through a net. Our Constitution was made only for a moral and religious people. It is wholly inadequate to the government of any other.[4]

Ted R. Weiland has studied its contents and compared them to that of the Scriptures. He asks:

Why do Americans, particularly Christians, have a love affair with the United States Constitution? Is it because they've been told repeatedly that it is one of the most important documents ever written by man? Is it because it was based upon biblical principles and is a great Christian document? Or because the victors in the culture war wrote our history the way they wanted us to perceive it? These are very hard questions but nevertheless they demand answers.[5]

Weiland was astounded by what he found. He again writes:

From the beginning of the Constitutional era, Christian historians have promoted the myth of the Christian origin of the Constitution. Philip Schaff, the most prominent American evangelical church historian of the late nineteenth century, summarized this view: We may go further and say that the Constitution not only contains nothing which is irreligious or unchristian, but is Christian in substance, though not in form. It is pervaded by the spirit of justice and humanity which are Christian.... Christians have a responsibility to uphold biblical principles in every aspect of life including government. We will never achieve a nation that honors God by promoting the Constitution. Why? The Constitution is not the biblically compatible document we have been told it is. It actually conflicts with Christianity and it is hostile to both God's sovereignty and morality.[6]

The "world" created by America's original Christian forefathers was turned upside down by the constitutionalists in the late 1700s. For the Constitution not to mention religion at all represented a rejection, an extremely controversial decision not to make the United States a Christian nation. It wasn't contemporary liberals who upset the Founders' religious ideas about the United States; it was the Founders who upset the Puritans' ideas.[7]

According to Abraham Lincoln, constitutionalism is a religion in and of itself, demanding absolute devotion and obedience to the Constitution and all laws made in pursuance thereof:

Let every American, every lover of liberty, every well wisher to his posterity, swear by the blood of the Revolution, never to violate in the least particular, the laws of the country; and never to tolerate their violation by others...to the support of the Constitution and Laws, let every American pledge his life, his property, and his sacred honor;--let every man remember that to violate the law, is to trample on the blood of his father, and to tear the character of his own, and his children's liberty. Let reverence for the laws be breathed by every American mother, to the lisping babe, that prattles on her lap--let it be taught in schools, in seminaries, in colleges; let it written in Primers, spelling books, and in Almanacs;--let it be preached from the pulpit, proclaimed in legislative halls, and enforced in courts of justice. And, in short, let it become the political religion of the nation; and let the old and the young, the rich and the poor, the grave and the gay, of all sexes and tongues, and colors and conditions, sacrifice unceasingly upon its altars.[8]

Most Americans, non-Christians and Christians alike, have precisely done just that. According to David Barton:

America's Constitution has been so successful that it is the longest on-going constitutional republic in the history of the world. It was an original and uniquely American document; it was not a compilation of the best clauses of other constitutions from across the world. It contained simple ideas that had never before embodied in written constitutions—politically new and novel practices such as the separation of powers, checks and balances, and full republicanism.[9]

Where did the Founding Fathers get their specific ideas for this most successful of all constitutions? In an attempt to answer this question, Barton writes:

Political scientists embarked on an ambitious ten-year project to analyze some 15,000 writings from the Founding Era. Those writings were examined with the goal of isolating and identifying the specific political sources quoted during the time surrounding the establishment of American government. If the sources of the quotes could be identified, then the origin of the Founders' political ideas could be determined. From the 15,000 writings selected, the researchers isolated some 3,154 quotations and then documented the original sources of those quotations. The research revealed that the single most cited authority in the writings of the Founding Era was the Bible: thirty-four percent of the documented quotes were taken from the Bible—a percentage almost four times higher than the second most quoted source.[10]

For example, George Washington and Alexander Hamilton acknowledged that the principle undergirding the separation of powers was the same principle found in Jeremiah 17:9. This was a principle that had been the subject of numerous sermons during the Founding

Era. Many other Bible verses and principles also found embodiment in the Constitution.

For example, compare Article I, Section 8's provision on uniform immigration laws with Leviticus 19:34; compare Article II, Section 1's provision that a president must be a natural born citizen with Deuteronomy 17:15; then Article III, Section 3's provision against attainder (an item of legislation without judicial process) with Ezekiel 18:20. Notice that Isaiah 33:22 defines the three branches of government, whereas Ezra 7:24 establishes the type of tax exemptions the Founders gave to our churches (and that still exist today). The concept of republicanism set forth in Article IV, Section 4—electing American leaders at the local, county, state, and federal levels—has its origin in Exodus 18:21.[11]

But others like Gary Barnet don't agree with this analysis. Why is this? It is because the U.S. Constitution is one of the most misunderstood documents in history. He writes:

> Even though it is filled with contradictions, it is accepted and revered by most people in America. As I have said many times in the past, it is literally worshipped in this country. This attitude has obviously gone unrewarded, but it is also telling of the success of the indoctrination process that has been going on for the past 200 plus years.... Things are always done for a reason, and in my opinion, the constitution was drafted so as to expand the powers of the national government, and weaken the powers held by the individual states and the people. This has certainly been the end result. I think it is important to remember that many of the Founders of this country, while courageous in their fight to free themselves from English rule, were still politicians, and such had their own agendas. These agendas did not always run parallel with individual freedom, especially considering the Hamiltonians. While this may be hard to swallow for some, it is nonetheless true.... One single reading of Article 1, Section 8 of the current U.S. Constitution should literally scare the living daylights out of all who believe in freedom and liberty.... In Article 1, Section 8

of our current Constitution, the federal government has virtually an unlimited power to tax. This fact alone should have been reason enough to not ratify the Constitution 223 years ago. Of course, most of the rest of those powers given to Congress in Article 1, Section 8 should have also caused great concern for anyone sympathetic to liberty.[12]

The Concept of Freedom and Liberty

The liberty and justice enjoyed by the people in the Western world and in other countries are increasingly seen as the products of a benevolent, secular government that is the provider of all things.[13] Unfortunately, there is no awareness that the liberties and rights that are currently operative in the free societies of the West are to a great degree the result of Christian influence. "All previous architects of civic freedom and justice drew extensively from the Christian perspective regarding humanity's God-given freedoms, which had for most of human history never really been implemented."[14]

Christianity's accent on the individual was a necessary condition for freedom and liberty to surface in the Magna Carta (1215), in England's Petition of Rights (1628), in the Bill of Rights (1689), and, of course, in the American Bill of Rights (1791). Political, economic, and religious freedom can only exist where there is liberty and freedom of the individual. Group rights that determine a person's rights on the basis of belonging to a given ethnic or racial group, as presently advocated by multiculturalists and by affirmative action laws, nullify the rights of the individual.[15]

Individual rights and group rights are mutually exclusive; we cannot have it both ways. Ethnicity, race, sex, or party affiliations today increasingly determine a person's rights. This is reminiscent of Hitler, who once said, "The individual is nothing. The group [the Nazi Party] is everything."[16] When group rights get the upper hand, gone are the "unalienable rights" given to the individual by his or her Creator so admirably expressed in the American Declaration of Independence.[17]

The problem is that although 2 Corinthians 3:17 states, "Where the

Spirit of the Lord is, there is liberty," and inscribed on America's Liberty Bell are these words, "Proclaim liberty throughout the land unto all the inhabitants thereof" (Leviticus 25:10 KJV), the Spirit of the Lord cannot be found in the Constitution because God and His perfect laws of liberty were flagrantly disregarded. Instead of liberty, the Constitution provided us with bondage: dishonest and reprobate legislators, ever-expanding debt, an ungodly court system, an unnecessary and inept prison system, corruption, licenses, permits, countless registrations, ungodly wars, in addition to taxes on nearly everything. None of these atrocities occur under God's system of law.[18] R. J. Rushdoony pointed out the subtly deceptive reasoning of governments based upon freedom when he wrote:

> A society which makes freedom its primary goal will lose it, because it has made, not responsibility, but freedom from responsibility, its purpose. When freedom is the basic emphasis, it is not responsible speech which is fostered but irresponsible speech. If freedom of press is abolished, libel will be defended finally as a privilege of freedom, and if free speech is abolished, slander finally becomes a right. Religious liberty becomes a triumph of irreligion. Tyranny and anarchy take over. Freedom of speech, press, and religion all give way to controls, totalitarian controls. The goal must be God's Law and order, in which alone is true liberty.[19]

The Constitution might have been ratified only for religious people as John Adams stated to the Massachusetts militia in 1789, but today "many supporters of socialism, communism, fascism, and other highly centralized governmental systems have a strong distaste for the freedom of the individual because such freedom hampers and impedes authoritarian/totalitarian governments from controlling the expressions and movements of its citizens. Without freedom of the individual there is no freedom, whether it is on the economic, political, or religious level."[20]

Jesus strongly emphasized the importance and significance of the individual person. He proclaimed, "For God so loved the world that

He gave His only begotten Son, that whoever believes in Him should not perish but have everlasting life" (John 3:16). According to the Lord Jesus Christ, salvation is a personal and individual choice. No one gets into heaven unless he or she believes in the atoning merits of what He did on the cross. Paul reiterated this by saying that God is personal and very close to each one of us.

> God, who made the world and everything in it, since He is Lord of heaven and earth, does not dwell in temples made with hands. Nor is He worshiped with men's hands, as though He needed anything, since He gives to all life, breath, and all things. And He has made from one blood every nation of men to dwell on all the face of the earth, and has determined their preappointed times and the boundaries of their dwellings, so that they should seek the Lord, in the hope that they might grope for Him and find Him, though He is not far from each one of us; for in Him we live and move and have our being, as also some of your own poets have said, "For we are also His offspring." (Acts 17:24–28)

As I have already noted, whether all the Constitutional framers were individually Christians or not we don't know; but what we do know was that there was a general consensus of theism among them—the belief that God existed—but they probably didn't have a personal, intimate relationship with Jesus Christ. In other words, some of them didn't have a personal revelation of the Lord in their hearts that is common today within Christendom. Real faith comes from knowing God personally and individually in the person of the Lord Jesus Christ. It springs from the heart. God through the Holy Spirit dwells in the hearts of men. Jeremiah reminds us, "And you will seek Me and find Me, when you search for Me with all your heart" (Jeremiah 29:13).

The purpose of our God-given liberty is to worship and serve God. The Lord delivered the Israelites from under the burden of Pharaoh so that they would worship and serve Him:

> For long ago [in Egypt] I broke your yoke and burst your bonds [not that you might be free, but that you might serve Me] and long

ago you shattered the yoke and snapped the bonds [of My law which I put upon you]; you said, I will not serve and obey You! For upon every high hill and under every green tree you [eagerly] prostrated yourself [in idolatrous worship], playing the harlot. (Jeremiah 2:20 AMP)

And when the children of Israel had come to the Wilderness of Sinai, the Lord revealed the reason why He rescued them from slavery, which is not too different from us today. The Bible tells us these things befell them as an example and warning to us all (see 1 Corinthians 10:11).

And Moses went up to God, and the Lord called to him out of the mountain, Say this to the house of Jacob and tell the Israelites: You have seen what I did to the Egyptians, and how I bore you on eagles' wings and brought you to Myself. Now therefore, if you will obey My voice in truth and keep My covenant, then you shall be My own peculiar possession and treasure from among and above all peoples; for all the earth is Mine. And you shall be to Me a kingdom of priests, a holy nation [consecrated, set apart to the worship of God]. These are the words you shall speak to the Israelites. (Exodus 19:3–6 AMP; see 1 Peter 2:9–10).

Conclusion

Christianity in the West has laid the foundation of civil and religious liberty. Alvin Schmidt said, "In whatever nations where the heritage of Christianity has had a prominent presence, there has been marked improvement in liberty and justice as opposed to societies that have been, or continue to be, dominated by non-Christian religions."[21]

We could not find a better example of liberty and justice than in the United States of America. This is because American liberty and justice has been profoundly influenced by Christian principles. Alexis de Tocqueville was right when he said, "There is no country in the world where the Christian religion retains a greater influence over the souls of men than in America."[22] Or as one Jewish author has noted, "The American civilization rests on the basic principles of Christian morality which have their origin in the Hebrew Scriptures."[23] The great emphasis on liberty and justice in the United States is not mere happenstance. It exists because the American architects of liberty and justice were influenced to a large degree by Christianity's biblical values and beliefs. "Remove the Bible as the constellation that guides the American Ship of State and the whole edifice of American civilization collapses."[24]

And regarding Western countries outside the United States, the historian Carlton Hayes has remarked, "Wherever Christian ideals have been generally accepted and their practice sincerely accepted, there is a dynamic liberty; and wherever Christianity had been ignored or rejected, persecuted or chained to the state, there is tyranny."[25] At the present time we are seeing an unprecedented acceleration of tyranny in the history of the United States and the West in general. Some are speculating that we almost now live in a police state that is run by an "elite" group who pass laws for the people but exempt themselves from those same laws.

This is happening because most Christians no longer believe in God's Word as the basis of justice. Or to say it another way, nothing will restore true liberty to the West unless, and until, there is a return to God and His revealed Word. The West should not abandon the Christian principles that made them great; we cannot continue violating the moral laws of God without any consequences. We are now at a moment in time at which we Christians and our leaders must devote ourselves to a time of prayer, fasting, repentance for a true revival and a Great Awakening, and to once again acknowledge that we surely cannot survive unless God Himself intervenes.

Endnotes

[1] Harry Elmer Barnes, *History and Social Intelligence* (New York: Alfred A. Knopf, 1926), 347–348. Cited in Ted R. Weiland, *Bible Law Versus The United States Constitution*, 79.

2 David Barton, *The Role of Pastors & Christians in Civil Government* (Texas: Wall Builder Press, 2003), 16–18.

3 Ibid.

4 *The Works of John Adams, Second President of the United States*, Editor Frances Adams (Boston: Little Brown and Company, 1854), vol. 1, X, 229. "Letter to Massachusetts Militia," October 11, 1798.

5 Ted R. Weiland, Preface, 2–3.

6 Ted R. Weiland, Preface, 2–3.

7 Nicolas Lehman, *The New Republic*, quoted in Isaac Kramnick and R. Laurence Moore, *The Godless Constitution: The Case Against Religious Correctness* (New York: W. W. North & Company, 1966), 1.

8 Abraham Lincoln, "The Perpetuation of Our Political Institutions: Address Before the Young Men's Lyceum of Springfield, Illinois, January 27, 1838," Abraham Lincoln Online Speeches and Writings, accessed from *http://showcase.netins.net/web/creative/Lincoln/speeches/lyceum.htm*.

9 David Barton, 16–18.

10 Ibid.

11 Ibid.

12 Gary D. Barnett, "I'm Fed Up With Constitution Worship," accessed from *http://www.lewrockwell.com/barnett26.1.html*.

13 Alvin J. Schmidt, *How Christianity Changed the World* (Grand Rapids: Zondervan, 2004), 248.

14 Ibid.

15 Ibid., 259.

16 Ibid.

17 Ibid.

18 Ted R. Weiland, 79.

19 R. J. Rushdoony, *The Institutes of Biblical Law* (The Presbyterian and Reformed Publishing Company, 1973), 581.

20 Alvin J. Schmidt, 258.

21 Ibid., 270.

22 Alexis de Tocqueville, *Democracy in America*, 314.

23 Kevin Abrams, *The Pink Swastika: Homosexuality in the Nazi Party* (Keizer: Founders Publishing Corporation, 1996), viii.

24 Ibid.

25 Carlton J. H. Hayes, *Christianity and Western Civilization* (Stanford University Press, 1954), 21.

Part IV: A Brief Look at the Slave Trade

CHAPTER 23

The Roots of Slavery in Britain and America

Man is born free; and everywhere he is chains one thinks himself the master of others, and still remains a greater slave than they.

—*Jean Jacques Rousseau*

Is Slavery Normal?

Before the time of the Romans, the practice of slavery was normal in what was called Britannia. It continued to be accepted as part of society under the Roman Empire. Slavery in the British Isles was practiced before Roman occupation, and in North America it was firmly established by the time of the United States Declaration of Independence was formed. The question most people ask is, How could America, which was founded by Christian Pilgrims, be involved in slavery? During its struggle with Great Britain, American leaders often admitted that slavery was contrary to the principles for which they fought—among these was liberty—and a number of reformers warned that the revolution could be justified only by a decision to rid the land of slavery.[1]

Dr. Frederick K. C. Price, who courageously tells it all in his well-researched work *Race, Religion, and Racism*, asks further ethical questions regarding this sensitive issue. But before we look at those questions, I have to point out that some have accused Dr. Price's books and teachings about this issue of slavery of inhaling racial animosity and teaching blacks to hate whites. I have read two volumes of his, but I didn't find any racial overtones in them.

I cannot be imprisoned in the life of resentment and bitterness toward whites regardless of what happened to me because of racism or slavery. Besides, most of the problems I've had in my life were self-inflicted: I sinned and made the wrong choices not because I am black but because of my own wrong actions. So I don't blame others but take full responsibility for all my choices. One of the reasons I have included this subject in this book is that many people have asked me so many questions regarding the issues of race and slavery, and as someone has rightly said, "We all don't know our subjects, the most we can know is where and how to find out the things we don't know."[2]

Therefore I hold no grudge or animosity against the West because of the issue of slavery. I am very proud of my African heritage, but I am also proud to be a British citizen (as of now), and to live in a country that raised people who had the good sense and decency to abolish slavery, send missionaries to spread the gospel, and to fight for other human rights.

Black People Were Considered Inferior

Edmund Morgan and David Brion, in their book *The Problem of Slavery in Western Culture,* explain that the promotion and protection of personal liberty was the highest virtue of man. After taking slavery for granted since the beginning of its history in the West, in a remarkably short period of time during the eighteenth century, slavery was redefined as the greatest evil, a moral and socioeconomic scourge that had to be exterminated.[3] Historians and economists have debated the economic effects of slavery for Great Britain and the North American colonies. Many analysts suggest that it allowed the formation of capital that financed the Industrial Revolution, although the evidence is unconvincing.

Dr. Price asks, "We know that slavery was an economic proposition, but what were the conditions that allowed some Christian men and women to condone it? What entered the minds of intelligent, rational people that caused them to mistreat a whole race of people who had never done anything negative to them? What allowed them to treat a whole race of people in a way in which they themselves would never have wanted to be treated?"[4] Furthermore, why do blacks behave the way they do?

The first answer, of course, to these many questions is a big lie that black people are inferior and not fully human, and therefore they needed to be segregated from the whites. In fact, the slave traders used Darwin's theory of evolution as philosophical justification for the slave trade, just as Hitler did for the Holocaust. This was an obvious lie, but a lie told often enough eventually becomes the truth.

Phillip Yancey tells us that he grew up as a racist and remembers well when the South practiced a perfectly legal form of apartheid. Stores in downtown Atlanta had three restrooms: one for white men, one for white women, and one for colored people. Gas stations had two drinking foundations, one for whites and one for colored. Certain motels and restaurants served white patrons only. And when the Civil Rights Act made such discrimination illegal, many owners closed their businesses instead of serving colored people.

He also tells of a time when he visited the Holocaust Museum in Washington, D.C., and was deeply moved by its depiction of Nazi atrocities against the Jews. What struck him most, however, was a section early in the exhibit that demonstrated how the early discrimination laws against the Jews—the "Jews only" shops, park benches, restrooms, and drinking fountains—were explicitly modeled on segregation laws in the United States.[5]

Religion and Evolution

Secondly, Price says blacks believe the way they do because slavery could never have happened without the consent of the church. But how can religion, which we associate with the Word of God, be a perpetrator of something evil like racism? The answer is that religion is not necessarily equated with the Word of God; religion is very often the word of man *about* the Word of God, and that has been the problem. While religion can mean the service or worship of God, it is also defined as a personal set or institutionalized system of religious attitudes, beliefs, and practices. Men have distorted the Word of God to foster their own racist attitudes, beliefs, and practices.[6]

Even Hitler had a religion called Nazism. There is even a picture of him leaving church that was distributed as part of his support to control the churches in Germany. The air Adolf Hitler and most Western people breathed in their childhood was soaked in the conviction that imperialism is a biologically necessary process, which according to the laws of nature, leads to the inevitable destruction of the lower races. It was an experiment that had been tried before in human history, and that had cost millions of lives before Hitler ever arrived on the world scene.

This acceptance of the theory of evolution is still held by many people today, and it has been the main position that underlies much of the attack on the authority of the Bible as the inspired Word of God during the past seventy years. This accepted theory is based on a materialistic assumption of atheism—that there is no need for a supernatural God or an Intelligent Designer of creation, and that everything in our universe, including humans, has evolved from dead, inanimate matter by random chance over many billions of years. Furthermore, many scholars have rightly noted that this generation of believers in the Western world is the first generation in the last 2,000 years of the Christian church to have faith in Christ and the Word of God and yet have deep reservations about the scientific accuracy of the Bible, especially the book of Genesis regarding God's creation of the heavens and earth, and ultimately the creation of man and woman in His image.

Darwin's Theory of Evolution

Charles Darwin (1809–1882) was a British scientist whose theories about evolution and natural selection became the foundation of our modern biology. The idea of evolution wasn't new with Darwin; it has been claimed that other scientists had explored it before him, including Darwin's grandfather, Erasmus Darwin, who had proposed a theory of evolution in the 1790s. But it was Charles Darwin who presented evolution in a more convincing way through a process he termed "natural selection."

He wrote a book in 1859 entitled *On the Origin of Species by Means of Natural Selection or the Preservation of Favored Races in the Struggle for Life*. In this book he wrote about the evolution of animals, and later in 1871, he applied his same ideas to humans in his book *The Descent of Man and Selection in Relation to Sex*. He believed that when animals compete in this life and struggle for food, the strongest survive and the weak are eliminated, which has been termed as "survival of the fittest." According to his theory, the natural breeding process works by selecting the best and letting others die out, resulting in a slow but steady evolution.

Darwin's ideas had huge consequences for intelligent design. His theory of evolution assumed that various living creatures developed over millions of years, but the Bible says that "God saw everything that He had made, and behold, it was very good (suitable, pleasant) and He approved it completely. And there was evening and there was morning, a sixth day" (Genesis 1:31 AMP). So Darwin's theory of natural selection disregards God's creative order according to the Holy Scriptures.

These were Darwin's theories that encouraged racism, and which contributed to slavery. They allowed scientists and biologists to ignore intelligent design and to apply absolutely no value to other human beings they deemed undesirables. The Darwinists believe that only the fittest survive. Regardless of whether their philosophy is mainstream or not, the genetic implication of Darwinism is that there must be a master race, and thus inferior ones.

The Famous Scopes Trial

For example, the racism associated with evolution was exposed during the famous 1925 Scopes Trial: The State of Tennessee vs. John Thomas Scopes. It is perhaps better known by its other name, "the monkey trial." It was about a teacher who broke the state's law against teaching the theory of evolution in a public school. The main debate about the trial was the relationship between faith and science in the United States.

The book that Scopes was using to teach the theory of evolution was George William Hunter's *A Civic Biology*. In that book, he talked about the evolution of man and how there once lived races of men who were much lower in their mental organization than the present inhabitants.[7] Excerpts from the book give the author's views about white supremacy, eugenics, contempt for people with disabilities, and impatience with charity.

Improvement of Man. --- If the stock of domesticated animals can be improved, it is not unfair to ask if the health and vigor of the future generations of men and women on the earth might not be improved by applying to them the laws of selection.... These are personal hygiene, selection of healthy mates, and the betterment of the environment.

Eugenics. --- When people marry there are certain things that the individual as well as the race should demand. The most important of these is freedom from germ diseases which might be handed down to the offspring.... The science of being well born is called eugenics.

Parasitism and its Cost to Society. --- Hundreds of families such as those described above exist today, spreading disease, immorality, and crime to all parts of this country. The cost to society of such families is very severe.... They not only do harm to others by corrupting, stealing, or spreading disease, but they are actually protected and cared for by the state out of public money. Largely for them the poorhouse and the asylum exist. They take from society, but they give nothing in return. They are true parasites.

The Remedy. --- If such people were lower animals, we would probably kill them off to prevent them from spreading. Humanity will not allow this, but we do have the remedy of separating the sexes in asylums or other places and in various ways preventing intermarriage and the possibilities of perpetuating such a low and degenerate race. Remedies of this sort have been tried successfully in Europe and are now meeting with some success in this country.[8]

In regards to the races of men, the trial spoke of five races: "At present there exist upon the earth five races of man, each very different from the other in instincts, social customs, and, to an extent, in structure. These are the Ethiopian or Negro type, originating in Africa; the Malay or brown race, from the islands of the Pacific; the American Indian; the Mongolian or yellow race, including the natives of China, Japan, and the Eskimos; and finally, the highest type of all, the Caucasians represented by the civilized white inhabitants of Europe and America."[9] George William Hunter therefore concluded that the Caucasians are the "highest type of all."

The Forgotten Heritage

Thirdly, Price says that some American or British blacks behave the way they do because they don't understand their history; it is only by understanding history that we can understand the present situation we find ourselves in. Much of what is going on today stems directly from the past.[10] Dr. Kenneth Stamp explains this further by suggesting that slaves were conditioned to feel "that their color was a badge of degradation."[11] Up to this day many blacks think they are inferior to other races. They were taught to degrade themselves in every possible way; they were not considered fully human and a sense of complete dependence on others was instilled within them. It was easy for slave owners to politically and economically subjugate blacks because they were not considered persons with a conscious or feelings. But blacks have feelings just like any other human race. The Bible tells us: "And He has made from one blood every nation of men to dwell on all the face of the earth" (Acts 17:26).

The fourth reason many blacks act the way they do is because the government gave black people emancipation, but the damage had already been done. The government permitted black people to be taken from their native lands, made them into slaves, and then stripped them of their heritage and family ties so that they could not find agreement and strength with each other. And that is the reason why so many blacks are ashamed of their race and ancestry. Africans and blacks in general should get rid of this same mindset and learn how to live according to what God and His Word says about them rather than what man says or the circumstances look like.[12]

Blacks should understand that God is no respecter of persons (see Acts 10:35). We have been portrayed in the media as people who are primitive and backward, and that is why many don't want to know anything about Africa. The government made it perfectly legal for black fathers to be sold in one direction, their wives sold off in another, and their children sold off in still another direction, breaking all family bonds and generations of families.

Many of these people were torn away from their families, traditions, and cultures, and given up to survive in a world with no historical definitions to guide them. This has greatly impacted the men who have been stripped of their human dignity, sense of manhood, and the purpose of why they were created. The outcome of this has been very disastrous as many of the men who are supposed to be the leaders of families have lost hope, self-esteem, and meaning in life.

They see themselves as victims of history, with no sense of what a real man or woman is supposed to be. From 1619 until 1865, black people were taken from Africa, made into slaves, and taught absolutely nothing. The majority of them could not read or write, and they could barely speak the language. Then the government opened the gate and set them free, and acted amazed because they did not compete with whites. They could not read, because for all those years it was against the law to teach a black person to read. But we should not forget that there were many wonderful, good, precious, and honest white Christians who taught their slaves to read, at the risk of their own lives.

The Scientific and Biblical View

The universe and all of humanity were created purposely by an intelligent God. The Scriptures declare, "In the beginning God created the heavens and the earth" (Genesis 1:1). The existence of God as our Creator is overwhelming concerning the truth about the purpose and meaning of our existence in the universe. So the question is, Who created this complex heaven and earth, which includes the complicated biological life that flourishes on this beautiful planet? It is God Almighty who created it all.

But then we may ask, Where did He come from if He wasn't born? Or if no one created Him, how did He begin to be who He is? The Bible tells us that God eternally existed, that He has always been there and will always be there, and that He is who He is. He was always the Creator and never a creature. In Hebrews 11 we read that it is by faith we understand that the worlds were framed by the word of God, so that the things which are seen were not made of things which are visible (see Hebrews 11:3). Then, a few verses later in the same chapter, we read that "he who comes to God must believe that He is, and that He is a rewarder of those who diligently seek Him" (Hebrews 11:6).

We cannot scientifically prove whether God exits or not. The Bible says we are to believe that God is there and He wants us to seek Him and find Him, know Him, love Him, and serve Him. We do not need to explain the existence of God because eternity cannot be mentally comprehended. Our minds are finite, prohibited from grasping everlasting concepts. Scripture declares that God infinite: "Before the mountains were brought forth, or ever You had formed the earth and the world, even from everlasting to everlasting, You are God" (Psalm 90:2). As we meditate on this, we'll frustrate our intellectual reasoning since "no one can begin to understand eternity" (Job 36:26 TLB). The Amplified Bible says, "Behold, God is great, and we know Him not! The number of His years is unsearchable"(Job 36:26 AMP).

To see how complex we are, just consider one part of the human body—the brain—as described by researcher and Bible teacher Grant Jeffrey:

Of all of the glorious examples of God's intelligent design is the creation of a human body. Your body (whether your skin color is white, black, yellow, or pink) is a structural masterpiece more amazing than science fiction.... The complexity and intricate order found in the human brain almost defies our comprehension.... In less than one second, your brain can calculate the trajectory of a football thrown at thirty miles an hour toward you by your friend without any prior warning whatsoever. Your brain instantly calculates your position and the ball's trajectory, and sends detailed electronic messages to the muscles in your arms and legs at more than three hundred miles a second to move you into a position to catch the ball. Despite billions of dollars and fifty years of advanced research on the brain by computer scientists seeking to duplicate its functions, there is no computer on Earth that can equal this marvelous instantaneous computing that is required to allow you to catch a football! Any fair-minded observer will conclude that the awesomely designed human brain must have been designed and created by God exactly as revealed in the Bible.[13]

That is exactly why the psalmist wrote: "You made all the delicate, inner parts of my body and knit me together in my mother's womb. Thank you for making me so wonderfully complex. Your workmanship is marvelous—how well I know it" (Psalm 139:13–14 NLT).

The apostle Paul describes the underlying spiritual reasons why human beings choose to reject the overwhelming evidence that points to the existence of a Creator. Writing to the Romans, he says no one has an excuse for not believing in God. Through everything God created, people can clearly see His invisible qualities, eternal power, and divine nature; therefore, we have no excuse for not knowing God or obeying His commandments.

God is the force of life that holds the worlds, the universe, and the smallest particles yet to be discovered, in place. His glory indeed covers the entire earth. If we discern correctly, we will see His presence everywhere we look. This is why Paul tells us:

For since the creation of the world His invisible attributes are clearly seen, being understood by the things that are made, even His eternal power and Godhead, so that they are without excuse, because, although they knew God, they did not glorify Him as God, nor were thankful, but became futile in their thoughts, and their foolish hearts were darkened. Professing to be wise, they became fools. (Romans 1:18–22)

In Him all things consist and have their being. Paul said again, "And He has made from one blood every nation of men to dwell on all the face of the earth…for in Him we live and move and have our being, as also some of your own poets have said, 'For we are also His offspring'" (Acts 17:26, 28). Without Him nothing was made (see John 1:3). He is love, but He is also energy. When He manifests His glory, energy is released—pure light, creative power, and life force radiate from His being. He is the giver of life and He is the light of the world: "For everything comes from Him and exists by His power and is intended for His glory. All glory to him forever! Amen" (Romans 11:36 NLT). This proves that we shrink into insignificance in the light of the magnificence of the great Creator of our universe. If our eyes are opened to the majesty of God's creation and His wisdom, there would be no room for pride but only the fear of the Lord to dwell in our hearts.

Created in God's Image

Life is a combination of two parts: the physical or natural life, and the spiritual or eternal life. We are complete beings made up of a body, soul, and spirit. Two thirds of a person—the spirit and the soul—are hidden from the visible realm. Only the body is visible to the naked eye, and that is because it is made from dust (see Genesis 2:7).

It has been proved that the same essential chemical elements found in man and animal life are found in the soil as well. We did not know this scientific fact until recent times, but God displayed it here in the creation of humanity. The body was taken from dust, the soul is the life which man then becomes, and the spirit is the life God gives to him. The body has world-consciousness and is an instrument of the life of the soul.

Since Adam and Eve sinned, the body seeks evil more easily than good.

The soul implies a self-conscious life. Our soul is the seat of our affections, desires, emotions, and active will. It is where our choices are made that bring either light or darkness into our lives, and these choices are based on who or what power we have allowed to be in control of us.

And the spirit is the part of us that has God-consciousness, and it is the part of man that "knows" his own mind. Because man is a spirit, he can communicate with God, who is also a Spirit. The Bible says that "there is a spirit in man, and the breath of the Almighty gives him understanding" (Job 32:8; see Psalm 18:28). Man's spirit is the spring of his inmost thoughts and intents.

The spirit and the soul are not the same thing—they are different. With our bodies we contact the physical realm, with our spirits we contact the spiritual realm, and with our souls we contact the soulish realm, which houses our intellect will and emotions. The Bible says, "God created mankind in His own image; in the image of God He created him; male and female He created them" (Genesis 1:27). That means whether we're white or black, we are created in God's image.

Christ died for all the races and tribes of the world, and we are all beautiful and precious in His sight: "He made from one [common origin, one source, one blood] all nations of men to settle on the face of the earth, having definitely determined [their] allotted periods of time and the fixed boundaries of their habitation (their settlements, lands, and abodes)" (Acts 17:26 AMP). And the book of Revelation says, "After these things I looked, and behold, a great multitude which no one could number, of all nations, tribes, peoples, and tongues, standing before the throne and before the Lamb, clothed with white robes, with palm branches in their hands, and crying out with a loud voice, saying, 'Salvation belongs to our God who sits on the throne, and to the Lamb!'" (Revelation 7:9–10).

So if the Bible says that we are all created in God's image, then we are also made in His likeness. The Hebrew word *tselem* (which is translated as image) also means "likeness." Another word for this is "resemblance" or "representation." If God the Father, the Son Jesus Christ, and God the Holy Spirit are a Spirit, then we are also spiritual beings since we are created in His image. Since God is a Spirit and man is flesh, that means our likeness to Him is not in physical resemblance. Rather, God has endowed all human beings, regardless of the color of their skin, with spiritual, intellectual, and moral likeness unto Himself.

Being created in His image means that God gave us His spiritual and moral nature, which means we possess His attributes, character, and nature. Because we are all created in the image and likeness of God, we were not created to be slaves, but to "be fruitful, multiply, and fill the earth, and subdue it [using all its vast resources in the service of God and man]; and have dominion over the fish of the sea, the birds of the air, and over every living creature that moves upon the earth" (Genesis 1:28 AMP).[14]

Black Is Beautiful

Noah's comments about Canaan being cursed (see Genesis 9:25) have been wrongly used to support racial prejudice and even slavery. The Chaldeans were one of the many Kushite tribes of the region (Kushite means "black"). The Kushites descended from Kush son of Ham. Noah's curse according to biblical and historical experts was not directed toward any particular race, but rather at the Canaanite nation itself. The Lord knew that this nation would become wicked. The curse was fulfilled when the Israelites entered the Promised Land and drove the Canaanites out as recorded in the book of Joshua.[15]

Marriage with a Canaanite was forbidden, but not with a Kushite or Egyptian, who were both black races. In fact, Joseph married an Egyptian wife (see Genesis 41:45). If at all the black race was cursed, as some people claim, then the Lord would not have become angry with Miriam and Aaron for criticizing Moses because of his Kushite wife, who was black. The Bible tells us that God asked them:

> "Why then were you not afraid to speak against My servant Moses?" So the anger of the Lord was aroused against them, and He departed. And when the cloud departed from above the

tabernacle, suddenly Miriam became leprous, as white as snow. Then Aaron turned toward Miriam, and there she was, a leper. (Numbers 12:6–10)

The Bible doesn't tell us why Miriam criticized this Kushite woman, but God would not allow bigoted comments against people of color. In fact, King Solomon, the wisest of all men, noted in the Song of Songs, that black is beautiful: "I am dark (black) but beautiful, O women of Jerusalem—dark as the tents of Kedar, dark as the curtains of Solomon's tents" (Song of Solomon 1:5 NLT).

According to a legend recorded by Josephus in the second century, before Moses became the Jewish liberator, he served as a general in the Egyptian army, fighting a war against Ethiopia. After he became victorious, he took an Ethiopian princess as a bride—the very same Kushite wife mentioned in the Bible. The offspring from that union are the original Beta Israel, also known as the Falasha. One historian suggested that before the advent of Christianity, at least half the inhabitants of Ethiopian blacks worshiped "the God of Abraham, Isaac, Jacob, and Moses."[16] The Ethiopian rulers took pains to claim descent from Menelek I, the supposed offspring of the union between Solomon and the Queen of Sheba. Some people even claim the Ethiopian Orthodox Church is almost as much Jewish as it is Christian, reflecting the tremendous influence of Judaism on Ethiopian culture.[17] According to Rabbi Benjamin Blech: "Clearly, Jews must have played a very powerful role with the blacks of Ethiopia from earliest times, which is why some claim that Jewish beginnings in Ethiopia go back to the tribe of Dan that was the first of the lost ten tribes of Israel."[18]

Michael L. Brown made an interesting observation when he wrote, "I personally believe that there is a special relationship between African-Americans (blacks) and Jews: Both are liberated slaves, both have been and are still persecuted minorities, both have special 'soul,' a unique personality and gifting. One day I believe we will see that we desperately need each other."[19]

In the meantime, we should be encouraged that Jesus Christ breaks down all racial barriers and accepts all people regardless of race, social standing, or gender:

> [In this new creation all distinctions vanish.] There is no room for
> and there can be neither Greek nor Jew, circumcised nor
> uncircumcised, [nor difference between nations whether alien]
> barbarians or Scythians [who are the most savage of all], nor slave
> or free man; but Christ is all and in all [everything and
> everywhere, to all men, without distinction of person].
> (Colossians 3:11 AMP)

Two Opposing Accounts

Many well-meaning people have unconditionally accepted that the theory of evolution as taught in schools and colleges must be scientifically true. If it is true, then the Bible's account of creation as recorded in the book of Genesis must be false and nothing more than a myth. These opposing accounts cannot coexist together. Either creation or the theory of evolution is correct—not both.

At some point, Christians place their faith and trust for their salvation and eternity in the truthfulness of the teachings, life, death, and resurrection of Jesus Christ as recorded in the New Testament. But if they have been taught that the Bible's statements about God's creation in Genesis are false, then how can they logically and confidently place their faith and trust for salvation and eternity in heaven upon the authority of Christ's promises of salvation as recorded in the Holy Scriptures?

Grant Jeffrey explains: "The problem is that millions of Christians in our generation who believe that evolution has been proven scientifically to be true have tremendously weakened their faith in Christ, whether or not they talk about that logical contradiction or even think about it clearly."[20] The reason Christians believe in evolution is because we've been taught it from our childhood.

Richard Wumbrand was a Jew who converted to Christianity and suffered under the Nazis and the communists. He was strictly anti-evolutionist and declared it strange that the communists accepted the teachings of Sir Charles Darwin. He said, "If you believe you were created by God, you will try to become Godlike. If you believe you sprang from apes, you are in danger of turning into a beast."[21] And A. W. Tozer said so beautifully,

> God made you in His image whether you are black or white or yellow, and you're stuck with it. God did not make the chimpanzee in His image. He did not make the horse, that symphony in motion, in His image. God did not make that beautiful bird that the poet says "sings darkling," His nocturnal note in His image. God made him beautiful, but He didn't make him in His image. God made only you in His image and you're stuck with it, sinner and Christian both, black and white. You're made in the image of God, and nothing short of God will satisfy you.[22]

Charles Finney and Oberlin College

Of course there were many other voices in the American church that did not believe in the theory of evolution too—they renounced slavery as a sin. One such voice was Evangelist Charles Finney, president of Oberlin College, which admitted both black and white students as equals decades before the Civil War. As a matter of fact, the students from the college where Finney was president not only became some of the most active conductors of the Underground Railroad but also started several of America's black colleges and universities.[23]

In one of his articles, "The Argument that Great and Good Men have been and are Freemasons, Examined," Charles Finney said that the same argument Masons were attempting to sustain their institution was that same one that sustained the practice of slaveholding. He is reported to have said:

> Why, how many wise and good men, it was said, were slaveholders. The churches and ecclesiastical bodies at the North were full of charity in respect to them but they could not denounce slaveholding as a sin. They would say that it was an evil; but for a long time they could not be persuaded to pronounce it as a moral evil, a sin. Why? Because so many doctors of divinity

were slaveholders and were defending the institution. Because a large portion of the church, of nearly every denomination, were involved in the abomination. "They are good," it was said; "they are great men—we must be charitable." And so, when this horrid civil war came on, these great and good men, that had sustained the institution of slavery, sustained and stimulated the war. Many of them took up arms, and fought with desperation to sustain the institution. But what is thought now—at least throughout all the North, and throughout all the Christian world—of the great and good men who have done this thing? Who does not now admit that they were deluded? That they had anything but the Spirit of Christ? That they were in the hands of the devil all along?[24]

Oberlin College doctrine held firm that slavery was a sin, based on the Bible and according to modern standards of Christian brotherhood. Oberlinites read with approval Theodore Weld's tract *The Bible Against Slavery,* first published in 1837, then Beriah Green's *The Church Carried Along* (1836), Charles Fitch's *Slaveholding Weighed in the Balance* (1837), J. G. Fee's *The Sinfulness of Slaveholding* (1851), and the anti-slavery theological writings of Wesleyans like Luther Lee, LaRoy Sunderland, and Lucius Matlack. When the Church Anti-Slavery Society offered a prize "for the best tract on the teaching of the Bible respecting slavery," the contest was won by an Oberlin student, Isaac Allen, for an essay entitled "Is Slavery Sanctioned by the Bible?"

In 1862 Reuben Hatch published his elaborate study *Bible Servitude Re-Examined,* in which he attempted to prove that slavery in the modern sense was not sanctioned in the sacred Scriptures. Oberlin Christians renounced their allegiance to all Christian benevolent societies that did not take part in the battle against the sin of slavery. The most important result of this action was the establishment of the American Missionary Association, a powerful Christian anti-slavery agency which sent its representatives into every important anti-slavery battleground.[25]

The root of slavery in Britain and America was racism. The West found it very hard to choose between the ideal of equality and reality of racism and slavery. They contradicted what the Bible has to say about people being created in God's image and likeness (see Genesis 1:27; Acts 17:26), and also contradicted what the Declaration of Independence affirms—that we're all created equal. The signers of this document believed that human rights were God-given, and, as such, they were universal and absolute—they were the rights of all people, in all places, at all times, regardless of their nationality, background, disability, race, or religion. No one is an accident. What the signers of the Declaration forgot was that the rights that are given by men can easily be taken away as we shall examine in the next chapter.

Endnotes

[1] Edmund Morgan and David Brion, *The Problem of Slavery in Western Culture* (Oxford University Press, 1996), 3.

[2] I am quoting one of my lecturers from my school days.

[3] Morgan and Brion, Ibid.

[4] Dr. Frederick K. C. Price, *Race, Religion & Racism, Volume 1: A Bold Encounter with Division in the Church* (Faith One Publishing, 1999), 169.

[5] Philip Yancey, *What Is So Amazing About Grace?* (Grand Rapids, Michigan: Zondervan Publishing, 1997), 130.

[6] Ibid.

[7] George William Hunter, *A Civic Biology: Presented in Problems* (University of California Libraries, 1914), 195–196.

[8] Ibid., 261–265.

[9] Ibid.

[10] Ibid.

[11] Kenneth M. Stampp, *The Peculiar Institution: Slavery in the Ante-Bellum South* (New York; 1964), 145.

[12] Ibid., 86–88.

[13] Dr. Grant R. Jeffrey, *Creation, Remarkable Evidence of God's Design* (Frontier Research Publications, Inc., 2003), 36–39.

14 Dr. Myles Munroe, *The Purpose and Power of God's Glory* (Shippensburg, PA: Destiny Image Publishers, Inc., 2000), 8. He writes, "Ruling over other human beings, particularly in an oppressive manner, is not within the original God-given jurisdiction of any person. Human government of laws was a necessary consequence of man's fall, instituted by God to protect the innocent and the helpless and to restrict the spread of sin. Therefore if at all human beings were created to rule the earth under God's overall sovereignty, it would be a contradiction for Him then to decree that any of us should be relegated to a life of subservience to anyone else."

15 J. P. Lange, *A Commentary: The Amplified Bible* (Zondervan Corporation, 1987), 11. "That Noah placed a curse on his youngest grandchild, Canaan, who would naturally, be his favorite, can only be explained on the ground that in the prophetic spirit he saw into the future of the Canaanites. God Himself found the delinquency of the Canaanites insufferable and ultimately drove them out or subdued them and put the descendants of Shem in their place. But Noah's foresight did not yet include the extermination of the Canaanite peoples, for then he would have expressed it differently. He would not merely have called them "the servant of servants" if he had foreseen their destruction. The form of the expression, therefore, testifies to the great age of the prophecy."

16 Rabbi Benjamin Blech, *The Complete Idiot's Guide to Jewish History and Culture* (New York: Alpa Books, 1999), 262.

17 Ibid.

18 Ibid., 263.

19 Michael L. Brown, *Our Hands Are Stained with Blood: The Tragic Story of the Church and the Jewish People* (Shippensburg, PA: Destiny Image Publishers, 1992), 175

20 Dr. Grant R. Jeffrey, *Creation, Remarkable Evidence of God's Design* (Frontier Research Publications, Inc., 2003), 16–17.

21 Richard and Sabina Wumbrand, *A Biography of the Rev. Richard Wumbrand and His Wife Sabina* (Jack Cole, 2000), 163

22 A. W. Tozer, *The Attributes of God: A Journey Into the Father's Heart, Volume 1* (Wing Spread Publishers, 2003), 33.

23 David Barton, *Setting the Record Straight: American History in Black and White* (Wall Builder Press, First Edition, 2004, Second Edition, 2010), 134.

24 Character, Claims and Practical Workings of Freemasonry 1869, Part 3. Accessed from *http://www.matthew548.com/FFree3.html*.

25 Robert Samuel Fletcher, *A History of Oberlin College From Its Foundation Through the Civil War*, accessed from *http://www.gospeltruth.net/oberlinhistory.htm#19*.

CHAPTER 24

Slavery and the Founders

The Issue of Slavery

There has been a lot debate about the issue of slavery throughout the years, precisely because it raises a lot of questions about America's reputation as the defender of human liberty, equality, and freedom. Colonial accounts record that slavery began in the English North American colonies in 1619 when a Dutch ship arrived at Jamestown and "sold us twenty niggers." By the time of the Revolutionary War, there were nearly 700,000 slaves in a total population of 2.5 million people. At the time of the American founding, there were about a half million slaves in the United States, mostly in the five southernmost states, where they made up 40 percent of the population.

During the Civil War in 1860 there were almost 4 million slaves. A number of the leading American Founders—most notably Thomas Jefferson, George Washington, and James Madison—owned slaves, but some did not. Benjamin Franklin thought that slavery was "an atrocious debasement of human nature," and "a source of serious evils." He and Benjamin Rush founded the Pennsylvania Society for Promoting the Abolition of Slavery in 1774.[1]

Jon Jay, who was the president of a similar society in New York, believed:

> The honor of the states, as well as justice and humanity, in my opinion, loudly call upon them to emancipate these unhappy people. To contend for their own liberty, and to deny that blessing to others, involves an inconsistency not to be excused.[2]

John Adams opposed slavery his entire life as a "foul contagion in the human character" and "an evil of colossal magnitude."[3] James Madison owned slaves yet he called slavery "the most oppressive dominion ever exercised by man over man."[4]

George Washington

From his first thoughts about the Revolution to his command of the Continental Army, and even to his presidential administration, George Washington's life and letters reflect a statesman struggling with the reality and inhumanity of slavery in the midst of the free nation being constructed. In 1774 Washington compared the alternative to Americans asserting their rights against British rule to being ruled "till custom and use shall make us as tame and abject slaves, as the blacks we rule over with such arbitrary sway."[5]

However, George Washington owned slaves. He is considered to be a southern traditional planter as he depended on slave labor to make his farm pay. To profit from his farm, he worked his slaves hard, divided their families so they could work more efficiently, punished them by whipping or selling them, and provided them with as little resources as possible.[6]

During his presidency (1789–1797), Washington lived at the President's House in Philadelphia. In 1780 Pennsylvania had passed "An act for the Gradual Abolition of Slavery," which prohibited non-residents from holding slaves in the state longer than six months. In an attempt to circumvent this law, Washington and his wife, neither of them permanent residents of Pennsylvania, rotated their slaves in and out of Pennsylvania so that none of them established continuous residency for six months. This practice violated the Pennsylvania Act, but the Washingtons were never prosecuted under it.[7]

Eventually, however, Washington found slavery to be morally abhorrent, and by 1786 he vowed never to buy another slave again. He freed his slaves in his will, which he wrote secretly; and upon the death of his wife Martha, all slaves under his control were to be educated. He did this even though Martha and his family bitterly opposed it.[8]

During the Revolutionary War, George Washington recruited free blacks into the Continental Army, and by the time of the Battle of Yorktown, African-Americans constituted 25 percent of the army.[9] In a draft of his first inaugural address, he expressed the desire for the country to "reverse the absurd position that the many were made for the few."[10] However, Washington did not seek to abolish slavery immediately or consider it as an issue of emergency. Despite freeing his slaves and not purchasing another slave after 1786, Washington believed slavery would be abolished by "slow, sure and imperceptible degrees."[11]

Thomas Jefferson

Thomas Jefferson condemned slavery and passionately opposed its expansion. In his book *Notes on the State of Virginia*, Jefferson called slavery an inhumane practice that commenced with the Spaniard's first discovery of America. In his first term in the Virginia House of Burgesses, Jefferson proposed a law to free Virginia's slaves.[12] In 1774 he was selected to draft the instructions for the Virginia delegation to the first Continental Congress. He urged the Virginia delegates to abolish the slave trade, saying,

> The abolition of domestic slavery is the great object of desire in those Colonies where it was unhappily introduced in their infant stage.... Previous to the enfranchisement of the slaves we have... to exclude all further importations from Africa...[13]

Furthermore, when Jefferson wrote a draft constitution for the state of Virginia that forbade the importation of slaves, he also in a draft of the Declaration of Independence complained of Britain's introduction of slavery and the slave trade to the colonies:[14]

> Yet our repeated attempts to effect this by prohibitions and by imposing duties which might amount to a prohibition, have been hitherto defeated by his majesties negative; thus preferring the immediate advantages of a few British corsairs to the lasting interests of the American States, and to the rights of human

nature, deeply wounded by this infamous practice.[15]

Jefferson should be admired for instilling in America the democratic principles that we hold so sacred today. But despite him being so outspoken against the issue of slavery, it is also important to know that he owned slaves.[16] At the time he wrote that "all men are created equal," he owned about 200 slaves, and slavery played an integral role in his life. Slaves constructed his classical home and even his personal coffin.[17]

Eventually, however, Thomas Jefferson freed five of his slaves in his will. Even though Virginia law mandated that freed slaves leave the state within a year of their emancipation, Jefferson petitioned the Virginia assembly to permit his freed slaves to remain "where their families and connections are." The Virginia assembly honored Jefferson's request.[18]

He also inserted in the Declaration of Independence a clause that would have freed the slaves, but Congress made numerous changes that resulted in reducing his original draft by approximately 25 percent. His clause condemning the enslavement of the inhabitants of Africa was struck out in deference to South Carolina and Georgia.[19] Although Jefferson is rightly acknowledged for his attempt to insert that clause, he was also tainted by the bigoted views of his time. He thought blacks were inferior to whites in terms of beauty and reasoning intelligence. The opinion that they are inferior in the faculties of reason and imagination must be hazarded with great diffidence.[20]

According to Jefferson, African-Americans were certainly different from whites. He observed the physical differences between blacks and whites and wrote negatively and positively about African-American behavior.[21] For example, Jefferson noticed that as compared to whites, blacks required less sleep but were more innovative than whites.[22] In analyzing their mental capacity, he observed that blacks had better memories than whites but could not reason nearly as well.

Jefferson knew that southern laws prohibited white people from teaching slaves to read, and that there had also been no such laws in ancient Rome where slavery had also been practiced. He insisted the reason some slaves in ancient Rome were philosophers or scientists whereas African-American slaves were not was because these ancient slaves "were of the race of whites."[23] He concluded, "It is not their condition then but nature, which has produced the distinction. Blacks could never be educated to the level of whites, not because they were slaves but because they were black."[24]

However, with respect to moral sense, he believed that God created all men equal. Regardless of his ideas on the equality of men, Jefferson believed that blacks and whites could not coexist as equals.[25] He feared that if whites usurped their individual responsibilities and liberties of choice, there would be a race war resulting in the black race overtaking the whites, just exactly as Tocqueville predicted.[26] He therefore supported the concept of gradual emancipation, as he feared their presence in the slave society would contribute to a slave revolt.[27] Jefferson stated: "There is not a man on earth who would sacrifice more than I would, to relieve us from this heavy reproach.... We have the wolf by the ear, and we can neither hold him, nor safely let him go. Justice is in one scale, and self-preservation in the other."[28]

Miller explains that to a degree, which might have astonished Jefferson himself, the dogma of black inferiority proved to have persisted for several years in the American anthropological, sociological, and historical scholarship.[29] Furthermore, Jefferson wrote that "nothing is more certainly written in the book of fate than that (slaves) are to be free," and he believed that African-Americans had "natural right" to pursue freedom.[30]

He admitted that the black man, in whose favor no laws of property existed, probably feels himself less bound to respect that freedom made in favor of others. This unfortunate difference of color, and perhaps of faculty, was a powerful obstacle to the emancipation of these people.[31] Jefferson did not have to look far to find evidence that hatred of slavery was perfectly compatible with hatred of blacks themselves. Arthur Lee, a Virginia patriot and slave owner himself, considered blacks to be "a race the most detestable and vile that the earth ever produced," and therefore unfit to mix with the white race.[32]

From the beginning, Jefferson wouldn't see a workable solution to ending slavery. Historian David Brion Davis states that in the years after 1785 and "Jefferson's return from France was his immense silence…in addition to having internal conflicts about slavery, Jefferson wanted to keep his personal situation private; for this reason, he chose to back away from working to end slavery."[33]

Thomas Jefferson's 1784 draft plan of government for the western territories prohibited slavery and involuntary servitude after the year 1800. The final Northwest Ordinance of 1787, passed by the Confederation Congress and passed again two years later by the First Congress and signed into law by President George Washington, prohibited slavery in the future states of Ohio, Indiana, Michigan, Illinois, and Wisconsin. That same year, Jefferson published his *Notes on the State of Virginia*, which included a section about slavery and race.

In his *Notes*, Jefferson ends with his famous quote about liberty being secure only if people would realize it as "the gift of God." This quote wasn't meant to encourage religion in America, rather, it was an expression of fear that a slave revolution similar to what happened in 1791 would occur in America. Jefferson believed the outnumbered southern slaveholders would face slaughter and enslavement by blacks, a scenario that even prayer wouldn't change:

> God who gave us life gave us liberty. And can the liberties of a nation be thought secure when we have removed their only firm basis, a conviction in the minds of the people that these liberties are the gift of God? That they are not to be violated but with His wrath? Indeed I tremble for my country when I reflect that God is just and His justice cannot sleep forever: that considering numbers, nature and natural means only a revolution of the wheel of fortune, an exchange of situation is among possible events: that it may become probable by supernatural interference! The Almighty has no attribute which can take side with us in such a contest.[34]

On December 2, 1806, in his annual message to Congress, which was widely reprinted in most newspapers, Thomas Jefferson denounced the "violations of human rights" attending the international slave trade and called for its criminalization on the first day that was possible (January 1, 1808). He said:

> I congratulate you, fellow-citizens, on the approach of the period at which you may interpose your authority constitutionally, to withdraw the citizens of the United States from all further participation in those violations of human rights which have been so long continued on the unoffending inhabitants of Africa, and which the morality, the reputation, and the best interests of our country, have long been eager to prescribe.[35]

Later, on March 2, 1807, President Jefferson signed the Act Prohibiting the Importation of Slaves. This act stated that no new slaves were permitted to be imported into the United States, it ended the legality of the transatlantic slave trade, and it took effect in 1808, the earliest date permitted by the United States Constitution. It states:

> The Migration or Importation of such Persons as any of the States now existing shall think proper to admit, shall not be prohibited by the Congress prior to the Year one thousand eight hundred and eight, but a tax or duty may be imposed on such Importation, not exceeding ten dollars for each Person.[36]

Just before his death, Thomas Jefferson, while referring to slavery, asserted that all eyes are opened, or are at least opening, to the rights of man.[37]

Emancipation Proclamation: Abraham Lincoln

As a result of signing the Emancipation Proclamation, Abraham Lincoln became almost a messiah to the Negro race. He was uncomfortable with such adulations and he felt it was the fearless abolition leaders who had paved the way for him. He refused to take the credit and he reportedly said it was God who deserved all the glory.

Many people believe that Abraham Lincoln freed the slaves because of a heartfelt desire to do what was right in the sight of God.

But others were not amused. They argued that many politicians made similar claims, for words come easily to political office seekers, but when we consider all the words of Lincoln's addresses, it is difficult to discount his spirit of dedication.[38]

Historian Philip Ostergard records that almost 6,000 people in Lewiston heard him speak on the Declaration of Independence and the Founders' belief that all men were created in God's image. Abraham Lincoln, giving a speech at Lewiston, Illinois, on August 17, 1858, said:

> We hold these truths to be self-evident; that all men are created equal; that they are endowed by their Creator with certain unalienable rights; that among these are life, liberty and the pursuit of happiness. This was their majestic interpretation of the economy of the Universe. This was their lofty, and wise, and noble understanding of the justice of the Creator to His creatures. Yes, gentlemen, to all His creatures, to the whole great family of man. In their enlightened belief, nothing stamped with Divine image and likeness was sent into the world to be trodden on, and degraded, and imbruted by its fellows. They grasped not only the whole race of man then living, but they reached forward and seized upon the farthest posterity. They erected a beacon to guide their children and their children's children, and the countless myriads who should inhabit the earth in other ages. Wise statesmen as they were, they knew the tendency of prosperity to breed tyrants, and so they established these great self-evident truths...so that truth, and justice, and mercy, and all the humane and Christian virtues might not be extinguished from the land.[39]

Scholar and historian Joe Wheeler has gone so far as to argue that Lincoln wanted to end slavery as a teenager but he had no power to do so and the moment was not right. Even if he would have had the power then, he wouldn't have been able to do it because many of the abolitionists were so hostile that to embrace abolitionism was often a political kiss of death.[40]

When Lincoln became president, however, he was still not granted the power instantly to end slavery. In 1860 and early 1861, when peace and war were teetering on the brink, a consensus on slavery would have been impossible to come to. Though many in the North despised slavery, they would never have responded to the call to arms had it been just to free slaves. What they volunteered to fight for was to save the republic.[41]

When Lincoln announced the Emancipation Proclamation to the nation on January 1, 1863, some black leaders distrusted the president's commitment to them as a people. They thought his promise to sign the Emancipation Proclamation might merely be a political ploy to gain advantage in the war; they thought the president did not personally care about colored people at all. And who could blame them for thinking that way? "This was an age in which whites in the South treated blacks as less than human, whereas most whites in the North treated blacks as non-existent."[42]

Philip Ostergard, who has spent years researching the faith of Abraham Lincoln, also writes, "Lincoln's challenge was to explain to the antislavery forces that, while he was in full agreement with their desire to end slavery, he could not immediately free the slaves without endangering the Republic and its Constitution. While he took no immediate action to free the slaves, his lawyer's mind was constantly wrestling with the issue. He began by recommending a most logical idea: offering full compensation for slaves through the federal treasury. If such legislation had passed, it might have saved the lives of 600,000 men and millions of dollars that was spent to maintain two fighting armies. It also would have spared the ravaging of southern plantations and property."[43]

Though it would not have much chance of acceptance, Lincoln urged acceptance with all his presidential power. He submitted a draft bill to Congress to compensate any state that abolished slavery, but slaveholders had gone too far and refused to consider the plan. The president then introduced his ideas of the black race colonizing in some other part of the country, asking them where they would be most happy. Lincoln expressed the biblical principle that man is created by and related to His Creator, and that fact gives him worth and dignity.[44]

His Address on Colonization to a Deputation of Negroes on August 14, 1862, was as follows:

> There is much to encourage you. For the sake your race you should sacrifice something of your present comfort for the purpose of being as grand in that respect as the white people. It is a cheering thought throughout life that something can be done to improve the condition of those who have been subject to the hard usage of this world. It is difficult to make a man miserable while he feels he is worthy of himself, and claims kindred to the great God who made him. In the American Revolutionary War, sacrifices were made by men engaged in it; but they were cheered by the future. Gen. Washington himself endured greater physical hardships than if he had remained a British subject. Yet he was a happy man, because he was engaged in benefiting his race— something for the children of his neighbors, having none of his own.[45]

By rejecting the proposition of compensation, the southern plantation owners would lose their total investment in slaves, their plantations would be torn up, and most tragically for them, they would lose their sons. The dollar cost of redemption of slaves was far less than the purchase of military arms and keeping the armies in the fields. Compensation was a sensible idea. It would have stopped the flow of blood and the number of widows and fatherless from rising. There would have been no battlefield deaths or amputations.[46]

The southern plantations would have been spared the waste and destruction, and we in our generation would have not known the legacy of bitterness that we have inherited. Still, to no one's surprise, the South rejected the idea. It is difficult to understand how anti-slavery, well-meaning people in the North were so dedicated to immediate emancipation that they could not even consider Lincoln's idea of compensation.[47]

A Clearer Understanding of Lincoln

In regards to further continued research and to gain a clearer historical understanding of slavery, I looked at Thomas J. Dilorenzo's book *The Real Lincoln*. Dilorenzo, who is a professor of history and political economics, has received severe criticism for the way he portrays Abraham Lincoln. He poses a question that almost no one has addressed in much detail: "Why didn't Lincoln do what much of the rest of the world did in the nineteenth century and end slavery peacefully through compensated emancipation?" He then answers, "Between 1800 and 1860, dozens of countries, including the entire British Empire, ended slavery peacefully; it was only in the United States that a war erupted."[48]

It is very likely that most Americans, if they had been given the opportunity, would have gladly supported compensated emancipation as a means of ending slavery as opposed to the almost unimaginable costs of the war: 620,000 deaths, thousands more maimed for life, and the near total destruction of approximately 40 percent of the nation's economy. "Standardizing for today's population of some 280 million (compared to 30 million in 1865), this would be roughly the equivalent of 5 million deaths—about a hundred times the number of Americans who died in Vietnam."[49]

Many doubt that Lincoln redefined the purpose of American government as the pursuit of equality rather than individual liberty. Lincoln is often hailed as a champion of the dictum in the Declaration of Independence that "all men are created equal." However, not all Lincoln scholars agree; many mock the idea that Lincoln was upholding the equality principle of the Declaration. Dilorenzo argues that this is a problematic interpretation because Lincoln stated over and over again that he was opposed to racial equality. His statement of opposition to racial equality was his response to Senator Stephen Douglass in an 1858 debate in Ottawa, Illinois:

I have no purpose to introduce political and social equality between white and black races. There is a physical difference between the two, which, in my judgment, will probably forever forbid their living together upon the footing of perfect equality; and inasmuch as it becomes a necessity that there must be a difference, I, as well as Judge Douglass, am in favour of the race to which I belong having the superior position. I have never said anything to the contrary.[50]

While adamantly opposing "social and political equality" of the races, Lincoln took the contradictory position of also defending—at least rhetorically—the natural rights of all races to life, liberty, and the pursuit of happiness, as enumerated in the Declaration of Independence, and referred to slavery as a "monstrous injustice." But blacks could never in fact achieve equality if they were denied all other rights that Lincoln wanted to deny them—to vote, to become jurors, and so on. "It was a textbook example of a masterful, rhetorically gifted, fence-straddling politician wanting to have it both ways—in favour of and opposed to racial equality at the same time—in an attempt to maximize his political support."[51]

Joe Wheeler has a different view altogether: "All his life Lincoln had detested the dehumanizing institution of slavery but had felt powerless to do anything about it—after all, it had been entrenched in America for 235 years, long before the birth of the nation itself. He had also gritted his teeth that constitutionally, though slaves were considered nonpersons, they gave their owners immense political power."[52] Therefore, "as one studies this time period, it is almost impossible to disagree with Lincoln's later perception that God, not man was orchestrating events with a script and timetable that were uniquely His own. For without that concept nothing made sense."[53] Then Wheeler concludes, "I know there is a God and that He hates injustice and slavery. I see the storm coming and I know that His hand is in it. If He has a place for me, and I think He has, I believe I am ready."[54]

Endnotes

1 Matthew Spalding Ph.D., *How to Understand Slavery and the American Founding,* The Heritage Foundation, *http://www.heritage.org/research/reports/2002/08/*, August 26, 2002.

2 Ibid.

3 Ibid.

4 Ibid.

5 Ibid.

6 Gordon S. Wood, "Slaves in the Family Published," accessed on December 14, 2003, from *https://www.nytimes.com/2003/12/14/books/slaves-in-the-family.html?pagewanted=all&srs=pm*.

7 Andrew P. Napolitano, *Lies the Government Told You: Myth, Power, and Deception in American History* (Thomas Nelson, 2010), 5.

8 Ibid., Gordon S. Wood.

9 Ibid.

10 Ibid., Matthew Spalding.

11 Ibid., Gordon S. Wood.

12 Ibid., Matthew Spalding.

13 Denise and Frederic W. Henderson, "How The Founding Fathers Fought For an End to Slavery" (Printed in The American Almanac, March 15, 1993), *http://American_almanac.tripod.com/ffslave.htm*.

14 Ibid., Matthew Spalding.

15 Denise and Frederic W. Henderson, "How The Founding Fathers Fought For an End to Slavery" (Printed in The American Almanac, March 15, 1993), *http://American_almanac.tripod.com/ffslave.htm*.

16 Andrew P. Napolitano, 3.

17 Alan Dershowitz, *America Declares Independence* (Hoboken, NJ: John Wiley & Sons, Inc., 2003), 124.

18 Andrew P. Napolitano, 5.

19 Frank Donovan, *Mr. Jefferson's Declaration: The Story Behind the Declaration of Independence* (New York: Dodd, Mead & Company, 1968), 93–96.

20 Thomas Jefferson, *Notes on the State of Virginia* (Richmond, VA: J. W. Randolph, 1853), 155. Accessed from *http://www.archive.org/details/notesonsatteofvi01jeff*. He said, "Whether further observation will or will not verify the conjecture, that Nature has been less bountiful to them in the endowments of the head, I believe that in those of the heart she will be found to have done them justice. That disposition to theft with which they have been branded, must be ascribed to their situation, and not to any depravity of the moral sense."

21 Alan Dershowitz, 128.

22 Ibid.

23 James Oakes, *Why Slaves Can't Read: The Political Significance of Jefferson's Racism in Thomas Jefferson and the Education of a Citizen*, James Gilreath, ed. (Washington, D.C.: Library of Congress, 1999), 180.

24 Ibid.

25 Ibid., 125.

26 Ibid.

27 John Ferling, *Setting the World Ablaze: Washington, Adams, Jefferson, and the American Revolution* (Oxford University Press, Inc., 2000), 290.

28 John Chester Miller, *The Wolf by the Ears: Thomas Jefferson and Slavery* (Charlottesville, Virginia: The Free Press, a division of MacMillan Publishing Company Inc., 1977), 241. He goes on to say, "Jefferson reflected the age-old belief that blackness was somehow a curse. As Henry Home, Lord Kames, an eighteenth-century Scottish philosopher whose writings influenced the development of Jefferson's philosophy, said, "The color of the Negroes... affords a strong presumption of their being a different species from the whites...." By expressing "suspicions" of the inferiority of blacks, Jefferson considerably weakened the impact of his appeal for freedom for the slaves. The alleged inferiority of blacks served as a justification for slavery; by raising doubts as to the slaves' capacity for freedom, it was possible to regard slavery as the proper condition of the non-Caucasian members of the human race. Slave owners made it a point to inculcate in the slaves a sense of their unworthiness, their helplessness, and their complete dependence upon the mercy of their masters. By creating a slave mentality, they hoped to instill in the blacks a fear of freedom. Indeed, until the conviction of inferiority had been thoroughly implanted in the slaves, southern slave owners could not account themselves secure in either their person or their property. White superiority and black inferiority were psychological imperatives of the system. In the nineteenth century, when slavery was acclaimed a "positive good" for both races, the biological inferiority of blacks was exalted into "an ordinance of Providence.""

29 Ibid., 58, 61–62.

30 Napolitano, 4.

31 Thomas Jefferson, *Notes on the State of Virginia*, 155.

32 John Chester Miller, 58, 61–62.

33 David Brion Davis, *Was Thomas Jefferson Anti-Slavery?* (New York: Oxford University Press, 1970), 179. Jefferson went on to write, "But it is impossible to be temperate and to pursue this subject through the various considerations of policy, of morals, of history, natural and civil. We must be contented to hope they will force their way into everyone's mind. I think a change already perceptible, since the origin of the present revolution. The spirit of the master is abating, that of the slave rising from the dust, his condition mollifying, the way I hope preparing, under the auspices of heaven, for a total emancipation, and that this is disposed, in the order of events, to be with the consent of the masters, rather than by their extirpation" (Thomas Jefferson, *Notes on the State of Virginia*, 175).

34 Ibid.

35 John Paul Kaminski, *A Necessary Evil? Slavery and the Debate over the Constitution* (Published by Rowman & Littlefield, 1995), 256.

36 U.S. Constitution: Article 1, Section 9, accessed from *http://www.usconstitution.net/xconst_A1Sec9.html*

37 Andrew P. Napolitano, 8.

38 Philip L. Ostergard, *The Inspired Wisdom of Abraham Lincoln: How Faith Shaped an American President* (Carol Stream, Illinois: Tyndale House Publishers, INC. 2008), 87–88.

39 Ibid.

[40] Joe Wheeler, *Stories of Our Most Admired President Abraham Lincoln: A Man of Faith and Courage* (Howard Books, 2008), 189–191.

[41] Ibid.

[42] Ibid.

[43] Philip L. Ostergard, 178–179.

[44] Kenneth P. Williams, *Lincoln Finds a General: A Military Study of the Civil War, Vol. 1* (New York: The Macmillan Company, 1949), ix.

[45] Philip L. Ostergard, 180.

[46] Ibid.

[47] Ibid.

[48] Thomas J. Dilorenzo, *The Real Abraham Lincoln: A New Look at Abraham Lincoln, His Agenda, and an Unnecessary War* (Three Rivers Press, 2002), 4.

[49] Ibid.

[50] Ibid., 11.

[51] Ibid., 13.

[52] Joe Wheeler, 120.

[53] Ibid., 121.

[54] Ibid., 120.

CHAPTER 25

Slavery and the Constitution

Alexis de Tocqueville's Prediction

When Alexis de Tocqueville traveled to America to study the American prison system, he wrote a book that has been regarded as one the greatest commentaries ever written on the American government and society. In it he explored the effects of the rising inequality of social conditions in the Western world. He noted the connection between slavery and the point of view held by many people at the time:

> Those who hope that the Europeans will ever mix with the Negroes, appear to me to delude themselves; and I am not led to any such conclusion by my own reason, or by the evidence of facts. Hitherto, wherever the whites have been the most powerful, they have maintained the blacks in a subordinate or a servile position wherever the Negroes have been strongest, they have destroyed the whites; such has been the only course of events which has ever taken place between the two races. I see that in a certain portion of the territory of the United States at the present day, the legal barrier which separated the two races is tending to fall away, but not that which exists in the manners of the country; slavery recedes, but the prejudice to which it has given birth remains stationary.... The modern slave differs from his master not only in his condition, but in his origin. You may set the Negro free, but you cannot make him otherwise than an alien to the European.... The moderns then, after they have abolished slavery, have three prejudices to contend against, which are less easy to

attack, and far less easy to conquer, than the mere fact of servitude: the prejudice of the master, the prejudice of the race and the prejudice of color.[1]

Tocqueville predicted that black Americans would eventually revolt at being deprived of their civil rights, including their social and economic rights. He prophetically saw that the country's past would determine its future:

> If ever America undergoes great revolutions, they will be brought about by the presence of the black race on the soil of the United States.... The Negro race will never leave those shores of the American continent, to which it was brought by the passions and the vices of Europeans; and it will not disappear from the New World as long as it continues to exist.... I am obliged to confess that I do not regard the abolition of slavery as "means of warding off the struggle of the two races in the United States." The Negroes may long remain slaves without complaining; but if they are once raised to the level of freemen, they will soon revolt at being deprived of all their civil rights; and as they cannot become the equals of the whites, they will speedily declare themselves as enemies.[2]

Thomas J. Dilorenzo draws attention to Lincoln's failure to live up to his expectations when he writes:

> Lincoln had no solution to the problem of slavery, except the colonization idea which he inherited from Henry Clay. When, before the war, he was asked what should be done with the slaves were they ever to be freed, he said, "Send them to Liberia, to their own native land." He developed plans to send back every last black person to Africa, Haiti, Central America—anywhere but the United States.... Lincoln approvingly quoted Clay as saying that "there is a moral fitness in the idea of returning to Africa her children" since "they will carry back to their native soil the rich fruits of religion, civilization, law, and liberty." How they would do this after having deprived of an education and of the fruits of

religion, civilization, law, and liberty in the United States was not explained.[3]

Meanwhile, Tocqueville concluded that the removal of the Negro population from America could not resolve the crisis, as he predicted that a civil war would break out:

> When I contemplate the condition of the south, I can only discover two alternatives which may be adopted by the white inhabitants of those states; that is either to emancipate the negroes, and to intermingle with them; or, remaining isolated from them, to keep them in a state of slavery as long as possible. All intermediate measures seem to me likely to terminate, and that shortly, in the most horrible of civil wars, and perhaps in the total extermination of one or other of the two races.[4]

But still some experts present arguments that the Civil War was a complicated political, economic, and social event. Though slavery was a key issue, the abolition of slavery was not a strong concern for the American public. The Civil War was not primarily over slavery; it was the first step in moving the United States from a decentralized government to a centralized one. While the war lasted only four years, its roots can be traced back to a great compromise forged during the Constitutional Convention when the delegates agreed to permit slavery. In 1922, during his remarks at the dedication of the Lincoln Memorial, President Warren Harding noted that this concession in the Constitution represented "an ambiguity which only a baptism in blood could efface."[5]

That is why in the summer of 1862, newspaper editor Horace Greeley published an editorial called "The Prayer of Twenty Millions." In it he upbraided the president for fighting against the evil of slavery while refusing to enact legislation to forbid it. Furthermore, he predicted that freeing the slaves would weaken the Confederacy. What Greeley did not know was that Lincoln had already drafted (and read to his cabinet) a preliminary Emancipation Proclamation.

Philip Ostergard, in his biography of Lincoln, demonstrated how the president was terribly concerned about the evils of slavery, yet he viewed the situation in light of all other challenges facing the Union at the time. Lincoln replied to Horace Greeley:

> Dear Sir, As to the policy I "seem to be pursuing" as you say, I have not meant to leave any one in doubt. I would save the Union. I would save it in the shortest way under the Constitution. The sooner the national authority can be restored, the nearer the Union will be "the Union as it was." If there be those who would not save the Union, unless they could at the same time save slavery, I do not agree with them. If there be those who would not save the Union unless they could at the same time destroy slavery, I do not agree with them. My paramount object in this struggle is to save the Union, and is not either to save or to destroy slavery. If I could save the Union without freeing any slave I would do it, and if I could save it by freeing all the slaves I would do it; and if I could save it by freeing some and leaving others alone I would also do that. What I do about slavery, and the colored race, I do because I believe it helps to save the Union; and what I forbear, I forbear because I do not believe it would help save the Union. I shall do less whenever I shall believe what I am doing hurts the cause, and I shall do more wherever I shall believe doing more will help the cause. I shall try to correct errors when shown to be errors; and I shall adopt new views so fast as they shall appear to be true views...[6]

What was the price for keeping the states within the Union? Lincoln promised to do nothing to interfere with slavery within their borders. Naturally, it was a difficult promise to keep, and his critics screamed, but Lincoln kept his word, convinced that failing to do so would have far more severe consequences. According to one historian, Greeley did not fully understand how intensely Lincoln had been agonizing over how to end the slaves' captivity.[7] Maybe that is why he is quoted to have said in a solemn voice: "It is a momentous thing to be the instrument under Providence for the liberation of a race."[8]

Historian David Barton has characterized the issue of slavery as a discrediting charge against the Founders: "The historical fact is that slavery was not the product of, nor was it an evil introduced by, the Founders; slavery had been introduced to America nearly two centuries before the Founders. In 1773, Pennsylvania passed a law to help bring slavery to an end, and other colonies were also making attempts to end slavery, but King George III vetoed those American laws."[9] The king was pro-slavery, the British Empire practiced slavery, and as long as America was part of the British Empire, it too would practice slavery. This position was a source of great discontent for many of the Founders.

Henry Laurens, president of Congress during the American Revolution, protested against this British position:

> I abhor slavery. [But] I was born in a country where slavery had been established by the British kings and parliaments...ages before my existence.... In former days there was no combating the prejudices of men supported by interest; the day, I hope a day is approaching when, from principles of gratitude as well as justice, every man will strive to be foremost in showing his readiness to comply with the Golden Rule ("Do unto others as you would have them do unto you," Matthew 7:12).[10]

Since the only way for America to end slavery was to separate from Great Britain, many of the Founders believed that separation would be an appropriate course of action. In fact, in the drafting of the Declaration of Independence, Thomas Jefferson personally penned the clause declaring that King George III "has waged cruel war against human nature itself, violating its most sacred rights of life and liberty in the persons of a distant people who never offended him, captivating and carrying them into slavery in another hemisphere or to incur miserable death in their transportation thither.... Determined to keep open a market where men should be bought and sold, he has prostituted his negative for suppressing every legislative attempt to prohibit or to restrain this execrable commerce."[11]

That is, not only had King George III engaged in slavery and the slave trade, he even opposed all efforts to stop it. Ending slavery was so important to so many of the Founders that when America finally did separate from Great Britain in 1776, several states began abolishing slavery right away—these included Pennsylvania, Massachusetts, Connecticut, Rhode Island, Vermont, New Hampshire, and New York.[12] Not every state immediately abolished slavery however. Even though the overwhelming majority of the Founders were anti-slavery, not all of them were. In fact, the delegates from Georgia and South Carolina complained about Jefferson's forceful denunciation of the slave trade in the original draft of the Declaration so strenuously that his clause was removed and a milder condemnation inserted instead.[13]

Nevertheless, the desire to end slavery was a major factor in the thinking of many of the Founders. Benjamin Franklin and Dr. Benjamin Rush (both of whom became signers of the Declaration of Independence) established an anti-slavery society two years before the separation from Great Britain, which was an act of civil disobedience because King George III said America could not end slavery. But these two Founders ignored that dictum and worked to end it anyway. Dr. Benjamin Rush led the anti-slavery fight for almost four decades and even headed the national abolition movement.[14]

For many Founders, their desire to end slavery was religiously motivated. This fact is illustrated by John Quincy Adams, who hated slavery and so crusaded against it that he was nicknamed "the hell-hound of abolition" for his unrelenting efforts to abolish that evil. In a famous speech, Adams cited the Bible passage from Luke 4 where Jesus declared that He had come to "proclaim liberty to the captives." He then noted that if this was the goal of the Savior, it should also be the goal of all Christians—they, too, should work to end slavery.[15]

Clearly such issues such as religious liberties and the desire to end slavery, as well as the removal of trial by jury, the impressments of American seamen by the British, the placing of the military power above the civilian power, and many others were important reasons behind the Founders' separation from Great Britain. Yet all that most Americans and British hear today is "taxation without representation."[16]

Was the Constitution a Pro-Slavery Document?

Why then did the Founders defend slavery and racism in the United States Constitution? Protecting the institution of slavery was necessary to gain the South's support for a new, centralized federal government. Yet there is also an assumption that the Constitution legitimized the ownership of some human beings by others. This was, of course, directly opposed the natural law values of the Declaration of Independence, which asserted that the rights of "all men" come from our Creator and are thus "unalienable." The Constitution contained express provisions recognizing slavery's existence, protecting it as a legal institution, and insulating it from regulation or interference by the federal government.[17] Three provisions of the Constitution implicitly recognize the existence of slavery.

The Fugitive Slave Clause (Article IV, Section 2, Clause 3) guaranteed the return upon claim of any "Person held to Service or Labor" in one state who had escaped to another. At the last minute, the phrase, "Person *legally* held to Service or Labor in one state" was amended to read, "Person held to Service or Labor in one state, under the Laws thereof." This revision emphasized that slaves were held according to the laws of individual states.[18]

The pro-slavery delegates wanted their slaves counted as whole persons, thereby according to their states more representation in Congress. It was the anti-slavery delegates who wanted to count slaves as less than human—not to dehumanize them but to penalize slaveholders. It was anti-slavery delegate James Wilson of Pennsylvania who proposed the three-fifths compromise. Also, this clause did not include blacks generally, as free blacks were understood to be free persons.[19]

It is significant to note that the words "slave" and "slavery" were kept out of the Constitution. Madison recorded in his notes that the delegates "thought it wrong to admit in the Constitution the idea that there could be property in men."[20] James Madison did not agree with the word *property*. He explained in the Federalist, No. 54, that we must deny the fact that slaves are considered merely as property, and in no respect persons.[21]

Historian and researcher David Barton looked deeply into this whole subject of the Constitution as a slaveholding document in his book *Setting the Record Straight: American History in Black and White*. He then came up with some credible evidence that needs to be considered in relation to this. Barton argued that "some have speculated that the Constitution was a pro-slavery document citing the Three-Fifths Clause which they interpret to mean that blacks are only three-fifths of a person."[22]

But one man who investigated this claim was the abolitionist Frederick Douglass, that great slave orator, whom was also born into slavery and remained a slave until he escaped to New York in 1838. He was born in Maryland to an enslaved black mother and a white man, and grew up on a plantation with his brothers and sisters, without shoes or stockings (even in the snow of winters), eating from a common trough. As a boy, he was sold to a Baltimore family whose mistress treated him kindly, gave him shoes and stockings, permitted him to eat with a spoon, and had taught him the first four letters of the alphabet when her husband spat out, "Learning would spoil the best nigger in the world; if you teach that nigger how to read the Bible there will be no keeping him. Next he will want to know how to write and then run away."[23] Douglass eventually did learn how to spell, read, and write. Then he also managed to escape to New England.

He became the most popular and widely heard black leader of his time, speaking out as far away as England about the institution of slavery. At his home in Rochester, New York, Douglass and his wife were part of the Underground Railroad. Like most Americans with negro blood (then and now), Douglass was extremely sensitive to patronizing whites who would espouse the abolitionist cause on principle but would not accept blacks on equal terms when interacting with them personally. It is reported that Douglass was a close friend of Abraham Lincoln, and what endeared Lincoln to Douglass was that he accepted him not because he was a famous abolitionist but because he was a brother, a fellow child of God. Douglass said:

In all my interviews with Mr. Lincoln I was impressed with his entire freedom from popular prejudice against the colored race. He was the first great man that I talked with in the United States freely, who in no single instance reminded me of the difference between himself and myself, of the difference of color.[24]

Three years after his escape, Douglass delivered an anti-slavery speech in Massachusetts. He was promptly hired to work for the state's anti-slavery society, and he also served as a preacher at Zion Methodist Church. During the Civil War, Douglass helped recruit the first black regiment to fight for the Union, and he advised Abraham Lincoln on the Emancipation Proclamation and other legislative issues. Following the Civil War, Douglass received presidential appointments from Republican presidents Ulysses S. Grant, Rutherford B. Hayes, and James A. Garfield. It is reported that Democratic president Grover Cleveland removed Frederick Douglass from office but Republican Benjamin Harrison reappointed him.[25]

During Douglass's first years of freedom, he studied at the feet of abolitionist William Lloyd Garrison, who taught him that that the Constitution was a pro-slavery document. Douglass accepted this claim, and his early speeches and writings reflected that belief. However, Douglass later began to research the subject for himself. He read the Constitution, read the writings of those who wrote the Constitution, and what he found revolutionized his thinking. He concluded that the Constitution was not a pro-slavery but an anti-slavery document.[26]

I was on the anti-slavery question...fully committed to [the] doctrine touching the pro-slavery character of the Constitution.... I advocated it with pen and tongue, according to the best of my ability.... Upon a reconsideration of the whole subject, I became convinced...that the Constitution of the United States not only contained no guarantees in favor of slavery but, on the contrary, it is in its letter and spirit an anti-slavery instrument, demanding the abolition of slavery as a condition of its own existence as the supreme law of the land. Here was a radical change in my opinions.... Brought directly when I escaped from slavery, into contact with a class of abolitionists regarding the Constitution as a slave holding instrument...it is not strange that I assumed the Constitution to be just what their interpretation made it.... But I was now conducted to the conclusion that the Constitution of the United States...was not designed...to maintain and perpetuate a system of...slavery...especially as not one word can be found in the Constitution to authorize such a belief.[27]

Douglass therefore concluded:

The Constitution is a glorious liberty document. Read its preamble; consider its purposes. Is slavery among them? Is it at the gateway? Or is it in the temple? It is neither.... If the Constitution were intended to be, by its framers and adopters, a slaveholding instrument, why neither *slavery, slaveholding,* nor *slave* can anywhere be found in it?... Now, take the Constitution according to its plain reading and I defy the presentation of a single pro-slavery clause in it. On the other hand, it will be found to contain principles and purposes entirely hostile to the existence of slavery.[28]

The Three-Fifths Clause

But if the Constitution is not a pro-slavery document, then what did the Three-Fifths Clause mean? Had Douglass not read that clause? Yes, he had. Then how could he conclude what he did about the Constitution? Douglass understood that the Three-Fifths Clause dealt only with representation and not the worth of any individual. The Constitution had established that for every 30,000 inhabitants in that state, it would receive one representative to Congress. The southern states saw this as an opportunity to strengthen slavery since slaves accounted for much of the southern population (for example, almost half of the inhabitants of South Carolina were slaves). Therefore, slave owners could simply count their slaves as regular inhabitants, and by doing so greatly increase the number of their pro-slavery representatives to Congress.[29]

The anti-slavery founders from the North opposed this plan. After all, the slave owners did not consider their slaves to be persons but only property; these slave owners were therefore using their "property" to increase the power of the slave states in Congress. The anti-slavery leaders wanted free blacks counted, but not slaves if counting slaves would increase the power of slave owners. They understood that the fewer the pro-slavery representatives to Congress, the sooner slavery could be eradicated from the nation.[30]

Many other founders like Governor Morris, Luther Martin, James Wilson, and Elbridge objected to counting slaves because they did not want to reward slaveholders and increase their power. The Three-Fifths Clause had nothing to do with the worth of any individual; in fact, free blacks in the North and the South were often extended the full rights of a citizen and regularly voted. The Three-Fifths Clause had nothing to do with representation: it was an anti-slavery provision designed to limit the number of pro-slavery representatives in Congress. This is why Frederick Douglass (unlike many Americans today who have never taken the time to study the Constitution) could therefore emphatically declare that the Constitution was an anti-slavery document.[31]

But some do not agree that all the Constitution was against slavery. For example, Judge Andrew Napolitano concludes, "The government that emerged from the American victory in the Revolutionary war however did not treat all men equally. The United States Constitution contained provisions that implicitly and explicitly recognized slavery's legitimacy and protected it as an institution and insulated it from regulation or interference by the federal government. In fact, the United States government permitted slavery for almost a hundred years after Thomas Jefferson wrote the immortal words that 'all men are created equal' language. It was not until recently that the government's behavior matched these words and African-Americans truly became equal under the law."[32]

Nevertheless, the Founders believed that slavery would meet its natural demise in the United States. At the Constitutional Convention, a Connecticut delegate, Roger Sherman, stated, "The abolition of slavery seemed to be going on in the United States…. The good sense of the several states would probably by degrees complete it."[33] Slavery, to some degree, ended but racism did not.

Endnotes

[1] Alexis de Tocqueville, *The Republic of the United States of America and Its Political Institutions, Reviewed and Examined,* translated by Henry Reeves, Two Volumes in One (New York: A. S. Barnes & Company, 1856), 273, 388–389, 409.

[2] Alexis de Tocqueville, 409.

[3] Thomas J. Dilorenzo, 17.

[4] Alexis de Tocqueville, 409.

[5] Philip L. Ostergard, 181.

[6] Ibid., 183.

[7] Ibid.

[8] Quoted in Joe Wheeler, *Stories of Our Most Admired President,* 191.

[9] David Barton, *The Role of Pastors and Christians in Civil Government* (Texas: Wall Builder Press, 2003), 5–7.

[10] Ibid.

[11] Ibid.

[12] Ibid.

[13] Ibid.

[14] Ibid.

[15] Ibid.

[16] Ibid.

[17] Andrew P. Napolitano, *Lies the Government Told You: Myth, Power, and Deception in American History* (Thomas Nelson, 2010), 6.

[18] 18 Matthew Spalding Ph.D., *How to Understand Slavery and the American Founding,* The Heritage Foundation, *http://www.heritage.org/research/reports/2002/08/,* August 26, 2002.

[19] Ibid.

[20] Ibid.

[21] Ibid.

[22] David Barton, *Setting the Record Straight: American History in Black and White* (Wall Builder Press, 2010), 9.

[23] Joe Wheeler, 188.

[24] Ibid., 189.

[25] David Barton, 10.

[26] Ibid.

[27] Ibid.

28 Ibid., 11.

29 Ibid.

30 Ibid.

31 Ibid., 13.

32 Andrew P. Napolitano, 1–2

33 Ibid., Matthew Spalding Ph.D.

CHAPTER 26

Racism and the Bible

Defining Racism

According to the *Merriam-Webster's Dictionary*, racism is defined as "a belief that race is the primary determinant of human traits and capabilities and that racial differences produce an inherent superiority of a particular race; racial prejudice or discrimination." You may be asking yourself, "Is racism still affecting us today in our tolerant culture and, if not, what does this kind of history have to do with my family and me?" I believe it is of significant importance for how we live our lives.

Marcus Tullius Cicero, the first-century Roman philosopher and writer, is quoted to have said, "There is very little that is more important for any people to know than their history, culture, traditions and language; for without such knowledge, one stands naked and defenseless before the world."[1] Calvin R. Robinson, Redman Battle, and Edward W. Robinson Jr., in their book *The Journey of the Songhai People,* addressed the issue of how races are programmed:

> Knowledge of race history is to the race exactly as an individual's memory is to that individual. The masses of African-Americans (and other Africans) suffer from partial cultural amnesia because of a certain deliberate program which wiped the slates of our memories clean of true African events prior to the cotton fields of America but those who perpetrated this cultural genocide were not satisfied. After wiping the memory slates clean, they wrote upon those slates a series of vicious lies. They wrote on the slates, of the minds of all, Black and White alike, that the African is

really an ape which can speak. They wrote on the slates, of the minds of all, that the African evolved in the heartland of the jungles of Africa where not even the faintest glimmer of the light of science and learning could penetrate. They wrote on those slates that African sub-human has neither the genetic ability to learn nor the ability to behave properly. They programmed all of this upon the minds of all Black and White alike.[2]

The history of our country certainly bears this out.[3]

Racism Is About Economics

Racism is not contained in genes or in the blood, but it is contained in the houses where children are raised. We are not born to be racist, but we have been taught it from our upbringing. Most of the racial seeds that have been planted in people's hearts were planted by their parents when they were young. Some white people find themselves uncomfortable or uneasy when they are with black people; likewise, some black people feel inferior and unwanted when they are with white people. The tendency to react in this way might have been planted within them when they were little children.

Most people have been programmed to think of blacks as inferior, different, and even dangerous; and even the media and some learning institutions have done a good job of portraying them as such. Racism is not necessarily the issue here; it is not about color, but about economics. It is how we respond to media distortions and the programmed self-hatred prevalent in our culture.

Dr. Anderson said much the same thing when he said the underlying reason for racism is not about the color of our skin, but about the power for the economic benefit of other people:

Racism is a power relationship or struggle between groups of people who are competing for resources and political power. It is one group's use of wealth and power and resources to deprive, hurt, injure, and exploit another group to benefit itself. Racism in practice never existed on earth until the 16th century when white nations began to commercially enslave black people.... There was slavery before that, but not racism; there is a big difference. That is why, as we have noted, slavery in America was called "the peculiar institution" because no slavery anywhere in the world was or has ever been exactly like slavery in America, which was based on skin color. Most people black and white don't know this…. Slavery is not new; racism is. Prior to the enslavement of black people, slaves were individuals who were the victims of religious persecution, prisoners of war, or personal indebtedness. Prior to the black enslavement practices, African blacks were clearly not at war with European whites, nor where they attempting to impose their religious beliefs on whites like some people today are doing. African blacks were not monetarily indebted to them, either. Enslaving an entire continent of people forever based simply upon their skin color was unheard of.[4]

How do we respond to all of this? The Bible doesn't distinguish by skin color but only by kindred, tongue, people, and nations. Let's look at some genetic scientific research regarding the origin of skin color.

What Does Science Tell Us About Skin Color?

Ken Ham, Karl Wieland, and Andrew Snelling authored a book called *The Answers Book: Answers to the 12 Most-Asked Questions on Genesis and Creation*. These men are all creation scientists with degrees in biology, geology, and medicine, respectively. They deal with the question of skin color in a very clear and conscious way that can be understood by any layman without a background in biology or science. They explain:

It is easy to think that since different groups of people have yellow skin, red skin, black skin, white skin, and brown skin, there must be many different skin pigments or colorings…. The fact is, however, that there is only one skin color: melanin. This is a brownish pigment which we all have in special cells in our skin…. If we produce only a little melanin; it means that we will be European white. If our skin produces a great deal of melanin, we will be a very deep black. And in between, of course, are all shades of brown. We also need to be aware that one is not born with a genetically fixed amount of melanin, but rather with a genetically fixed potential to produce a certain amount in response to sunlight. For example, if are Caucasian, you may have noticed that when your friends headed for the beach at the very beginning of summer, they may, if they spent all time indoors during winter, have more or less the same pale white. As the summer went on, however, some became much darker than others. Even very dark-skinned races are not born with such a skin color. It takes exposure to sunlight to switch on the melanin factories in the skin. In very dark-skinned people, the areas such as the palms of the hands and the soles of the feet, which are very rarely exposed to sunlight, generally stay much lighter than the rest of the body.[5]

They continue:

Let's look at a few observations which can help us to explain how many different skin colors can arise in a short time. (From here on, wherever we use such words as "different colors," we are strictly speaking, referring to different shades of the one color.) If a person from a very black race marries someone from a very white race, their offspring (called mulattos) are mid-brown. It has long been known that if people of mulatto descent marry, their offspring may be virtually any color, ranging from very black to very white. Understanding this gives us the clues we need for our overall question, so we must first look, in a simple way, at some of basic facts of heredity. Each of us carries in our body information which describes us in the way a blueprint describes a finished building, it determines not only that we will be human beings, rather than cabbages, or crocodiles, but also whether we will have blue eyes, short nose, long legs, etc. When a male sperm fertilizes an egg, all the information that specifies how the person will be built (ignoring such superimposed factors as exercise and diet) is already present…

The human blueprint is written in a code (or language

convention) which is carried on a very long chemical called DNA. The word "gene" means a small part of that information which carries the instructions for only one feature.... The fertilized egg —where does all its information, its genes, come from? One half has come from the father (carried by the sperm), and the other half from the mother (carried in the egg). Genes come in matching pairs...[6]

We know that skin color is governed by at least two (possibly more) sets of genes. Let's call them A and B, with the correspondingly more silent genes, *a* and *b*... (The small letters in this case code for a small amount of melanin.) So a very dark race which, on intermarriage, kept producing only very dark offspring would be AA BB; the same situation for a very fair-skinned race would be *aa bb*. Let's look at what combinations would result in a mulatto (the offspring of an AA BB and *aa bb* union).

What would happen...if two such mid-brown mulatto people were to marry? Surprisingly, we find that an entire range of color, from very white to very black, can result in one generation, beginning with this particular type of mid-brown parents.

Those children born with AA BB, who are pure black (in the sense of consistently having no other types of offspring,) have no genes for lightness at all. If they were to marry and migrate to a place where the offspring could not intermarry with people of different colors, all their children will be black—a pure "black line" will result. Those who are *aa bb* are white; if they marry other whites and migrate to a place where their offspring cannot marry other colors, a pure (in the same sense) "white line" will result—they have lost the genes which give them the ability to be black, that is, to produce a large amount of melanin.[7]

Adam and Eve could not have been white. If they had been white, they would have had no genes for any color other than white, and their offspring would have been only white children, just as blacks can only produce black children. They sum up their argument saying, "It is easily possible beginning with two middle-brown parents, to get not only all the colors, but also races with permanently different shades of coloring."⁸

So we see that Adam and Eve could have been mid-brown because only that combination of genes could produce all the varying colors we have in the world today. Frederick Price explains:

> Adam and Eve must have been mid-brown in skin color to have the genetic coding for white and black descendants…. God is a Spirit and He does not have a physical body. So He could have given to Adam His own genetic color code, because He does not have a color. Therefore when He created Adam and Eve, He had to make them mid-brown and place within them the genetic coding to produce every color of person there has ever been in the history of the world.⁹

How Should Parents Respond to Racism?

When some white people come into contact with black people, these reactions of superiority automatically come because others have subconsciously planted them in their minds. This doesn't mean that every white person is a racist—by no means! But "charity begins at home," which means that parents are the first role models in the lives of young children. We teach them by our words and by our deeds. They in turn study our words, body language, and our conduct, storing the information in their brains to learn more about the world we live in. As parents, we need to be very conscious of what we say and how we act to those around us. At the same time, our challenge as parents should be to teach our children about what happened in the past and teach them to respect all people, regardless of their racial, economic, or social backgrounds.

Racism and the Church

In Ephesians 2:11–22, the apostle Paul tells us that the church was founded upon the basic principle that all dividing walls have been destroyed by Christ's death. They continue to exist in the non-Christian world, but among the fellowship of believers such distinctions have no place. The racial conflict between Jew and Gentile was notorious in its day. Nevertheless, God, through the sacrifice of Jesus, overcame the enmity between them. That was a demonstration of the power of the gospel. And that same power is in the church today.

In addressing the issue of racial reconciliation in the church, Dr. Bruce W. Fong gives us some helpful observations from his analysis of Ephesians 2:11–15. He writes, "At the very heart of Christianity is God's acceptance of anyone through Christ regardless of race, language or class. Thus while in many cases the Church is a contributor to the problem, Christians with the gospel have the answer to the world's quest toward racial reconciliation."[10]

Before the church adopts a philosophy that addresses the issue of race, it must first examine and then articulate the New Testament foundation of the church's existence. Included in the explanation of its existence are two essentials: unity and fellowship. Dr. Bruce concludes by saying, "The divisions of Christendom will finally be overruled for a deeper and richer harmony, of which Christ is the keynote. In Him and by Him all problems of theology and history will be solved.... God's people can never get together on human creeds and disciplines. They are too narrow and changeable. We have a foundation that is broad enough to hold all. Christ Himself is this foundation. In Christ, all God's people are one, irrespective of race, color, social standing or creed."[11]

The Gospel Leads to Christ

While addressing the baptized saints not long ago, a preacher once said, "As we look upon the Church divided, upon the sect-ridden multitude, none of whom can see alike, how our tried souls cry out for that original love. And we will never win the world on any other plain."[12] The heathen themselves said it about the early Christians: how these Christians love one another! While we are breaking up into sects, creeds, and doctrines, our love is dying among us. Our beautiful Pentecostal work, so full of promise, where God has designed to come in and fill souls and wonderfully baptize them in the Holy Spirit, is broken and peeled and ruined for lack of love. "It is a common thing to read in the daily papers such words as these, 'Only union men need apply.' And it is becoming a common thing to read in church papers: 'Affiliating brethren are invited.' What is the difference? No difference, except one is a secular union, the other is a religious union."[13]

Every fresh division of race or party in the church gives the world a contradiction as to the oneness of the body of Christ and the truthfulness of the gospel. Multitudes are bowing down and burning incense to a doctrine rather than Christ. The many sects in Christendom are, to say the least, evidence to the world that Christians cannot get along together. Written creeds only serve to publish the fact that we cannot understand the Word of God and get together on it. Is the Word of God, then, hard to understand? They who establish a fixed creed bar the way to further progress.

It was said of the mighty evangelist Charles G. Finney, that he "forged his theology on the anvil of prayer in his own heart."[14] He was not bound by the systems of his day. We all belong to the whole body of Christ, both in heaven and on earth. God's church is one body, united across national borders. It is a terrible thing to go about dismembering the body of Christ.

The petty differences between Christians will appear foolish and wicked in the light of eternity. Christ is the "issue," not some particular doctrine about Him. The gospel leads to Him and Him alone. It exalts Christ, not some particular doctrine. To "know Christ" is the Alpha and the Omega of Christian faith and practice.[15] Maybe this lack of unity has been one of the reasons why revival tarries and has evaded us for so long. Yet when we are united according to the true New Testament church, we create an atmosphere necessary for the Lord to send a revival which we so desperately need.

Azusa Street Revival

Church historians believe that in 1906 God gave the church the opportunity to unify itself, to bring all Christians of every ethnicity and color together as one, to make a statement to the world. During that year God poured out His Spirit at a place called Azusa Street in Los Angeles, California, through a black, one-eyed preacher named William J. Seymour. He was born as a son of emancipated slaves in the County of Bayou, Louisiana, in 1870. As a young man, he was a member of the all-black Methodist Episcopal Church.

Brother Seymour was recognized as the leader of the revival and there was no pope or hierarchy within the revival. They were all brethren—they had no human program—the Lord Himself was leading the revival. They had no priest class nor priest craft. They were all on one level, brothers and sisters in Christ. The ministers were servants, according to the true meaning of the Word of God. Brother Seymour generally sat behind two empty boxes, one on top of other. And he usually kept his head inside the top one during the prayer meeting.[16]

There was no pride evident there either. Great emphasis was placed on Christ's blood. Divine love was wonderfully manifested in the meetings. They would not even allow an unkind word to be said against those who opposed them or the churches in the area. The message was the love of God. The baptism of the Holy Spirit did not allow them to think, speak, or hear evil of any person. The Spirit was very sensitive, tender as a dove.[17] They knew the moment they had grieved the Spirit by an unkind thought or word—they seemed to live in a sea of pure divine love.[18]

At the Azusa Street Revival, the color line was washed away in blood of Jesus. Nearly every account of the revival that sparked the American Pentecostal Movement notes that at Azusa, all people—Blacks, Whites, Asians, and Indians—worshiped freely together. Never in history had any such multiracial group surged at one time into one single church. This alone was miraculous, but for all of them to come together under the leadership of a black man made this revival particularly noteworthy. But such unity was not to last long. Some claim that others played on Seymour's ethnicity and doctrinal differences to establish their own churches.

But a firsthand account of the revival from Frank Bartleman says a different story: The work had gotten into a bad condition. The missions had fought each other almost to a standstill. Little love remained. A cold, hard-hearted zeal had largely taken the place of divine love and tenderness of the Spirit. The leader abused his privilege, and the meetings began to be run in appointed order. There were some poor illiterate Mexicans who had been saved and baptized in the Spirit, but the leader deliberately refused to let them testify. Every meeting was now programmed from start to finish. Disaster was bound to follow, and so it did.[19] The Holy Spirit was grieved and eventually left.

So this coming of the Holy Spirit, which gave rise to the Pentecostal movement, was disrupted by disunity and racial differences. Instead of the church remaining together in esteem, respect, affection, and friendship, most of the church did not fulfill Christ's prayer for unity (see John 17). It is only the Holy Spirit who can change an individual's heart. The whites suffer from a superiority complex and the blacks suffer from an inferiority complex; and it is only the Holy Spirit who can bring this love from heaven and fill us all.

It is this love that can change our nature and racial prejudices. Another writer has said that the apostasy of the early church came as a result of a greater desire to see the spread of its power and rule than to see new natures given to its individual members. He said, "The moment we covet a large following and rejoice in the crowd that is attracted by our presentation of what we consider truth, and have not a greater desire to see the natures of individuals (regardless of ethnicity) changed according to the divine plan, we start to travel the same road of apostasy that leads to Rome and her daughters."[20]

Carl Wells has some extreme words for my white brothers:

Certainly the white conservative Bible-believing church has a lot to answer for, in our relations with the black Bible-believing church. We should have been there to help the black church.... If we had simply acted out in faith, in their relations with black people, both black and white churches would have been greatly strengthened. The history of our country would be vastly different and better. We missed an opportunity to show that Christianity was a supernaturally revealed religion, the one true religion, the religion whose fruit is love and reconciliation.[21]

In his special bulletin about the lessons of Hurricane Katrina, Rick Joyner agrees that we still have very serious racial problems in America and within the church, which cannot be overlooked. But he believes that often those who use the racist card to manipulate others or gain political advantage are the worst racists themselves:

> I am still very alarmed at how many of the black leaders of this country operate out of such obvious wounds and obvious racism…. Those who are wounded operate out of hatred and disrespect for others and they will never be able to sit at the real table of power. If they did, it would result in tyranny…. Like it or not, the job won't get done without the trust of the white people, too. Most are not going to continue being manipulated by racist accusations, just as you should not continue to be oppressed by them. We both need freedom.[22]

Yes, we all need freedom. The cultural system has programmed black people through some of their leaders to always blame the whites, that they are ones who are racist. To give into this temptation of blaming everyone for our woes renders us unwilling to face life's challenges head-on and accept responsibility. We need to pray against the spirit of racism, and pray for racial healing in our respective nations so that this spirit of racism doesn't block the last great revival. Jesus Himself taught and predicted that there will be race wars in the last days (see Matthew 24:7), but He prayed for the unity of His church to be one just as He and the Father are one.

Endnotes

1 Calvin R. Robinson, Redman Battle, and Edward W. Robinson Jr., *Through the Pan African Federation Organization: The Journey of the Songhai People* (Philadelphia: Farmer Press, 1987), 26. Cited by Dr. Frederick K. C. Price, *Race, Religion & Racism, Volume 1: A Bold Encounter with Division in the Church* (Faith One Publishing, 1999), 170–171.

2 Ibid.

3 The authors ask an important question and then answer it superbly: Why study modern history or any history at all? "Two of the greatest benefits that can be derived from the knowledge of history is not only the receiving of a better understanding of the present, but more importantly, that knowledge of history will provide the information with which to shape the future. Place yourself in the position of a successful businessman who as a result, has a sudden loss of your memory. You would not know where your office is, nor how to get there. You would not know what successes you had achieved, what you are supposed to do today, nor how to plan for future successes. For all of your knowledge and experience would be entirely lost. You would have to start all over again. You would not know the reasons for your present situation. You could not call on experience and knowledge to plan for a successful future. If your business rivals stole your records, they could tell you all kinds of falsehoods. They could reduce you to an impoverished, blubbering idiot. That condition is called amnesia. Amnesia is not just limited to individuals. A whole race can have amnesia. It is a truism that 'history is to the human race, what memory is to the individual'" (Ibid).

4 Dr. Claud Anderson, "Powernomics," Teaching Seminar, Crenshaw Christian Center, May 29–30, 1997. Quoted by Dr. Frederick K. C. Price, 160–161.

5 Ken Ham, Andrew Snelling, and Karl Wieland, *The Answers Book: Answers to the 12 Most-Asked Questions on Genesis and Creation/Evolution*, revised ed. (Green Forest, Arizona: Master Books, 1990), 133–137.

6 Ibid.

7 Ibid., 141–143.

8 Ibid., 143.

9 Dr. Frederick K. C. Price, *Race, Religion & Racism, Volume 1: A Bold Encounter with Division in the Church* (Faith One Publishing, 1999), 135–139.

10 Bruce W. Fong, "Addressing the Issue of Racial Reconciliation According to the Principles of Ephesians 2:11–22," JETS 38/4 (December 1995), 565–580. Accessed from *http://www.etsjets.org/files/JETS-PDFs/38/38-4-pp565-580_JETS.pdf*.

11 Compiled by Roberts Liardon, *Firsthand Accounts of the Revival: Frank Bartleman's Azusa Street* (Shippensburg, PA: Destiny Image Publishers, 2006), 121.

12 Ibid.

13 Ibid.

14 Ibid.

15 Ibid., 122.

16 Ibid., 57–58.

17 The Holy Spirit is symbolized as a dove.

18 Ibid., Liardon, 54.

19 Ibid., 111–113.

[20] Roberts Liardon, *Firsthand Accounts of the Revival*, 50.

[21] Carl Wells, *The Christian Betrayal of the United States* (Author House, 2010), 160.

[22] Rick Joyner, "The Lessons of Hurricane Katrina, Part 1," 2005 Special Bulletin #8. Accessed from *http://www.morninstarministries.org/resources/special-bulletins/2005/lessons-hurricane-katrina-part-1#.UKE2VGd32So.*

CHAPTER 27

Eugenics: The Myth of Feeble-Mindedness

Eugenics Becomes Popular

To be able to really understand racism, we need to know the root cause of it: eugenics. The idea of eugenics became popular in the nineteenth century, officially beginning in 1863. A British man named Sir Francis Galton (1882–1911), who was a cousin of Charles Darwin, believed the human race should be judged on the basis of inequality. And the way he would achieve this was to use "eugenics." He coined the term using Greek words that expressed an original Greek concept, meaning "well," and "born." He further defined his new word as "the study of agencies under social control that may improve or impair the racial qualities of future generations whether physically or mentally."[1]

One of the ideas that Galton promoted was that eugenics is the theory that the human race can influence its own development through selective breeding. One of his theories was that if talented people married other talented people, the result would be even more talented offspring. These ideas were not his own, he claimed, but he was building on the ideas of other people like Thomas Malthus, Plato, and his cousin Charles Darwin.[2]

He described his ideas in an article that was published in two parts in the *MacMillan's Magazine*,[3] expressing his disappointment that no one was breeding the best offspring. He was planning to improve society through marriage using mathematical methods to determine which couples would produce better offspring. Unfortunately, his studies backfired, and his ideas were imported into the United States.

Among those that were influenced by Galton's scientific studies was a woman by the names of Margaret Sanger, who was a nurse and married the American oil tycoon Noah Slee. She was the founder of the American Birth Control League, which was renamed Planned Parenthood in 1943. Margaret Sanger was a feminist who espoused the thinking of eugenicists. She put many abortion clinics in minority neighborhoods, or what she called "inferior neighborhoods." She testified before the U.S. Senate in 1916 and called for the establishment of the Population Congress that would seek to employ what could be termed as Negative Eugenics to separate humanity. This was a study of or belief in the possibility of improving the qualities of the human species or a human population, especially by such means as discouraging reproduction by persons having genetic defects or presumed to have inheritable undesirable traits. Whereas positive eugenics is encouraging reproduction by persons presumed to have inheritable desirable traits.[4]

Her proposals of forced segregation for American citizens were the views of many eugenicists who wanted a superior and more intelligent race. Similar to the advocates of birth control, the eugenicists were seeking to assist the race toward the elimination of the unfit.[5] These words were spoken by a woman who is admired by women's groups all over the world. She's been described as the mother of Planned Parenthood and believed in "selective breeding" as a solution for a better human race by preventing reproduction of the unfit. She said, "We are paying for and even submitting to the dictates of an ever increasing, unceasingly spawning class of human beings who never should have been born at all."[6]

Eugenics and Feminism

Both feminists and eugenicists had different goals but agreed on some of the same things. Sanger led the feminist movement, and her ideology led to eugenic crimes around the world, including Nazi Germany. Her writings, which were very offensive, were not easily obtained until the copyright of her books finally expired and it became legal for the public to publish them. Two of her main books were *The Pivot of Civilization* and *Woman and the New Race*, the latter showing exactly what Sanger believed and taught.

Margaret Sanger had views similar to Darwin's "survival of the fittest," believing the genetic makeup of blacks, the poor, and other minorities were inferior to those of white people. She knew that some blacks would figure out her plot, so she decided to take the plan to the clergy of the black community to have them deliver the message to their congregations. In a letter to Dr. Clarence Gamble, Sanger wrote:

> We should hire three or four colored ministers, preferably with social-service backgrounds, and with engaging personalities. The most successful educational approach to the Negro is through a religious appeal. We don't want the word to go out that we want to exterminate the Negro population. And the minister is the man who can straighten out that idea if it ever occurs to any of their more rebellious members.[7]

Margaret Sanger also accepted the Malthusian theory that overpopulation is the root of all evil. She wrote, "No despot ever flung forth his legions to die in foreign conquest, no privileged-ruled nation ever erupted across its borders, to lock in death embrace with another, but behind them loomed the driving power of a population too large for its boundaries and its natural resources. No period of low wages or of idleness with their want among the workers, no personage or sweatshop, no child-labor factory, ever came into being, save from the same source. Nor have famine and plague been as much 'acts of God' as acts of too prolific mothers. They, also, as all students know, have their basic causes in over-population."[8]

She had contempt for human individuals, saying that "caught in this vicious circle, a woman has, through her reproductive ability, founded and perpetuated the tyrannies of the earth. Whether it was the tyranny of a monarchy, an oligarchy, or a republic, the one indispensable factor of its existence was, as it is now, hordes of human beings; human beings so plentiful as to be cheap that ignorance was their natural lot."[9]

Although some women celebrate her legacy, her writings contain many scornful remarks about women. Here is but one of them:

The creators of overpopulation are the women, who, while wringing their hands over each fresh horror, submit anew to their task of producing the multitudes who will bring about the next tragedy of civilization. While unknowingly laying the foundations of tyrannies and providing the human tinder for racial conflagrations, woman was also unknowingly creating slums, filling asylums with insane, and institutions with other defectives. She was replenishing the ranks of the prostitutions, furnishings grist for the criminal courts and inmates for prisons. Had she planned deliberately to achieve this tragic total of human waste and misery, she could hardly have done it more effectively.[10]

In the last chapter of *Woman and the New Race*, Sanger described her goals by asking a question and offering three possible solutions: "What is the goal of woman's upward struggle? Is it voluntary motherhood? Is it general freedom? Or is it the birth of a new race? For freedom is not fruitless, but prolific of higher things. Being the most sacred aspect of woman's freedom, voluntary motherhood is motherhood in its highest and holiest form. It is motherhood unchained; motherhood ready to obey its own urge to remake the world."[11] Her focus was on feminism and an improved race. She wrote,

It is the essential function of voluntary motherhood to choose its own mate, to determine the time of childbearing and to regulate strictly the number of offspring. Natural affection upon her part, instead of selection dictated by social or economic advantage, will give her a better fatherhood for her children. The exercise of her right to decide how many children she will have and when she shall have them will procure for her the time necessary to the development of other faculties than that of reproduction.

She will give play to her tastes, her talents and her ambitions. She will become a full-rounded human being. Thus and only thus will woman be able to transmit to her offspring those qualities which make for a greater race. Her blueprint not only brought death and destruction for unborn children but made preparations to build a master race. Great beings come forth at the call of high desire.

Fearless motherhood goes out in love and passion for justice to all mankind. It brings forth fruits after its own kind. When the womb becomes fruitful through the desire of an aspiring love, another Newton will come forth to unlock further secrets of the earth and the stars.... These and the free race that is to be in America wait upon a motherhood that is to be sacred because it is free.[12]

Her purpose in promoting birth control was "to create a race of thoroughbreds," and how to limit and discourage the over-fertility of the mentality and physically defective.[13] She believed that, for the purpose of racial "purification," couples should be rewarded who chose sterilization.[14]

The Myth of Feeble-Mindedness

Another American eugenicist, Henry H. Goddard, wrote a book titled *The Kallikak Family: A Study in the Heredity of Feeble-Mindedness*. He began his book by tracing the descendants of a man whom he called Martin Kallikak. According to Goddard's account, Martin seduced a feeble-minded girl, and she produced a feeble-minded son, who had 480 descendants. Of the 480, Goddard said, 33 were sexually immoral, 24 were drunkards, 3 were epileptics, and 143 were feeble-minded. To clarify the case, Goddard claimed that Martin married a young woman of normal intelligence, and they had 496 descendants with no feeble-minded children at all. Goddard's study provided evidence for a link between bad genes, feeble-mindedness, and immoral behavior. He concluded that a variety of mental traits were hereditary and society should limit reproduction to people possessing these traits.[15]

Goddard was one of the pioneers in the effort to measure intelligence, and his work was such a tremendous success that it attracted many publishers. Writers used Goddard's study to stir up prejudice against the disabled and to build support for eugenics programs. In her book *Woman and the New Race*, Margaret Sanger wrote,

"The offspring of one feebleminded man named Jukes has cost the public in one way and another $1,800,000 in seventy-five years. Do we want more such families?"[16]

Like Galton before him, Goddard believed that intelligence was an innate ability rather than a set of abilities a child develops under supervision and training. He also believed that intelligence could be measured on a sliding scale. Galton's ideas about measuring intelligence attracted researchers in both Europe and America. In France, Alfred Binet (1857–1911) developed tests to measure intelligence, and Lewis Terman (1877–1956) of Stanford University revised them for the United States. Lewis Terman was also a member of the Advisory Council of the American Eugenics Society (AES). The Stanford-Binet tests are still used to measure one's intelligence quotient, or IQ, today.[17]

Goddard did research at the Training School for the Feebleminded Boys and Girls in southern New Jersey, and he invented the word "moron," which is a Greek word for fool, to describe people with an IQ of 50 to 75. Goddard was also on a committee that developed IQ tests for the Army in World War I. Robert Means Yerkes (an AES member) organized IQ testing for 1.7 million U.S. Army recruits in 1919, and summarized his findings in "Psychological Examining in the United States Army." This was the report that led to Henry Fairfield Osborn's remark that World War I was worth the bloodshed because this book came out of it, and showed "once and for all that the negro is not like us."[18]

That is why many black women were subjected to nonconsensual forced sterilization during that time. Some did not know they were sterilized until they unsuccessfully tried to have children. Charlene Israel, who serves as a CBN *700 Club News* reporter, covered a story about eugenics on the program of the *700 Club*.[19] Her report tells us that for decades, a nationwide eugenics program sterilized some 60,000 Americans against their will. This movement specifically targeted the poor and minorities. Elaine Riddick, an African-American, is one of those victims.

She was just 13 years old when she was raped by someone she could not identify. She told CBN news that the person who raped her just jumped from a building and dragged her to a car where she was brutally raped. This rape led to a pregnancy and nine months later Riddick gave birth to a beautiful baby boy. She said "they immediately sterilized me at the same time without my knowledge or without my consent." I kept really, really sick. I was hemorrhaging. I would walk in the street and I would pass out for no reason at all. After that, I started going to a private doctor and the doctors told me that I had been butchered.[20]

The problem is that many generations have been destroyed as a result of this cruel act. The report goes on say that when Riddick was just 19, she got married. It wasn't until she and her husband tried to start a family that she learned she could no longer bear children. She says:

"I found out that when they went in to sterilize me they had so severely damaged my fallopian tubes until they could only patch one back up and the other one, I don't know what happened to it." It was later revealed that the state of North Carolina ordered her to be sterilized after a decision by the state's Eugenics Board. The North Carolina Justice for Sterilization Victims Foundation, reports that from 1929 until 1974, an estimated 7,600 North Carolinians, women and men, many of whom were poor, uneducated, institutionalized, sick or disabled, were sterilized by choice, force or coercion under the authorization of the North Carolina Eugenics Board program. When Riddick asked them why they did this to her, the response is because she was "feeble-minded."[21]

Buck vs. Bell Case

In 1927 Oliver Wendell Holmes, who served as an Associate Justice of the Supreme Court of the United States from 1902–1932, wrote that the majority opinion of a woman in the Buck vs. Bell case that upheld the forced sterilization was claimed to be of below average intelligence. In support of his argument, that the interest of the states in a "pure" gene pool outweighed the interest of individuals in their bodily integrity, he argued:

> We have seen more than once that the public welfare may call upon the citizens for their lives. It would be strange if it could not call upon those who already sap the strength of the State for these lesser sacrifices, often not left to be such by those concerned, to prevent our being swamped with incompetence. It is better for the entire world, if instead of waiting to execute degenerate offspring for crime, or to let them starve for their imbecility, society can prevent those who are manifestly unfit from continuing their kind. The principle that sustains compulsory vaccination is broad enough to cover cutting the Fallopian tubes.[22]

He concluded his argument by declaring, "Three generations of imbeciles are enough."[23]

The new American eugenics, according to Edwin Black, "saw traits as poverty, prostitution, alcoholism, and criminality as genetically transmitted from generation to generation. One could never rise above adverse social circumstances. The flows in your blood will bring you down."[24] The eugenicists believed that by eliminating the physical existence of minorities, the social ills of society would eventually disappear. To this end, American eugenicists were determined to populate the earth with vastly more of their own socio-economic and biological kind, and fewer—or none—of everyone else. "They wanted only the superior species that resembled their own forefathers—blond, blue-eyed 'Nordic' types. This group alone, they believed was fit to inherit the earth."[25]

For example, Lothrop Stoddard believed that millions of years of evolution were at stake, and that the work of evolution could be lost if the racial heritage of the intelligent people was lost. He also believed that he had identified the most valuable people on earth: white people. He wanted to protect their heritage with vast schemes, which included laws restricting immigration and more laws against marriages between whites and non-whites. He wanted to contain the spread of Asians and maintain white power over the wealth of developing nations.

All of Darwin's followers in the early twentieth century believed that the greatest achievement of the evolutionary process was the white race. By their understanding of the process, if whites were the best, then it was acceptable to ignore the welfare of non-whites, or even hasten their extinction. By measuring intelligence, it puts everyone on a sliding scale of measurable value, and makes it tempting to encourage those with higher IQs while setting aside—and even phasing out—those with lower IQs.[26]

Stoddard argued that race and heredity were the guiding factors of history and civilization, and that the elimination or absorption of the white race by colored races would result in the destruction of Western civilization. He, like Madison Grant, the author of *The Passing of the Great Race*, promoted white supremacy and divided the white race into three main divisions: Nordic, Alpine, and Mediterranean. He considered all three to be of good stock and far above the quality of the colored races, but he argued that the Nordic was the greatest of the three and needed to be preserved by way of eugenics.[27]

In the process, American eugenicists intended to subtract Blacks, Indians, Hispanics, Eastern Europeans, Jews, dark-haired hillbillies, poor people, the infirm—essentially, anyone outside the gentrified genetic lines drawn up by American race theory. They did it by identifying the so-called "defective" family trees and subjecting them to lifelong segregation and sterilization programs to kill off their bloodlines. Edwin Black, who is also an investigative historian, said, "The grand plan was to wipe away the reproductive capability and continued existence of the 'unfit'—those deemed weak and inferior. Their assets would be seized to repay society for the many hospitals and prisons required to house and accommodate them."[28]

According to a CBN report, Edwin Black recently testified before the U.S. House Judiciary Committee's subcommittee about the history of racist eugenics in America, saying:

The genocidal actions of the American eugenicists were not conducted by men in white sheets, burning crosses at midnight, but by men in white lab coats and in three-piece suits in the fine corridors of our great universities in the State House, in the courthouse, and in the medical society. This was all subject to the rule of law.[29]

Eugenics is also being blamed for paving the way for today's selective abortion practices, in which babies are aborted because of their race or sex. Congressman Trent Franks (R–Arizona) has also said that "the result of abortion on-demand in America today is that between 40 and 50 percent of all African-American babies, virtually one in two, are killed before they born."[30] Penny Nance, president of Concerned Women for America, added, "I think it is outrageous in a nation where we're so interested, and appropriately so, in protecting women and minorities, yet we turn a blind eye to the fact that children are being aborted just based on their skin color, just based on the fact that they're little girls."[31] This is what you wish never happened in a free country. But unfortunately, it is promoted by the state that is meant to be God's servant in executing justice and fighting for the weak in society.

Endnotes

[1] John Cavanaugh-O'Keefe, *The Roots of Racism and Abortion: An Exploration of Eugenics* (Xlibris Corporation, 2000), 38–39.

[2] Galton's studies about eugenics continued after his death; he was the inspiration for the Eugenics Education Society which was founded in 1907. The name was changed in 1989 to the Galton Institute. The society has brought many influential people from various educational backgrounds to discuss ideas about eugenics in some British and American universities.

[3] Volume 11, November 1864 and April 1865, 157–166, 318–327.

[4] Accessed from *http://dictionary.reference.com/browse/negative+eugenics*.

[5] Margaret Sanger, *Birth Control and Racial Betterment* (Birth Control Review, February 1919), 11.

[6] Margaret Sanger, *Pivot of Civilization,* 187. This book is now in the Public Domain.

7 Linda Gordon, *Woman's Body, Woman's Right: Birth Control in America* (Penguin Books: Revised and Updated edition, 1990).

8 Margaret Sanger, *Woman and the New Race* (New York: Truth Publishing Company, 1920), 4. This book is now in the Public Domain.

9 Ibid.

10 Ibid.

11 Ibid

12 Ibid., 60.

13 Birth Control Review, November 1921, 2.

14 David Kennedy, *Birth Control in America: The Career of Margaret Sanger* (Yale University, 1970, 1971), 117.

15 John Cavanaugh-O'Keefe, *The Roots of Racism and Abortion*, 63.

16 Ibid.

17 Ibid.

18 Ibid., 64.

19 This took place on the show that aired on October 1, 2012.

20 Charlene Israel, Eugenics: America's Past Genocide of Poor Minorities, accessed from *http://www.cbn.com/cbnnews/healthscience/2012/January/Eugenics-America-Past-Genocide-of-Poor-Minorities*, January 9, 2012.

21 Ibid.

22 Ibid

23 Buck vs. Bell, 274 U.S. 200 (1927). Case Preview Full Text of Case, 274. U.S. 207 U.S. Supreme Court No. 292. Argued April 22, 1927. Decided May 2, 1927. 274 U.S. accessed from *http://supreme.justia.com/us/274/200/case.html#207*.

24 Edwin Black, *Nazi Nexus America's Corporate Connections to Hitler's Holocaust* (Dialog Press, 2009), 21.

25 Ibid.

26 John Cavanaugh-O'Keefe, *The Roots of Racism and Abortion*, 61.

27 Lothrop T. Stoddard wrote, "We want above all things to preserve America. But 'America' as we have already seen, is not a mere geographical expression; it is a nation, whose foundations were laid over three hundred years ago by Anglo–Saxon Nordics, and whose nationhood is due almost exclusively to people of North European stock—not only the old colonists and their descendants but also many millions of North Europeans who have entered the country since colonial times and who have for the most part been thoroughly assimilated. Despite the recent influx of alien elements, therefore the American people is still predominantly a blend of closely related North European strains, and the fabric of American life is fundamentally their creation." Lothrop T. Stoddard, *Re-forging America: The Story of Our Nationhood* (New York: Charles Scribner's Sons, 1927), 101.

28 Edwin Black, 21.

29 Charlene Israel, Eugenics: America's Past Genocide of Poor Minorities, accessed from *http://www.cbn.com/cbnnews/healthscience/2012/January/Eugenics-America-Past-Genocide-of-Poor-Minorities*, on January 9, 2012.

30 Ibid.

31 Ibid.

CHAPTER 28

God Meant It for Good

Frederick Douglass and Sojourner Truth

It was David Barton who noted that "the story of African-Americans and the British is not unlike that of God's chosen people, the Jews. Their ancestors came to England and the United States against their will, and now these are their only countries and their only flags. They have shown themselves anxious to live for it and die for it. They have triumphed and prospered—or, in the words of Joseph whose brethren sold him into slavery: 'You intended evil against me, but God turned it for good.'"[1]

The story is told that Frederick Douglass once said in a mournful speech when things looked dark for his race, "The white man is against us, governments are against us, the spirit of the times is against us. I see no hope for the colored race. I am full of sadness." Just then, a woman rose in the audience and said, "Frederick, is God dead?"[2]

"I have borne thirteen children and seen 'em mos' all sold off into slavery, and when I cried out with a mother's grief, none but Jesus heard…"[3] These were the words of a Negro woman named Sojourner Truth (1797–1883), who was born as a slave to slave owners in New York. She was separated from her family, sold twice before the age of twelve, and eventually freed by her master in 1827. Sojourner admitted that she once hated white people, but once she met her Master Jesus, she was filled with love for everyone. Many slaves thought that everyone ignored their fate and the Lord had forsaken them in their suffering. However, He did hear the cries of many slaves like Frederick Douglass and Sojourner Truth.

John Newton's Engagement in the Slave Trade

John Newton (1725–1807), most widely known and recognized songwriter of "Amazing Grace," engaged in the lucrative but brutal African slave trade for a number of years. Newton became Wilberforce's spiritual director and his expertise on the slave trade and his abhorrence of it, belatedly pricked by his conscience, made a powerful impact on Wilberforce. The famous words, "God Almighty has placed before me two great objects: the suppression of the slave trade and the reformation of manners (morals)" were written by Wilberforce in his diary at the end of a long day (October 28, 1787), which he had spent largely alone in Newton's company.[4] The Newton–Cowper Museum at Olney, Buckinghamshire, has the framed text that hung on John Newton's study wall bearing the words: "Remember that you were a slave in the land of Egypt." Newton never forgot where God had brought him from, and this motivated him forward in dedication.

His public testimony on the slave trade to the Privy Council, to a Select Committee of the House of Commons, and in his sensational pamphlet *Thoughts upon the African Slave Trade* (1788) made him a great ally in Wilberforce's abolitionist cause, and his testimonies had an effect on the public opinion as Newton described details of the inhumane treatment of slaves. He acknowledged portraits of the unmerciful whippings and other stories too awful to be read.

One of these was a heartrending story of a young mother with a baby in her arms who had been taken into slavery on board a longboat. While being rowed out to the slave ship, the baby's crying disturbed the longboat's mate who threatened to silence the child. Eventually this mate became so furious that he did indeed silence the child—by tearing it from the mother and hurling it into the sea.[5]

Newton also referred to the frequent sexual abuse of the women slaves on board the ship. "When the women and girls are taken on board a ship, naked, trembling, terrified, perhaps almost exhausted with cold, fatigue, and hunger, they are often exposed to the wanton rudeness of white savages," wrote Newton. The word "rudeness" was a euphemism for sexual pre-selection, as the continuation of his eyewitness report made clear:

> In imagination the prey is divided upon the spot and only reserved till opportunity offers...the solicitation of consent is seldom thought of...such is the treatment that I have known permitted, if not encouraged in many of our ships—they (the African women) have been abandoned, without restraint, to the lawless will of the first comer.[6]

Newton, who in his youth had been one of these first comers, held back the details of the abuses to which the slaves were subjected, although with phrases such as, "This is not a subject for declamation" or "for my readers' sake I suppress the recital of particulars," he made it clear that he was censoring the worst abuses from his account. At the end of the section of his pamphlet that dealt with the sexual exploitation of African female slaves, Newton challenged those who condoned these practices to defend them in front of their own English womenfolk, writing, "Surely if the advocates of the Slave Trade attempt to plead for it before the wives and daughters of our happy land, or before those who have wives and daughters of their own, they must lose their cause."[7]

Those who rejected such arguments and allowed the slave trade to continue rested on the bizarre notion that what would be regarded as cruelty to Europeans need not be regarded as cruelty to Africans. This, said Newton, was based on the belief that "the African women are Negroes, savages, who have no idea of the nicer sensations that obtain among civilized people."[8] Newton rejected this racist nonsense and those who talked it with commendable vigor. "I dare contradict them in the strongest terms," he wrote. "I have lived long and conversed much among these supposed savages. I have often slept in their towns...with regard to the women in modesty and even delicacy that would not disgrace an English woman."[9]

Newton's assertion that African women deserved to be respected as much as their European equivalents in matters such as personal modesty and honor was a revolutionary view of his time. But he, William Wilberforce, and other leading figures in the abolitionist movement, knew that they were in the business of overturning misguided attitudes toward the African people as well as putting an end to what Newton in the final line of his pamphlet called "a commerce so iniquitous, so cruel, so oppressive, so destructive as the African Slave Trade."[10]

Newton provided several dark but fascinating glimpses of the slave trade. He said that he himself had purchased many hundreds of slaves in the area of Shebro River, picking them up two and three at a time. He had bought them from both African and European traders, but he was of the opinion that "a very considerable part of the slaves sold to the ships and boats are kidnapped or stolen."[11]

One member of the committee asked Newton whether the slaves showed "great apprehension or reluctance on being sold?" Newton replied, "They are often under great apprehension at the sight of the sea; they imagine they are bought to be eaten."[12] In another exchange about the customs and behavior of the native people in that part of Africa, Newton said:

> The people are gentle when they have no communication with the Europeans. They are naturally industrious and might be easily managed if they thought the Europeans had their interest at heart, but the slave trade naturally has a tendency to make both the natives and the people employed in it ferocious.[13]

The most painful moment in Newton's evidence to the House of Commons Select Committee came when he was asked, "In selling the cargo was any care taken to prevent the separation of relations?" "It was never thought of," answered Newton, pausing before he concluded this part of his evidence with the chilling sentence: "They were separated as sheep and lambs are separated by the butcher."[14] Indeed, he testified of the sadistic execution of slaves by a fellow slave-ship captain whom he had known:

> Two methods of his punishment of the poor slaves, whom he

sentenced to die, I cannot easily forget. Some of them he jointed; that is, he cut off, with an axe, first their feet, then their legs below the knee. Then their thighs, in like manner their hands, then their arms below the elbow, and then at the shoulders, till their bodies remained only like a trunk of a tree when all the branches are lopped away; and, lastly, their heads. And, as he proceeded in his operation, he threw the reeking members and heads in the midst of the bulk of the trembling slaves, who were chained upon the main deck. He tied around the upper parts of heads of others a small soft platted rope, which the sailors all a point, so loosely as to admit a short lever: by continuing to turn the lever, he drew the point more and more tight, till at length he forced their eyes to stand out of their heads: and when he had satiated himself with their torments, he cut their heads off.[15]

Newton's testimony shocked the committee members when his letter was read to them. He was asked why he had not included his account of this sadistic captain's outrages against the slaves in his own pamphlet, *Thoughts upon the African Slave Trade*. In response, he said:

My chief reason for suppressing it was that it is the only instance of its kind I had knowledge of, and I would hope the only one that ever was heard of. He added that compassion for his readers' feelings had been another cause for his reluctance until he was influenced by "the respectable judgment of the friends" who had advised me to mention it.[16]

Steve Turner observes that what was missing from Newton's growing spiritual consciousness was the intrinsic evil of his own occupation slave trading:

Like almost everyone of his generation he saw nothing inherently wrong with slavery and therefore no inconsistency in participating in it as a follower of Jesus. Of all the Christian denominations only the Quakers and Anabaptists had denounced slavery. Powerful traders belonged to the church—Joseph Manesty owned half a pew at St. George's Church in Derby Square, Liverpool—

and some Christians argued passionately that slavery was God's way of rescuing Africans from their barbaric practices and heathen beliefs and introducing them to Christianity. Using this perspective, slavery could easily be harmonized with Christianity. The only improvements a Christian trade might make would be to treat the slaves more compassionately.[17]

Years of further spiritual growth would lead Newton to a new awareness of slavery as a moral evil. He became the spiritual mentor of William Wilberforce, who led the anti-slavery campaign in Great Britain. It would take thirty years of tireless efforts in Parliament for abolition to become a reality, but in March 1807 the Bill for the Abolition of Slavery became law. Newton, judging himself too old to actively campaign, contributed to the cause with his first public attack on slavery, a 10,000-word essay entitled "The Thoughts upon the African Slave Trade."

He wrote, "I hope it will always be subject of humiliating reflection to me, that I was once an active instrument in a business at which my heart now shudders."[18] His wholehearted condemnation of the trade recognized, however, that he was "bound in conscience to take shame to myself by public confession, which, however sincere, comes too late to prevent or repair the misery and mischief to which I have, formerly, been accessory."[19] Newton had prayed that he would live to see the law passed, which he did. It was fifty-three years after he had given up the trade and twenty years after he wrote a tract supporting the campaign. He died in December of 1807.[20]

God Meant It for Good

But now, do not be distressed and disheartened or vexed and angry with yourselves because you sold me here, for God sent me ahead of you to preserve life. For these two years the famine has been in the land, and there are still five years more in which there will be neither plowing nor harvest. God sent me before you to preserve for you a posterity and to continue a remnant on the earth, to save your lives by a great escape and save for you many survivors. So now it was not you who sent me here, but God; and He has made me a father to Pharaoh and lord of all his house and ruler over all the land of Egypt. (Genesis 45:5–8 AMP)

And Joseph said to them, Fear not; for am I in the place of God? [Vengeance is His, not mine.] As for you, you thought evil against me, but God meant it for good, to bring about that many people should be kept alive, as they are this day. (Genesis 50:19–20 AMP)

Although Joseph's brothers had wanted to get rid of him, God used their evil actions to fulfill His ultimate plan in the earth. He had sent Joseph ahead to preserve their lives, to save Egypt, and to prepare the way for the beginning of the nation of Israel.

God is absolutely sovereign. His plans are not dictated by human actions. When others intend evil toward us, we should remember that they are only God's tools. Look at the sermon of Stephen preaching to the Sanhedrin the whole plan of salvation:

As they were gazing intently at him and saw that his face had the appearance of an angel. Brethren and fathers, listen to me! The God of glory appeared to our forefather Abraham when he was still in Mesopotamia, before he [went to] live in Haran.... But when Jacob heard that there was grain Egypt, he sent forth our forefathers [to go there on their] first trip. And on their second visit Joseph revealed himself to his brothers and the family of Joseph became known to Pharaoh and his origin and race. And Joseph sent an invitation calling to himself Jacob his father and all his kindred, seventy-five persons in all.... Until [the time when] there arose over Egypt another and different king who did not know Joseph [neither knowing his history and services nor recognizing his merits.... Which of the prophets did your forefathers not persecute? And they slew those who proclaimed beforehand the coming of the Righteous One Whom you now have betrayed—You who received the Law as it was ordained and set in order and delivered by angels, and [yet] you did not obey it! (Acts 7:1–4, 7–14, 18, 52–53 AMP)

Stephen's review of Jewish history gives a clear testimony of God's faithfulness and sovereignty. Despite the continued failures of God's chosen people and the swirling world events at the time, God was working out His plan of salvation for the whole human race.

John Newton made an interesting observation when he said:

> It is in these seemingly unfortunate circumstances that the ruling power and wisdom of God are most evidently displayed in human affairs. How many such casual events in the history of Joseph later had a necessary influence on his ensuing promotion? If he had not dreamed or if he had not told his dream; if the Midianites had passed by a day sooner or day later; if they sold him to any person but Potiphar; if his master's wife had been a better woman; if Pharaoh's officers had not displeased their Lord; or if any or all these things had taken place in another manner or time than they did, all that followed would have been different. The promises and purposes of God concerning Israel—her slavery, deliverance, organization, and settlement in the land—would have failed. If history had not been as it was according to God's plan, then the promised Savior, the Desire of all nations, would not have appeared. Mankind would be still in their sins, without hope, and the counsels of God's eternal love in favor of sinners defeated.[21]

Thus we may see a connection between Joseph's first dream and the death of our Lord Jesus Christ with all its glorious consequences. So strong, though secret, is the connection between the greatest and least important events in our lives and throughout world history. What a comfortable thought this is to black people, the Jews, and the Russians who died in the Gulags; the Armenian Christians, the Cambodians, the people of Rwanda, the Muslims in Arab nations, and people everywhere who have undergone and are still suffering from all kinds of terrible massacres, persecutions, and injustices, both believers and non-believers alike: to know that amid all the various interfering plans of men, the Lord has one constant goal, which He cannot and will not miss, namely, His own glory in the complete salvation of His people.

God is wise, strong, and faithful to make and promote those things that seem contrary to this plan. If we consider the larger picture, we can still rest on the wisdom and providence of God's ways: "We are assured and know that [God being a partner in their labor] all things work together and are [fitting into a plan] for good to and for those who love God and are called according to [His] design and purpose" (Romans 8:28 AMP).

What About Amazing Grace?

Someone once wrote that grace is the only force in the universe powerful enough to break the chains that enslave generations. Grace alone melts ungrace. I cannot go into detail about this sensitive issue—in fact, this topic could be expanded into a book all by itself. Most importantly, however, we should not blame only white people as if this sin has been only committed by them. Slavery was indigenous to African and Arab countries before it ever came to Europe. As a matter of fact, it was also practiced by the tribes of the American Indians before Columbus discovered the New World. In addition, Dr. Anderson noted:

> Blacks did not have sufficient wealth and power to use it to enslave, exploit or deny whites the necessities of life.... Black enslavement not only displaced wealth out of Africa and into Europe, but it gave whites a monopoly of wealth and power that makes it very easy for them to keep black people enslaved or noncompetitive.[22]

What would have happened if blacks had sufficient wealth and power to enslave whites? It was not only white people that exploited Africans in the slave trade, but one African tribe would sell another into slavery, and the fruits of that are still being seen today in tribal conflicts and in positions of leadership in African nations.

As Historian David L. Edwards argued when he wrote that the strength of economic arguments in favor of shipping slaves could be seen by anyone who meditated on one fact: it had been more profitable for the slave owners to buy more labor from slave shippers than for them to make elementary arrangements needed to ensure that their existing slaves had plenty of healthy children who could grow up to be useful laborers.[23] It was also pointed out that Africans themselves supplied the slaves whom the British shipped—and did not have equally desired products to exchange for the English and European goods which they coveted.[24]

Therefore, we've all sinned and God calls every one of us to repent and accept His amazing grace. Paul explained to the men of Athens about an unknown God and about how His purpose for creating them was to seek Him and find Him though He is not far from each of us, whether black or white or yellow. He is close and intimate to every one of us, for in Him we live and move and exist and have our being. Therefore, God overlooked our ignorance and sins about all these things like slavery and racism, but He now commands everyone everywhere to repent of our sins and turn to Him. Why? Because He has set a day for judging the world with justice by the Man He has appointed for that task, and He has proved to us who this Man Jesus Christ is by raising Him from the dead (see Acts 17:24–31).

I am not trying to put anyone in the bondage of guilt, especially when it comes to the issue of slavery; but neither should some people who have suffered racial discrimination or any kind of injustice use this as an excuse to be hostile to white people, or anyone for that matter. Reactions of racism is not a sign of strength, but rather indications of weakness. Carl Wells gives the black church some food for thought in this area:

> We all like to blame someone else for our problems.... Nevertheless, the racism of the white, conservative, Bible-believing church, while to be deplored and plainly having had terrible consequences, cannot be the major reason for black failure. 100% of the problem of black failure is the failure of the conservative, Bible-believing black church, to preach and insist upon a fully biblical Christian lifestyle among its members.... If you wait for white bigots to stop being racists as a way for your

problems to be solved, I promise you that you will wait until the end of time, with no material benefit to show for it.[25]

So if we have experienced any racial abuse at all, we must realize that people who are bigoted and racist are the ones who have the problem, not us. So let them worry about their own sin. God made us all different even though we are the same—our skin color is just a sixteenth of an inch, and we have the same blood flowing through our veins. We need also to remember that people are not really bad people, whether white or black, they are just doing what they were taught and raised up to do. Everyone—regardless of the color of their skin—is selfish and self-seeking if they are not truly born again. We all need the saving grace of Jesus Christ to save us from our sins, fill us with His Spirit, and put the love of God in our hearts so that so that we can obey the first and the second commandment: To love the Lord our God with all our heart, souls, minds, and strength, and to love our neighbor as ourselves. There is no commandment greater than these.

Endnotes

[1] David Barton, Foreword, *Setting the Record Straight, American History in Black & White* (Wall Builders, 2004, 2010), 3.

[2] Quoted in Dwight L. Moody, *The Overcoming Life* (Florida: Bridge-Logos Foundation, 2007), 63.

[3] Sojourner Truth, "A'nt I a Woman?" (1861), in John Hollitz, *Thinking Through the Past* (Boston: Houghton Mifflin Co., 2001), 250.

[4] Jonathan Aitken, *John Newton: From Disgrace to Amazing Grace* (Wheaton, Illinois: Crossway Publishing, 2007), 23.

[5] Ibid., 320.

[6] Ibid., 320–321.

[7] Ibid., 321.

[8] Ibid.

[9] Ibid.

[10] Ibid., 321–322.

[11] Ibid., 324.

[12] Ibid.

13 Ibid.

14 Ibid., 327.

15 Ibid., 326.

16 Ibid.

17 Steve Turner, Foreword by Judy Collins, *Amazing Grace: The Story of America's Most Beloved Song* (Harper Perennial: reprint edition, 2003), 50.

18 Ibid

19 Ibid.

20 Dennis R. Hillman, *Out of the Depths by John Newton: The Autobiography of John Newton,* Revised and Updated for Today's Readers by Dennis R. Hillman (Kregel Publications, 2003), 103.

21 Ibid., 63.

22 Quoted by Dr. Frederick K. C. Price, 160–161.

23 David L. Edwards, *Christian England, Volume 3, From the 18th Century to the First World War* (London: Fount Paperbacks, 1985), 89.

24 Ibid.

25 Carl Wells, 168–170.

CHAPTER 29

The Power of Forgiveness

We Need to Forgive One Another

Jesus told us, "Love your enemies, bless those who curse you, do good to those who hate you, and pray for those who spitefully use you and persecute you" (Matthew 5:44). We are commanded by the Lord to forgive and pray for those who have used and persecuted us. But how do we do that? We pray from our heart for these people that God would forgive them and bless them and prosper them as though they've never done anything wrong at all.

Dr. R. T. Kendall has written two excellent books about forgiveness: *God Meant It for Good* and *Total Forgiveness: Achieving God's Greatest Challenge*. In both of these books, which I highly recommend to anyone wanting to read more about this subject, Dr. Kendall draws many lessons from the life of Joseph. God has instructed and convicted me about many areas of my own life through his books, especially in the area of self-pity, the desire to be vindicated, God's timing, and total forgiveness.

Dr. Kendall goes on to explain that the reason why God exalted Joseph to the lofty position of the prime minister of Egypt is because Joseph learned how to forgive those around him. Dr. Kendall listed four proofs to know for sure that we have forgiven those who have hurt us: The first is that we don't want the other person to be afraid of us or what they've done to us. Joseph said to his brothers, "Do not be afraid, for am I in the place of God?" (Genesis 50:19). When we have totally forgiven another person, we don't want them to be afraid of us.[1]

The second way of knowing that we have really forgiven someone is that we refuse to take advantage of any superior position we might be in. Joseph could not use his position to make his brothers fear him all the days of their lives. He wanted to be transparently open with them. We are really putting ourselves in the place of God if we force another to respect us.[2] When Joseph's brothers acknowledged their sin, Joseph replied to them, "You meant evil against me; but God meant it for good, in order to bring it about as it is this day, to save many people alive" (Genesis 50:20).

The third proof that we have really forgiven another person, writes Dr. Kendall, is that we bind up the wounds so completely that we show that all that happened was really meant to be. Now Joseph had already said, "But now, do not therefore be grieved or angry with yourselves because you sold me here; for God sent me before you to preserve life" (Genesis 45:5). More than anything else, this helps the other person save face.[3]

The final proof that we have really forgiven the other person is that we keep on forgiving them even when they continue to hurt us. Now it's one thing to do it once and mean it. But we are not finished with forgiving one time! How do we know that we have forgiven another person? The answer is that we keep doing it. Joseph continued to comfort his brothers and spoke kindly to them, "'Now therefore, do not be afraid; I will provide for you and your little ones.' And he comforted them and spoke kindly to them" (Genesis 50:21). Thus, all that he said to them proved that he forgave them—not only that day but the next day and the day after that. We know we really have forgiven, and that is not just a burst of emotional feeling, because we keep on doing it. Dr. Kendall writes, "Total forgiveness holds two months later. Six months later. Two years later. Forever."[4]

Why Forgive at All?

Why does God ask us to forgive? Because that is what God the Father is. He is a merciful, forgiving, and gracious God. That is the way God forgives us and it is the way He expects us to forgive each other;

that is the way we need to forgive. Through this study of forgiveness, we discover that unless we totally forgive, we will never get out of prison until we forgive from our hearts, not just in our minds—every person who has ever been betrayed, sexually abused, molested, divorced, racially abused, or hurt us in anyway. Asking for forgiveness from the Lord and extending that forgiveness is integral for as long as we live, because it is guaranteed that others will sooner or later hurt us or we will hurt others. When Joseph finally forgave his brothers, the pain did not disappear, but the burden of being their judge fell away. He left everything in the hands of God, who knows what to do in all situations.

It is now being reported that it is more acceptable for blacks to make threats or even commit acts of violence against conservative white people, but never against liberal black people. If you are a black person doing this, you have to remember you have to totally forgive the injustices done against you. Until you forgive the white people, you will be in far greater chains than your ancestors ever experienced. God forgives our debts as we forgive our debtors. Release the white man and you will be released as well.

Wherever there has been a hurt, the human reaction is usually one of rebellion, hatred, and unforgiveness—the biggest bondage of these three is hate. When we hate, we give away our heart and mind because bitterness only hurts ourselves. It is true that without knowledge of history, humans are socially, intellectually, and emotionally rootless. And this is why Africans and other minority groups are bitter when they look back at their history and what has been done to them. But there is no sin or past action that is unforgivable.

Forgiveness is not easy—that is why it's an act of faith. When we forgive someone else, we are leaving the injustices in God's hands, who tells us not to take revenge.

> Repay no one evil for evil. Have regard for good things in the sight of all men. If it is possible, as much as depends on you, live peaceably with all men. Beloved, do not avenge yourselves, but rather give place to wrath; for it is written, "Vengeance is Mine, I

will repay," says the Lord. Therefore "If your enemy is hungry, feed him; if he is thirsty, give him a drink; for in so doing you will heap coals of fire on his head." Do not be overcome by evil, but overcome evil with good. (Romans 12:17–21)

As black people, we need to reject the legacy of bitterness that resides in our hearts. We have to love and forgive one another, even if we've suffered racial discrimination. We are all fallen people who hurt and disappoint one another. We all make mistakes and we all sin. Scripture tells us that we have all sinned, that we have fallen short of the glory of God (see Romans 3:23). The closer we get to each other, the more we see each other's faults and the more we can hurt each other. Everybody's normal till we get to know them.

How do we avoid this? The answer again is to develop an intimate relationship with the Lord. We also need the grace to die to the racial offenses that might be committed against us, which might increase because of multiplied lawlessness. It is only by living in the stream of God's grace that we will find the strength to respond with grace toward others. "A dead man or woman," quoting one writer, "does not react to an offense."[5] It is a special grace given by Jesus Christ to forgive; and we need to pray for it all the time. That is why Jesus told Peter to forgive up to seventy times seven (see Matthew 18:21).

An Example of Forgiveness

A story is told of an elderly black woman who experienced racial prejudice at about seventy years of age. She was facing a man in court named Mr. Van der Broek. He was guilty of brutally murdering her husband and son, who were all the family she had. In court the judge asked her, "How should justice be done to the man who murdered your family?" Her response was this: "I want three things: First, I want to gather the ashes of my husband (who the accused man had burned to death while she watched) and bury them. Secondly, since my husband and son were my only family, I want this man, Mr. Van der Broek to become my son. I would like him to come to the ghetto where I live twice a month and spend the day with me so that I can pour whatever love I have left in me on him. Lastly, I would like to cross the courtroom and take Mr. Van der Broek in my arms and embrace him and let him know he is truly forgiven."[6]

Bitterness Is Dangerous

We need to remind our black brothers and sisters that resentment or bitterness causes trouble and bitter torment, and many become contaminated and defiled by it (see Hebrews 12:15). Those who are embracing bitterness against whites should remember that many white people died fighting to end slavery, and many voted to put the first black (mixed-race) president in the White House. Blacks should understand that many white people are standing up for the God-given freedom and liberty of blacks in America and around the world, while the corrupt white and black leadership is profiting off the hatred they foster within the black community.

Author and pastor Paul McGuire tells us:

The main reason why many African-Americans are totally committed to this illusion is because they have psychological anchors of racial hatred passed down from previous generations who remember slavery and discrimination. Unable to step out of their programming due to racial hatred, they are setting themselves up to be slaves again. They are willing to give up their freedoms because they see government as God. They have been conditioned to see government as the source of meeting all their needs.[7]

Those who are harboring hatred because of what happened in the past are poisoning themselves, believing that it will kill the whites. We blacks are blaming whites as being the racists, forgetting the fact we are also harboring hatred and racist negative attitudes in our own hearts toward them. How many of us genuinely reach out to the white community to serve them? Look at the racist statements that flow from black politicians with the exception of a very few, which serves to further divide the races. Booker T. Washington had a great deal to say about how black leaders exploit their own race for financial and political gain. In his book *My Larger Education*, he wrote:

> There is another class of colored people who make a business of keeping the troubles, the wrongs, and the hardships of the Negro race before the public. Having learned that they are able to make a living out of their troubles, they have grown into the settled habit of advertising their wrongs—partly because they want sympathy and partly because it pays. Some of these people do not want the Negro to lose his grievances, because they do not want to lose their jobs.[8]

I feel sorry for those of us who are using hate, division, and revenge by twisting the truth for material and political gain. When we stand before the judgment seat of Christ, there will be no one to blame except ourselves. Our power, party, influence, and riches will all fail us —we can be assured of that. It won't matter whether we made a million dollars and made ourselves a name by selling our soul and others; what will be important is our relationship with Jesus Christ and how we served Him in the way we treated our neighbor—whether black or white—during our lifetime. All the applause and accolades we are now receiving will mean nothing in eternity.

The Sin of Racial Idolatry

Let's face it: most black leaders and pastors have a lot of soul-searching to do. Many blacks have fallen prey to identity politics— blacks for blacks and whites for whites. Alan Keyes asks whether or not black America is reaping a harvest of racial idolatry. That means that we put the idol of false racial pride above our respect for God and His Word. Now these black Christians are seeing the fruits of their idolatry:

> Joshua said to the Israelites: "Choose this day whom you will serve." American Christians of all ethnic backgrounds face the same choice. Will we serve the idols of human self-worship—of racial pride, mammon and the lust for power? Or will we serve the God who created the heavens and the earth, whose worship

inspired America's creed, and whose grace and forgiveness may yet renew the unity and strength of her people?[9]

Creating an idol is forbidden by the third of the Ten Commandments (see Exodus 20:3). Examples of blacks being addicted to the cult of black leadership and personalities have been admitted by many. There is even a book by a professor saying the president, a mere mortal man, was reelected to help the middle-class and poor Americans experience "heaven on earth."[10] If we are putting our faith in any human leader or president, we are going to be terribly disappointed. He is a human being who needs to be prayed for just as Paul admonishes us in his first letter to Timothy (see 1 Timothy 2:1–5).

Any human leader, either Republican or Democrat, Conservative or Liberal, will always disappoint us. How can we put trust in a mere mortal man and set our affections on a person, as if a human being would always be there for us? Bonhoeffer warns us at this point:

> Innumerable times a whole Christian community has broken down because it has sprang from a wish dream.... God will not permit us to live even for a brief period in a dream world. He does not abandon us to those rapturous experiences and lofty moods that come over us like a dream. God is not a God of emotions but the God of truth.... He who loves his dream of a community more than the Christian community itself becomes a destroyer of the latter, even though his personal intention may be ever so honest and earnest and sacrificial.[11]

Bonhoeffer further warned that if the church should ever substitute one Lord for another, if the cross of Christ was replaced by any other cross, the gospel would be betrayed and the church judged.

In January 1933 Hitler had just been elected as chancellor of Germany. The very next day Bonhoeffer who was not duped by the Führer's intentions, gave a radio address in which he warned that when a people idolize a leader, "then the image of the leader will inevitably become the image of the 'misleader.' Thus the leader makes an idol of himself and mocks God."[12] Bonhoeffer kept reminding anyone who would listen:

> The church has only one altar before which it must kneel and that is the altar of the Almighty. The pride of the church, he said, must be rebuked by the humiliation of the Cross. God's victory means our defeat, it means our humiliation; it means God's mocking anger at all human arrogance, being puffed up, trying to be important in our own right. It means the Cross above the world...the cross of Christ, that means the bitter scorn of God for all human heights, bitter suffering of God in all human depths, the rule of God over the whole world...with Gideon we kneel before the altar and say, "Lord on the Cross, be thou alone our Lord. Amen."[13]

My black brothers, there is only one Lord and His name is *Yeshua HaMashiach* (Jesus Christ), the Son of the living God who died on the cross to save us from our sins. The Bible says that every knee shall bow to Him, including all earthly rulers or presidents: "As I live, says the Lord, every knee shall bow to Me, and every tongue shall confess to God" (Romans 14:11).

Divide and Rule

History teaches us that when any government generates a racial war between different color groups, or a class war between the rich, middle-class, and the poor, it finds it easier to take emergency action measures to secure national peace. Believers in Jesus Christ are the only group of people standing between the rising tide of hate and destruction in the West. If we think this is too far-fetched of a message, just consider that Hitler would not have become führer of Germany without the cooperation of Germany's evangelical churches. Out of almost 13,000 pastors and churches, only 750–800 had the courage to oppose him. Why? He divided most of them.

It has been noted that while white America elected the first black president, it also brought out the worst in some black Americans, preachers, and other Christians who acted out instead of using their

God-given faculties to discern the times we live in. Hitler is quoted to have said: "How fortunate for governments that the people they administer don't think."[14] The only people who truly benefit from the race division are those who claim to be fighting for justice. There is no point of playing the politician's game of "divide and rule," using the old race card. We are all human beings created in the image of God, and we should love one another as brothers and sisters, regardless of the color of our skin.

We should all strive to love, serve, and glorify Christ, and enjoy Him forever. We should try to be the kind husbands, wives, mothers, and fathers the Lord expects us to be, serve our fellow men, and be productive and useful citizens of our respective countries.

White racism exists, but it is not the cause of our problems. God did not create one race to be inferior to another; there are tens of thousands of intelligent, productive black people. Many have arisen from humble beginnings to lead successful lives. Black people are exactly like white people in the area of natural intelligence—some very bright, some of ordinary good intelligence, and some slightly or seriously below average.[15] Statistics show black males are more than one-third of prisoners in state and federal prisons, even though they make up only 10 percent of the population.[16] In the United States alone, the black poverty rate is over 2.34 times higher than the white rate.

In the U.K. report on Black Mental Health, U.K. experience reveals: "It is in the field of forensic psychiatry that racial injustices and cultural oppression are felt most acutely by African service Caribbean service users. People from black and minority ethnic (BME) groups suffer poorer health, have reduced life expectancy, and have greater problems with access to health care than the majority of the white population."[17]

Abortion in African-American Communities

It has been documented that in the United States alone, African-Americans are the ones who are being targeted for abortion, most sexually transmitted diseases kill black people, and a third of all abortions in the U.S. are black babies. Yet the African-American church is so involved in earthly affairs that they don't seem to care anymore. When people forget what happened yesterday, they don't know who they are today or what they are trying to do. We are trying to do a futile thing if we do not know where we have come from or what we have been about.

Statistically, for every 1.3 live births in the black community, one child is aborted. This is not liberation. This is a deliberate elimination by Planned Parenthood's design, not of an entire race, but of a socio-economic class of people whom the abortion industry considers undesirables. Black women have abortions at nearly three times the rate of white women and significantly more abortions than Hispanics, despite lower representation in the U.S. population.[18]

I don't think we would have all these statistics (whether accurate or not) if blacks took the time to read, study, and learn the truth of the Word of God. But we've become so lazy and disinterested in learning the truth that we cannot think critically and make informed decisions for ourselves. This should not be. We should be a people who learn and excel in all that we do.

Blacks Encourage Learning and Excellence

The black church needs to encourage its people to love and respect learning. Black kids who work hard to get an education should not be classified as "acting white." Black Christians should encourage one another to pursue intellectual excellence. The welfare system exploits blacks and the poor by keeping them dependent on the system while stealing their intellectual and economic future.

If we encourage one another to respect learning, then we could have the freedom and liberty to determine our God-given destiny that is full of hope and promise in Jesus Christ. Maybe we could emulate Ben Carson's mother, who did not allow the system to dictate her life. She was a divorced single mother with only a third-grade education, but against all odds she determined to see her two boys succeed. She made a rule in the house, where these two boys could not watch no more than three programs a week. She decided how they could spend their free time when they were not watching television. She told them:

> "You boys are going to go to the library and check out books. You're going to read at least two books every week. At the end of the week you'll give me a report on what you've read." "Bennie," she said again and again, "if you can read, honey, you can learn just about anything you want to know. The doors of the world are open to people who can read. And my boys are going to be the best readers in the school."[19]

Was it easy for these two black boys? Not at all. In fact, as Ben Carson says, "we grumbled and complained, making the journey seem endless. But Mother had spoken, and it didn't occur to either of us to disobey. The reason we respected her."[20] Indeed, she was right and her lessons to these two young boys paid off. Today, Dr. Ben Carson is a professor and a widely acclaimed neurosurgeon, and his brother Curtis is an engineer.

Being black and coming from a broken home doesn't mean that everything is stacked against us. The factors that brought most of us immigrants to Britain and America were professional and economic development opportunities. Most of us have made very painful personal sacrifices so that our children can have better opportunities than we had. Let us use these opportunities that the Lord has afforded us while we still have the chance, or while the Lord tarries. We all know the pain of black history, but we must not allow race and color to trump our Christian principles. If you think I am just hard on my fellow blacks, remember "faithful are the wounds of a friend, but the kisses of an enemy are deceitful" (Proverbs 27:6).

Conclusion

Joseph said, "But as for you, you meant evil against me; but God meant it for good, in order to bring it about as it is this day, to save many people alive" (Genesis 50:20–21). The first thing we need to do as blacks is to forgive our white brothers for slavery and other racial injustices. Maybe God couldn't exalt Joseph to the position he had until he was willing to totally forgive his brothers. His brothers probably feared that he would take revenge on them—after all, many years had passed before his father Jacob had died.

But what did Joseph say to them? "You meant evil against me; but God meant it for good." The people who engaged in the brutal African slave trade for a number of years meant evil against blacks, but God in His ruling power and wisdom wanted to save many lives. Secondly, blacks in America and Britain should be very thankful to God and also express our gratitude to these countries. Many of us felt welcomed and doors of opportunities to preach the gospel were opened to us, which would have been impossible in other parts of the world. Many of our black brothers and sisters in Africa live in abject poverty and generally suffer from tyrannical regimes that are propped up by some corrupt politicians in the West.

Lastly, black churches that are still preaching the liberation theology social gospel should repent and preach the true gospel of Jesus Christ. The overall emphasis of black liberation theology is the black struggle for liberation from various forms of "white racism" and oppression. The social gospel of good deeds rejects the biblical concept of regeneration. I agree with Gary DeMar on this point:

> Advocates of this liberal social gospel see "a one divided realm, the state, as the true order of God and man. The state is given the overall jurisdiction and sovereignty over church, school, family, business, farming, and all things else which belong only to God. It should be remembered that white or black evangelicals who opposed the social gospel believed that Christians should influence society.... They believed the first step in societal transformation must come through repentance for sin and total dependence on God's grace supplied to us in the sacrificial death of Jesus Christ. Instead, the social gospel had degenerated into "religious morality" that is, morality without Christ.[21]

The only hope for future black prosperity is for the pastors to preach the true gospel of Jesus Christ and Him crucified for our sins, to preach repentance, to stand up for truth, righteousness, and justice, and finally to restore the traditional black family according to biblical standards. Carl Wells, in his book *The Christian Betrayal of the United States*, has some insights which I believe might be of interest to black Christian readers. He writes,

> Mature adult Christians, who are living disciplined, godly lives, should reach out much more intentionally to black children and young people who have no godly examples in their lives. Black and white girls, Christian or non-Christian, need godly men and women to befriend them. Spend time with them, love them, and hold them accountable. This is discipleship and it starts with one person at a time.[22]

Endnotes

[1] Carl Wells, 231.

[2] Ibid., 232.

[3] Ibid., 233.

[4] Ibid., 234.

[5] Quoted in Alice Smith, *Beyond The Veil: Entering into Intimacy with God Through Prayer* (Renew Books, 1996), 106.

[6] Quoted from *Enjoying Everyday Life Magazine,* Joyce Meyer Ministries, October 2005.

[7] Paul McGuire, November 5, 2012, "Election Day: Who will rule tomorrow?" accessed from *http://www.newswithviews.com/McGuire/paul146.htm.*

[8] Booker T. Washington, *My Larger Education: Being Chapters from My Experience* (New York: Double Day Page & Company, 1910, 1911), 118.

[9] "Black America: Reaping Harvest of Racial Idolatry?" Exclusive: Alan Keyes asks if minorities "Christian conscience" will sleep forever. Accessed from *http://www.wnd.com/2012/09/black-america-repaing-harvest-ofracial-idolatry.*

[10] Barbara A. Thomson, *The Gospel According to Apostle Barack: In search of a More Perfect Political Union as Heaven Here on Earth* (Author House, 2012).

[11] Dietrich Bonhoeffer, *Life Together* (New York: Harper & Row Publishers, 1954), 26–29.

[12] Erwin W. Lutzer, *When a Nation Forgets God: Seven Lessons We Must Learn from Nazi Germany* (Moody Publishers, 2010), 132.

[13] Mary Bosanquent, *The Life and Death of Dietrich Bonhoeffer* (London: Hodder & Stoughton, 1968), 121–122.

[14] Erwin W. Lutzer, 81.

[15] Carl Wells, 158–160.

[16] Ibid.

[17] Accessed from *http://www.blackmentalhealth.org.uk/index.php/stats-and-facts*.

[18] Maafa 21: A Documentary Film, *Black Genocide in 21st Century America* (Life Dynamics, Inc.), Accessed from their website *http://www.maafa21.com*.

[19] Ben Carson, *Gifted Hands: The Ben Carson Story* (Zondervan, 1990), 33–34.

[20] Ibid.

[21] Gary DeMar and Peter Leithart, 319. R. J. Rushdoony, *The Foundations of Social Order: Studies in the Creeds and Councils of the Early Church* (Nutley, NJ: Presbyterian and Reformed, 1968), 134–35.

[22] Carl Wells, 168–170.

Conclusion

In this volume we have examined how Christianity was introduced to England earlier than the period of Roman occupation. It is an undeniable fact that England has a long and rich Christian biblical heritage. In fact, as we've seen, Christianity was established in England as early as the Roman occupation in AD 43, which was only ten years after Pentecost.

The Lord raised up, sustained, and made Great Britain through many national revivals and awakenings, and it has became one of the greatest empires in the history of the nations. During the eighteenth and nineteenth centuries, hundreds of missionaries carried the gospel throughout the world, and tens of thousands came into an experience of saving faith in Jesus Christ as a result. The nation was filled with hundreds of martyrs, some who were executed primarily for being responsible for printing the Bible. They would not renounce God's name, His truth, or His holy Word.

England was given the privilege of dispensing the Great Charter of the Liberties of England, which is known as the Magna Carta. This charter is widely known throughout the English-speaking world as an important process that led to the rule of constitutional law in England, spreading to the rest of the world. In spite of all its weaknesses, it was still one of the most just and righteous empires in the history of the world. The nation raised up leaders who abolished the slave trade because of their belief that slavery was an offense against God.

The Lord has not forgotten those who gave up everything for the sake of the gospel. But the nation that God has raised up and sustained has somehow forgotten Him. Today many people in the West have little sense of how their lives have benefited from their biblical heritage, and from the revivals and great awakenings that took place there. It is very unfortunate that in our microwave, fast-paced culture, we don't stop and take time to look back and learn from past generations, either through their writings or their personal lives.

In most of America's institutions of learning, the Puritans, Calvinists, and Pilgrims are often portrayed only as separatists. But as we've seen throughout this volume, a close examination of the lives and writings of the early American colonists clearly reveal that their intent was to seek liberty for themselves and their little ones, and to walk with God in a Christian life, for the rules and motives of such a life were revealed to them from God's Word.

They were determined to escape the religious persecution of Europe. Bradford made it clear that the Pilgrims' purpose was to labor to have the right worship of God and discipline of Christ established in the church, according to the simplicity of the gospel, without the mixture of men's inventions. The original group of believers in Nottinghamshire, Lincolnshire, and Yorkshire joined themselves by a covenant to the Lord into a church estate, in the fellowship of the gospel, to walk in all ways made known unto them, according to their best endeavors, whatever it cost them, with the Lord assisting them. Most importantly we also have to remember that great hope and inward zeal they had of laying a good foundation for the propagating and advancing of the gospel of the kingdom of Christ in those remote parts of the world.

History demonstrates that the Pilgrims were willing to put biblical and Christian principles in government to the test. Both spiritually and politically, they rose up foundations of many generations. Four hundred years later, the people of the United States are still building on this great heritage that the Pilgrims laid. What about the Founders, whom some historians believe just made a mockery of the Christian faith in order to avoid persecution? Yes, one cannot marginalize the influence of Freemasonry upon them, but some of these Founders had fled repressive countries in which they risked arrest, imprisonment, or torture from tyrannical monarchs of eighteenth-century Europe.

So they decided to craft a mechanism of checks and balances by creating the executive, legislative, and judiciary branches of the government. They championed individual human rights and the idea of equality under the law, argued that all human beings have natural rights to life, liberty, and property, and that all people ought to be treated equally. They understood that all people have unbridled corrupt passions, and so they had to set up a system that would keep them from having unchecked power.

What motivated them to do such a thing? They acknowledged the overruling power of God in the affairs of men and nations. As had been already stated, it is impossible to examine all the Founders' private convictions in detail. What we might assess, however, is that these men had a godly conscious and were willing to put Christian principles in government to the test. We also have to bear in mind that any office of responsibility is ordained by God. It is He who governs the affairs of mankind and decides the outcome of history. Despite the weaknesses of some of these Founders, God delighted to use them for His purposes.

For instance, the pattern set by Pilgrims of proclaiming public days of fasting and humiliation was followed by subsequent generations of these leaders. George Washington, John Adams, and James Madison all issued proclamation days of solemn humiliation, fasting, and prayer for the entire nation. Under the sixteenth president, Abraham Lincoln, three separate days of national humiliation, prayer, and fasting were proclaimed throughout the nation. His second proclamation on the March 30, 1863, acknowledged these unique blessings enjoyed by the American people. He said:

> We have been the recipients of the choicest bounties of Heaven. We have been preserved, these many years, in peace and prosperity. We have grown in numbers, wealth and power, as no other nation has ever grown. But we have forgotten God. We have forgotten the gracious Hand which preserved us in peace, and multiplied and enriched and strengthened us; and we have vainly imagined, in the deceitfulness of our hearts, that all these blessings were produced by some superior wisdom and virtue of

our own. Intoxicated with unbroken success, we have become too self-sufficient to feel the necessity of redeeming and preserving grace, too proud to pray to the God that made us.[1]

Lincoln knew that these blessings could have brought an attitude of pride and self-sufficiency that are the main causes of any national crisis. Today, as we look back, we should ask ourselves this question: How many blessings and privileges, which God has bestowed upon the West and which were obtained for us by the sacrifice of the early colonists, are now being taken for granted?

Though I am not a historian by training, I needed to go back and research everything I could find about this rich biblical heritage of freedom, because when a people forget their heritage, they are easily persuaded to lose their identity. I have also read histories of how dictators came to power and stripped people of all their personal liberties. We've forgotten that everything is under God's jurisdiction, and without the lordship of Christ in every sphere of our lives, even a democracy inevitably leads to tyranny.

The more I read how the West became a beacon of light, righteousness, and justice in the world, the more compelling reasons I had to remind the West that much of what forms the foundation of Western civilization—the family, economics, education, the media, culture, arts entertainment, human rights, and all moral standards—stems from the Bible. And this is what will be further examined in the second volume of this work.

Endnote

---

[1] Philip L. Ostergard, *The Inspired Wisdom of Abraham Lincoln* (Tyndale House Publishers, Inc. 2008), 205.

Printed in Great Britain
by Amazon